CULTURE AND THE KING

SUNY Series in Mediaeval Studies
Paul E. Szarmach, editor

CULTURE AND THE KING

The Social Implications of the Arthurian Legend

Essays In Honor of Valerie M. Lagorio

edited by
Martin B. Shichtman
and
James P. Carley

STATE UNIVERSITY OF NEW YORK PRESS

Cover art: William Dyce, *Generosity: King Arthur Unhorsed Spared by Sir Launcelot* (1852). Fresco. British Crown Copyright with Permission of Her Britannic Majesty's Stationery Office.

Published by
State University of New York Press, Albany

For information, address the State University of New York Press,
State University Plaza, Albany, NY 12246

Library of Congress Cataloging-in-Publication Data

Culture and the king : the social implications of the Arthurian legend
/ edited by Martin B. Shichtman and James P. Carley.
　　p.　　cm. — (SUNY series in medieval studies)
　　Includes bibliographical references.
　　ISBN 0-7914-1863-4 (CH : Acid-free). — ISBN 0-7914-1864-2 (PB :
Acid-free)
　　1. Arthurian romances—History and criticism.　2. Arthurian
romances—Adaptations—History and criticism.　3. Literature,
Comparative—Themes, motives.　4. Social ethics in literature.
5. Conduct of life in literature.　I. Shichtman, Martin B.
II. Carley, James P.　III. Series.
　　PN685.C85　1994
306.4—dc20　　　　　　　　　　　　　　　　　　　　93-10552
　　　　　　　　　　　　　　　　　　　　　　　　　　CIP

CONTENTS

v

Part II
Reinventing the Middle Ages

VALERIE M. LAGORIO: A TRIBUTE

Valerie Lagorio remembers vividly the moment when Kurt Adler of the San Francisco Opera Company asked her, a young woman in the chorus, to perform as the Grail Maiden in *Parsifal*. "I had a very nice voice and could work in four languages," she explains, "and I could follow the German prompts." The role of Grail Maiden was the high point of her four years with the Opera Company, and it shaped— subconsciously perhaps—her subsequent career in literature.

Valerie Lagorio was born in 1925 in Iowa City, Iowa, where her father was captain of the University of Iowa ROTC program. Her mother was a concert pianist. Soon after her birth the family moved to San Francisco, where Valerie went to school and studied voice.

Her first professional role was as a civilian actress technician, "C.A.T.," in "Swingtime Fiesta," with a company that toured military bases in Germany. Her next role in the touring company was in "Song of the Island," where she was billed as Uilani, Queen of Maui. "I only performed classic hula," she insists.

When this show finished, she left Europe to return to San Francisco, but soon moved to Honolulu, where she was a disc jockey for an armed services' radio station, as "Your Pal Val." Returning once more to San Francisco, she auditioned for Adler and began singing in the chorus and performing small parts, working part time to pay for voice lessons. But she worked so hard that she strained her voice and had to give up her career in opera.

Her next job was with military intelligence, for which her linguistic skills well suited her—and in this her career parallels that of other distinguished Arthurians: Eugène Vinaver, Armel Diverres, and Faith Lyons. She returned to Europe and was stationed in Berlin. When questioned about her adventures in this role, she explains, "I was only a secretary in the office. But with Russian zones and all, it was a touch-and-go situation."

Following her two years in intelligence, she was an executive secretary for the American Presidents Line, a major steamship company to the Orient, until again the government called her. This time she was asked to set up a "Welcome to the United States" program for the U.S.

Immigration Service. She recruited and trained bilingual young women, staffing seventeen airports around the United States.

Soon afterwards her father suggested that she return to school. In four years she earned a B.A., M.A., and Ph.D. in English from Stanford University. Her dissertation, directed by R. W. Ackerman, was on "The Legend of Joseph of Arimathea in Middle English Literature."

Valerie Lagorio's teaching career began at San Francisco College for Women in 1966, and included six subsequent years at the University of Missouri, St. Louis, from 1967 to 1972. She became an associate professor at the University of Iowa in June 1972, and was promoted to full professor in 1975—the first woman so honored by the English department in forty years. She was recipient of the University of Iowa Council on Excellence in Teaching Award in 1988. She has received many awards and fellowships, beginning with the Stanford Wilson Dissertation Fellowship in 1966, and most recently a Fulbright Travel Grant to Montpellier, France in 1988.

Valerie Lagorio's energies have gone into professional associations as well. She has been on the Publications Committee of the Medieval Academy of America and was elected a councilor from 1980 to 1982. She serves on the review panels of a number of major grant-proposing institutions, including NEH, ACLS, and Fulbright-Hays. She was vice president for the North American Branch of the International Arthurian Society from 1975 to 1979 and president from 1988 to 1991.

Her responsibilities in the area of editing and publishing have been notable. She has been a member of the editorial or advisory boards of *Manuscripta, Philological Ouarterly, Index of Middle English Prose, Religion and Literature, Vox Benedictina, Avalon to Camelot, Fifteenth-Century Studies, Bear & Co., Arthurian Interpretations,* and *Quondam et Futurus.*

Valerie Lagorio's relationship to *Quondam et Futurus* has been particularly valuable. She and Ackerman had been interested in sponsoring a newsletter for the North American branch of the International Arthurian Society and they asked me if I would help. We presented the proposal at the following branch meeting, only to have it rejected because of the cost. At this point we decided to go forward with the newsletter on a subscription basis, and it has been published quarterly since 1989. She has continued to be active on the advisory board and has accepted the same responsibility for the merged *Quondam et Futurus. A Journal of Arthurian Interpretations.*

Valerie Lagorio's most important contribution as editor has been in her sixteen years of producing *Mystics Quarterly,* which grew out of her early research, with Sister Rita Mary Bradley, on the extensive— but rather neglected—body of work in Middle English prose in this area.

Originally entitled *Fourteenth-Century Mystics Newsletter*, the journal soon expanded beyond England and the fourteenth century and the new, lasting title reflected this change. The journal is now ecumenical and international, contemporary as well as medieval.

When I asked her why she worked in two such unrelated areas— Arthurian romance and medieval mysticism—she replied: "It is the Grail of course. Without the Grail, the Arthurian legend would be nothing more than a story of the rise and fall of a well-remembered king. With the quest of the Holy Grail at the center of his reign, Arthur becomes a figure of the apocalyptic Last Emperor, the once and future king. The Grail quest itself is mystic in its call for spiritual perfection. It is no coincidence that the interest in Arthur and the resurgence of interest in mysticism began in the nineteenth century and continues today. These have been years of stress and change. People are looking for fresh applications of old truth. Arthur has returned in a time of need." Perhaps it is this spirituality, as well as her insistence on the vitality of the Arthurian legend, that has brought so many of us to think of Valerie Lagorio as professor, advisor, editor, and most of all friend.

Mildred Leake Day
Quondam et Futurus
Gardendale, Alabama

Introduction
The Social Implications of the
Arthurian Legend

———————— *Martin B. Shichtman and*
*James P. Carley**

The history of Arthurian scholarship has for the most part been based on the assumption that the various elements constituting the legend contain inherent meaning, meaning that could be recovered through appropriate scrutiny of the legend's origins. The desire to understand these origins has led to a multitude of studies, including those focusing on Celtic mythology, cult ritual, Jewish ceremony, Gnostic philosophy, Samartian culture, depth psychology, and medieval debates concerning the Eucharist.[1] Archaeological expeditions have attempted to uncover the location of the "real" Camelot.[2] Predictably, the different arguments suggesting that consistent meanings inhere within the structure of the legend have, despite their claims to accuracy, produced contradictory results. In *Culture and the King*, we would like to distance ourselves from the notion of a consistent and recoverable Arthurian past. Our aim, instead, is to study the legend as a set of unstable signs appropriated by differing cultural groups to advance differing ideological agendas. The essays within this collection are primarily concerned with the issue of re-vision, how cultures alter inherited texts and are, in turn, changed by them. They also consider the ways in which various cultures have empowered the Arthurian legend so that power might be derived from it. The purpose of this volume, then, is to suggest that the vitality of the Arthurian legend is not to be found in some obscure and still unrecovered past but rather in its ability to be transformed and to transform, in its nearly protean potential to promote the imperatives of widely divergent social groups.

Culture and the King is divided into two parts. The eleven essays which comprise part I, "The Middle Ages: Inventing a Lost Past," attempt to address the medieval social conditions responsible for the creation of not a single, monolithic Arthurian legend, but rather a multiplicity of Arthurian legends. Louis Montrose has recently argued that:

> to speak of the social production of "literature" or of any particular text is to signify not only that it is socially produced but also that it is socially productive—that it is the product of work and that it performs work in the process of being written, enacted, or read. Recent theories of textuality have argued persuasively that the referent of a linguistic sign cannot be fixed; that the meaning of a text cannot be stabilized. At the same time, writing and reading are always historically and socially determinate events, performed *in* the world and *upon* the world by gendered individual and collective human agents. We may simultaneously acknowledge the theoretical indeterminacy of the signifying process and the historical specificity of discursive practices—acts of speaking, writing, and interpreting.[3]

In his article, "Marie de France's Arthurian *Lai*: Subtle and Political," David Chamberlain suggests that the Arthurian legend, even in its earliest literary manifestations, is structured by shifting social conditions. He locates Marie de France's criticisms of the Arthurian legend both in the intellectual environment of the twelfth century and in political pressures exerted by the court of Henry II. According to Chamberlain, Marie's *Lanval* functions as a response to Henry's political critics, a group whose authorization of the Arthurian legend was intended to undermine the king's claim to the throne; her learned de-glamorization—and to some extent de-historization—of Arthur would simultaneously flatter Henry II and prove the arguments of his opponents specious.

Chamberlain hints at Arthurian romance's thematization of the twelfth-century aristocracy's anxieties concerning genealogical progression. This becomes, to some extent, the subject of Donald Maddox's article. Maddox extends Claude Lévi-Strauss' hypothesis that Grail narratives embody "a myth of interrupted communication." For Lévi-Strauss, heroic achievement of the Grail involves the restoration of communications subverted prior to and during the quest. Maddox maintains that in many early French Arthurian narratives—and in many early French narratives, in general—the heroic adventure which is depicted as being adequate to the task of restoring axiological continuity involves an encounter with a narrative enclave, or relatively brief segment of narrative, which embodies ritualized protocols that must be fulfilled by the hero in order to restore continuity with the anterior order—a restoration often associated with reintegration in a genealogical network. He argues that the textual communities that sustained Arthurian fictions emphasizing this recuperation of an idealized anterior order did so not because such narratives constitute a psychological archetype but rather to allay real concerns about genealogical disruptions which might dilute claims to aristocratic privilege.

It has been the practice of Arthurian scholars to seek associations between Welsh narratives mentioning Arthur and the Arthurian romances of twelfth-century France. The primary purpose of such investigations has been to ascertain where the legend originated. Armel Diverres takes a different approach in his study of the Welsh *Culhwch and Olwen* and the romances of Chrétien de Troyes, an approach suggesting a reconsideration of the datings of these texts. Like Chamberlain and Maddox, Diverres suggests that specific renderings of the Arthurian story grow out of particular political situations. Diverres places the writing of *Culhwch and Olwen* at about 1100, and contends that the text's portrayal of Arthur, and its interest in heroic ideals, reflects the conservatism of the Welsh aristocracy, a conservatism fostered, at least in part, by the geographical isolation of Wales at the beginning of the twelfth century. Diverres also analyzes Chrétien's changing attitude towards Arthur from the early romances, *Erec* and *Cliges*—in which the king is presented as a regal figure—to later compositions, *Lancelot, Yvain,* and *Perceval*—in which he seems weak and ineffective. Diverres attributes this inconsistency to France's shifting political position in relation to Henry II, and claims that *Erec* and *Cliges* must have been written before 1186, their depiction of Arthur coinciding with French enthusiasm for Henry. *Lancelot, Yvain,* and *Perceval*, however, were likely written after 1186, after the treaty of Amiens freed Philip Augustus of France from the headaches of internal rebellions and allowed him to turn his attention to undermining Henry's authority.

Both Elspeth Kennedy and Edward Donald Kennedy focus on the reception of the Arthurian legend, on the horizons of expectation of medieval readers and listeners. Elspeth Kennedy examines the verbal echoes from Arthurian romance—and in particular from the Prose *Lancelot*—in some "nonfictional" writings of three prestigious thirteenth-century knights, Philippe de Novare, Philippe de Beaumanoir, and Ramon Lull, as well as Geoffroi de Charney of the fourteenth century.

In her view, Philippe de Novare, Philippe de Beaumanoir, and Ramon Lull found in Arthurian romance support for their own—largely legalistic—thoughts concerning feudal loyalty and the role of the knight in defending justice and the Church; these three apparently cared little about Arthurian romance as a literature of love. Geoffroi de Charney, on the other hand, writing in an entirely different political climate, made use of Arthurian romance to explain the role of the lady in creating a good knight. Edward Donald Kennedy considers medieval principles of translation and adaptation in his discussion of the French *La Mort le Roi Artu* and its influence on the fourteenth-century English stanzaic *Morte Arthur.* He argues that for the English poet, translation and adaptation become reinterpretation, a process incorporating an evaluation of audience values and expectations. The changes the English poet makes in the French text—specifically, the changes that are made in the depiction of Arthur—are therefore designed to reinforce the audience's conception of itself as a social and political entity.

Donald L. Hoffman and James P. Carley suggest that the Arthurian legend holds enormous propagandistic potential, that it can not only be utilized to reconfirm a culture's self-perception, it can bring about shifts in that self-perception and perhaps even in how the culture is viewed by others. Hoffman deals with the political use of Merlin in the thirteenth-century Italian context of the conflict between Frederick II and the pope. While Frederick's propaganda mill incorporated the prophesies of Merlin to convince the populace that the emperor was humanity's millennial hope, the pope looked to the same source to denounce Frederick as the beast of the apocalypse. From the writings generated by this standoff, the figure of Merlin joined, at least within the popular imagination, prophets whose historicity was believed and respected. Carley, editing an as yet unpublished account of an excavation in 1419, offers fresh evidence of the interest demonstrated by the monks of Glastonbury in "finding" Joseph of Arimathea's burial place and displying his relics. A letter written in 1421, in response to an inquiry from Henry V, hints—but does not actually say—that an excavation of the Glastonbury cemetery uncoverd Joseph's coffin and bones. Carley maintains that it is possible Henry himself commissioned this excavation, hoping to gain for England the status—with all of its attendant political advantages—of *natio* at the Council of Constance. Indeed, Carley speculates that only Henry's death in 1422 prevented the revelation of this astonishing "discovery."

Felicity Riddy's essay on *Sir Gawain and the Green Knight* (*SGGK*) addresses the dialogical tensions underpinning the social discourses involved in the creation of the text. Arguing that *SGGK* represents an intersection of aristocratic rhetorical culture and the understandings of thirteenth-century academic science regarding human physicality, Riddy examines the poem's emphasis on, almost obsession with, speech. According to Riddy, *SGGK* is informed both by courtly society's insistence that speech— and courtly speech, in particular—differentiates people from animals and by the writings of thirteenth-century scientists recognizing biological associations between humans and beasts. For Riddy, the poem ultimately undermines the pretensions of the politically powerful in its almost democratizing appreciation of the limitations of the body.

The final three essays in this section consider the various cultural forces giving form to Sir Thomas Malory's fifteenth-century Arthurian vision. Martin B. Shichtman begins with a discussion of the *Queste del Saint Graal*, Malory's likely source for "The Tale of the Sankgreal." Whereas scholars have often pointed to the Cistercian spirituality of the *Queste*, they have overlooked its political possibilities. Shichtman maintains that the *Queste* served to mediate escalating hostilities between the Cistercian monastic movement and members of the knightly classes. This mediation functioned both to benefit the Cistercians, who were largely dependent on knightly patronage for their order's expansion in the eleventh and twelfth centuries, and the knights, who, during this same period gained respect and authority, at least in part through their associations with monasteries. The Cistercian bias of the *Queste* offered knights certainty, almost as a commodity, in exchange for obedience. Shichtman argues that Malory's Grail story, on the other hand, reflects the social disruptions of fifteenth-century England and deviates from its source by suggesting the unreadability and even duplicity of semiotic systems. Bonnie Wheeler looks both to medieval and contemporary discussions of alchemy in her discussion of Malory's "Tale of Sir Gareth." Wheeler suggests that Gareth's development as a character follows the processes described in medieval alchemical handbooks as necessary for the creation of gold. She then turns to C. G. Jung's discussion of alchemy as a metaphor which structures and images human change and growth. According to Wheeler, Malory's incorporation of the alchemical process serves to describe Gareth's growth as a knight—his physical development in the physical world—and to mark his journey to psychological self-realization. Maureen Fries challenges the often reiterated assertion that Malory sees marriage as compatible with worship and knighthood. Her essay, which includes an analysis of fifteenth-century discussions of conjugal issues and dilemmas, demonstrates that Malory's England had witnessed, from a number of highly publicized cases, the collapse of the belief that marriage would necessarily function as a solution to social, political, or even emotional problems. In the fictional world of Malory's *Morte Darthur*, Fries claims, knights are forced to acknowledge that marriage is a hindrance rather than an asset to the pursuit of a chivalric career. In fact, a knight is much more likely to achieve success by taking a mistress than by taking a wife.

Norman F. Cantor has recently argued that attempts by twentieth-century scholars of medieval civilization to recuperate the past have only produced so many reinventions of the Middle Ages.[4] Cantor contends that in a number of ways these reinventions say more about the cultures of the scholars than they do about the subjects of their researches. The second part of *Culture and the King* looks at various appropriations of the Arthur story by postmedieval societies. In this part authors suggest that postmedieval popularizers had to reinvent the Arthurian legend as well as the Middle Ages in general to meet the needs of their audiences. Laurie A. Finke's essay, for example, examines the implications of the political mysticism—the combination of allegory, romance, antiquarianism, religion, and epic—of Edmund Spenser's *Faerie Queene*. Incorporating the writings of contemporary sociologists and anthropologists, Finke demonstrates that for both Spenser and his audience, the Arthurian legend functions as a kind of cultural capital, exchangeable under specific conditions for wealth, recognition, and power. According to Finke, Spenser profits from an invocation of the medieval past which functions to identify England as a sovereign nation, whose sovereignty is associated with the person of the monarch, and which participates in the sixteenth-century creation of an "imagined community" of the sort Benedict Anderson maintains is necessary to the development of nationalism.

Whereas Finke sees Spenser's *Faerie Queen* as reflecting England's sixteenth-century dynastic ambitions, David R. Carlson turns to two seventeenth-century texts, the Blome-Stansby edition of Malory and *Brittains Glory* to demonstrate the political instability of a nation embroiled in the discourses of revolution. Carlson suggests that the 1634 Blome-Stansby edition of Malory prepares the way for the revolution of 1640 through its manipulation of the Arthurian legend to criticize the monarchy. The preface, or "Advertisement," which begins the Blome-Stansby edition, is of particular interest to Carlson. In this "Advertisement," the editors/publishers clarify the differences between illegitimate and legitimate monarchies and insist upon the rights of society to remove an illegitimate government, by force, if necessary, in favor of a legitimate one. *Brittains Glory*, published in 1684, avocates, on the other hand, the restoration of the English monarchy dethroned by revolution. Although almost certainly influenced by Malory's *Morte Darthur, Brittains Glory* de-emphasizes all internal conflicts in the Arthurian court. Within this text, all political opposition to Arthur is derived from external sources. The point of *Brittains Glory,* then, is to aggrandize political stability under a strong monarch.

Debra N. Mancoff and Rebecca Umland discuss the "romantic revival" of the nineteenth century. Mancoff explores the pictorial presentation of the Arthurian legend in the frescoes of William Dyce. Dyce, prior to his commission to paint a series of Arthurian frescoes for the Queen's Robing Room at the new palace at Westminster, had little experience with the legend and found it a problem and an embarrassment once he began his study. Searching for "chivalric greatness," Dyce encountered instead, especially in Malory's rendering of the Arthurian legend, a catalogue of human failings as well as the glorification of Catholicism, a religion for which he held little regard. Dyce responded with a kind of historical revisionism which enabled him to depict the various characters of the legend as representative of particular virtures. Mancoff maintains that Dyce re-authorized the Arthurian legend both for himself and his aristocratic patrons by imposing a "moral signification" which reformed characters' vices while celebrating their virtues, by transforming Lancelot's adultery, for instance, into a celebration of "Generosity." Umland focuses on the concerns of the conservative middle class in her analysis of Tennyson's *Idylls of the King.* Following Michel Foucault's suggestion that Victorian England did not repress sexuality but rather transformed sex into "discourse" so that it might be regulated, Umland discusses Tennyson's depiction of Vivien as an attempt to achieve some social control over women's bodies, particularly over the bodies of the enormous number of women who formed the ranks of England's prostitutes. Umland demonstrates that prostitution was considered England's most significant social problem during the nineteenth century: while authorities debated the enactment of Contagious Diseases Acts, well over 8,600 women of the evening walked the streets of London. Tennyson enters this highly charged environment with a portrait of Viven—which would bring him both praise and criticism from his contemporaries—ultimately condemning those women he sees as being destructive to the very fabric of his society.

The final two essays in our volume deal with contemporary renderings of the Arthurian story. James Noble argues that beneath what appears as feminist rhetoric—and sympathetic liberalism—in Marion Zimmer Bradley's extraordinarily successful *The Mists of Avalon* (1982), lurks a very conservative and, at times, homophobic agenda.

He contends that in Bradley's depiction of Lancelot, a character confused by ambivalent sexual desires, there is no attempt whatsoever to portray homosexuality as a potential source of pride or power. In fact, Bradley's message seems to be just the opposite. Lancelot, having finally acknowledged his sexual orientation, must witness that orientation criticized both by men, who embody the narrow-mindedness of the patriarchal order, and, amazingly enough, by women, who are supposed to represent a liberating alternative to patriarchy's restrictiveness. For Noble, Bradley's attempts to demythologize homosexuality result in at best tokenism and at worst a misleading representation of suffering and disempowerment. In the concluding essay, Charles T. Wood reveals the importance of *Camelot 3000*, a series of twelve comic books, first published between 1982 and 1985, in redefining the Arthurian legend for a number of different audiences. Wood's article entertains the possibility of the creation of a whole new Arthurian genre, complicated by the structural problems posed by the re-release of the series in 1988 as a single paperback book, classified by its publisher, Warner Books, as science fiction. He also maintains that *Camelot 3000* must be taken seriously for its insertion of the Arthurian legend into contemporary controversies relating to gender, economics, and politics—both national and international.

It is almost universally acknowledged by scholars that even if a king named Arthur did once exist, all efforts to portray either what he or his court were really like have failed. The scholars who have contributed to *Culture and the King* recognize that perhaps such a portrayal cannot be made. They recognize the Arthurian legend as continuously changing, continuously undergoing transformation to respond to social pressures. To study the shifts in the Arthurian legend demands involvement in such diverse disciplines as literature, history, art, politics, economics, and gender study. To study the shifts in the Arthurian legend demands an understanding that the boundaries the academy routinely erects around these disciplines must be crossed, if not destroyed altogether. This collection offers a number of approaches to the ways in which the Arthurian legend has been appropriated and how it has brought about social change. There remains yet much to be done in recognizing the significance of the legend's relationship to Western society.

We dedicate *Culture and the King* to Professor Valerie M. Lagorio, upon her retirement from the University of Iowa. We hope that the focus of our collection serves to honor this distinguished Arthurian, whose career in so many ways continuously emphasized the vitality of the legend in its transference across cultures and time.

Notes

* The editors would like to acknowledge Randolph Harnett, who went carefully through the manuscript at various stages and whose suggestions ranged from details of punctuation to significant revision of text. We would also like to thank Michael Sturdy for his help with the index.

1. For an overview of the various theories concerning the origins of the Arthurian legend, see Marylyn J. Parins, "Modern Arthurian Scholarship," in *The Arthurian Encyclopedia*, ed. Norris J. Lacy et al. (New York, 1986), pp. 479–94.

2. See Leslie Alcock, *Was This Camelot? Excavations at Cadbury Castle, 1966–1970* (New York, 1972); also "Cadbury-Camelot: a Fifteen-Year Perspective," *Proceedings of the British Academy* 68 (1982), 355–88.

3. Louis Montrose, "Professing the Renaissance: The Poetics and Politics of Culture," in *The New Historicism*, ed. H. Aram Veeser (New York, 1989), p. 23.

4. See Norman F. Cantor, *Inventing the Middle Ages: The Lives, Works, and Ideas of the Great Medievalists of the Twentieth Century* (New York, 1991).

PART I

The Middle Ages: Inventing a Lost Past

Marie de France's Arthurian *Lai*: Subtle and Political

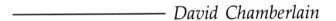 *David Chamberlain*

Marie's one *lai* involving King Arthur, *Lanval*, offers two problems still not explained adequately in terms of Marie's own culture: the harsh portrait of Arthur and the nature of Lanval's love affair. This essay focuses mainly on the love affair, and it offers new interpretations of both problems. Why does Marie unexpectedly present an Arthur who is highly unjust and shallow? This harsh view is especially surprising since *Lanval* is one of the earliest Arthurian works, after Wace's *Brut* (1155) but before Chrétien's *Erec* (c. 1170).[1] In earlier Arthurian authors, Geoffrey and Wace, Arthur has faults, but none that explain Marie's harshness. Possibly she took Arthur over from a source "en Bretans,"[2] but such an Arthur is not justified by surviving Brythonic material. Quite likely, she modified sources for her own purposes, given her wit and opportunity.[3]

This essay proposes that Marie's flawed Arthur was intended as praise and indirect counsel for King Henry II (1154–89). She wrote the *Lais* "in honor" of Henry, her "noble reis," "pruz e curteis," in whose heart "tuz biens" take root (prologue, 43–48). Henry was deeply involved in legal procedure, which is a major aspect of *Lanval*. He was an intellectual king, "remarkably polished in letters."[4] He was greatly concerned about succession to kingship, also a theme in *Lanval*. He and Eleanor received Wace's *Roman de Brut* in 1155. From 1157 to 1171, he had notable trouble with the Welsh princes, including three military failures,[5] and quite likely he was annoyed by constant Welsh talk of Arthur's return to rule.[6] Later, that talk motivated him to tell the monks of Glastonbury where to dig for Arthur's bones, which were supposedly

15

found late in his reign.[7] To praise Henry as a soldier, husband, and royal judge, and to scotch Welsh fantasies, Marie needed an unjust Arthur. To develop a subtle love theme, she also needed a ruler of Carlisle with an adulterous wife.

Unfortunately, criticism of *Lanval* suffers from one overriding defect: it largely ignores Marie's cultural context. Book after book neglects Marie's own *Fables* and *Espurgatoire* and hardly mentions twelfth-century moral philosophy, religion, historical works, or literary theory.[8] The same is true of articles, except for focused studies of particular topics.[9] Most interpretations of *Lanval* actually contradict general twelfth-century values. Jean Rychner is typical: Marie's purpose is "pur de surcharge didactique et morale,"[10] which contradicts all her prologues. Although E. Mickel emphasizes Marie's assertion of religious love in *Eliduc* and *Le Fresne*, in *Lanval* he finds simply the theme of "loyal lovers" overcoming "obstacles."[11] Jacques Ribard offers a brief reading that would have been recognizable to a twelfth-century audience, a mystical reading of the supernatural lady as divine grace, but it too is hardly compatible with the poem or medieval common sense.[12]

Marie herself, however, offers specific guidance for reading her *Lais*. In the prologue, she makes five related points: (1) "knowledge and . . . eloquence" are given by God to be used willingly (1–4); (2) ancient custom was to write "very obscurely" so that those who came later can "gloser la lettre/E de lur sen le surplus mettre" (15–16);[13] (3) philosophers knew that "the more they studied the subtler their minds would become to avoid errors" (17–22); (4) to avoid "vice" and "great suffering," one "should study. . . and do difficult work"; and (5) the *lais* must be remembered (34–40), an idea she repeats frequently later.[14] If "aventures" (36) are not held "pur remambrance" (35), implicitly they cannot be used to avoid the "vice" and "great sorrow" Marie speaks of. Here she draws on the Augustinian three faculties of the soul—reason, will, and memory—and similar emphasis on memory appears in John of Salisbury, Henry II's friend, Walter Map, and others.[15] Marie's term "aventures" draws on the Boethian tradition of fortune, of adversity and prosperity, which pervades twelfth-century thought.[16] Marie's prologue hardly implies that the *Lais* will contradict the commonplace norms of piety and wisdom. Her other works show a similar theory. The *Fables* (c. 1175) were written "par moralité" and to "give back her soul" to God.[17] The idea is relevant to *Lanval*. In passages of the *Espurgatoire* (c. 1185) not in her Latin source, Marie wishes "in the name of God" to put into French "the pains of Purgatory" "for remembrance" out of "great love to serve God," for the sake of "the laity," who should pray "to cleanse our sins."[18] These were not superficial sentiments in the twelfth century, and they cohere well with recent research on twelfth-century literary theory.[19]

The *contents* of the *Fables* and *Espurgatoire* provide an excellent introduction to Marie's world view. The *Fables* encourage wisdom, justice, and other virtues; they warn against folly, false counsel, and other vices. She wrote them for an uncertain "Count William, most valiant of this realm. . .the flower of chivalry and learning,"[20] indirectly a norm for *Lanval*. In specific fables, it is folly to leave an old country for a new unknown one (22) and folly to leave human society (23), both of which Lanval does. Intelligence is a greater aid than wealth or lineage, and women can deceive better than the devil (45), both points relevant to Marie's *lai*. "Many follow their wills so much they do not see what harsh *aventure* will follow" (63.6–9); the shrewd easily deceive the fool (70.72–76); and the wise person believes only the truth (83.47–48): three ideas relevant to *Lanval*. The wise person prays to do as God, not the changeable heart, wishes (99.21–26). Lanval obviously had not read the *Fables*.

Marie's *Espurgatoire seint Patrice* reminds us vividly of the religious side of her culture. She translates a Latin prose account of a journey through purgatory (from Station Island, Lough Derg, Donegal) by an Irish knight, Owein. It emphasizes faith, sacraments, devils, gruesome punishments, the earthly paradise, and pious clergy. The following themes are especially relevant to *Lanval*. Souls are rewarded and punished after death (49–60). Owein saves himself from the "evil allurements" of demons with the name "Jesu" (780, etc.). The "shield of faith" and sword "of the Holy Spirit" defeat devils and their false counsel of pleasure. Marie does not say what sins are being punished, but among those "nailed down," "dismembered," "flailed," "whirled," "boiled," only those "hanging by genitals," over "roasting fires" are recognized by Owein as former "campaignuns,"[21] clearly sexual offenders of noble rank. The miseries of the world are as nothing compared to these torments (1401–4), and whoever "remembers" them "will never delight in the vanity of. . .this world" (1415–19, 25). Owein wishes to become a monk, but Marie *changes her source* so he remains a knight because as such "he can serve God well" (1930). This ideal of knighthood reflects adversely on several knights in the *Lais*. The *Fables* and *Espurgatoire* embody twelfth-century views that critics should keep "en remembraunce e en memoire" (*Espurgatoire*, 5). To neglect them misrepresents Marie's culture.

The setting of *Lanval* has never been analyzed from a twelfth-century viewpoint. Arthur "sojourns" at Carlisle ("Kardoel," 5) literally because "the Scots and Picts" are "destroying" England, but this reason is never mentioned again. Carlisle is not a conventional seat for Arthur since Geoffrey and Wace never place him there. It may have been the setting in a lost north British source;[22] but an Avalon near Carlisle does not cohere with the lady's distant land (111–12). Carlisle did have recent and annoying associations for King Henry. He was knighted there at Pentecost in 1149 by King David of Scotland, but he declined to knight Malcolm IV there in 1158 because of Malcolm's growing hostility.[23]

Marie is making use of the common figurative meaning of the far north. Carlisle is the northernmost Brythonic city, and ubiquitously the far north is associated with the devil. We find it in scripture, Dante, Boccaccio, Chaucer, and Milton.[24] In the twelfth century, *Brendan*, Bernard, Walter Map, John of Salisbury, and many others use the idea.[25] To think Marie did not intend such connotations is to make her obtuse. Therefore, the most likely reason she does not mention again the "Scots and Picts" is that they signify the real enemies attacking Arthur's realm, that is, spiritual enemies in the soul and without, Paul's "spirits of wickedness" (Eph. 6:12) or John's "evil spirits" who ravage those "without wholesome faith."[26] Marie describes them at length in the *Espurgatoire*.

The time of Pentecost (11) also embodies meanings relevant to the action but ignored by critics. In Geoffrey and Wace, Pentecost offers the supreme example of Arthur's splendor and piety, but Marie's Arthur lacks virtues they describe.[27] Her Arthur gives nothing to Lanval (18), but Wace's Arthur gives rich gifts to all "stranger knights" who serve him.[28] Marie's Arthur gives "women" as well as "land" (17), like infidel Baligant of Babylon in *Roland*, but Arthur in Wace and Charlemagne do not.[29] Pentecost celebrates, of course, the Holy Spirit, particularly for its inspiration of the apostles (Acts 1–2). The Holy Spirit is associated especially with charity, and it is offended especially by envy.[30] But envy is just what most of Arthur's court, and implicitly Arthur himself, feel towards Lanval (23). Marie also refers to the "table roünde" (15), which was designed by Arthur specifically to prevent envy, according to Wace, who first describes it.[31] So Marie's Arthur violates his own ideal of the Round Table and profanes the feast of Pentecost. These offenses create Lanval's adversity: no gifts, no friends, and no counsel far from home.

But Marie also implies that Lanval has some responsibility for his plight and some obvious remedies. She never calls him "wise" ("sages"), as she does other characters.[32] Implicitly, he is improvident in "largesce" (21), spending all his wealth (30) without precaution. As the son of a "rich King" of "great nobility" (27, 232), though at present "far from his heritage" (28) and a temporary "vassal" of Arthur (363, 29), Lanval has several options. He can send home for funds, or return home, which is strongly encouraged in such situations by *Fables* and *Espurgatoire*, or make up a troop to punish the Scots and Picts, as Henry II, Eliduc, or Milun would have done, and thus oblige Arthur to reward him. But Lanval can do nothing.

Pentecost also implies another remedy for Lanval, and Marie invites readers to understand it by the words she uses: "dolent," "descunseillez," "ne seit sucurs quere" (34–38). Spiritual "conseil" and "sucurs" are available at Pentecost to those who seek them. One of the seven gifts of the Holy Spirit is "counsel" ("consilium"), so to be "descunseillez" at Pentecost is really to need and invite "sucurs" of the Holy Spirit. Abelard names his famous oratory "The Paraclete," for its great "comfort" in his distress, which was vastly worse than Lanval's.[33] To Map and John the Holy Spirit is a "source of continual joy," and Marie's Owein is defended and solaced by the Holy Spirit.[34]

"Counsel" is related to the whole Trinity, of course, and constitutes a major theme of medieval literature that begins in scripture, abounds in Marie's three works, and perhaps culminates in Chaucer's *Melibee*. Abelard repeats to Heloise Solomon's words, "do nothing without counsel and you will have no regrets."[35] In the *Jeu d'Adam* great harm comes from false counsel,[36] and Venus, or libido, "denudes anyone of counsel."[37] Lanval is oblivious to this commonplace source of aid, which Marie skillfully signals with "pentecuste," "descunseillez," and "sucurs."

Also related to Pentecost is Marie's important comment that Lanval is "far from his heritage" (28). Literally, he is many miles from his father's kingdom or his own earthly inheritance. Receiving it is a privilege and duty that his father and his subjects naturally expect Lanval to accept and that Marie emphasizes in other *lais*.[38] By the end of the *lai*, however, Lanval is forever separated from this "heritage," a situation that was abhorrent to medieval lords and subjects, and especially to Henry II, who made careful early plans for the succession of "the Young King," Henri au Cort Mantel.[39]

But "heritage" also has commonplace figurative connotations: the heritage or inheritance of all Christians is heaven or salvation. All should be "heirs of God" (Rom. 8:17), "heirs of eternal life" (1 Pet. 3:22), having an "eternal inheritance" (Ps. 36:18). The meaning is vivid in the twelfth century.[40] Princes inherit "eternal blessedness," says John, but they lose that "eternal heritage" by "acts of illicit fornication," says Andreas Capellanus.[41] Marie had no need to explain the obvious implication. Lanval is "far from" his spiritual "heritage" at the beginning of the *lai*, but he is permanently separated from it at the end.

Just before Lanval's meeting with the mysterious lady, or "fairy," as most critics call her, Marie portends her nature. Lanval's horse "trembles extremely" (46) by a running stream, and critics recognize this as evidence of the supernatural.[42] Like the stag that would rather die than enter Grendel's mere, Lanval's war horse ("destrer," 41) shows the reaction of innocent nature to malice. It has more sense than its master, who "does not give a thought to his horse" (78–79). Lanval's condition also is portentous. For some time, he has been impecunious (30), unhappy (34), without counsel (36), and unsure where to seek aid (38), and now, he is alone, idle and bored on his back, seeing nothing that pleases him (44–52). At this moment two beautiful maidens appear, richly dressed, tightly laced, and carrying two basins and a towel (53–66). Lanval's condition invites trouble. We do not need Stephen Vincent Benét, Faust, or Theophilus to tell us who exploits adversity.[43] John epitomizes tradition: "the Enemy should find you occupied . . . for idleness banishes all interest in virtue."[44]

From the start, Marie uses verbal irony to signal her attitude. Arthur is no more "pruz e . . .curteis" (6), than Equitan is "noble barun" (1) and "mut . . .curteis" (11). Marie praises Lanval's "valur" (21) and "prüesce" (22), but he shows neither. She says she "will tell [us] the truth" about the golden basins, but she never does. She is pushing us to discover the hidden "truth." She reminds us of wisdom when the maidens call their lady "pruz e sage e bele" (72), but she herself never says it, since neither Lanval nor the Lady is "wise." Again, why would maidens tell a knight of "prowess" (22, 113) they will escort him "safely" (75) to a visible tent, unless Marie wants to suggest that the journey is not so safe? Other adverbs were available.

But the description of the mysterious lady herself most vividly conveys her nature. Marie's allusion to Queen Semiramis (82) powerfully discredits the lady. Yes, Semiramis had power ("puissance"), but she hardly had wisdom ("saveir," 84). Paulus Orosius was a major source: Semiramis was "burning with lust and thirsty for blood . . . in the course of continuous adulteries," killed her lovers, "shamelessly . . . had incestuous relations with her son," and abolished all laws against incest.[45] Fulgentius, Peter Comestor, Dante, Boccaccio, and Chaucer take the same view.[46] Babylon was also associated with the infidelity of Islam, as in *Roland* and many other works.[47] If the mysterious lady were beneficient, no writer sensitive to connotations would compare her to Semiramis.

The allusion to "the emperor Octavian" (85) also derogates the supernatural wealth of the lady, but it may be a double reminder. John praises Octavius for resisting Cleopatra but blames the Romans as "victims of vainglory and greed beyond all people."[48] Linked with Semiramis, Rome especially implies an evil pagan source for the "lady's" inconceivable wealth. This staggering wealth is not an aspect of "fairy" lore in the twelfth century, but it does suggest "the prince of this world," who tempts with all the kingdoms of earth (Mt. 4:8; Lk. 4:5), and Marie's wording actually implies that the lady's tent cannot be purchased for any sum.[49]

Minor details confirm subtlely the obvious implications of Semiramis and supernatural wealth. The lady's beauty surpasses "the young lilies and roses of spring" (93–94), certainly ironic since lilies and roses are the well-known crowns of the martyrs, for chastity and charity. The lady's mantle of "purpre alexandrine" (102) is a sign of infidelity. Like Babylon, Alexandria was associated with "exterminating the Christian faith."[50] In *Roland*, both pagan Marsile and traitor Ganelon wear "Alexandrine brocade" (408, 463), and the emir of Babylon assembles his fleet at "Alexandre" (2626). Peter the Venerable of Cluny, who kindly counseled Heloise, laments that through Mahomet, Satan has delivered "to eternal death almost one-third of the human race."[51] When Marie wants to signify with cloth the noble virtue of Le Fresne, she uses a "brocade de Costentinoble" (123–25).

In this context, the basins and towels of the maidens suggest the "truth" (63) that Marie does not "tell." After pleasure in bed till "vespers" (156) and new rich clothing, Lanval washes his hands in the basins before eating (178–79). Although literally good manners, the washing suggests ironically the familiar washing of hands in the Mass, beginning "I will wash my hands among the innocent and encompass thy altar, O God" (Ps. 25:6). The prayer asks protection against the impious, whose hands are "filled with gifts" (25:9–10), just what the "fairy" offers Lanval. The washing, the new clothing, and the "commandemenz" of the lady (129) imply both the faith Lanval is abandoning and the impiety he is embracing. Sensual delights to the wise, says Henry's witty *familiaris* Walter Map, are a "honeyed poison" held out by "the cupbearers of Babel."[52]

Other details deftly confirm the folly of Lanval's "love." The lady is "whiter than the thornflower" (106), but throughout medieval poetry, the thorn or hawthorn, with its long spikes, worthless fruit, and unpleasant odor, is a sign of lechery.[53] In *Roland*, it is associated only with Baligant (3521) at a point when his death, false gods, and bestial followers are emphasized (3513–30). Later, Lanval vows to perform all the lady's "commandments," whether "Turt a folie u a seveir" (126), which clearly foreshadows folly. Equitan uses exactly the same words before attempting murder (340). Lanval foolishly ignores the lady's sudden appearance, distant land, immeasurable wealth, and inexplicable love. He sees only beauty (117), feels instantly the "spark"

(118) of "Amurs," and without a thought commits himself wholly to sensuality and opulence. When the lady grants "her love and body" (133), Marie comments "ore est Lanval en dreite veie" (134), drawing ironically on the familiar *via recta* and related imagery of scripture and liturgy. She also comments ironically twice, "Now Lanval is well lodged" (140, 154) when he gets the lady's wealth and bed. For three weeks, Lanval revels in money and coitus. Though he shows largesse (205–214), he does not give to the poor. John encapsulates the norm: "Pleasure is indeed a spurious source for virtue," and Map illustrates vividly that "he who controls his flesh escapes wrath."[54] If the lady truly loves Lanval "above anything" (116), why does she need to ask "If you are valiant and courteous?" (113). She ought to know already, as ladies do in Wace (10511–20). The only evidence she requires is secrecy, but numerous authors show that the virtuous do not practice sexual secrecy.[55] John concludes that secrets "destroy peace of mind" and lead "countless people...into hell" (3.12). The view that *Lanval* illustrates "la nécessité du secret en amour" begs the question.[56] The lady commands secrecy because she wants Lanval to violate it.

Why does the lady grant Lanval enormous wealth? He could be happy with much less. He could then go home to his "heritage" and marry her, which does happen with "fairies" (see below). The *Fables* show that he should leave Arthur's court.[57] Whatever the lady's motive, the effect of the wealth is predictable: "riches bring many friends" (Pro. 19:4), and the lady knows that popularity will arouse the queen.

Who, then, is this mysterious lady? No critic provides an answer convincing in a twelfth-century context. Twelfth-century fairies do not control immeasurable wealth or provide instant money and coitus. Geoffrey and Wace do not mention fairies. Though Merlin is the son of an "incubus demon," who moves boulders and disguises an adulterer, he does not have the lady's powers, and neither do fairies in *Eneas* and Chrétien.[58] Gottfried's "goddess" from the "fairy land of Avalon" removes sadness with Petitcrieu, but does not provide immense wealth or remove people from society.[59] Map tells of knights who seize fairies, beget children, and live happily, but that is all.[60] Fairies are beautiful in Marie's *Guigemar* (704), in *Narcisus* (450, 678), and in *The Romance of the Rose*, and show libido, pride, and generosity in Adam de la Halle, but not such supernatural powers.[61]

Indeed, the lady is not a fairy but a devil or succubus. Twelfth-century thought abounds in "assaults of demons," as Abelard warns Heloise.[62] Demons have individual vices in Peter Lombard, as does "Caucaueresard," the female demon of *luxuria* in Reginald of Durham.[63] When Philippe Ménard rhapsodizes over "La mystérieuse profondeur, tout emplie d' êtres. . .de l'Autre Monde," he unwittingly evokes the unromantic world of Peter the Venerable and many others, where devils abound, over four hundred and sixty times in Peter's works, with sixty different epithets.[64] Map refers to devils over fifty times and includes several beautiful devils that deceive knights.[65] Most telling is his tale of Gerbert, later Pope Sylvester II (999–1004), and the "sucubus demon. . .Meridiana," who appears at noon when Gerbert is wretched from poverty. She wants love, provides great wealth, delights him with pleasure and wisdom, requires a promise that Gerbert breaks, and scorns him so she can bind him tighter.[66] Lanval's lady shows just the same behavior, but Gerbert finally escapes "through repentance." The succubus knows that a woman will desire Gerbert when he is famous and that he will break his promise, just as Lanval does. "Meridiana" is a version of the "mid-day demon" ("demonium meridianum") of Psalm 90:6, called in the *Ancrene Wisse* the "shining devil" who deceives men in a "woman's body."[67]

Marie's demon knows the weaknesses that will capture Lanval forever. Great wealth will bring Lanval popularity, so Guinevere will feel desire, Lanval then rebuff her, Arthur grow angry, and Lanval feel he desperately needs aid. She can easily foresee that Guinevere will lack temperance, Lanval lack prudence and fortitude, and Arthur lack justice.

Again, the setting for Guinevere's proposition is highly relevant, the feast of St. John the Baptist (24 June), two to four weeks after Pentecost. The Baptist evokes not only the story of a queen wanting someone's head, but also the themes of the "dreite veie," heavenly "heritage," initiation by water ("uns bacins"), and the Holy Spirit ("pentecuste").[68] Critics emphasize Potiphar's wife, but "la feste seint Johan" (220) is explicit and more thematic. Place also is significant, since Guinevere proposes adultery not only in an orchard ("vergier," 223, 247), but in one where the number "thirty" is emphasized (221, 247). It implies both the Fall and Judas' betrayal of Jesus for thirty silver pieces.[69]

Critics emphasize Guinevere's vice, but they overlook subtleties. She is considerably worse than Potiphar's wife, given her motive, haste, and virile husband. Marie's humorous litotes for the meeting of thirty knights and ladies, "Cil parlemenz n'est pas vilains" (252), cleverly foreshadows Guinevere's imminent, villainous, *parlemenz* with Lanval. The queen disguises her desire by saying she has "greatly honored" Lanval (263–64), but this honoring quickly becomes vilification and even sanctimony as she declares that Arthur will "lose God" (286) because of Lanval. With this brilliant illogical touch, Marie brings out the crucial theme of losing God, which relates mainly to Lanval.

Lanval's folly is equally impressive. He cannot socialize affably for a couple hours, but must mope by himself "if he did not have his own delight" (258). He rebuffs the queen (267) crudely for one who is supposedly "pruz e curteis" (113) and "not at all foolish or boorish" (177). Map recounts vividly knight Galo's "respectful" evasion of his queen's libido and malice, until "purged in the furnace of Venus, he shone as a pattern of continence."[70] After Guinevere's pederasty jeer, Lanval is cruder, giving the insult that motivates the rest of the *lai*: his lady's poorest maiden is worthier "in beauty and goodness" than the queen (297–302). The succubus knew when Lanval rashly embraced herself that he would be a fool again. Other details evoke the theme of losing God, expressed already by Guinevere. Lanval will not "betray faith" to his lord Arthur (272–74), but he certainly "betrays faith" to his father and his Lord God, whose two heritages he should cherish. He loves the woman who "ought to have renown above all others" (293–94), but that implies the Virgin. Ironically, he "cries mercy a hundred times" (343) of his lady, but such language evokes Mary or Christ.

The trial (352–470) and rescue (471–646) can be discussed more briefly, though Marie introduces brilliant new qualities of legal realism and humorous suspense. Legal procedure interested twelfth-century nobility, and especially Henry II, "a subtle deviser of novel judicial process," says Map, and later considered the father of the common law.[71] The contrast between Marie's accurate legal terminology and the behavior of Arthur and Lanval is highly amusing.

Arthur would have seemed ludicrous to Henry II. Driven by the queen's malice, he vows death for Lanval without questioning anything—there were sixty witnesses—or reflecting that *vilté* is grounds for acquittal.[72] He does not see that the queen acts more like one rebuffed than one rebuffing: if *she* were rebuffed, then his insult would create her vindictiveness. Like the queen (316–24), Arthur is more upset by the insult than the proposition (363–70). In Cornwall's "medial judgment" (433–46), the queen's anger (442, 454) is driving the trial as much as the king's honor (439–40, 447–48). She impatiently pushes him (468–69) and angers at the delay of her lunch (545–46).[73] Arthur should direct his wrath at the "Scots and Picts" or restrain it, as Charles does in *Roland*. He angers instantly at Guinevere's charge (325), angrily "appeals" Lanval (362), angrily sends for his household (382–85), and angers at delay in the trial (500, 541–46). Henry II too had a "distinct problem" with anger, but he also "observed mercy. . .even to those whom he disliked," says Map.[74]

Arthur's vacuity and wrath create much injustice. He demands excessive bailsmen ("plegges") and excessive bail (397–404). He ignores the fact that "felunie" (439) requires an additional "appealer" and also the ordeal of battle, as Glanvill says and Cornwall implies (443–46).[75] Since none of his knights offer ordeal of battle, as Thierry does in *Roland*, the case is too weak to support. Before the trial, more than a hundred think Lanval is "very wrongly" accused (420–23). The case should never have gone to trial, let alone to a plenary court. Lanval has not committed *felonia* as defined by Glanvill,[76] and in no law records or chronicles does an insult to a queen's beauty violate fealty to a king. It should have been settled informally.

Marie presents an ideal of judicial virtue in the Count of Cornwall, probably to please Henry II. In Geoffrey and Wace, Gorlois and Cador of Cornwall are distinctly virtuous, and Earl Reginald of Cornwall served Henry II notably until 1175.[77] Marie's Cornwall clarifies and softens the proceedings in his "medial judgment."[78] Justice will be done he says, whoever dislikes it, implying Arthur and Guinevere (334–36). He distinguishes clearly the charges of "felunie" (439) for the proposition and "mesfait" (440) for the insult (441–42), but in truth, he says rightly, the charges deserve no "respuns" (446) because no one "appeals" except the king (443). One should honor his lord, however (443–48), that is, respond to him. Therefore, simply an oath can clear Lanval of the *felunie* charge (449–50). Such an oath clears Iseult in Beroul, though actually she lies.[79] And Cornwall declares that displaying the beauty of the lady as "guarant" (451) or proof can clear Lanval of "mesfait" or "vilté" (456). Without "guarant," Lanval must depart the king's service, but the reader and Cornwall know that this is no punishment at all, since Lanval has been treated abominably.

Lanval himself is a consummate wimp from the arraignment to his "rescue." He grieves only for his "amie," without a thought of his honor or "heritage." He faints often (342) and tears his hair (347–48). He hopes to be killed (358), and may kill himself (414), which would impoverish his bailsmen. He does "defent" (371) the charges clearly, "de mot en mot" (373), but he makes no effort to argue his innocence, though sixty witnesses had seen the queen pursue him. Others know that the queen began the event in the orchard, and many know Lanval has been busy with largesse (205–14) and shows no interest in women (279–80). He has attended court less than other knights because of pleasure with the demon. Thus, the facts gainsay the queen's charges, whereas Lanval's beauty (22), aloofness, new wealth and popularity are a likely recipe for her erotic interest.

Worse than not arguing, Lanval does not claim his right to battle at either arraignment or trial. When felony is denied, says Glanvill, "the plea shall be settled by battle."[80] In *Roland*, Ganelon first defends himself with argument, and then depends on battle by Pinabel (3757–79). Even Gottfried's cowardly steward illustrates Lanval's "right to judicial combat."[81] As the innocent heir of a king, Lanval should assert this right. If no one accepts for Arthur, there should be no trial. Instead, all the feckless one can do is grieve until the demon has him forever.

Marie develops the "rescue" with unusual irony, iconography, and humor. The two sets of maidens prepare the way for the mock "savior" who appears third, which imitates ironically John the Baptist's role and Christ's redemption on the third day. The retinue of two, appearing three times, suggests "departure from truth," in John's words, especially since nominal Christians in the *lai* use retinues of three.[82] "Departure from truth" is suggested more obviously by the emphasis on sensuality (476, 527–32, 561). Marie satirizes the doting admiration of Arthur's barons: they gape willingly (477), they eagerly help the maidens and "pay no attention to the mules" (540), and every judge "becomes warm with true joy" (584). The ambiguity of *esgarder* is explained astutely by Elizabeth Poe, so when Lanval is spared by the judges' "esgart" (629), "we are not sure if their wisdom or lust has saved him."[83]

Other details are more portentous. The servants command Arthur to prepare lodging (491, 535), but the lady "has not mind to stay" (614)—implicitly, she fears discovery. The first maidens are dressed in "violet" (475), which signified high rank, grief, or repentance,[84] all relevant to the "Prince of this World." The second two damsels are in "Phrygian brocade" (511) and mounted on "Spanish mules" (512). The Phrygian mode was the "abyss of lust and corruption,"[85] and the best known Phrygian was Paris, who destroyed his "heritage" for Helen. Mules were considered devilish, and "Spanish mules," like "purpre alexandrine" (102), connote Saracen infidelity, as in *Roland*.[86] The demon now appears as a hunter, with sparrowhawk and greyhound (573–74). The details are pointless except to reinforce Marie's theme. Hunting signifies destructive eroticism in *Equitan* and provides the occasion of Dido and Aeneas' "guilty...desires."[87] In Ovid, pursuing pleasure is the hunt of Venus; and throughout the Middle Ages, the devil is a hunter.[88] Again, ironic details imply the values Lanval lacks. Friends call him "li pruz et li hardiz" (516), but he never shows either. Ywain says, "For the love of God, speak to us" (520), but Lanval never acts from "love of God."

Lanval's unexpected departure confirms the portents. Amusingly, he leaps "at full speed" (640) from the dark mounting block onto the palfrey behind "la pucelle." The "dark marble" stone (634) implies evil, like the "dark stone" that cannot break Roland's Durendal and the "grey marble" where Beroul's Tristran tells lies egregiously.[89] The palfrey and

Lanval's position "detriers" (639) imply loss of knighthood, fore-shadowed earlier in forgetting his warhorse (41, 46, 78). Marie's vigorous knights are associated with *destriers*, not palfreys; Eneas rides a palfrey when Dido falls; and Chrétien's Gawain knows that palfreys and arms do not mix.[90] Lanval also no longer holds the reins, that is, the guidance of reason. Realistically, in twelfth-century terms, this heir to a kingdom loses his lordship to a wholly unknown party and ironically becomes her "seisine" (150), or legal possession, rather than vice versa. The greater irony is Lanval's loss of "seisine" to the lordship of Satan.

Marie also implies tersely that Lanval's destination is not the place of marvelous happiness that critics imagine. She comments that "the Bretons tell us" they go to "the beautiful isle" of "Avalun" (641–43), which signals skepticism.[91] To disappear forever from human society is not a twelfth-century ideal. Henry II would have been stupefied if the Young King had pulled such a trick. Even Gottfried's Tristan and Isolde cannot be happy for long in the *Minnegrotte*. In Marie's *Fables*, departure from society is either punishment or folly. Moreover, Avalon in Geoffrey and Wace is a place of healing so Arthur can *return*, and the "Lord of Avalon" in Chrétien's *Erec* (1957) partakes in human society.

But Avalon has other religious and philological associations. As scholars know, the Isle of Avalon was identified widely with the venerable abbey of Glastonbury. After 1179, the name acquired further pious connotation through saintly Hugh of Avalon, near Grenoble. Obviously, such holy Avalons were anathema to Lanval's lady. Marie's "Avalun" also implies something else. By analogy to "aval lez" (54), meaning "down beside," "aval luin" or "aval lunc" would mean "far down" or even "a val luin" "to the far valley," related to the underworld "valee" in *Espurgatoire* (930). "Val" appears nine times in *Roland* in infidel place-names, such as Val Tenebrus (2461), Val Metas (1502), where devils give spears, and Val Serre (3313).[92] Thus, this final place-name probably coheres with the opening in Carlisle.

Marie's subtlety, theme, and political relevance are more impressive than scholars have seen. The iconography of Carlisle, Pentecost, "heritage," and Semiramis establish a theme that is elaborated skillfully in plot, character, and many later signs. Brief comments and details direct ironic wit at Lanval and Arthur. The themes of vice and folly, adversity and seeming prosperity, in an *aventure* of demonic capture are serious aspects of twelfth-century culture. Marie compliments her king indirectly for his obvious superiority to the greatest legendary Briton, and she proves the absurdity of Welsh hopes for Arthur's return. She compliments Eleanor of the 1160s by contrast to the famous Guinevere, and in Lanval himself portrays the dangers of pleasure and irresponsibility for young Henri au Cort Mantel.[93] Truly, she created an Arthurian story closely related to Angevin culture.

Notes

1. See the discussion of date in G. S. Burgess, *The Lais of Marie de France: Text and Context* (Athens, Ga., 1987), pp. 32–34.

2. *Lanval*, line 4, in *Marie de France: Lais*, ed. A. Ewert (Oxford, 1960). All references are to Ewert's edition, but all are checked against *Le Lai de Lanval*, ed. J. Rychner (Geneva, 1958), who transcribes all four manuscripts. On a possible lost British source, see C. Bullock-Davies, "Lanval and Avalon," *Bulletin of Celtic Studies* 23 (1969), 128–42.

3. See M. H. Ferguson, "Folklore in the *Lais* of Marie de France," *Romanic Review* 57 (1966), 3–24; and E. Poe, "Love in the Afternoon: Courtly Play in the 'Lai de Lanval,' " *Neuphilologische Mitteilungen* 84 (1983), 301–10.

4. W. T. Warren, *Henry the Second* (London, 1973), p. 208, quoting Gerald of Wales. See C. H. Haskins, "Henry II as a Patron of Learning," *Essays in Medieval History Presented to Thomas Frederick Tout*, ed. A. G. Little and F. M. Powicke (Manchester, 1925), pp. 71–77.

5. Warren, *Henry the Second*, pp. 62–66.

6. See Gerald of Wales, *The Journey through Wales and the Description of Wales*, trans. L. Thorpe (New York, 1978), pp. 265, 274.

7. Gerald of Wales, *De principis instructione* 1.20 and *Speculum ecclesiae* 2.8–10, trans. L. Thorpe in *The Journey through Wales...*, appendix 3, pp. 281–284; Warren, *Henry the Second*, p. 208.

8. *The Lais of Marie de France*, trans. R. Hanning and J. Ferrante, (New York, 1978), pp. 8–11, emphasizes Marie's other works but does not use them adequately; Burgess, *The Lais of Marie de France: Text and Context*, uses some literary, but no intellectual context; *The Lais of Marie de France*, trans. G. S. Burgess and K. Busby (New York, 1986) emphasizes "the mainstream of medieval culture" (p. 23) but does not use it. See also E. Hoepffner, *Les Lais de Marie de France* (Paris, 1935); E. J. Mickel, Jr., *Marie de France* (New York, 1974); P. Ménard, *Les Lais de Marie de France: contes d'amour et d'aventure du moyen âge* (Paris, 1979); E. Sienaert, *Les Lais de Marie de France: du conte merveilleux à la nouvelle psychologique* (Paris, 1978). Mickel and Ménard use a little more cultural context than the others.

9. See notes 2 and 3; see also A. Knapton, "La poésie enluminée de Marie de France," *Romance Philology* 30 (1976), 177–87; E. A. Francis, "The Trial in *Lanval*," in *Studies in French Language and Mediaeval Literature Presented to Professor Mildred R. Pope*, no editor (Manchester, 1939), pp. 115–24; P. Hyams, "Henry

II and Ganelon," *Syracuse Scholar* 4 (1983), 24–35 (whom I thank for quickly sending me an offprint).

10. J. Rychner, "La présence et le point de vue du narrateur dans deux récits courts: le *Lai de Lanval* et la *Châtelaine de Vergi*," *Vox Romanica* 39 (1980), 86–103, at 87. See also *Les Lais de Marie de France*, ed. J. Lods (Paris, 1959), p. xxv, and passim; and A. Maraud, "Le *Lai de Lanval* et la *Chastelaine de Vergi*: la structure narrative," *Romania* 93 (1972), 433–459, esp. 448. All writers on *Lanval* cited earlier take the same view.

11. E. J. Mickel, Jr., "A Reconsideration of the *Lais* of Marie de France," *Speculum* 46 (1971), 39–65, at 51, 64; see also Mickel, *Marie de France*, p.121.

12. J. Ribard, "Le *Lai de Lanval*: essai d'interprétation polysémique," in *Mélanges de Philologie. . .offerts à Jeanne Wathelet-Willem*, ed. J. de Caluwe (Liège, 1978), pp. 529–44.

13. Scholars disagree over the precise meaning of line 16. Ménard partly summarizes the debate, *Les Lais*, p. 18. Hanning and Ferrante translate "gloss the letter/ and supply its significance from their own wisdom" (p. 28).

14. Marie de France, *Equitan* 7–10; *Bisclavret* 3, 318; *Chaitivel* 1; *Eliduc* 1183. All references are to Ewert's edition (see note 2).

15. Augustine, *On the Trinity*, 10.11.17, 14.8.11, 11.1.1; *Confessions* 7 emphasizes reason, 8 will, and 10 memory; John of Salisbury, *Policraticus* 7.13, trans. J. B. Pike, as *Frivolities of Courtiers and Footprints of Philosophers* (Minneapolis, 1938), p. 271 (hereafter *Policraticus*, trans. Pike); also Walter Map, *De nugis curialium: Courtiers' Trifles* 1.31, ed. and trans. M. R. James, rev. by C. N. L. Brooke and R. A. B. Mynors (Oxford, 1983), p. 129, and 5.7, p. 505.

16. Map, *Courtiers' Trifles*, pp. 245–47, same image, pp. 261–63 and 309–11; similar ideas pp. 47, 129, 211, 279, 405–7; John of Salisbury, *Policraticus*, trans. Pike, esp. pp. 251–57, also 7, 9, 35, 55. Henry II's tutor, William of Conches, wrote an important commentary on *The Consolation of Philosophy*.

17. *Marie de France: Äsop*, ed. and trans. H. U. Gumbrecht (Munich, 1973), prologue, lines 7, 12–16, epilogue, 20–22. All references are to this edition.

18. *Das Buch vom Espurgatoire S. Patrice der Marie de France und seine Quelle*, ed. K. Warnke, Bibliotheca Normannica 9 (Halle, 1938), lines 1–8, 25–26, 2300. All references are to this edition.

19. A. J. Minnis, *Medieval Theory of Authorship*, 2nd ed. (Philadelphia, 1988); P. Rollinson, *Classical Theories of Allegory and Christian Culture* (Pittsburgh, 1980).

20. Marie de France, *Fables*, prologue, ll. 30–32; epilogue, 9–12, 16–18.

21. Marie de France, *Espurgatoire*, ll. 771, 975; 864, 960; 863–68, 939–92; 1037–44; 993–1015; 1121–59; 1181–1202; 1229–52; 1105.

22. See note 2.

23. Warren, *Henry the Second*, pp. 36, 80, 182–83.

24. Isaiah 14.14; *Inferno*, canto 34; *Friar's Tale* 1413; *Par. Lost* 7.755; Boccaccio, *The Book of Theseus*, trans. B. M. McCoy (New York, 1974), pp. 196–97.

25. *Navigatio sancti Brendani abbatis*, ed. Carl Selmer (Notre Dame, 1959), chap. 22–23, pp. 61.41, 63.36; Bernard of Clairvaux, *The Life and Death of Saint Malachy the Irishman*, trans. R. T. Meyer, Cistercian Fathers 10 (Kalamazoo, 1978), p. 35; Map, *Courtiers' Trifles*, p. 319; John of Salisbury, *Policraticus* 8.7, trans. Pike, p. 336; Gregory, *Moralia, PL,* 76, 26.

26. John of Salisbury, *Policraticus* 6.17, in *The Stateman's Book*, trans. J. Dickinson (New York, 1927), p. 230; see also *Policraticus,* 2.27, trans. Pike, pp. 139–41. Dickinson translated the political parts of John's *Policraticus* in 1927, Pike the other half of the work in 1938. See note 15.

27. Geoffrey of Monmouth, *The History of the Kings of Britain*, trans. L. Thorpe (Baltimore, 1966), pp. 225–30; Wace, *Le roman de Brut*, ed. I. Arnold, 2 vols. (Paris, 1938–40), lines 10197–620.

28. Wace, *Brut*, lines 10597–620, esp. 10617–20.

29. *La chanson de Roland*, ed. F. Whitehead (Oxford, 1957), 3398 and 340.

30. On charity, Augustine, *City of God* 11.27–28, *On the Trinity* 11.3.3, 14.12.15; Peter Lombard, *Sententiae* 1.10, *PL* 192, 549–50; Dante, *Inferno* 3.5–6 and *Convivio* 3.5.8; on envy, Lombard, *Sent.* 2.43.10, *PL* 192, 755; Chaucer, *Parson's Tale*, 485.

31. Wace, *Brut*, lines 9747–60.

32. For instance, king and counselor in *Bisclavret* 222, 239; Le Fresne at 254, 482; Guildelüec in *Eliduc* 9, 710.

33. Abelard, *History of My Calamities*, in *The Letters of Abelard and Heloise*, trans. B. Radice (Baltimore, 1974), pp. 90–92, 96–97.

34. Map, *Courtiers' Trifles* 1.1, p. 5; John of Salisbury, *Policraticus* 3.1, trans. Pike, p. 154; Marie de France, *Espurgatoire* 649–64, 805, 1817–30.

35. Abelard, *The Letters*, trans. B. Radice, letter 7, p. 225, citing Prov. 11:14 and 12:15.

36. *Jeu*, lines 46, 68, 71, 188, 197, 292 (Latin), 322, 356, 374–75, 478, 528 (including evil counsel of the devil), in *Medieval Drama*, ed. and trans. D. Bevington (Boston, 1975), pp. 82–103; also *Narcisus*, 254–75, in *Three Ovidian Tales of Love*, ed. and trans. R. Cormier (Boston, 1975), pp. 104, 114–16.

37. Third Vatican Mythographer, *Scriptores rerum mythicarum Latini tres. . . ,* ed. G. H. Bode, 2 vols. (Celle, 1834; repr. Hildesheim, 1968), 1:159. Also, Bernard, *Malachy*, p. 20.

38. Marie de France, *Equitan* 195–204; *Le Fresne* 313–27, *Bisclavret* 303, *Yonec* 18.

39. Warren, *Henry the Second*, pp. 108–11 and passim.

40. *Brendan*, chap. 1, pp. 5.33–35, 7.73, chap. 7, esp. p. 16.15, 21; Anselm, *The Prayers and Meditations*, trans. B. Ward (New York, 1973), p. 202; Aelred of Rievaulx, *Mirror of Charity* 1.31.87, trans. E. Connor, Cistercian Fathers 17 (Kalamazoo, 1990), p. 40; Bernard, *Malachy*, p. 12.

41. John of Salisbury, *Policraticus* 4.2, trans. Dickinson, p. 48 (and rest of chapter); Andreas Capellanus, *De amore* 3, ed. E. Trojel (Copenhagen, 1892; altera editio, Munich, 1964), pp. 315, 327.

42. G. S. Burgess, *The Lais of Marie de France*, p. 171; Ménard, *Les Lais de Marie de France*, pp. 70, 90, 174; and others.

43. S. V. Benét, "The Devil and Daniel Webster"; Roswitha of Gandersheim, "Theophilus" (c. 970) in *Hrotsvithae Opera*, ed. H. Homeyer (Munich, 1970), pp. 154–70; and Rutebeuf, *Le miracle de Théophile* (c. 1261), in *Medieval French Drama*, trans. R. Axton and J. Stevens (Oxford, 1971), pp. 170–76.

44. John of Salisbury, *Policraticus* 1.8, trans. Pike, pp. 37.

45. Paulus Orosius, *Seven Books of History Against the Pagans*, trans. I. W. Raymond (New York, 1936), pp. 49–50.

46. *Fulgentius the Mythographer*, trans. L. Whitbread (Columbus, 1970), pp. 193–195; Peter Comestor, *Historia scholastica*, PL 198, 1108d; *Inferno* 5.52–60; Boccaccio, *On Famous Women* 2; Chaucer, *Man of Law's Tale*, 358–64.

47. See C. M. Jones, "The Conventional Saracen of the Songs of Geste," *Speculum* 17 (1942), 201–225.

48. John of Salisbury, *Policraticus* 3.10 and 2.14, trans. Pike, pp. 182, 80. Of course the attitude toward pagan and even Christian Rome was a complex love-hate situation.

49. Suz ciel n'ad rei ki[s] esligast/ Pur nul aver k'il i donast" (91–92). A similar tent in *The Quest of the Holy Grail* signifies the sinful world, and its beautiful owner is the devil (trans. P. M. Matarasso [Baltimore, 1969], p. 132).

50. Jean Bodel, *Le jeu de s. Nicholas* (c. 1200), in *Medieval French Drama*, lines 232, 391. Dante puts Mohamet and Ali in *Inferno*, canto 28.

51. J.-P. Torrell and D. Bouthillier, *Pierre le Vénérable et sa vision du monde: sa vie, son oeuvre, l'homme et le démon* (Leuven, 1986), pp. 334–35.

52. Map, *Courtier's Trifles* 4.3, p. 289. Many others could be cited.

53. See S. S. Eberly and D. Chamberlain, " 'Under the Schaddow of the Hawthorne Greene': The Hawthorn in Medieval Love Poetry," in *New Readings*

of Late Medieval Love Poems, ed. D. Chamberlain (Lanham, Md., 1993), pp. 15-43. William IX associates hawthorn with hands under a lady's cloak, Marcabru with noble wives' appetite for peasants, and Beroul with oath-breaking and ass' ears (pp. 26-27).

54. John of Salisbury, *Policraticus* 1.4 and 7.24, trans. Pike, pp. 24, 287; Map, *Courtiers' Trifles* 3.5, pp. 275-77, in the story of Resus, who wins his lord's wife but abstains.

55. Prudentius, *Psychomachia* 740-45, ed. and trans. A. J. Thomson, 2 vols. (Cambridge, 1962), 1:330; Chrétien de Troyes, *Philomela*, lines 771-76, in *Three Ovidian Tales*, p. 234; Capellanus' *amor* needs secrecy because it is illicit. Married embraces are not furtive because marriages are public knowledge.

56. Ménard, *Les Lais*, p. 456.

57. *Fables* 22, 23, 63, 100, 101 should be considered together.

58. Geoffrey of Monmouth, *History* 6.8, 8.12, 8.20, trans. L. Thorpe, pp. 168, 197-98, 206-07; Wace, *Brut*, 7445, 8143-162; *Eneas*, 4013-20, 7185-212; trans. J. A. Yunck (New York, 1979), pp. 136, 139, 200-5; Chrétien de Troyes, *Erec et Enide*, 6682-728, ed. M. Roques (Paris, 1981); *Arthurian Romances*, trans. D. D. R. Owen (London, 1987), pp. 89-90.

59. Gottfried von Strassburg, *Tristan*, trans. A. T. Hatto (Harmondsworth, 1960), pp. 249-50, 256.

60. Map, *Courtiers' Trifles* 2.12, 4.10, pp. 155-59, 359-60.

61. *Roman de la rose*, ed. F. Lecoy, 3 vols. (Paris, 1966-70), lines 3410, 9922, 17925-40. Cf. Augustine, *City of God* 15.23; Adam de la Halle, *Le jeu de la feuillée*, in *Medieval French Drama*, pp. 232-44.

62. Abelard, *The Letters*, trans. B. Radice, letter 7, pp. 199, 205, 206, 244, 260, 266.

63. Peter Lombard, *Sententiae* 2.6, *PL* 192, 602-3; Reginald of Durham, *De vita et miraculis S. Godrici...*, Surtees Society 20 (London, 1847), pp. 357, 90, 92, 334.

64. Ménard, *Les Lais*, p. 243. Torrell and Bouthillier, *Pierre le* Vénérable, pp. 240-41, 258-56, and passim.

65. Map, *Courtiers Trifles* 2.14, 4.9, pp. 161-63, 346-49, etc.

66. Map, *Courtiers Trifles* 4.11, pp. 351-63.

67. *Ancrene Wisse*, ed. J. R. R. Tolkien, EETS 249 (London, 1962), pp. 114.20, 115.20-116.29.

68. Vividly in Mt. 3.1-17, 11.1-15, 14.1-12; also Mk. 1.1-11, 6.4-29; Lk. 1.5-80; Jn. 1.6-7, 15-34.

69. Mt. 26.15, 27.3–9; Lk. 22.3, Jn. 13.27.

70. Map, *Courtiers' Trifles* 3.2, pp. 211–47 (at 211, 245), a superb story.

71. Warren, *Henry the Second*, pp. 360–61; Map, *Courtiers' Trifles* 5.6, p. 477. Francis, Hyams, and Rychner (pp. 78–84) discuss the trial, but none quite convincingly. See notes 2 and 9.

72. Warren, *Henry the Second*, p. 358, and the whole chapter "Royal Justice," pp. 317–61.

73. *Le lai de Lanval*, ed. Rychner, from mss. S & C: "Que trop lungement jeünot" (546), literally "fasted."

74. Map, *Courtier's Trifles* 5.6, p. 495; Warren, *Henry the Second*, pp. 388–89.

75. *The Treatise on the Laws and Customs of the Realm of England, Commonly Called Glanvill*, ed. and trans. G. D. G. Hall (London, 1965), pp. 171–73.

76. *Glanvill*, pp. 171–77.

77. Warren, *Henry the Second*, p. 366.

78. I borrow the term and others from Francis (p. 116) and Hyams (p. 27). See note 9.

79. Beroul, *The Romance of Tristran*, ed. A. Ewert (Oxford, 1946), lines 4159–266.

80. *Glanvill*, p. 172; Warren, *Henry the Second*, p. 357.

81. Gottfried, *Tristan*, trans. Hatto, pp. 186, 170, 172, 189–90.

82. John of Salisbury, *Policraticus* 2.27, trans. Pike, p. 234: Saul "was fittingly attended by a retinue of two," going to the Witch of Endor, "since he had departed from the supreme and true unity." Two is generally associated with errancy. The succubus' retinues of two at 55, 472, 510; retinues of three at 259 (Queen), 328 (Arthur), 477 (Gawain).

83. Poe, "Love in the Afternoon," p. 398 (see n. 3).

84. Knapton, "La poésie enluminée," pp. 183, 185 (see n. 9).

85. John of Salisbury, *Policraticus* 1.6, trans. Pike, pp. 32–33.

86. Athanasius, *Life of Antony*, trans. R. Meyer (Westminster, Md., 1950), pp. 88–89, the archetypal saint's life; Salisbury 1.3, trans. Pike, p. 49; *Roland* 185, 847, 862, 1000, etc. Though the French have mules, Saracen mules are prominent and crucial, bringing fraudulent gifts.

87. *Aeneid* 4.117–72; John of Salisbury, *Policraticus* 1.4, trans. Pike, p. 14; also *Policraticus* 6.22, trans. Dickinson, p. 248; *Eneas*, ll. 1391–538, trans. Yunck, pp. 84–87.

88. *Ars amatoria*, ll. 45–50; Gerald of Wales, *The Journey*, pp. 117–18, *re* devil; D. W. Robertson, Jr., "Why the Devil Wears Green," *Modern Language Notes* 69 (1954), 470–72; E. J. Mickel, Jr., "Marie de France's Use of Irony as a Stylistic and Narrative Device," *Studies in Philology* 71 (1974), 265–90.

89. *Roland* 2300, 2338; Beroul, *Tristran*, ed. Ewert, l. 235 (233–291).

90. *Milun*, ll. 12, 444 (also "cheval," 421, 425, 433); *Chaitivel* 101; *Eliduc* 283; *Guigemar* 636; *Eneas* 700, trans. p. 70; *Perceval* 6533–34, ed. Roach (Geneva and Paris, 1959), trans. Owen, p. 460.

91. See also R. Sturges, "Texts and Readers in Marie de France's *Lais*," *Romanic Review* 71 (1980), 244–64 (at 261).

92. *Roland*, ed. Whitehead, p. 175. Only "Valence" is a Christian name, and it does not imply the word "val."

93. Warren, *Henry the Second*, pp. 580–84. Marie had the wit to see Henri's weaknesses, when many did not.

Lévi-Strauss in Camelot: Interrupted Communication in Arthurian Feudal Fictions

Donald Maddox

Over the course of his prolific career, Claude Lévi-Strauss has addressed many issues of interest to literary scholars.[1] Potentially the most suggestive for medievalists has been his exploration of affinities between properties of myth and the grail theme, particularly in the works of Chrétien de Troyes, Wolfram von Eschenbach, and Wagner.[2] An important component of this inquiry involves comparisons between the literary usage of the grail theme in Western Europe and certain mythic traditions in other cultures.[3] Contrasting Oedipus and Perceval in terms of the types of communication their stories represent, Lévi-Strauss perceives a relation of "inverse symmetry" between what he calls "Oedipal myths" and "Percevalian myths." By penetrating the enigma of the Sphinx, Oedipus resolves a question awaiting an answer. This moment of optimal heroic communication is later valorized negatively, by instances of "acclerated communication," in the hero's unwitting incest and the plague that devastates Thebes and hastens pernicious natural cycles.[4] In contrast, the so-called Percevalian myths are marked by "interrupted communication," whereby the hero has been unaware of the identity of his lineage. Arriving in the realm of his forbears, a "wasteland" created by catastrophic sclerosis of the natural cycles, he encounters the obverse of an enigma, an answer awaiting his question. When finally asked, the question leads the hero to discovery of his kinship with the family of the grail, and defines his salutary role in restoring both their leader and their land.[5] In sum, communication in Oedipal myths harms both individual and community and destroys

35

cultural and natural properties; in Percevalian myths it integrates the hero into his communal heritage and harmonizes nature and culture. Lévi-Strauss links the Percevalian model with certain North American Indian tales that together would typify a myth devoted to "the theme of interrupted communication."[6] and he hypothesizes that all mythology may ultimately concern a problem of communication.[7]

These insights were not unnoticed by medievalists. Like Perceval, I myself encountered them, in the form of an answer proffered by Claude Lévi-Strauss himself, as I plied him with questions on other matters. This was in the fall of 1974, only a few months after he had completed his seminar at the Collège de France on "Le Graal en Amérique."[8] He expressed skepticism concerning the treatment of literary texts on the same plane as myth, explaining that his objective had been to see what the mythic "traces" he perceived in medieval grail texts might reveal about the behavior of myth. By extrapolating two mythic types from the stories of Oedipus and Perceval, he had never intended to create a new problematic awaiting a medieval scholar. Soon thereafter, however, a handful of articles proved that the implications of his views on the grail material were indeed of interest to medievalists.[9]

Their attention was confined largely to Chrétien's Conte du graal, in keeping with Lévi-Strauss' own notion of a Percevalian myth lying within the relatively limited sphere of medieval grail narratives.[10] In this essay I wish to move beyond that sphere, towards a broader horizon of medieval narratives to which his views seem equally pertinent. This move entails a series of disentanglements. We must above all disengage the story of Perceval—and, a fortiori, European grail narratives in general—from issues in comparative mythography that preclude study of medieval texts across a wider spectrum. We must set aside, at least temporarily, parallels between Perceval and Oedipus, thus ensuring that our perception of the medieval narratives not be governed by comparisons with the Greek "myth" on the basis of an extremely limited set of features.[11] We must also disentangle Perceval's story from loose comparisons with native American myths. Having thus moved away from mythic theory, we retain from Lévi-Strauss' investigation a single theme, whose ramifications in medieval narrative are more extensive than he assumed.

Let me consider a few works marginal or external to the "Percevalian" sphere that nonetheless thematize interrupted communication as described by Lévi-Strauss. Chrétien's romances, Renaut de Beaujeu's Le Bel inconnu, the cyclic Prose Lancelot, and the Roman de Mélusine are texts from the late twelfth through the fourteenth centuries that either directly involve Arthurian story or reflect the influence of

Arthurian tradition. Together they suggest that, in the fictional representations of medieval feudal culture, interrupted communication as theme plays a more significant and consequential role than we have heretofore supposed.

Interrupted Communication
in the Romances of Chrétien

Chrétien's first four romances all feature instances of interrupted communication that anticipate its usage in the final work. In both *Erec et Enide* and *Cligés* we find a harmful breach between royal court and courtly couple. In the penultimate episode of *Erec*, the "Joie de la Cort," a knight's bondage to selfish and destructive amatory service has long sapped the vitality of an entire realm.[12] By abolishing this nefarious symbiosis of love, prowess, and custom, Erec restores communication between the symbolic courtly couple and the courtly community that has stagnated during their seclusion.[13] Likewise, the ruseful retreat of Cligés with Fénice into the artificial idyll of tower and orchard leaves Constantinople bereft of its legitimate heir apparent; the remaining episodes restore the couple to Byzantine society and culminate in their recognition and coronation.[14]

While in *Erec* and *Cligés* the couple is isolated from society, in *Yvain* the communicative rift occurs within the couple. When Yvain does not meet his lady's deadline, she repudiates him and he falls into madness.[15] The couple's eventual reunion requires his progressive acquisition of honorable renown under the pseudonym of the "Knight of the Lion." As he makes his way back to lordship of his lady's domain, his adventures enable him to bring beleaguered individuals and communities into productive communication (3138–6516). In the *Chevalier de la charrete*, Arthur's court is bereft of his subjects imprisoned in Gorre.[16] Lancelot ultimately brings about their return, though his covert love affair with the queen implicitly sets them at odds with the court.

In Chrétien's *Conte du graal* the theme of interrupted communication pertains to both Perceval and Gauvain.[17] Both mediate between the Arthurian court, eagerly awaiting news of its heroic luminaries, and isolated domains anxiously awaiting a redeemer; both arrive at a remote locus where a remnant of their respective families holds answers to the questions they must ask. When this unfinished romance breaks off, it appears that Perceval's itinerary would have taken him back—as indeed it does in the Continuations—to the Grail Castle, to ask the requisite questions and assume leadership of the family of grail custodians.[18] Likewise, Gauvain ends the enchantments at the residence-in-exile of three generations of his family and assumes the functions of its lordship (7224–9188).[19]

In Chrétien's first four romances communication is disrupted between various parties on a strictly contemporaneous basis; only in the *Conte du graal* is there heroic mediation of *a communicative hiatus between generations in the hero's own lineage.* This function, identified by Lévi-Strauss as characteristic of Percevalian myths, is indeed a useful criterion for considering the *Conte du graal* and later works inspired by it that feature a grail hero, but it is equally pertinent to romances marginal to or outside of this sphere.

The Exalted Father

Consider in this regard Renaut de Beaujeu's *Le Bel inconnu.*[20] Profoundly indebted to Chrétien, *Erec et Enide* in particular,[21] this work makes restoration of interrupted communication the centerpiece of the fiction, situating it near the work's numerical midpoint.[22] Having in the first half of the poem undertaken and finally succeeded, moments earlier, in the supreme adventure of the Fier Baiser, the hero learns from a disembodied voice his own name, Guinglain, the name of his father, Gauvain, the paragon of Arthurian chivalry (3216–42), and the covert circumstances of his upbringing under the aegis of his fairy mother (3236–39).[23] After this parental link had been severed following his conception, the otherworld had secretly guided him toward the paternally symbolic order of chivalry.[24] In the second part of the romance Guinglain works through the conflict between the maternally associated enticements of the fairy otherworld and the feudal culture of the father and opts for a place in the latter.

Restoration of interrupted communication between the filial and the paternal generations is thus the fulcrum of the entire romance, the vital turning point that confers heroic identity and initiates the long process culminating in the hero's enculturation in Arthurian society. Along with self-recognition goes a sudden, overwhelming awareness that the most significant dimension of selfhood is overdetermined in highly consequential ways by a lineal design.

Clearly, the morphology of adventure in *Le Bel inconnu* could well have made of Guinglain another Perceval. Both were deliberately raised by maternal figures in ignorance of the name of the father; both were confronted by powerful amatory distractions on the road to their highest adventure.[25] The latter in both cases requires restoration of a feudal wasteland to prosperity by ending a long-standing enchantment, as well as the eventual assumption of the realm's lordship.[26] Above all, in both stories this magnificent achievement is associated with the hero's dramatic discovery of his kinship with an avuncular or paternal figure previously encountered.[27] In sum, Guinglain's story treats the theme of interrupted communication in a manner remarkably similar to its usage in *Le Conte du graal* and fulfills virtually all of the criteria of what Lévi-Strauss calls a Percevalian myth, even though it has nothing to do with either Perceval or the grail.

The Exalted Lineage

In the cyclic Prose *Lancelot*, interrupted communication plays a greater variety of roles within a more ambitious and complex format.[28] While retaining the motif of the son's discovery of the father's identity, the Prose *Lancelot* redeploys heroic restoration of interrupted communication at numerous other junctures, to achieve more ambitious ends. In successive revelations, Lancelot discovers the identity of his father, the exalted profile of a seemingly perdurable ancestry, and, progressively, his own eccentric place in a genealogy whose luminaries both precede and follow him.

His childhood follows the same formative pattern evident in the biographies of Perceval and Guinglain, all three of which, in their emphasis on selfhood, identity and origins, show affinities with the tale-type of the Fair Unknown.[29] Lancelot is raised by a nurturant creature from the otherworld, Ninienne—the Lady of the Lake—in ignorance of his identity and that of his noble and knightly forbears (VIa-21a).[30] She is ambivalent about the youth's maturation, deferring his entry into the chivalric world yet also providing vital assistance once this moment arrives.[31] When the lad is eighteen, Ninienne, in a *chastoiement*, an instructive discourse reminiscent of the advice Perceval heard from his mother, offers him wise counsel on the nature and ethical significance of chivalry (XXIa, 7–19);[32] Like Guiglain's mother, she arranges for the youth to appear at Arthur's court; having herself escorted him to Camelot, she even negotiates with the king the terms of his induction into knighthood (XXIIa, 9–12). All three heroes thus owe their early nurturance to a solitary feminine figure who, while sheltering the youth from communication with informants capable of providing news of the noble father, paradoxically becomes an auxiliary as he embarks on an itinerary that will in due course lead him to a full awareness of his chivalric lineage.[33]

In all three cases, the renowned assembly of the Arthurian court provides initial recognition of the hero's chivalric status, albeit awkwardly: Arthur never completes the knighting of either Perceval or Lancelot, and the three youths all encounter skepticism from within the court as to their capabilities.[34] Fulfilling no supreme goal, this initial sojourn at Arthur's court is, rather, the point at which a fateful itinerary is defined, a course on which the hero will eventually surpass the Arthurian chivalric standard, but only through establishment of communication with representatives of the hero's forbears. Like Perceval and Guinglain, Lancelot must acquire crucial knowledge about the lineage that engendered him; genealogy merges with teleology as he is called upon to assume a role in the stewardship of mandates and missions his family has sponsored through the ages.

The Prose *Lancelot* continues a tendency established by the *Conte du graal* and *Le Bel inconnu*, which is to place the moment of restored communication at the locus of a *merveille*—a supernatural phenomenon—as for example in the episode of the Carole Magique. In this adventure from the hero's mature phase (LXXXIII, 1–10), Lancelot ends an enchantment, a courtly dance that has lured countless knights and ladies into the euphoric lotus of its ceaseless round. The Carole Magique is also a message suspended in time: King Ban, Lancelot's father, had left his crown to the one who could finally abolish the enchantment and thus be recognized as the best and fairest of the world's knights (LXXXIII, 9). Indirect communication with a male ascendant signifies contrastively, however: Lancelot casts away his father's gold crown which he won upon breaking the spell, "por ce que signe de roi senefioit" [because it was an emblem of monarchy] (LXXXIII, 3). As do many others, this episode shows how Lancelot, wary of assuming temporal power, adheres to a unique ideal of knighthood.[35]

As in the case of Perceval, the secrets of lineage are unveiled to Lancelot in incremental stages. His highest adventure of self-definition, occurring soon after his first sojourn at the Arthurian court, recalls the principal adventures of Perceval and Guinglain. A remote feudal community is again the setting. Once prosperous, the Dolorous Guard has been reduced to a wasteland by an enchantment that has systematically annihilated knights seeking to abolish it (XXIVa, 1–4). Like its analogues in the *Conte du graal* and *Le Bel inconnu*, the abolished enchantment entails accession to lordship and provides the first details concerning identity. When in the cemetary at the Dolorous Guard Lancelot raises the tombstone to be lifted only by the castle's conqueror and reads therein: "Chi gerra Lancelos del Lac, li fiex au roi Ban de Benoÿc" [Here will lie Lancelot del Lac, son of King Ban de Benoyc] (XXIVa, 32)—past and future converge as the dead father is named at the site of the son's eternal repose. Less positive than the analogous moment in the careers of Perceval and Guinglain, Lancelot's uncovering of the paternal name in the depths of his own tomb crystallizes a motif of unsettling thanatopic discovery that will later recur at significant junctures.[36]

Indeed, the two tombs he discovers later on at the Saint Cimetière remind him of his earlier adventure: "et quant il voit les tombes, si li membre de la Dolerose Garde" [when he sees the tombs he remembers the Dolorous Guard] (XXXVII, 32). Appropriately enough, for this return to the tomb-opening motif places him before the tombs of his ancestors and thus into contact with the lineage of grail custodians. His success in opening the tomb of Galahad, the son of Joseph of Arimathea, bringer of the grail to the West, will eventually be apparent: in keeping with Merlin's prophecy (XXXVII, 30), Lancelot disinters and transposes to Wales the body of his ancestor Galahad, son of the agent of the grail's past fortunes; so too will he engender his own son Galahad, agent of the grail's future fortunes. Mediating between once and future Galahads, Lancelot restores communication among generations of the descendants of Joseph of Arimathea by providing a vital link in the lineal chain of grail keepers. Yet he is destined to fail in his attempt to open the second tomb, containing the body of Joseph's nephew Symeu, whose tormented entombment has been a protracted expiation of sin. Symeu will indeed be delivered one day, not by Lancelot, but by the conqueror of the Perilous Seat (XXXVII, 37-40). News from the tomb thus exalts the anticipated son at the hero's expense (XXXVII, 37). Although Lancelot embodies as much valor and prowess as is possible in any mortal, the father's one adulterous sin ensures his own exclusion from success in the supreme adventures reserved only for his son Galahad. Communication with ascendants thus acquires powerful negative overtones, signified by figures of purgatorial expiation and the visitation of paternal sin upon the son. Having served elsewhere to identify Perceval as the hero of the grail, communication with the lineal past now emphasizes Lancelot's inevitable failure in this role.[37]

As does yet another adventure involving an ancestral tomb, occupied by his grandfather, King Lancelot (XCIII, 1-23). Blood issuing from this tomb heals all who touch it; nearby, the king's severed head lies in the depths of a boiling spring. Lancelot successfully recovers the head and transposes the king's remains into the tomb of the lady whom he loved. If their story recalls his own—the elder Lancelot had also loved a married lady—Lancelot's *mise au tombeau* of King Lancelot and his beloved is no *mise en abyme* of the main story; contrasts outweigh resemblances. Unlike the hero, king and lady had shared a spiritual, wholly ascetic love until her jealous husband, failing to recognize its true nature, had slain the king, his kinsman. Though Lancelot pays tribute to this martyrdom of love, his heroism is again contrasted negatively with that of Galahad, who on account of his carnal purity is to succeed in dissipating the darkness that has reigned at the castle of King Lancelot's cousin since the time of the murder (XCIII, 17).

In an earlier sepulchral exploit, Lancelot had discovered the tomb of Galehaut (XLIX, 5–24), whose epitaph bespeaks a death induced by love: "Ci gist Galehout li fiz a la Jaiande, li sires des Lointaignes Isles, qui por l'amor de Lancelot morut" [Here lies Galehaut, the son of the Giantess and Lord of the Nether Isles, who died for love of Lancelot] (XLIX, 10). To dissuade Lancelot from the temptation to join his cherished friend in death, the Lady of the Lake had proposed a consoling alternative: that he transpose Galehaut's remains into his own tomb at the Dolorous Guard—Lancelot will lie eternally beside his beloved Galehaut. His reburial of King Lancelot with his lady in a common tomb therefore cannot be viewed as an analogue of his own love for the queen or of any ultimate destiny to lie beside her in death.[38]

Lancelot's fourfold communication with the remote past via tombs, as well as his threefold transposition of remains, first of Galahad the elder, then of Galehaut, and finally of King Lancelot, are highly significant as an ensemble. He discovers thereby two lines of communication restored between generations in the same illustrious family: one links the two Galahads, who across the centuries share in the lineally transmitted, spiritual brotherhood of the grail; the other associates the two Lancelots, who share in the affective adventure of love for a woman. Yet upon the hero Lancelot reflects none of the ancestral honor conferred by the hagiographic motif of remains transposed, for neither Galahad's solitary and saintly repose nor King Lancelot's interment with the object of a pure and innocent love resonates with Lancelot's destiny to lie in a tomb whose double occupancy exalts a temporal chivalric bond.

While the theme of lineal communication interrupted and restored names in successive stages Lancelot, his father, and his lineage, the work's cyclic architecture eventually uses the theme to underline Lancelot's own inadequacies and to prefigure his spiritually superlative son, the hero of the *Queste del saint graal*.[39] Although the larger cycle's concern with the grail is anticipated, Lancelot's career is ultimately at odds with the so-called Percevalian myth, for repeated use of the theme of interrupted communication to deepen the significance of his biography also sets him apart from the high design of his lineage and underlines the impossibility of his ever metamorphosing into a hero of the grail.[40]

The Dynasty's Bilineal Design

Although the late fourteenth-century prose *Roman de Mélusine* by Jean d'Arras is not an Arthurian work, it inherits numerous characteristics of earlier Arthurian fictions, as in the triple development of the motif of the unknown father or ancestor in ways reminiscent of its usage in the three Arthurian romances already discussed.[41] The main body of the romance details the marvelous achievement of the illustrious founder of the Lusignan dynasty, the fairy Mélusine, who marries the noble Raymondin and bears him a sizable number of male offspring, whose exploits are also recounted.[42] Like Perceval, Guinglain, and Lancelot, Raymondin enters manhood unaware of his father's identity. It is Mélusine who gives him a lengthy account of how his real father, a Breton nobleman named Hervy de Léon, was treacherously dispossessed of his patrimony and driven into exile. (Hervy's loss of his domain through betrayal is in some respects reminiscent of the tribulations of Lancelot's father, Ban de Benoÿc.)[43] Offering oracular prescriptions for success, Mélusine dispatches Raymondin to Brittany, where he eventually redresses the injustice done to his father and brings the paternal domain of Léon back into the lineal fold.[44] As at the midpoint of *Le Bel inconnu*, the fairy's role here is to enable the hero to recognize his own identity and mission through discovery of the name and the sphere of the previously unknown father.[45]

The second restoration of interrupted communication between generations instigated by a fairy occurs near the end of the work and involves the son of Raymondin and Mélusine, Gieffroy au Grant Dent, the heir of Lusignan. In pursuit of a marauding giant, Gieffroy finds his way into a mountain and discovers the tomb of his maternal grandfather, King Elinas of Albanie, where he reads a long account of the latter's life, lineage, and descendants.[46] Mélusine was the eldest of three fairy daughters born to Elinas and the fairy Présine. Because Elinas had violated a taboo Présine had imposed upon him—that he should never observe her during her confinement—Mélusine had conspired with her two sisters to imprison Elinas in the depths of a mountain. In turn, Présine punished her daughters by banishing them to disparate realms. When Elinas finally died, Présine constructed a magnificent tomb at the foot of which she placed his likeness, along with a golden tablet bearing an inscription of their entire history. This ancestral shrine was to be guarded by many generations of giants until the advent of Gieffroy au Grant Dent.[47] The hero's discovery of truths pertaining to his own lineage at the tomb of a male ascendant recalls our earlier analogues from the Prose *Lancelot*. As a result of this discovery, Gieffroy will come to recognize in Elinas and Présine the parents of his mother

Mélusine and in due course will reveal this kinship to his illustrious brothers. The tomb of Elinas is also reminiscent of the Carole Magique in the Prose *Lancelot* in that it too serves as a "time capsule" which, when its secret is finally unlocked, will reestablish continuity within the lineage, in this case between the first and the third generations.

The final episode of the *Roman de Mélusine* contains a third instance where a feminine agent of the *merveilleux* is instrumental in bringing a later generation into significant contact with an earlier one. This passage is a kind of epiloque, in that it takes place long after the death of the third son of Raymondin and Mélusine, King Guion of Albanie, during the reign of one of the latter's descendants. Once again, an ancestral shrine provides the decor for a dramatic recognition of kinship relations. At a castle containing a mural depicting the entire history of Elinas, Présine, and their three fairy-daughters, this descendant of the Lusignans attempts to win honor in the previously unconquered Custom of the Sparrow Hawk. The custom prescribes that if the challenger succeeds in remaining awake for three consecutive days and nights, he may receive any reward of his choosing *except* the privilege to consort with the winsome lady of the castle.[48] Upon fulfilling the terms of the custom, however, the king will settle only for the love of this forbidden lady, and when she refuses, he attempts to take her by force. In so doing he earns her malediction for attempting to violate, albeit unwittingly, the most fundamental of all taboos:

> Povre fol, n'es tu pas descendu de la lignie du roy Guion, qui fu filz Melusigne, ma suer, et je suis ta tante, et tu es si prez de mon lignaige, posé que je me voulzisse assentir a toy avoir, que l'eglise ne s'i vouldroit pas accorder.[49]

> Fool, are you not a descendant of King Guion, the son of my sister Mélusine? I am your aunt, then, and we are such close kin that, even if I were to consent to have you, the church would not allow it.

Because this descendant of Présine and Mélusine has attempted to rape the latter's sister, Melior, she pronounces a malediction upon the family's nine succeeding generations, culminating in the last generation's loss of the kingdom.[50] As with some of Lancelot's later encounters with ancestors, this communication is fraught with negative implications for the protagonist while also prefiguring future developments within the lineage.

The *Mélusine* thus makes highly sophisticated threefold use of the communication theme cultivated in earlier Arthurian romance. The main body of the romance tells how the sons of Mélusine and

Raymondin created a vast international network of contemporaneous lordships and monarchies; each instance of interrupted lineal communication, restored through the auspices of the feminine otherworld, provides a unique link between this world and other sectors of the lineage from which it has long been isolated. The first two illustrate Lévi-Strauss' Percevalian myth, though no associations with the grail are involved. Together they provide the dynasty with a lineal memory; both are analepses that provide crucial access thereto. On the one hand, Mélusine's revelation of the identity of Raymondin's father restores the family's link with the patrilineal, feudal ancestry; the other, provided by Gieffroy's subterranean discovery, reveals the matrilineal, supernatural ancestry. Together, they enable the progeny of Raymondin and Mélusine to trace both lines of their prestigious ancestry and to link their diverse realms and domains in Europe and the Near East with this doubly distinguished dynasty.

While these two episodes recall the dynasty's glorious, if turbulent, rise, the third, both as epilogue and prolepsis, briefly foretells the ninefold phases of its decline. Ironically, however, this final episode brings us full circle, for the two earlier instances of what Lévi-Strauss called a Percevalian myth of interrupted communication restored culminate tragically in precisely the kind of "accelerated communication" he identified with the Oedipal myth. For the royal descendant of Mélusine who violates the terms of the custom closely resembles Oedipus: like the latter, he unwittingly elects a forbidden sexual relation and in so doing violates the taboo of incest; this in turn initiates a long and destructive progression toward cultural decay and a perverted natural state. Here, then, we have a romance which, in reconstructing the dynastic infrastructure in its totality, makes use of interrupted communication in both the guises identified by Lévi-Strauss. It thus links the diegetic order of events in the main story as it unfolds with the protodiegetic order of events that preceded and conditioned it, then with the postdiegetic order of events that led to its extinction. While communication interrupted and restored provides the dynasty with an account of its remote and glorious origins, accelerated communication ushers in its decline and tells of its demise.

Unveiling the Past:
Literary and Cultural Perspectives

The "theme of interrupted communication" is clearly pertinent to a larger corpus of medieval narratives than that with which Lévi-Strauss originally identified it. Our limited sampling of texts permits a few closing observations concerning the literary and cultural implications of the theme's persistence over the centuries that saw the rise of courtly romance.

In the literary usage of this theme, self-perception occurs within the temporally deep context of lineage, giving access to an elusive past. As in Chrétien's last romance, emphasis is on the hereditary obligations of lordship, family, and manor. Initiation restores lineal memory and makes self-recognition as part of a genealogical continuum the basis of prestige, power, and rights while reaffirming the principle of degree of nobility in direct proportion to longevity of lineage. Some genealogical disclosures concern a dead father or ancestor whose example bestows empowerment, political as well as personal, in a moment of crisis, and whose ancestry traces back to biblical or supernatural figures. This brings to mind tendencies, in evidence since the eleventh century, of European nobility to construct genealogies emanating from illustrious though fictive ancestors. These efforts to glorify a lineage share with the romances examined here a similar concern with unveiling genealogical designs that have unfolded over the *longue durée* and whose temporality stems back to an originary grounding in the marvelous.[51]

Yet can we really speak of Chrétien's depiction of Perceval as being a seminal text where such narratives are concerned? The *Conte du graal* was by no means the earliest twelfth-century romance that might have held particular appeal for the *imaginaire généalogique* of a courtly textual community. Empowerment of the hero by means of a dramatic encounter with his dead father comprises a lengthy and crucial episode in a work that had already appeared several years before the *Conte du graal*. In the *Roman d'Enéas*, the eponymous hero journeys to the Underworld and encounters the shade of his father Anchises, who provides him with prophetic guidance concerning his foreordained role and that of his descendants in the foundation of a Latin empire to succeed the House of Troy.[52] In the very early, formative period of medieval courtly narrative, then, the sixth book of the *Aeneid* provides a significant classical subtext featuring the theme of interlineal communication interrupted and restored.[53] The *Conte du graal* is thus one of many texts—by no means all of them grail texts—that appropriated or rediscovered an archaic theme that could give expression to certain persistent concerns within various secular spheres of feudal culture.

What is the nature of these concerns? Along with a dramatic revelation of membership in an exceptional genealogy, the theme's usage typically involves disclosure of some social upheaval that interrupted communication between generations. For Lancelot and Raymondin as for Enéas and Perceval, loss of contact with the anterior lineal order traces back to events that took place within a turbulent and destabilized social setting; violence born of political or interpersonal struggle is commonplace in stories of forbears told to these heroes. The theme's longevity may result from anxieties about the fragility of lineal memory and genealogical continuity within an imperiled sector of medieval society. Others have documented ways in which the political and economic marginalization of the feudal nobility found expression in literary works, whether in portrayals of the deleterious effects of this process or else in compensatory fictions of empowerment.[54]

Restoration of communication with forbears is never an end in itself, however, nor is the theme implemented merely to record a catastrophe that befell a given line. After having limned the profile of the absent father or departed ancestor, the narrative does not simply make the hero's subsequent exploits replicate those of the ascendant. Instead, it moves him in some direction other than toward a return to things precisely as they were before the disruption of lineal continuity. The hero becomes the virtual or actual lord of a different domain, often one more positively valorized, or one more in keeping with the particular qualities of his growth. While this moment is compared with the profile of some predecessor in the line, it is invariably exceptional in its own right, the most significant juncture thus far in the hero's lineage. Although the Prose *Lancelot* is unique in this regard, to the extent that it *relativizes* the status of Lancelot with respect both to his ascendants and to his superlative offspring, thus making his career an accessory to, rather than the ultimate locus of, a major lineal juncture, it resembles other texts that develop the theme by virtue of its insistence on Lancelot's significant, indispensable role in a genealogical design. In many of these texts, communication disrupted and restored provides a retrospective account of the strife and anarchy that threatened the founding impulses or earlier phases of noble families; it also magnifies that critical point at which restoration of the consciousness of a lineal heritage makes possible the reconsecration of genealogy in terms of new, normally positive ideals.

The accounts of communication disrupted and restored that we have examined here are thus indicative of the enduring appeal in late fuedal culture of fictions which give expression in imaginary situations to remarkably similar aspirations and anxieties: aspirations to maintain the integrity and the continuity of noble genealogies, the backbone of feudal society, but also anxieties about their weakening and fragmentation, perhaps also about the vulnerability of lineal memory, as well as about the potential obsolescence of a system in which hereditary lordship was the mainstay of economic strength and autonomy.

In Arthurian tradition, excellent examples of how this theme may heighten the tensions between an exalted past and an indeterminate future are found in analogous passages from two manuscripts that link the prose *Merlin* of Robert de Boron with the Didot *Perceval*.[55] In the prose *Merlin*, Arthur himself has been raised in ignorance of his true parentage.[56] Not until after his definitive election to the monarchy does Merlin reveal, in the presence of the assembled barons, that the new king is descended from Uther and Ygerne. Moreover, Merlin discloses the grail's descendance through the lineage of Joseph of Arimathea, its passage into the West, and its current possession by the Fisher King; he reveals that the prophecies concerning the grail will be fulfilled by a member of the Round Table, the order Uther had founded. While this revelation, made to Arthur at the very inception of his rule, places his reign at the apex of two lineally transmitted ideas of order, one chivalric and temporal, the other spiritual, it also prefigures the bilineal bind that will both glorify and imperil the culture of the king.

This example of the theme's importance to the literary elaboration of the Arthurian legend lends further support to Lévi-Strauss' insight concerning the role of communication in medieval feudal fictions involving the grail. As this essay has attempted to suggest, however, our perception of the theme's full scope depends on recognition that stories of Percevalian heroes and of the lineage of the grail belong within a larger body of medieval stories: fictions that make revelation of kinship and genealogy the cornerstone of heroic action and social regeneration and in so doing address some of the most important concerns of a crepuscular, increasingly marginalized feudal nobility.

Notes

1. Much interest was kindled by his massive study of the native mythologies of South and North America: *Mythologiques: Le Cru et le cuit* (Paris, 1964); *Du Miel aux cendres* (Paris, 1966); *L'Origine des manières de table* (Paris, 1968); *L'Homme nu* (Paris, 1971).

2. Claude Lévi-Strauss, "De Chrétien de Troyes à Richard Wagner," in *Parsifal, Programmheft I der Bayreuther Festspiele* (Bayreuth, 1975), pp. 1–6; 60–65. Lévi-Strauss, *Le Regard éloigné* (Paris, 1983) contains a slightly expanded version of the same article, pp. 301–24.

3. His work in this area was featured in his seminar on Structural Anthropology at the Collège de France in 1973–74, abstracted in "Anthropologie sociale," *Annuaire du Collège de France. 74e Année*, 303–9 and republished in *Paroles*

données (Paris, 1984), pp. 129–37, with an addendum, pp. 138–40, by André Zavriew, "The Waste Land and the Hot House," summarizing Lévi-Strauss' lecture on Chrétien, Wolfram, and Wagner at the French Institute in London, on 3 October 1975. He mentioned Perceval as early as 1960, in his inaugural address at the Collège de France; see also Lévi-Strauss, *Anthropologie structurale deux* (Paris, 1970), pp. 31–35.

4. "Oedipal myths present the problem of communication that is first unusually efficient (the enigma resolved), then abusive when incest occurs: the sexual proximity of individuals who should remain separate from one another combines with the plague that ravages Thebes, accelerating and disrupting natural cycles." Lévi-Strauss, *Regard*, p. 314, trans. mine.

5. Lévi-Strauss, *Regard*, pp. 314–15; *Paroles*, pp. 136–37.

6. Lévi-Strauss, *Paroles*, pp. 129–35.

7. Ibid., p. 137.

8. Ibid., pp. 129–40.

9. Jean-Guy Gouttebroze, "L'Arrière-plan psychique et mythique de l'itinéraire de Perceval dans le *Conte du graal*," in *Voyage, Quête, pèlerinage dans la littérature et la civilisation médievales* (Aix-en-Provence, 1976), pp. 340–52; Charles Méla, "Perceval," *Yale French Studies* 55/56 (1971), pp. 374–440; and Sara Sturm-Maddox, "Lévi-Strauss in the Waste Forest," *L'Esprit Créateur* 18 (1978), 82–94.

10. This sphere includes numerous texts of the late twelfth and early thirteenth centuries—the Continuations; the works of Robert de Boron; *Perlesvaus*; the *Elucidation*; *Bliocadran*; and parts of the Vulgate Cycle (cf. *Regard*, pp. 306–7)—through Lévi-Strauss' conceptualization of a "mythe percevalien" relies primarily on the eponymous hero of Chrétien's *Conte du graal*.

11. Rapprochements between Perceval and Oedipus may restrict or distort insights into the grail narratives as an ensemble. According to Daniel Poirion, the *Conte du graal* evokes yet also diverges from the myth of Oedipus:"L'Ombre mythique de Perceval dans le *Conte du graal*," *Cahiers de Civilisation Médiévale* 16 (1973), 191–98.

12. Chrétien de Troyes, *Les Romans de Chrétien de Troyes. I. Erec et Enide*, ed. M. Roques (Paris, 1963), vv. 5319–6358.

13. For critical background, see Sara Sturm-Maddox, "Hortus non conclusus: Critics and the *Joie de la Cort*," *Oeuvres & Critiques* 5 (1980–81), 61–71.

14. Chrétien de Troyes, *Les Romans de Chrétien de Troyes. II. Cligés*, ed. A. Micha (Paris, 1965), vv. 6236–6638.

15. Chrétien de Troyes, *Les Romans de Chrétien de Troyes. IV. Le Chevalier au lion (Yvain)*, ed. M. Roques (Paris, 1965), vv. 2696–3015.

16. Chrétien de Troyes, *Les Romans de Chrétien de Troyes*. III. *Le Chevalier de la charrete*, ed. M. Roques (Paris, 1965), vv. 76–77, and passim.

17. Sturm-Maddox, "Lévi-Strauss," 90–92.

18. When Chrétien's romance abruptly ends, Perceval has in fact already fulfilled his vow to penetrate the castle's mystery and has learned the secrets of his lineage: Chrétien de Troyes, *Le Roman de Perceval, ou le Conte du graal*, ed. W. Roach (Geneva and Paris, 1959), vv. 4728–40; 6388–513. For Perceval's visits to the Grail Castle in the Continuations, see *The Continuations of the Old French Perceval of Chrétien de Troyes*, ed. W. Roach, vol. 4: *The Second Continuation*, (Philadelphia, 1971) E, vv. 32,265–32,594; P, 34,611–34,934; vol. 5: *The Third Continuation, by Manessier* (Philadelphia, 1983) 32,595–33,183; P, 34,935–35,551; 41,861–42,637; P, 44,605–45,374. Gerbert's Continuation begins with Perceval's second visit to the Grail Castle and ends with yet another: Gerbert de Montreuil, *La Continuation de Perceval*, vols. 1 and 2, ed. M. Williams (Paris, 1922; 1925), and vol. 3, ed. M. Oswald (Paris, 1975).

19. The last full episode in the works of Chrétien, portraying Gauvain's rise to lordship, is a rewriting of the "Joie de la Cour": see D. Maddox, *Arthurian Romances of Chrétien de Troyes: Once and Future Fictions* (Cambridge, 1991), pp. 108–18.

20. Renaut de Beaujeu, *Le Bel inconnu*, ed. G. Perrie Williams (Paris, 1929).

21. On reminiscences of Chrétien's works, see William H. Schofield, *Studies on Li beaus Desconus*, (Boston, 1895).

22. At the midpoint, v. 3133, "Hom ne vit onques sa parelle" [Nothing like it was ever seen] the hero is confronted by the redoutable *wivre*, the monster to whom he administers the requisite embrace, the "Fier Baissier" (v. 3186), thus ending the castle's enchantment.

23. See L. Harf-Lancner, *Les Fées au moyen âge: Morgane et Mélusine; La naissance des fées* (Paris, 1984), pp. 331–38.

24. "Si te dirai qui est ta mere:/ Fius es a Blancemal le fee;/ Armes te donnai et espee,/ Au roi Artus puis t'envoia..." [I shall tell you who your mother is: you're the son of Blancemal the fairy. I gave you armor and sword; then she sent you to King Arthur...] (vv. 3236–39).

25. Perceval and Blanchefleur, *Conte du graal*, vv. 1699–2747; Guinglain and the Pucele as Blances Mains, *Le Bel inconnu*, vv. 1871–2492.

26. On the beleaguered realm of the Grail Castle, see the *Conte du graal*, vv. 4669–83. In *Le Bel inconnu*, Blonde Esmeree's realm, called "la Cité Gaste" (v. 2775) and described as a wasteland—(vv. 2797–808, 2871–72): "En la cité homme n'avoit;/ Tote gaste la vile estoit" [There was not a soul in the fortified city, and the whole town was a wasteland]—is the site of numerous enchantments (vv. 2871–72).

27. *Conte du graal*, vv. 6413–19; *Bel inconnu*, vv. 3232–37.

28. *Lancelot, roman en prose du XIIIe siècle*, ed. A. Micha (Paris and Geneva, 1978-1983), 9 vols. References in paretheses are to this edition: the first number indicates the chapter, followed by the numbered sections within the chapters.

29. On the identity theme, see Elspeth Kennedy, *Lancelot and the Grail: A Study of the Prose Lancelot* (Oxford, 1986), pp. 10–48.

30. See Harf-Lancner, *Les Fées au moyen âge*, pp. 289–315.

31. See Micheline de Combarieu, "Le *Lancelot* comme roman d'apprentissage: Enfances, démesure et chevalerie," in *Approaches du Lancelot en prose*, ed. J. Dufournet (Paris, 1984), pp. 101–36.

32. Cf. *Conte du graal*, ed. Roach, vv. 510–94.

33. On the ambivalence of these feminine figures, see D. Maddox, "Specular Stories, Family Romance, and the Fictions of Courtly Culture," *Exemplaria* 3 (1991), 299–326.

34. See the *Conte du graal*, ed. Roach, vv. 1001-7 (Kay's mockery of Perceval); *Le Bel inconnu*, ed. Perrie Williams, vv. 229–40 (Hélie's skepticism about Guinglain's aptitude for the Fier Baiser); and *Lancelot* ed. Micha, XXIIa, 31 (Arthur's doubts that Lancelot can avenge the *chevalier enferré*).

35. See also Emmanuèle Baumgartner, "L'Aventure amoureuse dans le 'Lancelot en Prose'," in *Liebe und Aventure in Artusroman des Mittelalters*, ed. P. Schultze (Göppingen, 1990), pp. 93–108, at 104–6.

36. See also Daniel Poirion, "La Douloureuse Garde," in *Approches*, ed. Dufournet, pp. 25–48; and Charles Méla, *La Reine et le Graal: La Conjointure dans les romans du Graal, de Chrétien de Troyes au Livre de Lancelot* (Paris, 1984), pp. 385–86.

37. See also Elspeth Kennedy, "The Theme of Failure in Arthurian Romance," *Medium Aevum* 60 (1991), 16–32.

38. Lancelot's entombment: *La Mort le roi Artu*, ed. Jean Frappier (Paris, 1964), pp. 261–63. On the nature of Galehaut's love for Lancelot, See Frappier, "Le Personnage de Galehaut dans le *Lancelot* en prose," in *Amour courtois et table ronde* (Geneva, 1973), pp. 181–208; Christiane Marchello-Nizia, "Amour courtois, société masculine, et figures du pouvoir," *Annales: Economies, Sociétés, Civilisations* 36 (1981), 969–82, at 974–77; Emmanuèle Baumgartner, "Géants et chevaliers," in *The Spirit of the Court*, ed. G. Burgess and R. Taylor (Cambridge, 1985), pp. 9–22, at pp. 12–13.

39. On the revalorization of the love theme in the cyclic version, see, in addition to *Lancelot do Lac: The Non-Cyclic Old French Prose Lancelot*, ed. Elspeth Kennedy, 2 vols. (Oxford, 1980), E. Kennedy, *Lancelot and the Grail*, pp. 274–91;

and E. Kennedy, "The Re-writing and Re-reading of a Text: The Evolution of the Prose *Lancelot*," in *The Changing Face of Arthurian Romance: Essays on Arthurian Prose Romance in Memory of Cedric E. Pickford*, ed. A. Adams et al. (Cambridge, 1986), pp. 1–9.

40. On the question of the grail in the cyclic version, see Kennedy, *Lancelot and the Grail*, pp. 253–313.

41. Jean d'Arras, *Mélusine, roman du XIVe siècle*, ed. L. Stouff (Dijon, 1932). All references are to this edition. An Arthurian element is already apparent near the outset, when Présine takes her three daughters to Avalon. J. d'Arras, *Mélusine*, pp. 10–11.

42. On antecedent traditions, see Jacques Le Goff and Emmanuel Le Roy Ladurie, "Mélusine maternelle et défricheuse," *Annales: Economies, Sociétés, Civilisations*, 26 (1971), 587–622; Harf-Lancner, *Les Fées au moyen âge*, pp. 79–198; Claude Lecouteux, *Mélusine et le Chevalier au cygne* (Paris, 1982); and Françoise Clier-Colombani, *La Fée Mélusine au moyen âge* (Paris, 1991).

43. Cf. *Mélusine*, ed. Stouff, pp. 48–51, and *Lancelot*, ed. Micha, Ia–IIIa. In addition, like Tristan at the court of King Mark, Hervy, Raymondin's father, is victimized by the jealousy and calumny of envious barons.

44. *Mélusine*, ed. Stouff, pp. 51–76.

45. Notable among father-son resemblances, Hervy's story anticipated that of Raymondin: like his son, he had encountered and loved a beneficent fairy— who civilized the Forez as Mélusine later did in Poitou, though in the former case no offspring had resulted. *Mélusine*, ed. Stouff, p. 15. Cf. Harf-Lancner, *Les Fées au moyen âge*, 160–62.

46. *Mélusine*, ed. Stouff, pp. 265–66.

47. *Mélusine*, ed. Stouff, pp. 1–15.

48. *Mélusine*, ed. Stouff, pp. 302–7. Although its premises are unique, this Custom of the Sparrow Hawk recalls the initial segment of Chrétien's *Erec et Enide*, "Li premiers vers."

49. *Mélusine*, ed. Stouff, p. 305.

50. "Fol roy, par ta musardie te mescherra. Toy et les tiens decherront de terre, d'avoir, d'onnour et de heritaige, jusques a la IXe lingnie; et perdra par ta fole emprise le IXe de ta lignie le royaume que tu tiens. Et portera cellui roy nom de beste mue." ("Foolish king, this outrage will be your undoing. You and your kin will lose land, wealth, honor, and estate, from now unto the ninth generation; because of your foolhardiness the ninth descendant in your line will lose the kingdom over which you rule. And that king will be called Savage Beast.") Ibid., p. 305. On the figure of Melior, see Clier-Colombani, *La Fée Mélusine*, pp. 76–83.

51. See Georges Duby, "Structures de parenté et noblesse dans la France du Nord aux XIe et XII siècles," in *Hommes et structures du moyen âge* (Paris and The Hague, 1973), pp. 267–85; Gabrielle M. Spiegel, "Genealogy: Form and Function in Medieval Historical Narrative," *History and Theory* 22 (1983), 43–53; R. Howard Bloch, *Etymologies and Genealogies: A Literary Anthropology of the French Middle Ages* (Chicago, 1983), pp. 79–87; 203–17; Gabrielle M. Spiegel, *Romancing the Past: The Rise of Vernacular Prose Historiography in Thirteenth-Century France* (Berkeley and Los Angeles, 1993).

52. *Enéas: Roman du XIIe siècle*, ed. J. -J. Salverda de Grave (Paris, 1968), vv. 2161–218; 2839–996.

53. See Raymond J. Cormier, *One Heart, One Mind, The Rebirth of Virgil's Hero in Medieval French Romance* (University, Miss., 1973), pp. 178–87; and Jean-Charles Huchet, *Le Roman médiéval* (Paris, 1984), pp. 81–110.

54. See the recent discussion by Judith Kellogg, *Medieval Artistry and Exchange: Economic Institutions, Society, and Literary form in Old French Narrative* (New York, 1989).

55. For the pertinent passages from the two MSS, Paris, B. N. nouv. acq. fr. 4166 and Modena, Estense 3.39 , see Robert de Boron, *Merlin: Roman du XIIIe siècle*, ed. A. Micha (Paris and Geneva, 1980): pp. 293–98 (Modena), and 298–302 (Paris).

56. *Merlin*, ed. Micha, pp. 247–91.

Arthur in *Culhwch and Olwen* and in the Romances of Chrétien de Troyes

—————————————————————— *Armel Diverres*

In a volume devoted to the changing nature of the Arthurian legend, it seems appropriate to examine the manner in which Arthur's role and character have been treated in works that were almost certainly written less than a century apart, but against different cultural backgrounds. Here, I am referring to the anonymous middle Welsh *Culhwch and Olwen* on the one hand, and to the French verse romances of Chrétien de Troyes, on the other.[1] Since much has been written about Arthur in the Welsh *chwedl* [tale], and still more about his treatment by Chrétien,[2] it is impossible to deal with the subject without drawing extensively on previous studies and inevitably repeating points that have already been made by other scholars. However, to my knowledge, nobody has attempted a direct comparison of the figure of Arthur as envisaged by a Welshman around 1100 and a Frenchman some eighty years later.

Culhwch and Olwen is one of eleven middle Welsh tales composed for an aristocratic audience, and has been preserved in two fourteenth-century manuscripts, the White Book of Rhydderch and the Red Book of Hergest.[3] The latest editors, who have shown convincingly that the language includes more archaic features than that of the *Four Branches of the Mabinogi*, propose that the tale must have been first written down around the very end of the eleventh century.[4] It is true that the text contains a number of words of French origin, but Anglo-Norman barons had started to settle in Wales, particularly in the south, during the 1070s, no doubt beginning to influence the vocabulary of the native population in a short period, and this is the area in which *Culhwch and Olwen* in all probability originated.[5] It is of course difficult to be precise about the date of a text on purely linguistic grounds, since the age and idiosyncracies of scribes play a part. However, it would be hard to envisage a storyteller using prose as his medium in the eleventh or twelfth century, who would deliberately use archaic words and expressions in order to give an air of greater antiquity to a work designed for the entertainment of his audience. Transcribers of manuscripts tend to modernize exemplars by replacing obsolete words and constructions with contemporary ones, and this is illustrated by a comparison between the texts in the White Book and the Red Book, copied some forty or fifty years apart. I therefore find no reason to doubt the linguistic arguments in support of a date around 1100 for the archetype.

Arthur plays a role in the two quests which Culhwch undertakes and on which the tale is structured.[6] His help is sollicited by the hero in order to find Olwen as his bride, and he allows six of his leading warriors, including Cei, Bedwyr, and Gwalchmei, to accompany Culhwch in his search for her, though he merely initiates the expedition and takes no active part in it. Yspaddaden Penkawr, the girl's giant father, sets her suitor forty tasks, the accomplishment of all of which he himself evidently considers impossible, before he will grant the young man his daughter's hand. As Bromwich and Evans point out, many of these must be based on traditions drawn from various sources, others may be pure invention on the redactor's part. The achievement of these tasks makes up the second quest, though the completion of only twenty-one is described, some with very great brevity, and in a different order from the one in which they are set. Arthur himself joins in fourteen, sometimes taking the initiative, while Culhwch is relegated to the background. It would therefore be hazardous to apply the name "romance" to the work, since it is short and possesses relatively little *conjointure* (consciously developing narrative structure), the term used by Chrétien in the prologue of *Erec* (14) to distinguish between his work and the tales of the oral storytellers. The text of *Culhwch and Olwen* is loosely episodic and appears indeed to have preserved many of the characteristics, such as the use of folk material, usually found in oral narrative.[7]

On his arrival at Arthur's court, Culhwch, following his father's instructions, asks the king to trim his hair. According to the ninth-century *Historia Brittonum*, this appears to have been an acknowledgment of consanguinity,[8] and of course the two characters are first cousins, since they have a common maternal grandfather. However, in *Culhwch and Olwen* Arthur accedes to the young man's request before learning for certain of their kinship, which suggests that in this context the writer may have understood the tradition to be part of an initiation ceremony into manhood for a youth of aristocratic birth, into a status akin to knighthood. There is neither dubbing, nor, on Culhwch's part, any pledge of loyalty to his lord or payment of homage, though this may of course be implied. He next invokes of Arthur a boon in the name of all present, male and female, that is to say aid in obtaining the hand of Olwen, whose existence, as well as that of her lineage, is unknown to the king. It should be added that all mention of Arthur's own lineage in *Culhwch and Olwen* is to Welsh antecedents, which show no influence of Geoffrey of Monmouth.

In fact, there is no specific mention of any feudal relationship between Arthur and the members of his court, though his wide authority is suggested by the large number of warriors in attendance. Furthermore, he calls on some to accomplish particular tasks, such as on Cei, Bedwyr, Cynddylig, Gwrthyr, Gwalchmei, and Menw to accompany Culhwch on his search of Olwen (ll. 373–411). Cei and Bedwyr also appear in the Arthurian episode of the *Vita Cadoci* by Lifris of Llancarfan, dated at the latest near the beginning of the twelfth century. In neither text do the two warriors receive Normandy and Anjou as their respective apanages, as they do in the *Historia Regum Britanniae* (ch. 156). They are men of a certain age, since they both have sons who belong to Arthur's warband (ll. 283–85). One odd detail is that, when listing the forty tasks, Olwen's father claims that Arthur will not be persuaded to join in the hunt for Twrch Trwyth because "he is a man of mine" (l. 733). This would suggest that Yspaddaden considers himself to be the king's overlord, but perhaps the remark is intended merely to underline the giant's arrogance.

In the *Vita Cadoci* Lifris calls Arthur *rex illustrissimus Brittanniae*.[9] This establishes that his fame as the most important ruler in Britain in his day was widely known in Wales more than thirty years before Geoffrey's work. This title would correspond approximately to the one that is given to Arthur in *Culhwch and Olwen* namely *Penn Teyrned yr Ynys honn* [chief of the princes of this island],[10] whose authority is recognized by lesser princes in the isle of Britain, unlike Arthur in the *Historia Regum Britanniae*, who becomes an emperor of European stature. He controls a *teulu* [warband] made up of warriors, some with magical properties, drawn from the aristocratic families of Celtic Britain, some at least heroes long current in oral tradition.[11] The presence of two kings of France, Iona (l. 202) and Guilenhin (l. 294), and of the son of Flergant, king of Brittany (l. 216) at his court would underscore his prestige among the audience of the tale and does not indicate Arthur's dominion over the northwestern part of the continent of Europe.[12] Only once does he cross the Channel, and that is to Brittany, also part of the Celtic fringe, in order to acquire the two hounds of Glythmyr Ledewic, an episode recounted in a single sentence (l. 1007–9).

In *Culhwch and Olwen* Arthur is no longer depicted as the defender of the Britons against the Saxons, the Picts, and the Scots, as he is described in the *Historia Brittonum*. Now his battles are delivered against the figures of legend and monsters of folklore, in particular the giant boar, Twrch Trwyth, with which he had been associated at least since the ninth-century *Mirabilia*, appended to the *Historia Brittonum*.[13] Apart from his brief excursion to Brittany, his adventures are located in the isle of Britain, from Cornwall in the south to the old British North, and in Ireland. Though he plays an active part in the completion of fourteen of the twenty-one of those which are described, there is no suggestion that he is conquering territories outside his kingdom nor that his feats of arms earn him any merit in the manner of those performed by knights of courtly romance. There is one episode in which Arthur settles a vendetta between two warriors over an abduction. His solution is for the maiden to remain unmolested in her father's house, while the two protagonists are to fight each other on May-calends until doomsday, the victor on that day winning her (ll. 987–1004), a judgment that is more reminiscent of myth than of any customary law. Twice only is he described in person in the act of slaughter: in Ireland where he kills one of Twrch Trwyth's piglets (l. 1073), and in the final adventure, located in the old North, when he slices the Black Witch in two across her stomach (ll. 1225–29).

The one touch of courtliness in Arthur's personal conduct is to be found in the manner in which he overrides Cei's objections to Culhwch's entry into his hall until the meal is over, on the grounds that it would go against court protocol. "Not so, fair Cei," the king replies. "We are noble men as long as we are resorted to. The greater the bounty we show, all the greater will be our nobility and our fame and our glory" (ll. 135–38). In spite of Culhwch's unorthodox entry on horseback, Arthur does not chide him, but addresses him instead as *unben* [chief, lord] and bestows on him the privilege of *edling, gwrthrychyad teyrnas* [atheling, heir to a throne] (l. 149), though there is nothing to suggest that Culhwch is being considered by the king as his own heir. In fact, Culhwch would be excluded by the Welsh law of agnatic succession, and so the terms are purely honorific. Furthermore, Arthur has no hesitation in granting the young man a boon, provided it is not his ship, his arms or his queen (ll. 156–62). Such are the limits to his courtliness.

The queen and the ladies of the court are named, being described as "the gentle-torqued maidens of this Island" (ll. 356–57), but they are not described as playing any active part, neither choosing a champion nor inspiring the warriors to greater feats of arms, as they do at Caerleon, according to the *Historia Regum Britanniae* (ch. 157). How different and more luxurious is the life led in Geoffrey's Caerleon than at Arthur's court as described in *Culhwch and Olwen!*

There are several references to Christianity in the text, and it is clear that Arthur is a Christian king. Among the members of his court is Bitwini, "the bishop who blesses meat and drink" (l. 356), while the saints of Ireland bestow on him their blessing after he has given them his protection (ll. 1062–64). There are other references to Christianity but none refer specifically to Arthur or his court. Strikingly, the Virgin Mary is nowhere mentioned, nor are religious festivals, such as Easter and Pentecost, which are frequent times of the year for the start of courtly romances.

It is generally assumed that in *Culhwch and Olwen* Arthur's court is located at Celliwig in Cornwall.[14] It is true that his presence there is mentioned on three occasions later in the tale (ll. 975, 1024, and 1203–4), on the last of which he is said to have gone there to refresh himself after the hunt for Twrch Trwyth, which ended in Cornwall in any case. What seems odd is that Arthur's links with Celliwig are not mentioned before the tale is three-quarters over, nor is there any suggestion that it happens to be his principal seat. There is nothing to localize the court in Cornwall at the time of Culhwch's arrival, and in view of the practice of medieval rulers to move their court round their domains, it would be hazardous to assume that Arthur was in residence at Celliwig on that occasion.[15] Had *Culhwch and Olwen* been post-Geoffrey, one would have expected Caerleon to be named, but it is conspicuous by its absence throughout the tale.

Throughout *Culhwch and Olwen* Arthur appears as an active leader, capable of courtliness, while sharing with his warriors their adventures, occasionally even leading them in their successful completion and not plagued by temporary weaknesses. Although he does not always succeed in carrying out his threats, a feature that suggests the possibility of irony on the author's part, there is a greater sense of Arthur leading a team in combat than there will be in the romances of Chrétien de Troyes, to which I now turn.

The two main literary works between *Culhwch and Olwen* and Chrétien which were to have an undeniable influence on the latter were the *Historia Regum Britanniae*, written towards the end of the 1130s,[16] and its adaptation into Norman French by Wace, under the title of *Le Roman de Brut*, completed in 1155. The still greater emphasis on refinement in this work than one finds in the *Historia Regum Britanniae* might explain why, according to Layamon,[17] the author presented a copy to the new queen of England, Henry II's consort, Eleanor of Aquitaine. Wace's *Brut* is the earliest text to mention the Round Table, about which "Bretun dient mainte fable."[18] A little further on, Wace enlarges on the numerous tales about Arthur which circulated in his day, expressing his own disbelief of their veracity. It is clear that Chrétien must have had access to these and that his sources were not limited to Geoffrey, Wace, and other contemporary texts.[19]

Chrétien describes Arthur as the son of Uther Pendragon (*Erec*, l. 1767; *Yvain*, l. 663; *Perceval*, l. 445), and so his debt to the *Historia Regum Britanniae* and *Brut* is clear. Caerleon figures as one of his residences in *Lancelot* and *Perceval*, though only in the former as the location of the opening of the narrative, where the text reads in Foerster's edition

> A un jor d'une Asçansion
> Fu venuz devers Carleon
> Li rois Artus et tenu ot
> Cort mout riche a Camaalot (ll. 31–34)

However, the text of the Guiot manuscript (Paris, Bibliothèque Nationale, MS fr. 794) omits both place names. Since Arthur's residence is stated at the beginning of Chrétien's other romances, it would seem that the Foerster reading is the correct one. Yet a certain doubt must remain, because, apart from this occurrence, Camelot does not appear in Chrétien's romances.[20] The location of Arthur's residences at the beginning of Chrétien's other romances is Cardigan in *Erec*, Winchester in *Cligés*, in which Arthur's realm is described most closely to reality, and Cardueil, usually identified as Carlisle, in both *Yvain* and *Perceval*.[21] Other residences are named in the body of the romances, Carnant or Caruent and Nantes in *Erec*, London and Windsor in *Cligés*, Chester and Dinasdaron in *Yvain*, and Orquenie in *Perceval*.[22]

It is in *Erec* that we find the ideal of kingship that Arthur represented for Chrétien at the early stage of his career as a writer of romance. It is expressed in the sovereign's own words as part of a long speech at the time of the hero's return to Cardigan, accompanied by Enide, on whom he will bestow the kiss in accordance with the custom of the slaughter of the White Stag.

> Je sui rois, si ne doi mantir,
> ne vilenie consantir,
> ne fauseté ne desmesure;
> reison doi garder et droiture,
> qu'il apartient a leal roi

que il doit maintenir la loi,
verité, et foi, et justise.
Je ne voldroie an nule guise
fere deslëauté ne tort,
ne plus au foible que au fort;
n'est droiz que nus de moi se plaingne.
Et je ne voel pas que remaigne
la costume ne li usages
que siaut maintenir mes lignages.
De ce vos devroit il peser
se ge vos voloie alever
autre costume et autres lois
que ne tint mes peres li rois.
L'usage Pandragon, mon pere,
qui rois estoit et emperere,
voel je garder et maintenir,
que que il m'an doie avenir. (ll. 1749-70)

The emphasis in this speech is laid on the integrity of the sovereign, on his responsibility for the maintenance of customary law, truth, and good faith, on fair, loyal, honest conduct, based on reason and the rejection of all excess. In showing the king as the focus of an authority and power that had to be exercised within the letter of the law, the speech reflects ideal kingship as advocated by the political thinkers of the second half of the twelfth century, such as John of Salisbury in his *Policraticus*, and shows a vision of a stabler and more humanely organized society than the one depicted in *Culhwch and Olwen*.

In *Erec* Arthur lives up to this ideal, though he remains throughout a retiring figure, doing little more than presiding over his court, from which the hero starts on his adventures and to which he returns on their successful conclusion.[23] We learn, however, about the king's love of the hunt, a truly royal sport in which he indulges on other occasions too, for it is his decision to set out on the chase of the White Stag at the beginning of the romance which sets the plot in motion. This episode allows us as well to discover his insistence on his authority, that once he has made a decision, on no account may it be changed, even when warned of its possible divisive outcome (ll. 41–62). In this event, he is fortunate in being able to postpone this, in consultation with his council (ll. 311–42). Among his other distractions is to preside over tournaments, perhaps the most detailed of these being the one held outside Oxford, in which Cligés covers himself with glory (*Cligés*, ll. 4539–929).

Arthur is ruler of Britain, but there are several details in Chrétien's romances which suggest that his realm is visualized as corresponding to Henry II's dominions in Britain and northwest France, with client kings such as Lac, Erec's father and king of Estre-Gales, and Loth, king of Loenois (Geoffrey's *Lodonesia*, Lothian), who is Gauvain's father in *Yvain* (l. 6261). Loomis has identified Estre-Gales (in some manuscripts Outre-Gales) as the south Wales kingdom of Deheubarth, while Ritchie has pointed to it being the ancient British kingdom of Strathclyde.[24] Both of these identifications are perfectly plausible, though I prefer Ritchie's since the form found in manuscripts of *Erec* is clearly *estregales* or *outregales* and not *destregales*. In the case of *Erec*, however, a third possibility occurs to me, in view of the hero's connection with Brittany and his coronation at Nantes at the end of the romance, namely that Chrétien is using the name in this instance for the duchy, which had come under Henry II's control in 1158.[25] In *Cligés*, Arthur sails across the Channel, to be welcomed by the inhabitants of Brittany, now called by its correct name, as their liege lord (ll. 559–61). This title is also given to him in *Lancelot* (l. 3888), though here, as in *Erec*, *Yvain*, and *Perceval*, we find an indeterminate geography of Greater and Lesser Britain, with no indication of separation by the sea.

In one of Chrétien's romances only does Arthur show any initiative, and that is in *Cligés*, in which he spends a whole summer in Brittany, presumably on a royal progress, having left his island kingdom under the regency of the Earl of Windsor. On learning that the earl has taken over control of London, the king assembles an army, the only time that he acts decisively, and returns to Britain with his loyal Bretons. The defeat of the traitor owes nothing to him, for he merely performs a ceremonial role throughout. However, when the captured earl is handed over to him, Arthur dispenses retribution without delay, but shows mercy to his accomplices (ll. 2159–71). He then proceeds to reward Alexandre, Cligés' father, who had led his knights to victory, offering him any of his possessions, with the exception of his crown and queen (ll. 2180–86).[26] Near the end of the romance, when Cligés returns to beg Arthur's aid against his uncle, the emperor of Constantinople, the king promises to fill one thousand ships with knights and three thousand with men-at-arms to support the young man's claim. These are recruited in England, Flanders, Normandy, France, Brittany, and Aquitaine, all Angevin dominions, with the exception of Flanders, and France in its strict sense, the inclusion of both of which may have been included for metrical reasons. But the fleet does not sail because of the emperor's convenient death. Apart from a reference to his victory over King Rion in *Perceval* (ll. 851–52), this is the nearest that Arthur gets to going to war against a foreign power,[27] and Chrétien never suggests that he is personally involved in the search for the Grail.

The emphasis on the wealth and refinement of Arthur's court is to be seen at the beginning of Erec in particular (ll. 27–62, etc.), where it is attained not only by kings and knights, but also by rich ladies and maidens, noble daughters of kings. Queen Guenievre plays an important role in court life from the start, setting off with her husband on the hunt for the White Stag, attended by a king's daughter as lady-in-waiting, though the two women halt when the animal's scent has been detected. When the defeated Yder, who has allowed his squire to strike her handmaid, arrives at Arthur's court to surrender to the queen, at Erec's behest, he is treated with the utmost courtesy by her and told that she has no wish to punish him (ll. 1201–4). Similarly, she takes the shy and poorly dressed Enide in hand on her arrival (ll. 1567–661). Guenievre's role near the beginning of Cligés is equally important, for it is she who notices that Alexandre and Soredamor are in love and tactfully overcomes their reticence (ll. 1535–624). In both of these romances, she then fades into the background, but how different a character she has been shown to be than Gwenhwyfar in Culhwch and Olwen, who is but a name as Arthur's consort. Guenievre has become the courtly lady par excellence.[28]

Any examination of the depiction of Arthur by Chrétien must emphasize how he deteriorates after Cligés, and, from being a regal figure, albeit a retiring one, he is transformed into a feeble, even impotent, man. In Lancelot (ll. 43–67) he is incapable of protecting his wife against the demands of an unknown knight and is later cuckolded by the hero, who receives the queen's favors in a secret assignation for having defeated her abductor in combat (ll. 4653–86). This scene illustrates the courtly lady bestowing the ultimate reward on her lover for his services towards her, as well as exemplifying the concept that true love cannot be found in marriage. It has been suggested that Chrétien depicted Arthur in decline in order to provide Guenievre with a pretext for infidelity, and it is true that the husbands of courtly ladies in twelfth and thirteenth-century French literature are often described unsympathetically. However, since Chrétien continues to emphasize Arthur's weakness in Yvain and Perceval, though in neither is the queen shown to be unfaithful, this explanation appears inadequate. In the latter romance, just before the hero arrives at court to request the king to dub him, Arthur has failed to react to the arrogant demands for his territories made by the Red Knight. He merely broods and, lost in thought, fails to hear Perceval's greeting, even when repeated (ll. 907–26).

The situation at the beginning of *Yvain*, though somewhat different, discloses once more an effete Arthur. Now he has retired to his chamber to rest, accompanied by Guenievre, to the surprise of the court since never before has he left the company on a feast day. It happens that the queen detains him, lying at his side until he falls asleep (ll. 41–52), before returning to hear Calogrenant recount his adventure. This incident led Nitze to call Arthur a "roi fainéant," while Noble goes further and accuses the king of being "overcome with lust," which seems to be an exaggeration.[29] In all of the three romances Arthur subsequently acts very much as he does in *Erec* and *Cligés*, presiding over his court with little show of authority, except in the case of the litigating daughters of the lord of Noire Espine, where he finally decides to settle the dispute himself, passing a judgment by which the younger sister obtains her portion of their father's estate, but must swear to be the liege woman of the elder (*Yvain*, ll. 6396–440).

What is Chrétien's purpose in switching from the quietly regal Arthur of *Erec* and *Cligés* to the spent figure at the openings of *Lancelot, Yvain*, and *Perceval*? I venture to suggest that he is seeking to convey that the king is now an old man, who no longer possesses the physical strength nor the intellectual power to rule his realm effectively. Irony is apparent in these scenes, and nowhere more than in the contrast between the prologue of *Yvain* and the opening of the narrative which follows.

A further question posed by this transformation is whether it has any significance for the historical background against which all five romances were composed and also their dates. Noble suggests that Chrétien's increasing hostility to Arthur reflected the conflict between his patrons at the time at which he was writing his later romances, who happened to belong to the houses of Champagne and Flanders, and the royal authority.[30] Interesting though this is, I find myself unable to support it. The barons' revolt against Philip Augustus, led by, among others, Counts Henry of Champagne and Philip Flanders, took place between 1181 and 1186, when the precocious and strong-willed king was still in his teens and full of vigor. The treaty of Amiens in March 1186 brought reconciliation, Henry and Philip becoming once again his loyal vassals. From now on the king of France's struggle was against the Angevin king of England, whose continental empire he was determined to undermine. In view of Chrétien's possible equation of Arthur's realm with Henry II's empire, mentioned earlier, it seems to me that the change in Arthur in *Lancelot, Yvain*, and *Perceval* may indicate the king of England's decline and French hostility towards him. This could mean that all three were written after early 1186.[37] I would concur with the view that Chrétien's five extant Arthurian romances were written in a ten-year period preceding 1192,[32] *Erec* and *Cligés* by March 1186, and the three others later. An historical event that may have triggered off *Erec* is the marriage of Geoffrey Plantagenet to Constance, heiress of the duchy of Brittany, in 1181. Unfortunately, no chronicler that I have been able to consult, including Robert de Torigni, indicates where the ceremony was held, but many weddings of the ducal family were celebrated at Nantes, the location of *Erec's* coronation at the end of the romance. A link between the two is plausible, and it could even be that *Erec* was written to commemorate the event. Chrétien's close connection with the Angevin court at that time is not unlikely. The only evidence of the countess of Champagne's patronage is to be found in the prologue of *Lancelot*, in which the declining Arthur makes his first appearance.

The differences between the figure of Arthur in *Culhwch and Olwen*, on the one hand, and in the romances of Chrétien de Troyes, on the other, are considerable. In the Welsh tale the quests are undertaken by members of his warband forming a group, not by a single warrior, while the king participates in a number of them and plays the leading role in a few, particularly the hunt for Twrch Trwyth. The society which he heads is entirely male-orientated, and the social relationship that counts is that of kinship.

In *Erec* and *Cligés* Chrétien depicts a very different Arthur, the representative of the post *Historia Regum Britanniae* literary ideal of the late twelfth-century monarch, presiding over a court in which chivalry and refinement are predominant, the queen and her ladies being seen as arbiters of behavior. Even in *Cligés*, the romance in which the settings approximate closest to reality because the locations are given their proper names, there is no glorification of Arthur's own martial pursuits, merely those of his knights. The relationship that is now underlined is the feudal relationship between lord and vassal. I suggest that the king's decline in the three later romances may have reflected the antagonism between Philip Augustus and his vassals on the one hand and Henry II on the other during the second half of the 1180s.

That irony is used by both authors is undeniable, and this is particularly evident in *Culhwch and Olwen* but it is difficult for us today, separated as we are by eight centuries from the composition of these works, to be sure how much. The wide use of alliteration and assonance in the grouping of names, which may today appear deliberately comic, was perhaps not so to a twelfth-century native Welsh audience still steeped in an oral tradition, in which the two played such an important part.[33] Both the Welsh and the French works were intended for aristocratic publics and composed within a period of some eighty years if the dates I propose are approximately correct, yet the ethos of Chrétien's work has moderated the stark brutality of military prowess described in *Culhwch and Olwen*. Although Wales possessed codes of customary laws at the time, Arthur is only seen to dispense justice in one of the episodes, and then not according to custom.[34] How far is this accounted for by the fact that Welsh literary fashions of the early twelfth century had retained more of the ideals of the heroic age? No doubt, Wales's geographical position near the edge of the Western world would have been an important factor in this conservatism, being responsible for a more gradual acceptance by its literary tradition of influences emanating from Europe and beyond from the second half of the eleventh century onward.

Notes

1. Quotations from *Culhwch and Olwen* have been taken from *Culhwch and Olwen: An Edition and Study of the Oldest Arthurian Tale*, ed. Rachel Bromwich and D. Simon Evans (Cardiff, 1992), based on the late Idris Foster's transcription. The best known twentieth-century translation is the one in *The Mabinogion* by G. Jones and T. Jones (London, 1949). Quotations of phrases have been copies from this translation, followed by the line numbers of the Welsh text. Quotations from Chrétien de Troyes work have been taken from Chrétien de Troyes, *Les Romans de Chrétien de Troyes*. I. *Erec et Enide*, ed. M. Roques (Paris, 1963); *Les Romans de Chrétien de Troyes*. II. *Cligés*, ed. A. Micha (Paris, 1965); *Les Romans de Chrétien de Troyes*. III. *Le Chevalier de la charrette*, ed. M. Roques (Paris, 1965); *Les Romans de Chrétien de Troyes*. IV. *Le Chevalier au lion (Yvain)*, ed. M. Roques (Paris, 1965); *Le Roman de Perceval, ou le Conte du graal*, ed. W. Roach (Geneva and Paris, 1959). Throughout, I have reduced the titles of Chrétien's romances to the names of their heroes, *Erec, Cligés, Lancelot, Yvain,* and *Perceval*. I wish to thank the editors for their very helpful comments on the original draft of this essay.

2. Most recently Kenneth Jackson, Idris Foster, Roger S. Loomis, Erich Köhler, Richard Barber, Rachel Bromwich, Doris Edel, Jean Frappier, Jean Markale, Leslie Topsfield, Beate Schmolke-Hasselmann, Rosemary Morris, Madeleine Blaess, Stephen Knight, Barbara N. Sargent-Baur, Peter Noble, Donald Maddox, Brynley Roberts, and many others. I shall name those of their contributions whenever I refer to them directly.

3. The collection was inaccurately given the title of *The Mabinogion* by Lady Charlotte Guest in her English translation, published in its complete form in 1849, but individual tales had appeared from 1838 onwards. A detailed study of the manuscript tradition is to be found in the introduction of the Bromwich and Evans edition, pp. ix–xiii.

4. A larger number of archaic linguistic features appear in the first 564 lines than in the remainder (*Culhwch and Olwen*, ed. Bromwich and Evans, pp. xiv–xxv). See also Patrick Sims-Williams, "The Significance of the Irish Personal Names in *Culhwch and Olwen*," *Bulletin of the Board of Celtic Studies* 29 (1982), 600–20. His conclusion is that the Irish names indicate a date of the middle of the twelfth century at the very latest.

5. On the influence of Norman French on Welsh, see Morgan Watkin, *La Civilisation française dans les Mabinogion* (Paris, 1962).

6. See Doris Edel, *Helden auf Freiersfüssen* (Amsterdam, 1980), p. 17.

7. *Culhwch and Olwen*, ed. Bromwich and Evans, pp. xxvii–xxxiii, lxxi–lxxvi. This is further discussed by Brynley F. Roberts, who considers that "the author appears to have attempted to ensure some degree of coherence in the progress of the narrative," in "*Culhwch and Olwen*, The Triads, Saints' Lives," *The Arthur of the Welsh: The Arthurian Legend in Medieval Welsh Literature*, ed. Rachel Bromwich et al. (Cardiff, 1991), pp. 73–95, at 78.

8. See Nennius, *British History and the Welsh Annals*, ed. and trans. J. Morris (London, 1980), ch. 39, pp. 29, 71. See further David N. Dumville, "Nennius and the *Historia Brittonum*," *Studia Celtica* 10/11 (1975–76), 78–95, in which he shows that the attribution of the work to Nennius is unfounded; also "The Historical Value of the *Historia Brittonum*," *Arthurian Literature* 6 (1986), 1–26. Dumville is at present engaged in preparing a ten-volume edition of the work, of which three volumes have been published: *Historia Brittonum*, ed. David N. Dumville; vol. 3, *The Vatican Recension* (Cambridge, 1985); vol. 7, *The Sawley and Durham Recensions* (Cambridge, 1986); vol. 2, *The Chartres Recension* (Cambridge, 1988).

9. Text as reproduced by E. K. Chambers in his *Arthur of Britain* (London, 1927), p. 244. The title of *amherawdwr (imperator)* is given to Arthur in an *englyn* (a three-lined stanza), which has been dated linguistically to before 1100 (A. O. H. Jarman, "The Delineation of Arthur in Early Welsh Verse," *An Arthurian Tapestry: Essays in Memory of Lewis Thorpe*, ed. Kenneth Varty [Glasgow, 1981], p. 5). See also R. Bromwich, "Celtic Elements in Arthurian Romances: A General Survey," *The Legend of Arthur in the Middle Ages: Studies Presented to A. H. Diverres by Colleagues, Pupils and Friends*, ed. P. B. Grout et al. (Cambridge, 1983), pp. 41–55, 230–233 and P. Sims-Williams, "The Early Welsh Arthurian Poems," *The Arthur of the Welsh*, ed. Bromwich et al. pp. 33–71.

10. The English translation is the one given by Bromwich in her introduction, *Culhwch and Olwen*, ed. Bromwich and Evans, p. xxvii.

11. Some may be the author's invention in order to create an extended "run." See Brynley Roberts, "*Culhwch and Olwen*, The Triads, Saints' Lives," *The Arthur of the Welsh*, ed. Bromwich et al., p. 78–9.

12. Iona is purely fictitious, Guilenhin is usually thought to refer to William the Conqueror, while Flergant is likely to be Alain Fergant, duke of Brittany from 1084 until his deposition in 1112.

13. For the relevant portion of the text and a discussion of the episode, see *Culhwch and Olwen*, ed. Bromwich and Evans, pp. lxiv–lxvii. See also note 8 above.

14. On the possible sites of Celliwig, see O. J. Padel "Some South-Western Sites with Arthurian Associations," *Arthur of the Welsh*, ed. Bromwich et al., pp. 229–48, esp. 234–38.

15. In the Welsh Triads, Arthur is given three residences, Celliwig in Cornwall, Mynyw [Saint David's] in Wales, and Pen Rhionydd, an unidentified location in the old North. For the text, an English translation and a discussion of the triad, see *Trioedd Ynys Prydein; The Welsh Triads*, ed. and trans. R. Bromwich (Cardiff, 1961), pp. 1–4. In later triads Mynyw is replaced by Caerleon-on-Usk, e.g. Triad 85.

16. Geoffrey of Monmouth, *Historia Regum Britanniae: The First Variant Version*, ed. N. Wright, (Cambridge, 1985), Introduction, pp. ix–xx. See also Roberts, "*Culhwch and Olwen*, The Triads, Saints' Lives," *The Arthur of the Welsh*, p. 97; and John Gillingham, "The Context and Purpose of Geoffrey of Monmouth's *History of the Kings of Britain*," *Anglo-Norman Studies* 13 (1990), 99–118.

17. Layamon, *Brut*, ed. G. L. Brook and R. F. Leslie, 2 vols. (Oxford, 1963), 1: ll. 20–3.

18. *Le Roman de Brut, par Wace*, ed. I. Arnold, 2 vols. (Paris, 1938 and 1940), 2: ll. 9752. Henceforth, Wace, *Brut*.

19. Wace, *Brut*, 2: ll. 9786–98. It is in *Le Roman de Rou* that he gives his equally sceptical description of his visit to the forest of Brocéliande, which covered much of central Brittany in his day and was believed by many to be the abode of fairies. See *Le Roman de Rou*, ed. A. J. Holden, 3 vols. (Paris, 1970–3), 2: ll. 6373–98. On Chrétien's other possible sources, see R. Bromwich, "First Transmission to England and France," *The Arthur of the Welsh*, ed. Bromwich et al. pp. 273–98.

20. It appears for the first time elsewhere in Manessier's *Continuation* and *Le Chevaliers as deus espees*. See G. D. West, *An Index of Proper Names in French Arthurian Verse Romances, 1150–1300* (Toronto, 1969), p. 31. See also C. E. Pickford, "Camelot," *Mélanges. . . Pierre Le Gentil* (Paris, 1973), pp. 633–40.

21. It may seem surprising that he has not used the form *Kaerleïl*, to be found in both the *Historia Regum Britanniae* (ch. 28) and Wace's *Brut* (l. 1599). However, the form with *d* is also found in Marie de France's *Lanval* (line 5), Béroul's *Tristan* (ll. 650, 684), and in all later texts. Perhaps the change from *l* to *d* was made to avoid confusion with Caerleon, or merely by dissimilation. Cardigan in *Erec* is unexpected. It had been captured by the Welsh from the Anglo-Normans in 1165, and in 1176 the Lord Rhys held a great assembly of poets and musicians there. See R. R. Davies, *The Age of Conquest* (Oxford, 1991), pp. 53, 221. Could the reputation of this gathering have reached Chrétien's ears?

22. Erec is with Arthur at Tintagel when he learns of his father's death, and so this too may be one of the king's residences. It certainly is not so in *Perceval*.

23. Erec pays a fleeting visit to Arthur's camp in the forest, and this divides his quest with Enide in two (ll. 4171-252).

24. Beate Schmolke-Hasselmann has discussed Chrétien's equating of Arthur with Henry II in "The Round Table: Ideal, Fiction, Reality," *Arthurian Literature* 2 (1982), 41-75. On the identification of Estre-Gales, see R. S. Loomis, *Arthurian Tradition and Chrétien de Troyes* (New York, 1949), pp. 70-75; R. L. G. Ritchie, *Chrétien de Troyes and Scotland* (Oxford, 1952), pp. 10-11. The identification of the British kingdom of Strathclyde was made by E. Brugger, "Beiträge zur Erklärung der arthurischen Geographie," *Zeitschrift für Französische Sprache und Literatur* 27 (1904), 69-116. The list of guests at Erec's wedding includes many client kings and vassals (1879-956).

25. See A. L. Poole, *From Domesday Book to Magna Carta, 1087-1216*, 2nd ed. (Oxford, 1955), pp. 324-25. There seem to me to be other cases of Chrétien's use of the same name for different places, according to the romance, e.g., Logres, which may be part of Arthur's kingdom in *Lancelot*, but is certainly not so in *Perceval*, see also note 22 above.

26. This detail reminds one of Arthur's conditions for awarding the boon to Culhwch (ll. 156-62).

27. Rosemary Morris suggests that in this episode Chrétien is giving Arthur the status of Western Emperor: R. Morris, *The Character of King Arthur in Medieval Literature* (Cambridge, 1982), pp. 60-61.

28. On Chrétien's Guenievre, see Madeleine Blaess, "The Public and Private Face of Arthur's Court in the Works of Chrétien de Troyes," *Chrétien de Troyes and the Troubadours: Essays in Memory of the Late Leslie Topsfield*, ed. P. S. Noble and L. M. Paterson (Cambridge, 1984), pp. 238-48.

29. W. A. Nitze, "The Character of Gauvain in the Romances of Chrétien de Troyes," *Modern Philology* 50 (1953), 222. See also P. S. Noble, "Chrétien's Arthur," in *Chrétien de Troyes and the Troubadours*, pp. 220-37, esp. p. 228.

30. Ibid, p. 234.

31. Much has been written on the dates of Chrétien's romances since A. Fourrier's article "Encore la Chronologie des Oeuvres de Chrétien de Troyes," *Le Bulletin bibliographique de la Société Internationale Arthurienne* 2 (1950), 69-88. In it he proposed 1170 for *Erec*, because Henry II spent Christmas 1169 at Nantes, 1176 for *Cligés*, between 1177-81 for *Lancelot* and *Yvain*, and 1182-83 for *Perceval*. However, J. Misrahi ("More light on the Chronology of Chrétien de Troyes?" *Le Bulletin bibliographique de la Soc. Int. Arth.* 11 [1959], pp. 89-120) cast doubt on Fourrier's conclusions, stating that if an historical event is behind an episode

in a work of fiction, a lapse of some years may have occurred between the two. C. Luttrell dates the five romances between 1184 and 1190 in *The Creation of the First Arthurian Romance* (London, 1974), claiming the clear influence on *Erec* of Alain de Lille's *Anticlaudianus*, published in 1184. T. Hunt, ("Redating Chrétien de Troyes" *Bulletin bibliographique de la Société Internationale Arthurienne* 30 [1978], pp. 209–37) refuses to accept Luttrell's identification of the publication of the *Anticlaudianus* as the *terminus a quo* of *Erec*, on the grounds that the ideas in question were being discussed by other writers a few years earlier, but he concludes, "What Luttrell has shown is that all the necessary stimulus of Chrétien's activity is there in the period 1184–90" (p. 237).

32. I have expressed my arguments in favour of 1190 as the likely date for the start of *Perceval* in "The Grail and the Third Crusade," *Arthurian Literature* 10 (1990), 13–109, esp. 97–100.

33. For the view that *Culhwch and Olwen* is a parody of the *märchen* tradition and is entirely ironic, see J. N. Radner, "Interpreting Irony in Medieval Celtic Narrative: The Case of *Culhwch ac Olwen*," *Cambridge Medieval Celtic Studies* 16 (Winter 1988), 41–57. On irony in Chrétien, see D. H. Green, *Irony in Medieval Romance* (Cambridge, 1979), T. Hunt, *Chrétien de Troyes, Yvain* (*Le Chevalier au Lion*) (London, 1986).

34. See *The Latin Texts of the Welsh Laws*, ed. H. D. Emanuel (Cardiff, 1967). For a study of the importance of custom as a theme in Chrétien's romances, see E. Koehler, "Le Rôle de la 'costume' dans les romans de Chrétien de Troyes," *Romania* 81 (1960), 386–97; and Donald Maddox, *The Arthurian Romances of Chrétien de Troyes* (Cambridge, 1991).

The Knight as Reader of Arthurian Romance*

——————————————————————— *Elspeth Kennedy*

There is sometimes a tendency, especially among non-medievalists, to think of Arthurian romance as escapist literature, concerned with lost dreams and a past golden age, primarily written for women, in contrast with the "manly" epic. However, although there is indeed evidence from references to patrons and from the ownership of manuscripts that *dames* were amongst the avid readers or listeners to the reading of romances, there are also examples of interplay between life and Arthurian literature which concern knightly activities. A number of scholars have drawn attention to the general influence of the Arthurian stories on chivalric games or spectacles. For example, Roger S. Loomis (a pioneer in this field) wrote two articles on the subject.[1] More recently, Jonathan Boulton has pointed out that Arthurian literature was important in terms of providing a general background for monarchical orders of knighthood such as the Order of the Garter, founded on the model of the Round Table, although the romances themselves did not provide details for the organization of such bodies.[2] Nevertheless, I think that some serious works in the vernacular on contemporary society and on the theory and practice of chivalry draw more than has perhaps been realized from the great romances and in particular from the Prose *Lancelot*, one of the most widely read in the thirteenth, fourteenth, and fifteenth centuries.[3] Indeed, there seems to be evidence that there were knights of some standing who were as familiar with this text as were ladies, although their interest may well have been directed towards different elements within the romance. To illustrate this, I propose to examine some of the nonfictional works of two men, Philippe de Novare and Philippe de Beaumanoir of the thirteenth century, with a briefer look at a third, Ramon Lull, whose book on chivalry was very influential in the later Middle Ages, and a glance forward at the writings of Geoffroi de Charny of the fourteenth century. These men had trained as knights and were well known in relation to other forms of secular activity. I shall be looking for explicit allusions to or verbal echoes from Arthurian romance rather than a general background of Arthurian tradition.

Philippe de Novare (sometimes known as Philippe de Navarre) was born of a noble family in Italy about 1195 in Novaro, Lombardy. As a young man he went to Cyprus and seems to have spent the rest of his life in the Eastern Mediterranean. He served the Ibelins and took part in their war with the Emperor Frederick II. He was a good warrior, and apparently an able diplomat, as the Ibelins entrusted him with negotiations with the supporters of Frederick. He was also an expert in law, "le meilleur pledeour deça mer" according to one of his contemporaries, Hugues de Brienne. In his legal treatise, *Livre de forme de plait que Sire Felippe de Novaire fist pour un sien ami aprendre et enseigner coument on doit plaidoier en la haute court*,[4] he gives an interesting account of how he learned law, which, curiously enough, links up specifically with the reading of romances:

> Il avint que je fui au premier siege de Damiete, o messire Piere Chape, et messire Rau de Tabarie menga un jor o lui; aprés mengier, messire Piere me fist lire devant lui en un romans: messire Rau dist que je lisoie moult bien. Aprés fu messire Rau malade, et messire Piere Chape, a la requeste de messire Rau, me manda lirre devant lui. Issi avint que trois mois et plus y fu; et moult me desplaisoit ce que moult me deust pleire: messire Rau dormet poi et malvaisement; et quant je avoie leu tant com il voleit, il meismes me conteit moult de chozes dou royaume de Jerusalem et des us et des assises et disoit que je les retenisse. Et je qui moult doutai sa maniere, otreai tout. *(Assises de Jerusalem, 1:525)*

> It happened that I was at the first siege of Damietta with messire Piere Chape, and messire Rau de Tabarie dined with him one day; after the meal, messire Piere asked me to read from a romance in his presence: messire Rau said that I read very well. Later messire Rau fell ill and, at his request, messire Chape sent me to read to him. Thus it happened that for more than three months I was with messire Rau; and what should have pleased me very much displeased me: messire Rau slept little and badly; and when I had read as much as he wanted, he himself would tell me many things about the Kingdom of Jerusalem and about the customary law and the assises and

would say that I should remember them; and I, who was much in awe of him, submitted to all this.

There is also evidence of Philippe's interest in customary law in his other works. These are listed at the end of one of the manuscripts of his moral treatise, *Les quatre âges de l'homme*:[5] there he is named as the author of this book and two others. The first, of which only fragments survive, consisted of a collection of diverse material. The first part was about himself: how he came to the East and what he did there. This autobiographical account was followed by several rhymes and songs he composed himself, some about love. After this came an account of the conflict between the Emperor Frederick and the lord of Philippe, le seignor de Barut, Jean d'Ibelin the Old; this also contained verses by Philippe. The final part of this book was said by Philippe to bring together some songs and rhymes he composed in his old age. It has only been possible to piece together a fragment of the autobiography and the account of the struggle between Frederick and the Ibelins which has come down to us in the *Gestes des Chiprois*. These fragments of the work of Philippe de Novare have been edited under the title *Mémoires 1218-1243*.[6] The second book mentioned was the treatise on feudal law referred to above, which forms part of the *Assises de Jérusalem*. The third book was of course the "traité moral," known as *Les quatre âges de l'homme*, from which this list is taken, and which Philippe de Novare wrote, according to the first sentence in the work, when he was more than seventy years old.

I shall look first at the *Mémoires*, in order to place the Arthurian references in his work as a whole in the context both of his own experiences as a knight and of the interplay with other literary genres to be found in this particular text, an interplay which foreshadows the pattern of allusions to be found in his later work. In Philippe's description of the knighting in Cyprus of the Lord of Baruth's two elder sons, there is one of the earliest references to Arthurian games, held in 1223:

A cele chevalerie fu la plus grant feste et la plus longue qui fust onques desa mer que l'on sache. Mout i ot douné et despendu, et bouhordé, et contrefait les aventures de Bretaigne et de la Table ronde, et moult de manieres de jeus. (*Mémoires*, p. 7)

The festivities at this knighting were the greatest and longest ever known overseas. There was much giving and spending, much tourneying and re-enacting the adventures of Britain and of the Round Table and all manners of games.

This provides an example of the general use of Arthurian literature in relation to chivalric pursuits without any precise verbal allusions to a particular text. There are, however, in this text more specific references, not to romance, but to epic. When the lord of Baruth hears that his castle is under siege by the Longuebards, the term used to designate the supporters of the emperor Frederick II, he appeals for help to Henri de Lusignan, king of Cyprus, as his lord, reminding the king of the debt owed by him to the Ibelins and supports his plea by an allusion to the request for help made by Guillaume d'Orange to King Louis in a *chanson de geste, Foulque de Candie.*[7]

Philippe also inserts poems figuring characters from the *Roman de Renart* into his account of the conflict between the Ibelins and the Longuebards, and these too have epic resonances in that they recall passages from a number of branches of that work which, often for comic rather than strictly satirical purposes, present animals in the guise of epic heros. In Philippe de Novare, however, there is a clearly political significance given, as Renart and his allies are identified with the enemies of the Ibelins, whereas Philippe and his companions represent the opponents of the fox (he names himself as Chantecler the cock). It is significant that Renart is not presented here, as is usual in most branches of the *Roman de Renart,* as the hero/rogue who through his cunning nearly always comes out on top and avoids the punishment. His disrespect for authority would conflict with the emphasis on the need for loyalty to one's lord and on respect for mutual obligations which characterizes the *Mémoires* and which will be underlined in the Arthurian allusions in the next of his works to be examined.

Les quatre âges de l'homme, the last of Philippe's works, gives advice on the education and upbringing of children of noble birth, on the conduct of young men who should devote themselves to service, on the appropriate way of life for those in their prime, and finally on how best to live out one's old age honorably. In the "First Age" Philippe says that those educating the sons of great lords should teach them about the *estoires* and the books of the authors where there are many fine sayings and much good advice:

> eux faire apanre les estoires et les livres des autors ou il a mout de biaus diz, et de bons consaus. (*Les quatre âges,* p. 13)

Autors here may well refer to the *auctores,* the classical authors. There is a similar reference to the importance of reading and to the *actors* in Philippe's legal work.[8] Philippe knew Latin: he quotes St. Paul, *Romans* 12.3 in Latin (*Assises de Jérusalem,* 1:565), and there is one allusion to Lucan in the *Les quatre âges* (p. 88); but the majority of the allusions are to literature in the vernacular. For example, in the "Fourth Age," there is a lengthy quotation from the *Roman de Troie* to illustrate the importance of refraining from pride (*Les quatre âges*, p. 97).[9] There is also a long passage on the young Alexander which exemplifies the importance of *largece* for the "Second Age" (*Les quatre âges*, pp. 39–41), a quality required of knights and kings in Arthurian romance as well (for example, Prose *Lancelot*, pp. 72–73). It is also in the advice given to the *jone* that the direct allusion to the Prose *Lancelot* is made:

> Il est escrit ou livre Lancelot, ou il i a mout de biaus diz et de soutis, que uns prodons et sages et loiaus, qui avoit a nom Farien, avoit .j. sien neveu qui estoit apeleiz Lanbague; cil estoit viguereus et hardis et estalufrez. Andui furent a .j. mout grant consoil ou il avoit assez de viaus et de sages. Lambagues, li niés Farien, se hasta et parla devant les autres, et ses diz fu tenuz a mal et a folie.
>
> Li oncles l'an reprint mout, et li dist: "Biaus niés, je t'anseignerai .i. sens qui mout porra valoir a toi et as autres jones, se il est bien retenuz: garde, se tu te trueves en grant consoil, que ta parole ne soit oïe ne tes consaus, devant que li plus sage et li plus meür de toi et li greigneur avront parlé et dit lors senz: si en porras plus avisiement estre garniz a dire ton avis; et se tu viens en besoig d'armes, ou tu puisses fere .i. biau cop, garde que tu ja n'i atendes plus viel ne plus jone de toi, car granz honte et granz pechiez est de fol consoil doner hastivement, et granz honors est d'estre viguereus et hardiz, quant leus en est, et especiaument en jovant." (*Les quatre âges*, pp. 23–24)

It is written in the Livre Lancelot, where there are many fine and perceptive remarks, that a wise and loyal man of worth called Pharien had a nephew called Lambegues; the latter was vigorous, brave and impulsive. Lambegues, Farien's nephew, rushed in and spoke before the others, and what he said was held to be wrong and foolish.

His uncle reproved him severely for this and said: "Fair nephew, I will give you some advice which, if listened to, may be of value to you and to other young men: take care, if you are present at a great council, that you keep silent and refrain from giving advice until the wiser, riper in years, and higher in station than you have spoken and given their opinion; you will then be more qualified to give an informed view; and if you come to battle where you can strike a good blow, take care not to wait for those older or younger than you, for there is great shame and disgrace in putting forward foolish views hastily and there is great honor in being vigorous and bold on the right occasion, especially when young."

This passage paraphrases but does not quote in full advice given to Lambegues by Pharien. However it does echo certain phrases used in the Prose *Lancelot* which are italicized in the following passage:

"Biaus niés," fait Phariens, "de toi ne me mervoil ge pas, se tu mez po de raison en tes affaires, car l'an ne voit gaires avenir en nule terre que granz sens et granz proesce soient ensenble herbergié en cuer d'anfant. Et il est voirs que de la proesce as tu assez selonc l'aage que tu as, tant que tu en voiz un po mains cler el mireor de sapience. Si t'anseignerai ores un po de san, car g'i voi des ores mais plus cler que tu ne fais en la proesce. Se tu cest anseignement vels retenir, mout an porras amender, et tu et tuit li anfant qui en pris volent monter par grant proesce. *Et garde que tant com tu seras en enfances, se tu ies en leu o l'en consaut de granz affaires, que ja ta parole n'i soit oïe ne tes consauz jusqe la que tuit li plus ancien de toi avront parlé. Et se tu viens en bataille o en poigneïz de guerre ou en leu nul ou granz chevalerie soit assenblee, garde que ja n'i atandes plus juene ne plus viel de toi, mais fier devant toz les autres des esperons por faire un biau cop, la ou tu porras ataindre, car a pris et a honor d'armes conquerre ne doit nus atandre, ne lo juesne ne lo veillart.* Mais as granz consauz doner doivent li anfant entendre les plus meürs. *Et tant saches tu bien de voir, tres granz honors gist en morir par hardement et par proesce, et granz hontes et granz reproches vient en dire fole parole et fol consoil.* Cest essemple trai hore tant avant, por ce que tu m'as blasmé devant toz ces preudomes qui ci sont, qui miauz sevent que est sans et savoirs que tu ne feis." (Prose *Lancelot*, p. 85)

"Fair nephew," said Pharen, "I am not surprised if you do not behave very sensibly, for it is rare to find both good sense and great valour combined in the heart of a youth. It is true that you have a great deal of valour for one of your age, indeed so much that as a result you see a little less clearly in the mirror of wisdom. I will now teach you something about good sense, for at this point I have a clearer perception of that than you do of valour. If you will listen to this advice you will benefit from it, both you yourself and all young men who want to win high esteem through great valour. Take care that while you are still a youth, if you are present at a council concerned with important decisions, that no words of advice are heard from you until all those older than you have spoken. And if you come to a battle or armed skirmish or anywhere where a great number of knights are assembled, take care that you do not wait for those older or younger than you, but spur forward before everyone else to strike a good blow wherever you can, for no one should wait, neither young nor old, before winning honor in deeds of arms. But when important council is being given, the young should listen to the more mature. But I tell you truly that there is great honour in dying when undertaking brave deeds and feats and advice and great shame comes from speaking foolish words and giving foolish words and giving foolish advice. I draw your attention to this wise saying because you have reproached me before all the men of worth here present, who know better than you do what constitutes wisdom and good sense."

It might indeed be expected from the pattern of allusions to be found in the *Mémoires* that the part of the Prose *Lancelot* used by Philippe de Novare should be that which concerns Lancelot's childhood and that of his cousins, for this part of the romance deals with problems of the relationship between lord and vassal and of conflicting loyalty, themes characteristic of the epic and linking up with some of Philippe's own experiences and with his interest in feudal law. Indeed Pharien has much in common as the type of the good vassal with an epic hero such as Guillaume d'Orange[10] (referred to in the *Mémoires*), and there are a number of passages in the early part of the Prose *Lancelot* where the circumstances which might justify the renunciation of homage by a vassal are discussed. Pharien has to struggle hard to restrain his young nephew Lambegues from raising his hand against his lord Claudas, who has seized the children of their former lord, King Bohort of Gaunes. It is within this context that the episode concerning Pharien and Lambegues belongs. This point of loyalty to one's lord is picked up a little further on by Philippe de Novare, without a direct reference to Lambegues:

Et li jone home, qui qu'il soient, chevalier ou borjois ou autres, qui ont aucun pooir, se doivent mout garder que il ne se revelent as seigneurs; car trop est honteuse chose et vilainne d'estre contre seignor: comment que ce soit, a droit ou a tort, i a vilain blasme, et sovant en est on tenuz a traïtor, et po avient que l'an n'an vaigne a male fin.[11] (*Les quatre âges*, p. 26)

And young men, whoever they are, whether knights, townsmen (burghers) or others who have some power, should take great care never to rebel against their lords; for it is a dishonorable and wicked thing to be in opposition to one's lord; whether or not right is on one's side, there is great shame attached, and one is often held to be a traitor and can easily come to a bad end.

It is important to note that, although *Les quatre âges* allots a certain amount of space to the "Four Ages" of women, there are no allusions to their role as the inspiration for great feats of arms by young men, a constantly recurring theme in much of Arthurian romance and given great importance in the Prose *Lancelot* as well as in the love lyric. This is in spite of the fact that Philippe talks in *Les quatre âges* of the *chansons d'amour* (none surviving) which he has written; it is in marked contrast with a fourteenth-century writer such as Geoffroi de Charny who stresses the importance of a knight's love for a lady in spurring him on to great deeds and advancing his career as a knight. Indeed, Philippe advocates keeping women firmly in their place. Girls should be taught to sew and to spin, but not to read or write unless they are to become nuns:

> car par lire et escrire de fame sont maint mal avenu. Car tieus li osera baillier ou anvoier letres, ou faire giter devant li, qui seront de folie ou de priere, en chançon ou en rime ou en conte, qu'il n'oseroit proier ne dire de bouche, ne par message mander.
> (*Les quatre âges*, p. 16)

> for by a woman's reading and writing much harm can come: a letter containing wanton proposals in song, verse, or tale might be handed to, sent to or cast before a woman on behalf of someone who would not dare to make such proposals in person or by messenger.

There is an episode in an Arthurian romance, the Prose *Tristan*, which provides a good illustration of the the possible dangers of such correspondence between knight and lady: through letters exchanged between Kahedin and Iseut, writing in her own hand, Tristan goes mad and Kahedin dies of his love.[12] For Philippe the situation in relation to men is quite different. He states in *Les quatre âges* (p. 13) that it is important that the sons of great lords (*les riches homes*) should learn to read, and he underlines the importance of both being able to read and write in his legal work:

> Et ceaus qui ont poeir ou vollenté ou loisir de demourer longement o siecle, deivent aprendre au mains tant que il sachent lire et escrire; car lor segré en devra estre meaus celé. (*Assises de Jérusalem*, 1:565)

> And those who have the power or the will or the opportunity to remain for long in the world ought to study until they have at least learnt how to read and write, for this will mean that their secrets will be better kept.

The emphasis on the advantage of the greater confidentiality to be achieved through literacy is interesting, again in terms of the situation in the Prose *Tristan*. There the great knights such as Tristan and Lancelot, renowned for their armed prowess, also write private letters in their own hand; in addition and in contrast, they compose songs, both words and music, and perform them, and such compositions are destined to become widely known. These skills of Arthurian heros of romance may well reflect those of some thirteenth-century knights. Aristocratic *trouvères* such as Conon de Béthune who also took part in wars are to be found before the writing of the Prose *Tristan*; Philippe de Novare himself, according to his *Mémoires*, was, during a siege, referred to as "vostre chanteor," when it was thought he had been killed:

> Ceaus dou chasteau crierent: "Mort est vostre chanteor, tué est!" Et le tenoient ja si hennemi par le frein; mais son seignor le secorut, et le delivra mout vigourousement. Le soir après fist il deus coubles de chansons, et se fist porter devant le chasteau, a la roche, et les chanta en haut et dist. Adonc sorent il bien, cil dou chasteau, que il n'estoit mie mors. (*Mémoires*, p. 39)

> Those of the castle shouted: "Your singer is dead." And his enemies already held him by the bridle; but his lord came to his assistance and rescued him with great vigor. The next evening he composed two verses of songs, and had himself carried in front of the castle to the rock and sang them out loud, words and music. Then those in the castle knew indeed that he was not dead.

But Philippe does not present himself as the knightly lover, in spite of the reference in *Les quatre âges* (p. 122) to

> rimes et chançons plusors, que il meïsmes fist, les unes des granz folies dou siecle que l'an apele amors.

> rhymes and songs, which he himself composed, some on the great folly of the world which is called (courtly) love.

The contribution of love to chivalry is not an aspect of Arthurian romance to which he refers.

To sum up, what Philippe de Novare draws from Arthurian, romance accords with his own experiences when serving the Ibelin, with his interest in law, and with the pattern of literary references including his own compositions which he inserts within his work. He uses quite a wide range of allusions to literature in the vernacular, but gives particular importance to works which deal with feudal relationships and political problems; amongst these is the Prose *Lancelot*, particularly in the part dealing with the "enfances Lancelot." In fact, his work provides an interesting example of the complex interplay between life and literature characterized by a two-way traffic.

Our next knight, Philippe de Beaumanoir, was also deeply involved with the law. He was born about 1250 and is described as *miles* in documents. In the past, the general view was that as Philippe de Rémi he wrote two fictional works in verse when young, *La Manekine* and *Jehan et Blonde*, and also wrote a number of poems of various kinds. However, it has been suggested recently that these were probably written by the father of the legist, also called Philippe.[13] In 1279, our Philippe became *bailli* of Clermont and about the same time must have taken possession of Beaumanoir. He became in turn seneschal of Poitou, seneschal of Saintonge, Bailli de Vermandois, Bailli de Touraine, Bailli de Senlis, and died in 1296. His great legal work, *Coutumes de Beauvaisis*,[14] was probably begun about 1280 and finished in 1283, with subsequent additions and corrections.

An active interest in romance in general seems to have been part of the family tradition even if Philippe *fils* may not have been an author of verse fiction as well as a reader of romance, but his substantial and well known work is the lawbook. There is one direct reference to the Prose *Lancelot* in a *Fatrasie*,[15] which may again be by the father, but at least shows knowledge in the family of a Lancelot romance: "Grant reparlance est de l'enfance Lancelot." It is worth noting that once again the allusion is to the early part of the Prose *Lancelot*; two manuscripts of the romance itself (Paris, Bibliothèque Nationale, MS f. fr. 773 and MS f. fr. 1430) refer to the section of the story recounting Lancelot's early adventures as "les enfances Lancelot." The reading is to be found after Lancelot had completed his first knightly task as champion of the Lady of Nohaut and had defeated Alybon, the knight of the ford: "Et ci faillent les enfances de Lancelot" (here ends [the account of] Lancelot's deeds as a youth).[16] In spite of the fact that there is no direct reference to the Prose *Lancelot* in the work known to be by Philippe *fils*, there are nevertheless close verbal parallels with a passage which comes from the account of Lancelot's youth. The passage concerns the origin of kings and of *gentil homme*, which is in accordance with the usual medieval political theory concerning the origin of all human forms of government after the Fall:

Coutumes

§1453 Comment que pluseur estat de gens soient maintenant, voirs est qu'au commencement tuit furent franc et d'une meisme franchise, car chascuns set que nous descendismes tuit d'un pere et d'une mere. Mes quant li pueples commença a croistre et guerres et mautalent furent commencié par orgueil et par envie, qui plus regnoit lors et fet encore que mestiers ne fust, la communetés du pueple, cil qui avoient talent de vivre en pes, regarderent qu'il ne pourroient vivre en pes tant comme chascuns cuideroit estre aussi grans sires l'uns comme l'autres: si eslurent roi et le firent seigneur d'aus et li donnerent le pouoir d'aus justicier de leur mesfès, de fere commandemens et establissemens seur aus; et pour ce qu'il peust le pueple garantir contre les anemis et les mauvès justiciers, il regarderent entre aus ceus qui estoient plus bel, plus fort et plus sage, et leur donnerent seignourie seur aus en tel maniere qu'il aidassent a aus tenir en pes et qu'il aideroient au roi, et seroient si sougiet pour aus aidier a garantir. Et de ceus sont venu cil que l'en apele gentius hommes, et des autres qui ainsi les eslurent sont venu cil qui sont franc sans gentillece.

Although there are many different ranks of people now, it is true that at the beginning all men were free and of the same status, for everyone knows that we all descend from the one father and mother. But when the number of people increased and war and discord arose from pride and envy, which held greater sway than they should then, as they still do now, the general community of men, those who wanted to live in peace, saw that they could not do so as long as each man thought he was as great a lord as his fellows, so they elected a king and gave him authority over them and the power to bring them to justice for their misdeeds and to make them subject to laws; and in order that he could protect the people from enemies and from those who failed to maintain justice, they looked for those amongst them who were fairest in body, strongest and wisest and gave them authority over the people so that they might help to keep the peace and support the king and would serve under his rule and would assist him in the protection of the people. And from the men chosen to do this have descended those who are called *gentius hommes* (men of noble birth) and from those who chose them have descended those who are free, but not of noble birth.

This should be compared with the Lady of the Lake's account of the origin of chivalry:

Et tant sachiez vos bien que chevaliers ne fu mie faiz a gas ne establiz, et non pas por ce qu'il fussient au commencement plus gentil home ne plus haut de lignage l'un des autres, car d'un pere et d'une mere descendirent totes les genz. Mais qant envie et coveitise commança a croistre el monde et force commança a vaintre droiture, a cele hore estoient encores paroil et un et autre de lignage et de gentilece. Et qant li foible ne porent plus soffrir ne durer encontre les forz, si establirent desor aus garanz et desfandeors, por garantir les foibles et les paisibles et tenir selonc droiture, et por les forz boter arrieres des torz qu'il faisoient et des outraiges.

A ceste garantie porter furent establi cil qui plus valoient a l'esgart del comun des genz. Ce furent li grant et li fort et li bel et li legier et li leial et li preu et li hardi, cil qui des bontez del cuer et del cors estoient plain. Mais la chevalerie ne lor fu pas donee an bades ne por neiant, ençois lor en fu mis desor les cox mout granz faissiaus. Et savez quex? Au commencement, qant li ordres de chevalerie commança, fu devisé a celui qui voloit estre chevaliers et qui lo don en avoit par droiture d'eslection, qu'il fust cortois sanz vilenies, deboenneires sanz felenie, piteus vers les soffraiteus, et larges et appareilliez de secorre les besoigneus, prelz et appareilliez de confondre les robeors et les ocianz, droiz jugierres sanz amor et sanz haïne, et sanz amor d'aidier au tort por lo droit grever, et sanz haïne de nuire au droit por traire lo tort avant. Chevaliers ne doit por paor de mort nule chose faire o l'an puise honte conoistre ne aparcevoir, ainz doit plus doter honteusse chose que mort sossfrir.

Chevaliers fu establiz outreement por Sainte Eglise garantir, car ele ne se doit revenchier par armes, ne rendre mal encontre mal; et por ce est a ce establiz li chevaliers, qu'il garantisse celi qui tant la senestre joie, qant ele a esté ferue en la destre. (Prose *Lancelot*, pp. 142–43)

And understand this, that knighthood was not created and set up light-heartedly, nor because some men were originally more noble or of higher lineage than the others, for all people are descended from one father and one mother. But when envy and greed began to grow in the world, and force began to overcome justice, at that time all men were still equal in lineage and nobility. And when the weak could no longer withstand or hold out against the strong, they established protectors and defenders over themselves, to protect the weak and the peaceful and to maintain their rights, and to deter the strong from their wrongdoing and outrageous behavior.

To provide this protection, they established those who were most worthy in the opinion of the common people. Those were the big and the strong and the handsome and the nimble and the loyal and the valorous and the courageous, those who were full of the qualities of the heart and of the body. However, knighthood was not given to them frivolously or for nothing, but with it a great burden was placed on their shoulders. And do you know what that was? Originally, when the order of knighthood began, a man who wished to be a knight, and who was accorded that privilege by right of election, was told he should be courteous without baseness, gracious without cruelty, compassionate towards the needy, generous and prepared to help those in need, and ready and prepared to confound robbers and killers; he should be a fair judge, without love or hate, without love to help wrong against right, without hate to hinder right in order to further wrong. A knight should not, for fear of death, do anything which can be seen as shameful: rather, he should be more afraid of shame than of suffering death.

The knight was established wholly to protect the Holy Church, for she should not avenge herself by arms, or give back evil for evil; and for that reason the knight was established to protect the Church, who turns the left cheek, when she is struck on the right.

For Beaumanoir, who had spent much of his life in the service of the king of France as *bailli*, it is to be expected that the origin of kings is placed first, followed by that of *gentilhommes*, but the phrases describing the origin of *gentilhommes* are similar to those in the Prose *Lancelot* describing the origin of knights and the role of the two as defenders of justice also coincide. In the Prose *Lancelot* the king's role as defender of justice is stressed when a *preudomme* (wise man) comes to give Arthur advice on his shortcomings as king. More significant perhaps is the fact that the explanation given by the *preudomme* of the importance of the *bas gentilhommes* to the king for assistance in the governing of the kingdom also links up with the task given to *gentil hommes* by Beaumanoir:

"Cil te faillent de lor gré cui tu deüsses faire les granz onors et porter les granz seignories et les granz compaignies: ce sont li bas gentil home de ta terre par cui tu doiz estre maintenuz, car li regnes ne puet estre tenuz se li comuns des genz ne s'i acorde." (Prose *Lancelot*, p. 285)

"Those are failing you of their own free will to whom you should have done great honor and given noble treatment and good fellowship: that is the lesser gentry of your land, by whom you should be maintained, for the kingdom cannot be held without the consent of the common people."

Further on, the wise man also emphasises:

"Miauz seront les terres gardees par maint prodome, s'il les ont, qu'eles ne seroient par toi seul, car tu n'ies c'uns seus hom, ne tu ne puez se par aus non ce que tu puez. Et tu doiz miauz voloir que ti prodome tiegnent a enor de ta terre une partie que tu perdisses honteussement et l'une et l'autre." (Prose *Lancelot*, p. 288)

"Better care will be taken of the land by many men of worth, if they hold land, than it would be by you alone, for you are only one man, and whatever you can do, you can only do it through them. You should prefer that your men of worth hold a part of your land with honour than that you shamefully lose both it and them."

The adventures undertaken by Arthur's knights also often concern the maintenance of justice in relation to the King's vassals and their defence against attack, so that they fulfil the role of *gentilhommes* as described by Beaumanoir.[17]

The link in the form of verbal echoes between the passages in Beaumanoir and those in the Prose *Lancelot* describing the origin of chivalry and the function of knights/*gentilhommes* in relation to the maintenance of justice in the kingdom seems to be evident. Like Philippe de Novare, Philippe de Beaumanoir has drawn from the prose romance those elements which are in accord with his own experience and service to his lord, and again it is the early part of the *Lancelot* which is of the most immediate interest to him.

Ramon Lull too seems to have made use of the same passage from the Prose *Lancelot*. Lull was a thirteenth-century knight who served

James, son of James the Conqueror, king of Arragon. When young, he delighted in knightly pursuits and wrote songs. In 1263 he underwent a religious experience, gave up his old ways, and devoted his life to the conversion of Islam. He learned Latin and Arabic, journeyed a great deal, wrote a number of books, mainly on religious and philosophical subjects, and was stoned to death by Moslems he was trying to convert, appearing almost to seek martyrdom, in 1316. The book which is of interest to us, the *Libre del Orde de Cavallería*, was written in Catalan, probably between 1263 and 1276; it was widely read and translated into Old French, Castilian, Middle Scots, and into English by Caxton. The work has a prologue which introduces the treatise on chivalry in terms reminiscent of Arthurian romance. A squire rides through the forest on his way to the great court to be held by a wise and noble king for the making of knights. The squire loses his way and comes upon a cell of an aged hermit, who, as does the typical *rendu* in Arthurian romance, has withdrawn from the world after a long life spent in arms and chivalry. Like Perceval's uncle in the *Conte del Graal* of Chrétien de Troyes and many a hermit in the *Queste del Saint Graal* of the *Lancelot-Grail* cycle, the hermit finds himself in the presence of a young man ignorant of the true meaning of knighthood. He begins to read to him from a little book which explains the purpose and basis of chivalry and then presents him with the volume so that he can take it with him to the King's court and show it to the other young men who are to be knighted. There are close verbal parallels with the Lady of the Lake's discourse on chivalry, particularly in relation to its origin. Lull describes the beginning of chivalry as follows:

> Part Primera: la qual tracta del començament de cavallería.
>
> Defallí caritat, leyaltat, justicia e veritat en lo mon: comença enamistat, desleyaltat, injuria e falsetat, e per assò fo error e torbament en lo poble de Deu, qui era creat per so que Deus sia amat, conegut, honrat, servit e temut per home.
>
> 2. Al començament, con fo en lo mon vengut menyspreament de justicia per minuament de caritat, covench que justicia retornás en son honrament per temor: e per assò de tot lo poble foren fets milenaris, e de cascun .M. fo elet et triat un home pus amable, pus savi, pus leyal e pus forts, e ab pus noble coratge, ab més densenyaments et de bons nodriments que tots los altres.[18]

I give Caxton's translation below which was based on the Old French translation of the text rather than on the original Catalan:

The second chapytre is of the begynnynge of chiualrye or knighthode.

Whan Charyte, Loyaulte, Trouthe, Iustyce and veryte fayllen in the world, thenne begynneth cruelte, iniurye, desloyalte and falsenes. And therfore was erroure and trouble in the world in whiche God hath created man in intencion that of the man he be knowen and loued, doubted, serued and honoured. At the begynning whan to the world was comen mesprysion, justyce retorned by drede in to honour in whiche she was wonte to be. And therfore alle the peple was devyded by thousandes. And of eche thousand was chosen a man moost loyal, most strong and of most noble courage and better enseygned and manerd than al the other.[19]

Ramon Lull also makes some traditional points concerning the duties of knights, to be found not only in the Prose *Lancelot* but also in many other texts. For example, he says that it is the office of the knight to maintain and defend the Holy Catholic Faith (*Cavalleria*, p. 212) and to protect widows and orphans (*Cavalleria*, p. 217). The phrases he uses in relation to the knight's office to defend his earthly lord do, however, specifically recall those to be found in the Prose *Lancelot* (Prose *Lancelot*, p. 285, 288) and in Beaumanoir on the importance of the support of the *gentilhommes* for the king's maintenance of justice within his lands:

Offici de cavaller es, mantenir e deffendre senyor terrenal: car Rey ni princep ni null alt baró sens aiuda no poría mantenir dretura en ses gents. (*Cavalleria*, p. 214)

Thoffyce of a knyght is to mayntene and deffende his lord worldly or terryen, for a kyng ne no hyhe baron hath no power to mayntene ry3twysnes in his men without ayde and helpe. (Caxton, p. 29)

Like them, he stresses the duty of the knight to maintain justice:

Per los cavallers deu esser mantenguda justicia. (*Cavalleria*, p. 214)

By the knights ought to be maintayned and kept justice. (Caxton, p. 31)

Thus Ramon Lull, who, like Philippe de Novare, wrote poetry in the vernacular when he was young, in his maturity turned his attention to religion and philosophy, and it is the religious element in chivalry to which he gives particular emphasis, often in terms which would have resonances of Arthurian romance for his contemporaries. Once again, the context for these echoes of romance is a serious one, suggesting that the knight as reader of romance might find something more than just frivolity. This is in contrast with the warning against the deceiving vanity of Arthurian verse romances to be found in the prologue of an early thirteenth-century prose translation of the *Vie des Peres* dedicated to Blanche de Navarre. This prologue criticizes those other *dames* who commission the rhyming of lies and continues:

> Dame, de ce n'avez vos cure:
> De mençonge qui cuers oscure,
>   Corrompent la clarté de l'ame,
> N'en aiez cure, douce dame.
> Lessiez Cligés et Perceval,
>   Qui les cuers tue et met a mal,
> Et les romanz de vanité.[20]

Lady, do not concern yourself with this: pay no attention to lies which bring darkness to the heart and corrupt the pure light of the soul. Have nothing to do with Cligés and Perceval, who cause damage and harm to the heart, nor with the romances, which are works of vanity.

Romances in prose as opposed to verse were presented as worthier of attention, for they were deemed to contain more of the truth according to a prologue to a prose chronicle of the reign of Philippe-Auguste, written in 1221 or shortly afterwards:

> Issi vos an feré le conte
> Non pas rimé, qui an droit conte,
> Si eon li livres Lancelot
> Ou il n'a de rime un seul mot,
> Por mielz dire la verité
> Et por tretier sans fauseté;
> Quar anviz puet estre rimee
> Estoire ou n'ait ajostee
> Mançonge por fere la rime.[21]

Thus I will relate this not in verse but in prose, which gives an accurate account, like the book of Lancelot where there is not a single rhyme. I shall do this the better to tell the truth and to treat the subject without false deviations, for a history can rarely be told in verse without lying additions, made to furnish the rhyme.

Indeed, for these three knights of the thirteenth century, the verbal allusions are, above all, to the prose romances, especially to the Prose *Lancelot*. They draw in the main from Lancelot's early adventures, where problems of feudal loyalty were treated at length, and the role of the knight in defense of the Church and of justice was explored in ways which accorded with the experiences and particular interests of men such as Philippe de Novare, whose activities as a knight and legist were pursued in the Eastern Mediterranean, Philippe de Beaumanoir, another legist, who served the king of France, and Ramon Lull, who began his career in Catalonia and Arragon, travelled widely and died in Bougie. A central theme in Arthurian romance, the inspiration of love in relation to chivalry, plays no part in their textual allusions and echoes, although two of our knights are said to have written love songs when young.

The distinguished knight as reader of and quoter from romance is not just a thirteenth-century phenomenon. The *Livre de Chevalerie*[22] of Geoffroi de Charny (a knight closely connected with the founding of the order of chivalry, la Compagnie de l'Etoile, and killed at the battle of Poitiers), while drawing much from an earlier treatise, l'*Ordene de Chevalerie*,[23] and from Ramon Lull, also has verbal resonances of the Prose *Lancelot*. However, in these echoes there seems to have been a significant shift in emphasis away from feudal relationships and the role of a knight as champion of justice, a shift which may well be linked to the changing political situation and to the particular needs of the French king from his knights during the Hundred Years' War. In addition, the role of the lady in creating a good knight is now stressed in terms which recall passages in prose romance, and Guinevere is mentioned. Ramon Lull's book on chivalry, with its memories of the Prose *Lancelot*, was translated in the fifteenth century by Caxton, publisher of the work of another knightly reader of Arthurian romance, Sir Thomas Malory, whose view of chivalry and of what can be learned from the "French book" is, on the whole, rather different from that of my thirteenth-century knights.

Notes

* The translations from the Old French are mine, except where I have made use of *Lancelot of the Lake*, trans. C. Corley (Oxford, 1989).

1. "Arthurian Influence on Sport and Spectacle," in *Arthurian Literature in the Middle Ages*, ed. R. S. Loomis (Oxford, 1959), pp. 553–59; "Chivalric and Dramatic Imitations of Arthurian Romance," in *Medieval Studies in Memory of A. K. Porter* (Cambridge, Mass., 1931), 1, pp. 79–97.

2. *The Knights of the Crown: the Monarchical Orders of Knighthood in later Medieval Europe 1325–1520* (Woodbridge, Suffolk, 1987), pp. 107–08)

3. *Le Roman de Lancelot do Lac*, ed. E. Kennedy, 2 vols. (Oxford, 1980); abbreviated to Prose *Lancelot*.

4. *Les Assises de Jérusalem, ou, Recueil des ouvrages de jurisprudence composes pendant le XIIe siècle dans les royaumes de Jérusalem et de Chypre*, ed. A. Beugnot, 2 vols. (Paris, 1841–43), 1: 475–571 contains "Le livre en forme de plait que sire Felippe de Novaire fist pour un sien ami aprendre et enseigner coument on doit plaidoier en la haute court" [Book in the form of a legal plea which sire Felippe de Novaire composed to teach one of his friends how to plead a case in the high court]; abbreviated to *Assises de Jérusalem*.

5. Philippe de Novare, *Les quatre âges de l'homme: traité moral de Philippe de Navarre, publié pour la première fois d'après les manuscrits de Paris, de Londres et de Metz*, ed. Marcel de Fréville, (Paris, 1888): abbreviated to *Les quatre âges*.

6. Philippe de Novare, *Mémoires (1218–1243)*, ed. C. Kohler (Paris, 1913: rpt. 1970 with corrections), abbreviated to *Mémoires*. The editor states that he has removed the interpolations to be found in the text as it appears in *Les Gestes des Chiprois*.

7. *Mémoires*, p. 54. *Foulque de Candie*, ed. O. Schultz-Gora, 4 vols: vols. 1–3 [Dresden, 1909–36], vol. 4, introduction by U. Mölk (Halle, 1966).

8. "Et es livres des actors meismes peut l'on moult aprendre des fais dou siecle." (*Assises de Jérusalem* 1:565) [And in the books of the authors one can learn much of events in this world.]

9. This contains lines which correspond approximately with a selection of lines from a passage in *le Roman de Troie*, ed. L. Constans, 6 vols. (Paris, 1904), 1:6082–136. Philippe may here be paraphrasing his source in his own verse as he paraphrases the Prose *Lancelot* in his allusion to Pharien's advice to Lambegues.

10. See E. Kennedy, "Social and Political Ideas in the French Prose *Lancelot*," *Medium Aevum* 26 (1957), 90–106; J. Dufournet, "Un personnage exemplaire et complexe du *Lancelot*: Pharien," in *Approches du Lancelot en prose. Etudes recueillies par Jean Dufournet* (Paris 1984), pp. 137–56.

11. See also *Assises de Jérusalem* where Philippe de Novare also stresses the importance of not breaking one's faith with one's lord: "Et toujours dit l'om que entre seignor et home n'a que la fei, c'est a entendre que moult doit estre espeluchee et esclarzie et nete lor conscience si que la fei y soit sauvee ains que il entrent en querele" (1:491). It recalls the youthful chivalric ambition of the twelfth-century "jeune" described by G. Duby in "Les 'jeunes' dans la société aristocratique dans la France du Nord-Ouest au XIIe siècle," in G. Duby *Hommes et structures du Moyen Age* (Paris, 1973) and referred to by D. Maddox in relation

to the young knights of Chrétien's romances: "Their presence at court creates an enduring situation of potential anarchy that threatens the viability of authority based on communal consent." D. Maddox, *The Arthurian Romances of Chrétien de Troyes: Once and Future Fictions* (Cambridge, 1991), p. 15.

12. *Le Roman de Tristan en prose*. ed. R. Curtis, 3 vols. (Cambridge, 1985) 3:834, 871.

13. See S. Lécuyer in the introduction to her edition of *Jehan et Blonde de Philippe de Rémi: Roman du XIIIe siècle*, (Paris, 1984). She cites the arguments for and against attributing the romances to the jurist and comes to the conclusion that the probabilites are in favor of the attribution to the father rather than to the son. For a similar view, see B. Gicquel, "Le *Jehan et Blonde* de Philippe de Rémi peut-il être une source du *Willehalm von Orlens?*" *Romania* 102 (1981), 306–23. However, M. Shepherd, *Tradition and Re-creation in Thirteenth-Century Romance: "La Manekine" and "Jehan et Blonde" by Philippe de Rémi* (Amsterdam, 1990), pp. 9–15 inclines towards the view that the legist wrote the verse romances.

14. Philippe de Beaumanoir, *Coutumes de Beauvaisis*, ed. A. Salmon, 2 vols. (Paris, 1884–85, repr. 1976); a volume of commentary was later added: G. Hubrecht, *Philippe de Beaumanoir, Coutumes de Beauvaisis, t. III: Commentaire historique et juridique* (Paris, 1974). Abbreviated to *Coutumes*.

15. *Fatrasie* 43 in *Philippe de Remi, sire de Beaumanoir, Oeuvres poétiques*, ed. H. Suchier, 2 vols. (Paris, 1884–85), 2:279.

16. See Prose *Lancelot* 182, 11. 26–27 and the variant to these lines in vol. 2 of this edition, p. 147.

17. See E. Kennedy, *Lancelot and the Grail. A Study of the Prose Lancelot* (Oxford, 1986), pp. 102–10.

18. *Libre del orde de Cavalleria* in *Obres de Ramon Lull* ed. M. Antoni M. Alcover i D. Mateu Obrador i Bennassar, 20 vols. (Palma de Mallorca, 1906) 1:208. For a comparatively recent discussion of the importance of this book in the development of the theory of chivalry, see M. Keen, *Chivalry* (New Haven, 1984). Abbreviated to *Cavalleria*.

19. Caxton's translation, *The Book of the Ordre of Chyualry, translated and printed by William Caxton from a French version of Ramon Lull's "The libre del orde de caugleria." Together with Adam Louthet's Scottish Transcript Harleian MS. 1649*, EETS 168, ed. A.T.P. Byles, (London, 1926), pp. 14–15. I have added a little punctuation to make the translation easier to read.

20. Quoted in B. Woledge and H. P. Clive, *Répertoire des plus anciens textes en prose française depuis 842 jusqu'aux premières années du XIIIe siècle* (Geneva, 1964), p. 30.

21. Ibid.

22. There is an edition of this text in progress by R Kaeuper and E. Kennedy, based on the Brussels manuscript of the text. I shall be exploring further Geoffroi de Charny and Arthurian romance in a forthcoming paper.

23. K. Busby has edited the verse text in *Le Roman des Eles by Raoul de Hodenc and l'Ordene de Chevalerie* (Amsterdam, 1983). The editor points out (pp. 91–92) that it cannot be said with certainty whether Geoffroi de Charny was using the verse text of the *Ordene de Chevalerie* or one of the thirteenth-century prose redactions.

The Stanzaic *Morte Arthur*: The Adaptation of a French Romance for an English Audience

-------------------- *Edward Donald Kennedy*

The stanzaic *Morte Arthur*, a late fourteenth-century adaptation of the French Vulgate *La Mort le Roi Artu*, is the first English version of the Arthurian tragedy that included the love story of Lancelot and Guenevere. Although once studied primarily as a source for the final tales of Malory's *Morte Darthur*, it has in recent years been appreciated as one of the better Middle English romances;[1] yet most who have written about it have emphasized the roles of Lancelot and Guenevere,[2] and discussions of Arthur have been brief or have generally described him as a weak king who is a foil to the hero Lancelot.[3] The Arthur of the stanzaic *Morte*, however, is considerably different from the Arthur of the French source, and the changes that the English author made in his character reflect a different attitude toward Arthur in England than an author would be likely to consider in adapting a French romance. Although the Arthur of the English adaptation has flaws, he is not as weak a king as some have assumed, and a reexamination of his character can lead to a better understanding of a reinterpretation of a French Arthurian tragedy for an English audience.

Because of the hierarchical relationship of French and English styles in medieval England, J. D. Burnley points out, "the transition from French to English involved a cultural descent, or at the very least a broadening of appeal. Anglicisation often meant popularisation, adaptation to a new audience of less sophisticated tastes."[4] Differences between the stanzaic *Morte* and its French source indeed suggest that the English author was attempting to popularize the story for a less sophisticated audience and are typical of other Middle English adaptations of French romances: a simplified, more concise plot; fewer characters; and greater emphasis upon action and dialogue. Changes made in the character of Arthur and in the concluding scenes of the romance indicate, however, that in popularizing this work the author was concerned with factors besides narrative technique and had a conception of the Arthurian tragedy quite different from that of the French *Mort Artu*. The English version is, in fact, so different from the French that J. Douglas Bruce, believing that an English author would not add much to a French source, assumed that the stanzaic *Morte* was based upon some lost French romance.[5] More likely reasons for the differences, however, are the English author's creativity, his familiarity with other Arthurian literature, and his concern for the interests of his English audience.

Some differences between the French and English versions indicate that the English author had read Arthurian chronicles. At the beginning of the romance, for example, instead of referring, like the author of the French *Mort*, to the loss of knights on the Grail quest, the narrator describes the quest as a triumph[6] that would have recalled for an English audience Arthur's victories in the chronicles. Emphasis upon the treasonous nature of the Lancelot-Guenevere affair rather than upon its immorality, could suggest, in addition possibly to contemporary political views,[7] the influence of the politically motivated chronicles which stress Mordred and Guenevere's treason against Arthur. The treaty between Arthur and Mordred that makes Mordred heir to the kingdom (ll. 3261–63) is, as Göller points out, similar to the treaty found in the sixteenth-century Scottish chronicles of Hector Boece and William Stewart in which Arthur agrees to let Mordred succeed him;[8] although Göller suggests that Boece drew upon the stanzaic *Morte*, the author of the stanzaic *Morte*, who was from the Northwest Midlands, could have been drawing upon Arthurian historical material also known to later Scottish chronicles. Mordred's insistence that Arthur cede to him Kent and Cornwall (l. 3275) suggests the influence of Geoffrey of Monmouth's *Historia* and other chronicles in which Mordred controls Kent and flees to Cornwall before his last battle. The three battles between Arthur and Mordred in the stanzaic *Morte*, instead of a single battle at Salisbury in the French *Mort Artu*, reflect a chronicle tradition of three battles that originated with Geoffrey of Monmouth. The final battle's being caused by a knight's drawing a sword to kill an adder parallels an episode in the Arthurian section of the mid-fourteenth-century Spanish chronicle *Libro de las Generaciones*, and the English and Spanish authors could have drawn upon a similar Latin or French chronicle.[9] Arthur's tomb at Glastonbury is often mentioned in chronicles written after the discovery there in 1191 of what were supposedly the bodies of Arthur and Guenevere. And Guenevere's entering a convent because of remorse rather than because of fear of Arthur and Mordred, as in the French *Mort*, appears in Arthurian chronicles from the time of Wace.[10]

That the author of the stanzaic *Morte* would have known Arthurian chronicles is not surprising since they were widely read in England.[11] Rachel Bromwich, in fact, attributes the esteem in which Arthur was held in England to the "deeply entrenched belief in Arthur's historicity" and the concept of him "as the noblest and most powerful of. . . British kings. . . propounded. . . by Geoffrey of Monmouth."[12] In adapting a French Arthurian romance into English, an author would surely have considered the chronicles which the English accepted as part of their history. The treatment of the character of Arthur and of the Arthurian tragedy in the stanzaic *Morte* is what one might expect from an English writer who wished to bring the account in the French *Mort* more into line with accounts of Arthur's character and fall found in chronicles.

Another factor that could have shaped the English author's conception of Arthur was contemporary political theory. The portrayal of Arthur in the French source as an often capricious and apparently absolute monarch suggests that either the French author had little concern for the advice given to monarchs in popular medieval *speculum regis* literature or that he deliberately portrayed a king who had little concern for such advice. Some changes that the English author makes in Arthur's character, particularly in his reliance upon counsel, could reflect his concern with both *speculum regis* literature and late fourteenth-century English politics.

The author of the French *Mort Artu* drew upon several earlier accounts: the chronicles of Geoffrey of Monmouth and Wace; some version of the *Tristan*; the Vulgate *Lancelot* and *Queste del Saint Graal*; and possibly romances of Chrétien de Troyes.[13] The portrait of Arthur in a work drawn from so many sources has inconsistencies: although he is at times the strong king of the chronicles, he is also jealous and capricious and is similar to the often weak Arthur of the first part of the Vulgate *Lancelot en prose* and of Chrétien's *Charrette*: a *roi fainéant*, a jealous husband, a "pathetic figure" who "rarely. . . makes the right decisions."[14] Arthur of *Mort Artu* is at times like the weak King Marc of the early *Tristan* stories who vacillates between love and hatred;[15] he is an outraged husband who angrily condemns Guenevere to death at one moment and then pardons her later with little concern for whether or not she is innocent. He is 92 years old and often lacks the impassibility that should be, in Frappier's words, "la seule attitude digne d'un roi," and, in Frappier's opinion, his prestige is further diminished by his obeying Gawain's demands for vengeance and by his frequent tears and despairing apostrophes to God and Fortune.[16]

Although many factors bring about Arthur's fall in *Mort Artu* (the adultery of Lancelot and Guenevere, the envy of Agravaine and Mordred, the treachery of Morgan le Fay, the vengeance of Gawain, the workings of Fortune, possibly the punishment of Arthur for incest),[17] the tragedy is to a considerable extent due to Arthur's own failings.[18] He is a pawn in the hands of Gawain and is unable to resist Gawain's demand for vengeance after Lancelot kills Gawain's brothers. Overcome by jealousy, he repeatedly ignores sound advice: he decides to wage war upon Lancelot even though warned on one occasion that anyone who cared about his kingdom would not do so; on another, that he will be destroyed as a result of it; and on another, that he will accomplish nothing.[19] Arthur's flaws are still more pronounced when he later refuses to heed warnings to arrange a truce with Mordred and proceeds with the battle that leads to his death and the destruction of his realm.

The first warning occurs when, after Gawain's death, Arthur has a vision in which Gawain's spirit appears to him. Gawain warns him that if he fights Mordred, he will be mortally wounded and that he must seek Lancelot's help. Arthur ignores Gawain's advice: he will not postpone the battle because, he says, he would be a coward if he did not defend his land against a traitor, and he cannot believe that Lancelot would help him. Gawain repeatedly warns Arthur of the consequences of ignoring his advice: "Sire, gardez vos d'assembler a Mordret; se vos i assemblez, vos i morroiz ou vos seroiz navrez a mort"; "quel domage quant vos hastez si vostre fin"; "se vos a cestui besoing ne le [Lancelot] mandez, vos n'en poez eschaper sanz mort"; "ce sera granz domage a toz preudomes" (pp. 225–26). Arthur nevertheless makes no effort to arrange a truce. His desire to defend his land might seem honorable, were it not in defiance of a warning from heaven; and the refusal to send for Lancelot suggests pride and stubbornness. His response to Gawain's message is simply to pray that events will be changed and that God will grant him victory.

The next night in another vision he is seated on top of Fortune's wheel. Fortune throws him to the ground so roughly that he fears he has broken all of his bones. He realizes what the vision foreshadows: "Einsi vit li rois Artus les mescheances qui li estoient a avenir" (p. 227). Shortly after this an archbishop gives him a third warning: he tells him that he must postpone the battle until Lancelot arrives "por sauveté de vostre ame et de vostre cors et del reigne," and that he must turn back if he does not wish to be dishonored ("se vos ne vos voulez honnir"). Arthur, however, says that he cannot turn back. The archbishop then gives a fourth warning by citing Merlin's prophecy that this battle would orphan the realm of Logres. Arthur refuses to listen, saying that he shall never leave until God has granted him or Mordred victory; if he loses, that will be the result of his sin and folly (pp. 227-29). Arthur thus ignores four warnings, three of which—the visions of Gawain and Fortune and the prophecy of Merlin—are supernatural. Moreover, as Frappier points out, the archbishop's appeals to Arthur are appeals for moderation. He does not ask Arthur to renounce vengeance, only to wait for help from Lancelot. Arthur, Frappier comments, remains "sourd aux paroles de prudence."[20]

Although Arthur later admits that he was foolish not to ask Lancelot for help (p. 240), he continues to show the same blindness he had shown earlier. He asks how God could have let him see his best men killed, permitted the final battle to take place, and let him be brought so low (pp. 243-45), forgetting that he had been given the chance to change the course of events but had refused to do so.

After his death even the question of the salvation of Arthur's soul is unresolved. There is no certainty of this, as there is for Gawain, Lancelot, and Guenevere; nor is there certainty of damnation, as for Mordred, whose death wound is pierced by a ray of sunlight as a sign "de corrouz de Nostre Seigneur" (p. 245). There is some indication that God is displeased with Arthur: after the wounded Arthur spends the night following his last battle praying at a chapel, he embraces Lucan and accidentally crushes him to death in the chapel, an act that suggests God's disfavor, although Arthur blames Fortune (p. 247). The fact that Arthur is finally buried in consecrated ground could indicate that he has achieved salvation;[21] but the inscription on the tomb—"Ci gist li rois Artus qui par sa valeur mis en sa subjection XII roiaumes"— emphasizes not salvation but the transience of earthly power, and Arthur's being buried next to Lucan, whose tomb bears the inscription "Ci gist Lucans li Bouteilliers que li rois Artus esteinst desouz lui" (p. 251), reminds the reader that Arthur had crushed him to death and suggests God's disfavor.

Both Arthur and Lancelot in *Mort Artu* have flaws; but while Lancelot errs at the beginning of the romance when he resumes his affair with Guenevere but then steadily develops into an ideal Christian,[22] Arthur has good and bad traits throughout the romance. He vacillates from being heroic to being pathetic. Frappier comments on these contrasting qualities in his discussion of Arthur's final battle against Mordred: although Arthur at one moment seems interested in honor in its best sense of integrity, shortly thereafter he seems concerned with honor in the sense of earthly power; and although Arthur in this battle demonstrates "une grandeur farouche," Frappier nevertheless believes that "par son angoisse et ses faiblesses humaines...il est la victime la plus émouvante du Destin."[23]

The contrasting qualities that Frappier notes—the grandeur, the anguish, the weakness—are all present, but Frappier's emphasis upon Arthur as a victim of destiny is misleading. He is more than a victim; he is a flawed character, who, as Larry Benson writes in a discussion of the *Mort* in relation to Malory's *Morte Darthur*, is responsible for his own fall.[24] Arthur's responsibility is suggested in the dream of Fortune mentioned above, and Frappier's interpretation of this dream is questionable. Although Frappier finds weaknesses in Arthur's character, he nevertheless sees Fortune in this work as an impersonal force, as it often is in medieval literature, and its wheel as a symbol of the caprice that destroys kingdoms without concern for merit.[25] Fortune's appearance and speech suggest, however, that more than a universal law concerning the inevitable decline of earthly power is involved. Fortune in the *Mort* is a beautiful lady, "la plus bele qu'il eüst onques mes veüe el monde" (p. 226), not a grotesque and blind one that often appears in medieval art and literature to suggest her irrationality.[26] In the *Mort* she seems more like the clear-sighted and beautiful rational feminine guides of dream visions. She tells Arthur: "Tu vois as tu esté li plus puissanz rois qui i fust. Mez tel sont li orgueil terrien qu'il n'i a nul si haut assiz qu'il ne le coviegne cheoir de la poesté del monde" (p. 227). Fortune is, as Frappier points out, stating a universal law; but the reference to "orgueil terrien," combined with the fact that Fortune can see clearly, suggests that Fortune is not as indifferent to the individual's merit or lack of merit as Frappier suggests.

Although medieval writers often thought of Fortune as a blind, capricious goddess, they also sometimes portrayed her as a force that punished people for their sins, especially pride, and in these instances, her actions could be considered rational.[27] Thus, John Gower notes that man is "overal/ His oghne cause of wel and wo" and that which "we fortune clepe so/ Out of the man himself it groweth"; Lydgate, in describing the "fall off pryncis fro Fortunys wheel" remarks that "Off ther onhapp,.../Toward hemsilff the cause doth rebounde"; even Chaucer's Monk, whose frequently quoted definition of tragedy ignores the notion of sin and punishment, nevertheless presents some tragedies (Lucifer, Balthasar, Nero, Holofernes, and Croesus) that are punishments for the sin of pride.[28] On the basis of both Fortune's

warning about earthly pride and Arthur's actions, there is justification
for seeing in the French *Mort* a similar view of Fortune. Arthur's fall
seems due not to a universal law about the inevitable transience of
earthly power, as Frappier believes, but to his pride and consequent
failure to heed warnings to seek a truce and ask Lancelot for help.[29]

Since Arthur of the stanzaic *Morte* resembles in some ways the
Arthur of the French *Mort*, particularly in his inability to resist Gawain's
wish for vengeance, some scholars believe that the English author
presents an unfavorable picture of Arthur.[30] Some traits, however, that
suggest weakness today may not have done so in the Middle Ages, and
one can argue that in adapting the French *Mort* for an English audience
the author makes Arthur into a better king.

The English author retains most of the favorable traits of Arthur's
character in the French *Mort* (commitment to justice, love for Lancelot,
regret concerning the war against him) and removes many of the
unfavorable ones. He omits, for example, most allusions to Arthur's
jealousy that appear in the French source and emphasizes instead the
political problem of disloyalty.[31] Although some instances of Arthur's
anger appear in the English romance (see ll. 1716, 2070–74, 2118–23,
2500–07), several others in *Mort Artu* are omitted or modified. For
example, when Arthur hears Agravain and his brothers discussing the
adultery, although he "for wrathe was neghe wode" (l. 1716), he does
not threaten to kill Agravain if he does not tell him the truth, as he
does in the French *Mort* (p. 109). While in *Mort Artu* Arthur angrily
tells his men that they must condemn Guenevere to death ("sanz mort
n'en puet ele eschaper" [p. 120]), in the English romance there is no
reference to Arthur's anger, and the "Kynge and all hys knyghtis" take
"counselle" to decide "What was beste do with the quene" (ll. 1921–23).
Later, Arthur accepts the Pope's command to stop the war and take
the queen back, not because, like the French Arthur, he loves Guenevere
so much (*Mort Artu*, p. 153), but because he "Wolde...noght that
Ynglonde were shente" (l. 2273), a detail that adds to Arthur's stature
as king. Moreover, the author omits the scene in the French *Mort* in
which Arthur, after praying in a chapel, accidentally crushes Lucan to
death and instead has Lucan die when he attempts to lift the wounded
king (ll. 3430–41). He also omits the reference to Arthur's age of 92 which
Frappier believed was intended to make the Arthur of the French source
seem weak. As Wertime points out, Arthur becomes in the Middle
English work one of the characters who "are doing...the best
which...honorable persons can do to resolve their conflicts and
conquer their imperfections."[32]

Peter Korrel, who believes that the English author sympathizes with Arthur, nevertheless finds Arthur in this work basically weak and suggests that the frequent references to Arthur's sorrow (see ll. 684, 692–93, 1544–45, 1970–74, 2203–5, 2437) offer evidence of this. Frappier interprets the sadness of Arthur in the French *Mort* in the same way,[33] and most readers today would probably agree. A medieval audience, however, may have reacted differently to a leader's tears, as evidenced by the great amount of weeping and fainting in an epic like the *Song of Roland*.[34] Moreover, Lancelot, generally recognized as the hero of the stanzaic *Morte*, does his share of weeping (see ll. 2082–83, 2457, 3724–29, 3746–47); yet no one, to my knowledge, has interpreted this as weakness in his character.

Besides finding Arthur's tears a sign of weakness, Korrel believes that Arthur's reliance upon the advice of others in the stanzaic *Mort Artu* further detracts from his character. While the king of the *Mort Artu* vacillates between the weak Arthur dominated by Gawain and the proud Arthur who ignores advice not to fight Lancelot and Mordred, the English author's Arthur is "a weak-willed monarch, who never makes up his own mind, and who, even in matters of little importance, asks people for their advice and acts upon it."[35] Korrel here points to a significant change that the English author made in his acccount. His Arthur is always taking advice: Guenevere advises him to hold a tournament (ll. 17–40); Evwayne, to permit Lancelot to leave the court (ll. 105–36); Gawain, to bury the maid of Ascalot at court (ll. 1112–19); and Agravaine, to capture Lancelot and Guenevere (ll. 1744–51). While the Arthur of the French source tells his knights to decide what kind of death Guenevere should die, in the stanzaic *Morte* Arthur takes the advice of his knights (ll. 1921–25). While in the French source, Arthur agrees to let Mordred rule England after he volunteers to do so (*Mort Artu*, p. 166), in the English romance, Arthur's knights suggest that Mordred should be steward of England (ll. 2516–20, 2955–57). Some of these matters are trivial; others are not; but by presenting an Arthur who consistently takes advice, the English author removes from the king some responsibility for the tragedy. Even his following Gawain's advice to seek vengeance becomes more understandable in a work in which Arthur consistently relies upon the advice of others.

Moreover, an Arthur who relies upon advice is consistent with kings who follow advice in *speculum regis* literature. Kings in European countries were expected to rely upon counsellors, and there would have been no question by the late fourteenth century that an English king would have done so.[36] As Richard Firth Green has pointed out, handbooks for rulers such as the pseudo-Aristotelian *Secretum Secretorum* and Aegidius Romanus's *De Regimine Principum* were widely read in England in the late Middle Ages.[37] Chaucer's *Tale of Melibee* and book VII of Gower's *Confessio Amantis* are examples of such literature written for the court of Richard II. Even when a king followed "ffals counsel," it was customary to place blame for his actions upon the "euyl excitacion" of his advisors.[38] By presenting an Arthur who consistently seeks advice, the English author was presenting a king who was acting as one might expect an English king to act. Gawain's advice can be seen as the false counsel that a king should avoid; but other advice— including that concerning Guenevere's punishment for treason and the appointment of Mordred as regent—was based upon consultation with a number of knights. Such changes remove from Arthur the responsibility for making those bad decisions on his own.

Arthur's reliance upon advice is especially important to the conclusion to the stanzaic *Morte*; it makes Arthur less responsible for the tragedy than he was in the French *Mort*. Besides omitting the three warnings about the disastrous outcome of the war against Lancelot which the Arthur of the French *Mort* ignores (*Mort Artu*, pp. 134, 142, 168), the English author has Arthur react to the warnings of Gawain and Fortune quite differently from the way the Arthur of the French *Mort* reacts.

The English author reverses the order and changes the content of the visions. In the stanzaic *Morte* the vision of the wheel comes first, Gawain's warning second. While in the French *Mort* Fortune mentions "orgueil terrein," and hurls Arthur from the wheel, in the English work only the wheel, without the goddess and the warning about pride, appears. The English author's elimination of the goddess Fortuna from the dream has suggested to some that he had little interest in Fortune.[39] Lack of interest in Fortune, however, is not the most likely explanation for the change. Although the significance of some wheels in medieval art is elusive,[40] the wheel of Fortune was sometimes depicted without the goddess,[41] and, as Larry Benson observes,[42] the wheel in the stanzaic *Morte* would surely have suggested Fortune's wheel to a medieval audience. Just as many of the wheels of Fortune in medieval art show a crowned king on top of the wheel, in the English romance Arthur sits "rychely crownyd" on an enormous wheel; it turns suddenly and, falling off, Arthur is caught by "dragons" waiting below in "blake water" (ll. 3176–83). This fate is similar to that of other victims of Fortune who are cast off the wheel into the mud, an "vgly pit," or a dungeon where serpents bite them.[43] Presenting the wheel without the goddess could make Fortune seem more like an impersonal force than a goddess who is punishing Arthur for his pride. This concept of Fortune as an impersonal force would also account for the English author's omission of Arthur's description of Fortune as his stepmother (*Mort Artu*, pp. 221, 247), which suggests that the goddess has some malevolent interest in him. The vision of the wheel in the stanzaic *Morte* gives no reason for Arthur's fall; one only knows that the wheel turns.

While the English author's retention from his source of the wheel suggests that events in the romance are ultimately due to a Fortune that is impersonal, his changes in the final scenes of the romance give the impression that much that happens is due to the more chaotic force of chance or accident.[44] Immediately after the vision of the wheel, the spirit of Gawain appears to Arthur in a dream and tells him that he must make a truce for a month in order to give Lancelot time to come to help him (ll. 3192–223). While in the French *Mort* Arthur refuses to follow Gawain's advice, in the English work he heeds the warning: summoning his men, he tells them to ask Mordred for a month's truce. Mordred, however, insists that the battle shall take place, saying, in a line that echoes two of Arthur's statements in the Fench *Mort*, "The tone of us shall dye thys day."[45] When Arthur's men try to compromise by offering Mordred the kingdom after Arthur's death, Mordred insists that he immediately be given Cornwall and Kent. Mordred also insists that full armies of both sides be present (ll. 3280–87). When the two sides meet to negotiate, neither trusts the other; Arthur and Mordred tell their men to be ready to fight if they see a weapon drawn. As the leaders are about to sign the treaty, an adder stings one of Mordred's knights. When the knight draws his sword to kill it, Arthur's men assume that Mordred's side has begun the attack, and they start fighting. Thus the final battle begins not because of Arthur's refusal to heed warnings, but because of circumstances: Mordred's insistence that full armies be present at the signing of the treaty, the chance appearance of an adder, the drawing of a sword. The effect of such events is similar to the effect of the *aventure et mescheance* that dominate a French prose romance, the Post-Vulgate *Roman du Graal*: unlike the French *Mort*, this work shifts sympathy to Arthur by having much that happens be due simply to mischance.[46] Similarly, the final events of the stanzaic *Morte*, whether due to chance or ultimately to impersonal Fortune, help win sympathy for Arthur.

The English author also changes the account of the final battle. In the French *Mort* after the battle Mordred and almost 300 of his men are still alive, while on Arthur's side only Arthur, Sagremore, Lucan, and Girflet remain. After the deaths of Arthur, Mordred, and Sagremore, Lucan and Girflet have the unbelievable task of defeating almost 300 of the enemy. In the English version, before Arthur kills

Mordred, 100,000 men from the two armies have been killed; only Arthur and his severely wounded knights Lucan and Bedevere remain alive on one side and only Mordred on the other. At this point, when almost everything has been lost, Arthur in a rage attacks Mordred and in doing so receives his death blow. Arthur's act is immoderate, but unlike the Arthur of the French source who acts immoderately earlier, it is the final, desperate act of one who has little to lose. By this time there was little point in heeding Gawain's warning to wait for Lancelot; the battle that Arthur had tried to avoid had taken place, and his kingdom had already been destroyed.

The incestuous birth of Mordred is treated differently in the two works. The French *Mort* refers four times in the concluding scenes to Mordred's being Arthur's son (pp. 172, 176, 211, 245); and although incest is not emphasized in this work, these reminders of it[47] may have been intended to suggest that Mordred's killing of Arthur is retribution for sin. Two references during the last battle emphasize the horror of a father and son killing one another and contribute to the negative portrait of Arthur: he says that no father will ever do to a son what he will do to Mordred; and the narrator writes that the father killed the son, and the son gave his father a mortal wound (pp. 211, 245). By contrast the two references in the stanzaic *Morte* to Mordred's being Arthur's son explain why Mordred is chosen steward and emphasize his villainy. When Arthur goes abroad to fight Lancelot, his knights advise him to appoint Mordred regent because he was the "kynges soster sone. . . / And eke hys owne sonne" (ll. 2955-56). The English author's other reference to Mordred's being Arthur's son blackens Mordred's character. When Mordred tries to take over the kingdom, "Hys faders wyfe than wold he wedde/ And hyr hold with mayne and myght." In a scene not in the Vulgate *Mort*, the Archbishop of Canterbury rebukes Mordred for trying to wed his "faders wyffe"; Mordred replies by threatening to have the Archbishop drawn apart by wild horses (ll. 2987-3025). Although the author mentions on these earlier occasions that Mordred is Arthur's son, he omits the references to the father/son relationship found in the account of Arthur's final battle in the French *Mort* and thus omits the reminders of Arthur's sin that occur in the final scenes of that work. The effect is similar to that achieved in the Post-Vulgate *Roman du Graal* where, as Fanni Bogdanow points out, although Arthur is guilty of incest, emphasis on chance occurrences makes the reader pity Arthur as a "helpless victim of an internal strife for which he was in no way responsible."[48]

The stanzaic *Morte* includes a final scene between Lancelot and Guenevere that can help one understand the author's interpretation of the Arthurian tragedy. A similar scene is interpolated in one manuscript of the French *Mort*, Palatinus Latinus 1967, and some scholars assume that the stanzaic *Morte* was drawn from a French text related to it. The two scenes, however, may have had no relation to one another, and their similarities may be coincidental.

In the French Palatinus manuscript Lancelot finds Guenevere by chance at an abbey where she has become a nun because she feared Mordred's sons.[50] Lancelot tells her that he has killed the sons and she can now leave the abbey. She refuses because she believes that she and Lancelot should spend the rest of their lives doing penance. Lancelot replies that he wants what she wants and that he too will serve God. As he leaves the abbey, he asks her to pardon him for his misdeeds. She forgives him and chastely kisses him goodbye and embraces him, gestures undoubtedly intended to recall the first kiss between Lancelot and Guenevere in the earlier *Lancelot en prose*. Guenevere spends the remaining year of her life praying for the souls of Arthur and Lancelot. Although Lancelot weeps when he leaves, the scene is, on the whole, a restrained one.[51]

The English version is more emotional and emphasizes the guilt of the lovers and the consequences of their sin.[52] Guenevere becomes a nun not because of her fear of Mordred's sons but, as in the chronicles, because of remorse. While in the French text Guenevere says that she must not return to the secular life because she and Lancelot have done what they should not have done ("nous avons fait moi et vous tele chose que nous ne deüssiens avoir faite" [p. 265]), the English author stresses the guilt that she feels and the consequences of their adultery. She tells the abbess:

> . . . throw thys ylke man and me. . .
> All thys sorowfull werre hathe be!
> My lord is slayne that had no pere,
> And many a doughty knyght and free. (ll. 3639–42)

She expresses regret that "so many barons bolde/ Shuld for us be slayne away," and hopes that God will let her amend her sins so that she can achieve salvation. She tells Lancelot to leave her company, return to his kingdom, and marry. Lancelot makes no attempt, as he does in the French version, to persuade Guenevere to return to Arthur's kingdom; instead he protests that he could never marry anyone else and says that he too will "byde in penance. . ./ And suffre for god sorow and stryffe."

As he is about to leave, he again vows to lead a life of penance, but he asks for one last kiss. Instead of kissing him goodbye, like Guenevere of the French *Mort*, she tells him to "thynke on that no-more" but to think instead of Christ. She concludes with a reminder of the "warre and stryffe and batayle sore" that resulted from their love. The scene ends not with the relatively calm farewell of the French text, but with the characters weeping and wringing their hands. Guenevere faints and is carried to her chamber; Lancelot rides away, lamenting "Ryghtwosse God! what is my rede?/ Allas!...why was I borne?" (ll. 3649–741).

In his analysis of the scene in the Palatinus manuscript, Frappier points out that although this interpolation is not part of the original French *Mort*, for many readers it would have seemed a fitting conclusion; that a scribe chose to add it is not surprising. Citing Vinaver's belief at the time that Malory's source for the similar scene in *Morte Darthur* was a lost French romance, Frappier compares the scene in Malory with the one in the Palatinus manuscript. In his view, the similarities are not striking and could be coincidental; the differences between the two scenes, the "simplicité pathétique" of the French version in contrast to the "noblesse guindée" of Malory's, convinced him that the scene in Malory was not related to the French version. He felt, in fact, that such a farewell is so inevitable that Malory could have written it independently of any source.[53] Although Frappier's view that the French version is superior to Malory's is debatable,[54] his emphasis upon the differences between the two scenes and his belief that they were independent of one another deserve consideration.

Frappier knew that a similar scene is also found in the stanzaic *Morte*, but he had not read this version. If he had, he would have realized that Malory's version was based upon it.[55] Since Malory followed the scene in the stanzaic *Morte* closely, what Frappier wrote about the probable independence of Malory's version from the French would apply as well to the scene in the stanzaic *Morte*: the similarities between the scene in the French *Mort* and the stanzaic *Morte* could be coincidental and the contrasts suggest that they could have no direct relationship to one another.[56]

The two scenes appear to have been written for different purposes. While the French version alludes to the shame Guenevere feels, it appears to have been written to present a final, tender farewell between the two lovers to recall the scene of their first kiss in the Vulgate *Lancelot en prose* and to show what had been only briefly mentioned earlier in the French *Mort*, that Guenevere died a holy woman. The English version emphasizes instead the guilt of Lancelot and Guenevere for the death of Arthur and the destruction of the kingdom. Although the scene could have been suggested by the Palatinus version, it could as easily have been added without a source by an author who wished to emphasize Lancelot and Guenevere's share in the responsibility for the destruction of the kingdom. Chronicles in which Guenevere enters a convent out of remorse, rather than fear as in the French *Mort*, could have suggested the addition of this scene. While it increases the lovers' tragic stature and the audience's sympathy for them, it also helps remove from Arthur some of the responsibility for the tragedy that results in the French *Mort*. The approach is similar to that of the author of the Post-Vulgate *Roman du Graal* who increases Lancelot's guilt in order to win sympathy for Arthur.[57] The English author's other efforts to remove Arthur's responsibility for the tragedy suggest that this could have been his primary reason for adding this scene to his account. Dieter Mehl, in contrasting the stanzaic *Morte* and another English work, the alliterative *Morte Arthure*, writes that in the stanzaic *Morte* the fall of Arthur is "not, as in the alliterative *Morte Arthure*, presented as a just punishment for Arthur's pride, but as an inescapable destiny. . . deplored by all and for which Lancelot and Gaynor are ultimately responsible."[58] The comment could apply as well to the contrast between the stanzaic *Morte* and the French *Mort*.

The English author's changes in Arthur's character make Arthur less responsible than the Arthur of the French *Mort* for the destruction of his kingdom. Although the English author follows his source in having Arthur come under Gawain's influence in waging war upon Lancelot, the final tragedy would have been averted if Arthur had been able to arrange a truce; that his efforts are unsuccessful is due to circumstances over which he had no control. The more favorable portrait of Arthur and the different conception of the tragedy in the English version were probably due to the positive portraits of Arthur in English chronicles. Although chroniclers borrowed minor details from romances, the influence of romances upon them was relatively insignificant,[59] and their story of Arthur remained basically that of Geoffrey of Monmouth. The presentation of Arthur in some romances as an often weak king was not consistent with the chroniclers' view of Arthur, and they generally ignored this romance conception.

In the chronicles of Geoffrey of Monmouth, Wace, and Layamon, Arthur is too much an idealized nationalist figure to be portrayed as one punished for his sins;[60] and his fall is due to what Vinaver describes as a "natural consequence of a military disaster."[61] The same is true of the later chroniclers: when Arthur is abroad fighting the Roman emperor, he hears of Mordred's usurpation, returns, and, in defeating

Mordred, is killed. Although the suggestion that Arthur's fall is a punishment for sin appears in one English work derived from chronicles, the alliterative *Morte Arthure*, the story in the chronicles themselves is the story of a fall without guilt or punishment. An English author familiar with chronicle accounts of an Arthur whose fall is due to circumstances beyond his control would in all likelihood find this conception of Arthur more acceptable and more authentic than the one presented in the French *Mort*, and chronicle versions of the Arthurian story could in this way have influenced the English adaptor to change the ending in the way that he did. The attempt of the author of the stanzaic *Morte* to present Arthur more positively is, in fact, analogous to that of two other English writers, Robert Mannyng of Brunne, who wrote an early fourteenth-century English verse chronicle, and John Lydgate, who includes Arthur in his *Fall of Princes*. Both seem to have been trying to rectify the damage that romance tradition had done to Arthur's reputation.

Mannyng apparently knew French prose Arthurian romances since he expresses admiration for the "stile" of the "grete bokes" about Arthur that "ffrensche men wryten...in prose" that "we...here alle rede."[62] Instead of drawing upon them for his account of Arthur, however, he followed the version in the French verse chronicles of Wace and Pierre de Langtoft. While he at times supplemented the material in his sources, almost none of his additions can be traced to prose romances. One exception to this is a couplet concerning Arthur's pursuit of Mordred into Cornwall: "ȝyf Arthur hadde lenger abiden/þe sykerere myghte Moddred haue ryden."[63] Fletcher believes that Mannyng was replying "to the emphasis...[in *Mort Artu*] on Arthur's refusal to wait for reënforcements."[64] Mannyng's lines, intended to justify Arthur's final battle against Mordred, were probably directed at those who were familiar with the presentation of Arthur in the French *Mort* as a king who ignores advice and foolishly goes into battle. If Arthur had waited, Mannyng tells us, Mordred's forces would have become stronger. This brief comment, along with the fact that he borrows almost nothing else from the prose romances, suggests that his attitude toward them was not as positive as the lines expressing admiration for their style might lead one to believe. Moreover, the often excessive praise of Arthur that Mannyng adds to his account (the "doughtiest knyght," the "lordlyest of alle," "þe hardiest" who "ouer alle prynces þe pris he nam/ Of curteseye & of wysdam"),[65] may have been intended to counter the portrait of Arthur created by the "ffrensche men."

Lydgate's story of Arthur is a tragedy, but not one, like so many others in *Fall of Princes*, caused by "vicious lyuyng." In adapting

Laurence de Premierfait's French version of Boccaccio's *De Casibus Virorum Illustrium*, Lydgate made Arthur into a much more positive figure whose tragedy results from the "double goddesse" Fortune who "envied at his glorie" and from Mordred who treacherously rebelled against him.[66] He adds details that justify Arthur's actions: Arthur's earlier wars are fought for self-defense ("He droof Saxones out of his contre") or for other good reasons ("Wrouht bi counsail, and bi the ordynaunce/ Of prudent Merlyn"); instead of having Arthur refuse, as he does in the source, to pay the Romans the customary tribute that is due them, Lydgate maintains that the Roman demand for tribute is "forward & outraious" (ll. 2721, 2726–27, 2875–76). He enhances Arthur's reputation by describing him as the "wisest prince and the beste kniht" (l. 2667), "curteis, large, and manly of dispence," "Merour. . .off liberalite" (ll. 2717–18), "a briht sonne set amyd the sterris" (l. 2795). At the end Arthur is "crownid in the heuenly mansioun" as the most honored of the nine worthies. (ll. 3106–8). Arthur's fall was due not to any fault of his own but to "conspiracioun of vnkynde blood" (l. 3164). Lydgate omits the statement in his source, derived from the French *Mort*, that Mordred was Arthur's son and notes only that he is "cosyn," (l. 3000), which in Middle English could mean "nephew," and is thus consistent with the chronicles' presentation of Mordred as Arthur's nephew, not his son. Lydgate knew several chronicles[67] that could have given him a favorable opinion of Arthur and suggested details that enhance Arthur's reputation.[68]

In adapting the French *Mort Artu*, the English author was like other late medieval translators who turned to French sources for their material. Such a writer, Burnley suggests, did not think of "translation in the narrow sense we now use the word. . . .Rather. . .he might consider himself as involved in the business of *inventio*, seeking subject matter from sources which had not previously been exploited within his own cultural sphere. . . .He was concerned not with the text but with the story and its relation to its future audience."[69] Burnley's discussion of a medieval approach to translation can be aptly applied to the writing of the stanzaic *Morte*. The author turned to new *materia* for an English romance, the Arthurian tragedy caused in part by the love of Lancelot and Guenevere. He had before him a French source in which Arthur had some positive traits, but also many negative ones that contributed to the collapse of his kingdom. Like Mannyng and Lydgate, he apparently wanted to present a portrait of Arthur that would correspond more to the Arthur known to readers of chronicles. Arthur's greatest mistake, listening to Gawain's advice, remains, but since the war against

Lancelot was an essential part of the plot, it is difficult to see how it could have been omitted; there had to be a reason for Arthur's going to the continent and leaving Mordred in charge of the kingdom, and the Roman war, which accounted for this in the chronicles, was not an essential part of the plot of this romance.[70] He removed many other unfavorable traits found in the French *Mort* and changed the ending so that the tragedy results not from Arthur's pride or failure to heed warnings, but primarily from accident and impersonal Fortune. The stanzaic *Morte* thus presents a conception of the tragedy similar to that found in the chronicles. The English work also appears to have been influenced by contemporary political ideas. In consistently presenting Arthur as a king who takes advice, the author must have had in mind the emphasis of the political theorists upon the importance of a king's counsellors. This adaptation of the French *Mort* for an English audience presents an Arthur who is, to use Benson's description of Malory's Arthur, "relatively blameless."[71] Malory, it should be noted, found this portrait of Arthur more appealing than the one in the French *Mort*, for the stanzaic *Morte* became the major source for the conclusion to his *Morte Darthur*.[72] Although the stanzaic *Morte* is known primarily to specialists in Middle English, the author's portrayal of Arthur influenced through Malory the conception of Arthur that many readers have today.

Notes

1. See D. Mehl, *The Middle English Romances of the Thirteenth and Fourteenth Centuries* (London, 1968), pp. 186–93; R. A. Wertime, "The Theme and Structure of the Stanzaic *Morte Arthur*," in *Publications of the Modern Language Association* 87 (1972), 1075–82; S. E. Knopp, "Artistic Design in the Stanzaic *Morte Arthur*," *English Literary History* 45 (1978), 563–82; L. C. Ramsey, *Chivalric Romances: Popular Literature in Medieval England* (Bloomington, 1983), pp. 127–31; F. M. Alexander, " 'The Treson of Launcelote du Lake': Irony in the Stanzaic *Morte Arthur*," in *The Legend of Arthur in the Middle Ages*, ed. P. B. Grout, et al. (Cambridge, 1983), pp. 15–27; W. R. J. Barron, *English Medieval Romance* (London, 1987), pp. 142–47; J. O. Fichte, "Geschichte wird Geschichte: Überlegungen zum Realitätsbezug der homiletischen Artusromanze," in *Spätmittelalterliche Artusliteratur*, ed. K. H. Göller (Paderhorn, 1984), pp. 69–83.

2. See Wertime, "Theme and Structure"; Alexander, "The Treson"; V. B. Richmond, *The Popularity of Middle English Romance* (Bowling Green, Ohio, 1973), p. 141; *Le Morte Arthur*, ed. P. F. Hissiger (The Hague, 1975), pp. 7–11; *Medieval English Romances*, ed. A. V. C. Schmidt and N. Jacobs (London, 1980), 2:23.

3. See E. Ven-Ten Bensel, *The Character of King Arthur in English Literature* (Amsterdam, 1928), pp. 132–33; K. H. Göller, *König Arthur in der englischen*

Literatur des späten Mittelalters (Göttingen, 1963), pp. 69–70; Richmond, *Popularity*, pp. 132–33; P. Korrel, *An Arthurian Triangle: A Study of the Origin, Development and Characterization of Arthur, Guinevere and Modred* (Leiden, 1984), pp. 225–45.

4. Burnley, "Late Medieval English Translation: Types and Reflections," in *The Medieval Translator: The Theory and Practice of Translation in the Middle Ages*, ed. R. Ellis (Cambridge, 1989), p. 42.

5. *Le Morte Arthur*, ed. Bruce, EETS ES 88 (1903), xiii–xx.

6. *Le Morte Arthur*, ed. S. Noguchi (Tokyo, 1990), lines 9–16. Line references from this edition will appear within the text.

7. Mehl (*Middle English Romances.* p. 188) mentions the author's concern with treason. Barron asks if the love of Lancelot and Guenevere in this romance is "compatible with the dynastic ideal which Arthur embodied for an age which condemned sexual relations with the wife of the ruler as treason" (*Medieval Romance*, p. 144).

8. Göller, *König Arthur*, p. 71.

9. See *Libro de las Generaciones*, ed. J. F. Martinez (Valencia, 1968), p. 40; D. C. Menéndez-Pidal, *De Alfonso X al Conde de Barcelos* (Madrid, 1962), pp. 387–90; K. C. Jones, "The Relationship between the Versions of Arthur's Last Battle as They Appear in Malory and in the *Libro de las Generaciones,*" *Bibliographical Bulletin of the International Arthurian Society* 26 (1974), 197–205.

10. See *Le Roman de Brut, Wace*, ed. I. Arnold, 2 vols. (Paris 1938 and 1940) 2:689–90, ll. 13201–22.

11. The French prose *Brut* survives in at least 50 manuscripts; I list 172 of the English prose *Brut* in "Chronicles and Other Historical Writing," *A Manual of the Writings in Middle English*, gen. ed. A. E. Hartung, (New Haven, 1989), 8:2629–37, 2818–33. Felicity Riddy told me of another English *Brut* fragment: National Library of Wales, MS Brogyntyn 8, vol. 1r-18v.

12. See her review of J. D. Merriman, *The Flower of Kings*, *Review of English Studies*, n.s., 26 (1975), 329.

13. See J. Frappier, *Étude sur La Mort le Roi Artu*, 3rd ed. (Geneva, 1972), pp. 149–215.

14. E. Peters, *The Shadow King* (New Haven, 1970), pp. 204–6; A. Micha, "Le mari jaloux dans la littérature romanesque des XIIᵉ et XIIIᵉ siècles," *Studi Medievali* 17 (1951), 307–12; *The Death of King Arthur*, trans. J. Cable (Harmondsworth, 1971), p. 16.

15. Arthur is also similar to the villainous Marc of the later prose *Tristan*, a work that *Mort Artu* could have influenced.

16. Frappier, *Étude*, pp. 280, 328.

17. In *Mort Artu* Arthur says only that Mordred is his son, but the author probably expected his audience to recall a reference to the incest that occurs in the *Agravain* section of the Vulgate *Lancelot* (see *Lancelot: Roman en prose du XIIIᵉ siècle*, ed. A. Micha, 9 vols. [Paris and Geneva 1978–83] 5:223). Frappier's views on Arthur's incest in the Vulgate Cycle changed over the years; see *Étude*, pp. 32–37, "Additions et Corrections," p. 429; his 3rd edition *Le Mort le Roi Artu* (Geneva, 1964), pp. xvi–xvii.

18. See F. Bogdanow, "The Changing Vision of Arthur's Death," in *Dies Illa: Death in the Middle Ages*, ed. J. H. M. Taylor (Liverpool, 1984), p. 110.

19. *Mort Artu*, ed. Frappier, pp. 134, 142, 168. Subsequent references will appear within the text.

20. Frappier, *Étude*, p. 282.

21. Frappier, *Étude*, p. 251.

22. See Frappier, *Étude*, pp. 229–43, 324–26.

23. Frappier, *Étude*, pp. 282–83; also see Frappier, "La Bataille de Salesbieres," in *Amour Courtois et Table Ronde* (Geneva, 1973), pp. 214–15.

24. Benson, *Malory's Morte Darthur* (Cambridge, Mass., 1976), p. 239.

25. Frappier, *Étude*, p. 255.

26. See H. R. Patch, *The Goddess Fortuna in Medieval Literature* (1927; repr. New York, 1967), pp. 42–49.

27. See Patch, *Fortuna*, pp. 69–70; P. Tristram, *Figures of Life and Death in Medieval English Literature* (London, 1976), pp. 143–44; W. Matthews, *The Tragedy of Arthur* (Berkeley, 1960), pp. 123–26.

28. Gower, *Confessio Amantis*, in *The English Works of John Gower*, ed. G. Macaulay, 2 vols. EETS ES 81–82, (1900–01) 1:19–20; Lydgate, *Fall of Princes*, ed. H. Bergen, 4 vols. EETS ES 121–124 (1924–27), 2:332; Chaucer, *Monk's Tale*, *The Riverside Chaucer*, ed. L. Benson et al. (Boston, 1987), pp. 241, 244, 248, 249, 252. For French examples, see Patch, *Fortuna*, pp. 69–70.

29. K. J. Höltgen sees in *Mort Artu* the first suggestion in Arthurian legend that Fortune may be punishing Arthur, but he believes that the fall is brought about not by Arthur's pride but by Lancelot's love for Guenevere and the failure of the Grail Quest. ("König Arthur und Fortuna," *Anglia* 75 [1957], 42–43). M. Blaess argues that characters in *Mort Artu* are driven by "character, environment, upbringing and heredity, though chance also has its part to play" ("Predestination in Some Thirteenth-Century Prose Romances," *Currents of Thought in French Literature* [New York, 1966], p. 19).

30. See note 3 above.

31. On this point, see Mehl, *Romances*, p. 188.

32. Wertime, "Theme and Structure," p. 1080.

33. Korrel, *Triangle*, p. 228; Frappier, *Étude*, p. 238.

34. See D. Sayer's comments in her translation of *The Song of Roland* (Harmondsworth, 1957), p. 15.

35. Korrel, *Triangle*, p. 227.

36. See A. J. Carlyle, *A History of Medieval Political Theory in the West*, 3 (London, 1915), 153–56; E. F. Jacob, *The Fifteenth Century: 1399–1485* (Oxford, 1961), pp. 428–29, 432.

37. Green, *Poets and Princepleasers* (Toronto, 1980), pp. 140–43.

38. See the blame placed upon counselors of Edward II, Edward III, and Richard II in *The Brut*, ed. F. W. D. Brie, EETS 131, 136 (1906–1908), 1:225, 2:329–30, 346, 351, 356; also see Gower, *The Tripartite Chronicle, The Major Latin Works of John Gower*, trans. E. W. Stockton (Seattle, 1962), p. 290.

39. See Höltgen, "König Arthur," p. 50; Wertime, "Theme and Structure," p. 1075.

40. Wheels could symbolize such concepts as Heaven, Lust, Life, the Seven Deadly Sins, the Seven Works of Mercy, and the Five Senses. See E. W. Tristram, *English Wall Painting of the Fourteenth Century* (London, 1955), pp. 27–28; F. P. Pickering, *Literature and Art in the Middle Ages* (Coral Gables, Fla. 1970), p. 218.

41. See E. Mâle, *The Gothic Image*, trans. D. Nussey (1913; repr. New York, 1958), pp. 94–95; Patch, *Fortuna*, p. 147, plate 11, p. 166; Pickering, *Literature and Art*, pp. 202–3, 215; G. Heider "Das Glücksrad und dessen Anwendung in der christlichen Kunst," *Mittheilungen der K. K. Central-Commission zur Erforschung und Erhaltung der Baudenkmale* 5 (1859), 114–125.

42. Benson, *Morte Darthur*, p. 237.

43. Patch, *Fortuna*, pp. 160–61; for the "vgly pit," see James I, *The Kingis Quair*, ed. J. Norton-Smith (Oxford, 1971), p. 41, l. 1129.

44. On distinctions between chance and Fortune, see Patch *Fortuna*, pp. 4–26.

45. Lines 3248–55. Cf. Arthur's statements in the French *Mort*: "ge n'en partirai jamés jusques a tant que Nostre Sires en ait donee enneur a moi ou a Mordret" (p. 229); "Por amour de cest coup veu ge a Dieu qu'il couvient ici morir moi ou Mordret" (p. 245).

46. See Bogdanow, "Changing Vision," p. 112. The English author could have read the Post-Vulgate *Roman du Graal*; at least part of it—the *Suite du Merlin*—was known in England and was the source for Malory's first tale.

47. See note 17 above.

48. Bogdanow, "Changing Vision," p. 113.

49. See Hissiger, *Le Morte Arthur*, pp. 8–9.

50. In the French *Mort* Guenevere takes refuge at the abbey because she fears Mordred, who wants to marry her, and Arthur, who, she thinks, will believe that she has been unfaithful again (p. 218). At the time of the interpolated parting scene, Mordred and Arthur are dead, but she believes that Mordred's sons are alive.

51. The scene is in an appendix to Frappier's edition, pp. 264–66.

52. For studies of this scene in the stanzaic *Morte*, see J. and R. Beston, "The Parting of Lancelot and Guinevere in the Stanzaic *Morte Arthur*," *Journal of Australasian Universities Modern Language and Literature Association* 40 (1973), 249–59; S. L. J. Jaech, "The Parting of Lancelot and Gaynor: The Effect of Repetition in the Stanzaic *Morte Arthur*," *Interpretations* 15 (1984), 59–69.

53. "Sur un remaniement de *La Mort Artu* dans un manuscrit du XIVe siècle: Le Palatinus Latinus 1967," *Romania* 57 (1931), 214–22.

54. F. Whitehead, who believed that the scene in the stanzaic *Morte* was based upon a MS of *Mort Artu* with the Palatinus interpolation, preferred the versions in the stanzaic *Morte* and Malory to the French: see "Lancelot's Penance," *Essays on Malory*, ed. J. A. W. Bennett (Oxford, 1963), pp. 108–13.

55. See R. M. Wilson, "Malory, the Stanzaic *Morte Arthur* and the *Mort Artu*," *Modern Philology* 37 (1939–40), 125–38; E. T. Donaldson, "Malory and the Stanzaic *Le Morte Arthur*," *Studies in Philology* 47 (1950), 460–72.

56. See Beston and Beston, "Parting," above note 52. The authors believe there is no known source for the scene, but that it echoes two earlier ones in the stanzaic *Morte*.

57. See Bogdanow, "Changing Vision," pp. 113–14.

58. Mehl, *Middle English Romances*, p. 186.

59. Fletcher, *The Arthurian Material in the Chronicles, Especially Those of Great Britain and France*, 2nd edn, ed. R. S. Loomis (New York, 1966), p. 186.

60. See Höltgen, "König Arthur," pp. 41–42.

61. Vinaver, *Rise of Romance* (Oxford, 1971), p. 89.

62. Mannyng, *The Story of England*, ed. F. J. Furnivall, Rolls Series 87, 2 vols., (London, 1887), 1:383.

63. Mannyng, *Story*, 2:494.

64. Fletcher, *Arthurian Material*, p. 207.

65. Mannyng, *Story*, 1:341.

66. Lydgate's *Fall of Princes*, ed. H. Bergen, pt. I, EETS ES 121 (1924), bk. 2, line 46; pt. III, EETS ES 123 (1924), bk. 8, line 2868. References within the text will refer to pt. III, bk. VIII of *Fall of Princes*.

67. Bergen believed that Lydgate used, in addition to Laurence's text, Layamon, Geoffrey of Monmouth, Wace, Robert of Gloucester, and the prose *Brut* (*Princes*, pt. IV, EETS ES 124 [1927], p. 326). W. Perzl suggests that Lydgate used Geoffrey's *Historia* and other chronicles, but cites borrowings only from the prose *Brut* and Robert of Gloucester (*Die Arthur-Legende in Lydgate's Fall of Princes: Kritische Neu-Ausgabe mit Quellenforschung* [Munich, 1911], p. 91).

68. For Lydgate's treatment of Arthur, see Göller, *König Arthur*, pp. 131–36, and "Arthurs Aufstieg zum Heiligen," *Artusrittertum im späten Mittelalter*, ed. F. Wolfzettel (Giessen, 1984), pp. 93–94; R. A. Dwyer, "Arthur's Stellification in the *Fall of Princes*," *Philological Quarterly* 57 (1978), 155–71; J. Withrington, "The Arthurian Epitaph in Malory's 'Morte Darthur' " *Arthurian Literature* 7 (1987), 124–38.

69. Burnley, "Translation" (see above note 4), pp. 41–42.

70. In *Mort Artu* after Arthur has gone abroad to fight Lancelot and before he hears of Mordred's rebellion, the author inserts, out of deference to chronicle tradition, a brief account of the Roman war that is irrelevant to the plot (pp. 205–9); the English author omits it.

71. Benson, *Morte Darthur*, p. 238.

72. See my "Malory and His English Sources," *Aspects of Malory*, ed. T. Takamiya and D. S. Brewer (Cambridge, 1981), pp. 27–55.

Was Merlin a Ghibelline?
Arthurian Propaganda at the Court of
Frederick II

———————————————— *Donald L. Hoffman*

When a Cornish cripple fought with the canons of Laon, who had
sneered at the hope of Arthur's return,[1] he initiated an era of Arthurian
apocalypse that was not, perhaps, concluded until the Council of Trent
condemned the English Merlin's book of obscure predictions.[2] The
account of the mêlée provides our first record of the British hope of
Arthur's return, and reflects popular expectations of the millennium and
the Last World Emperor, who will preside over a reign of universal peace.

In Geoffrey of Monmouth, whether his primary purpose was to
encourage the Normans,[3] or praise the Welsh,[4] Arthur represents the
height of British imperial glory and his *exitus dubius*, his doubtful
departing, and hoped-for return, allows the dream to remain alive.[5] His
Arthur is praised as the third great British emperor, successor to
Brennus and Constantine, but, although he defeats the Roman emperor
Lucius, Mordred's rebellion prevents him from claiming the crown, thus
destroying the hopes of British imperial sovereignty and canceling the
possibility of Arthur's accession to the role of the archetypal Last World
Emperor. With the decision of the last British king to assure himself
of a heavenly rather than an earthly crown, the apocalyptic hope is
transferred from this world to the next and the advent of the secular
Messiah is deferred.[6] The hope is not entirely denied, however, for, as
the canons of Laon had clearly learned from the cripple, Arthur may
yet return.

When Geoffrey's *Historia* travelled from Britain to Italy, the muted
apocalyptic theme became embedded in an already rich context of

millenarian expectations. Apart from nonliterary traces,[7] Arthur and Merlin are first recorded in Italy in 1191, the same year that Arthur's tomb was unearthed in Glastonbury. But by 1191, when Godfrey of Viterbo completed his *Pantheon*, which includes Italy's first Arthurian narrative, the peninsula had already spent nearly a century anticipating universal calamities. It was at the beginning of that century that Ranieri, the archbishop of Florence, had announced that the Antichrist had already been born[8] and went on to identify him as Pope Paschal II.[9] The expectations aroused by Ranieri in the north pale in comparison to the frenzy of speculation, curiosity, and occasional lunacy inspired by the metaphysics of history produced by the Calabrian abbot, Joachim of Fiore. The textual intersection of Geoffrey of Monmouth and Godfrey of Viterbo is parallelled in the nearly synchronous meeting in the winter of 1190–01 of Joachim and Richard Coeur de Lion at Messina.[10] At this meeting with the English courtiers and clerics, Joachim explicated St. John's vision of the seven-headed dragon and expressed his belief that Antichrist was now fifteen years old and on his way to obtain the apostolic see.[11]

In continuing the tradition established by Ranieri of Florence, the identification of Antichrist with the papal see all but inevitably led, in the context of a heated rivalry between papal and imperial claims to universal sovereignty, to the conception of the emperor as the antidote to Antichrist. Thus, with the coronation of Henry VI, also in 1191, metaphysical historians began the process of embedding *Kaisergeschichte* within the narrative of *Endzeit-Erwartung*.[12] In such a context, Godfrey's history focused on Geoffrey's Merlin to express the rumor of Arthur's return, the expectation that he will not perish utterly (*nec perit omnino*), but will live on as an eternal king (*perpetus. . . rex*) beneath the sea (*maris. . . imo*). In recounting the prophecy of Arthur's advent,[13] he sounds an imperial theme that establishes Merlin as an imperial spokesman as soon as he arrives in Italy. In the midst of the struggles for the domination of the peninsula waged by the pope and the emperor, the conflict between the Guelfs and the Ghibellines that ravaged Italy from the twelfth to the fourteenth centuries, Merlin enters immediately as a partisan; he is a Ghibelline.

Godfrey may have had his patron Henry VI in mind when he penned his (probably commissioned) praise to imperial glory painted in Arthurian colors, but his praise of the father is merely prologue to his celebration of the son. In part to counter Sicilian hostility to a German emperor, the court poets seem to have taken full advantage of the messianic possibilities opened by the twelfth-century associations of the papacy with Antichrist. When a son was at last born to the

Emperor Henry and the Empress Constance, the child was greeted as a miracle. Godfrey in his *Friderici I. et Heinrici VI* regarded the infant *stupor mundi*, Frederick II, as "the future Savior foretold of prophets, the time-fulfilling Caesar;" with no less extravagance his contemporary, Peter of Eboli, updated Virgil's fourth eclogue to announce the birth of the miraculous child.[14] In later years, the emperor himself did little to squelch these expectations, taking full advantage of the suggestive accident of having been born in the town of Iesi, which he honored as "our Bethlehem...where our Divine Mother brought us into the world."[15] Most remarkably, however, Merlin himself was called upon to laud the child's "insperati et mirabilis ortus,"[16] his "unexpected and miraculous birth."[17] It is possible that this prophecy marks the emperor's propagandists' attempt to co-opt the prophetic authority of Merlin as a counterblast to the growing disaffection of the Guelfs and their profound and influential prophet, Joachim of Fiore.

The miracle of Frederick's birth, however, was capable of a less supernatural interpretation. The child praised by the court propagandists as the "future Savior" was dismissed as a bastard by others, who neither wanted a German emperor nor believed that the elderly empress could have legitimately conceived her first child in her fortieth year (her sixtieth, according to one scandal-mongering chronicler).[18] Suspicion was so widespread, in fact, that the empress, according to one report, was forced to quell the rumors by giving birth in an open tent in the marketplace.[19] The Franciscan Salimbene records the contemporary slander that the aging empress had only pretended to be pregnant and passed off as the imperial infant the son of a local. Salimbene assented to this belief for three (to him) compelling reasons: (1) Frederick's father-in-law once angrily called him the son of a butcher ("Fi de becer diabele"), (2) "trickery of this kind is common among women," and (3) Merlin himself had prophesied a miraculous and unexpected birth.[20] Thus, what had begun as a Ghibelline campaign to salute the advent of a Hohenstaufen messiah degenerated into a Guelph-sponsored epidemic of slander and suspicion.

Merlin does not, however, seem to have been entirely effective as a Ghibelline Virgil. As a consequence, the court buttressed Merlin's authority by appropriating that of the great contemporary prophet, Joachim of Fiore, who became a Merlin expositor[21] with a conveniently Ghibelline bias. Both Salimbene in 1283 and the fourteenth-century Venetian chronicler, Andrea Dandolo, record that it was necessary for the Emperor Henry VI to call upon his "friend," the Abbot Joachim, to supply an appropriate (*i.e.* Ghibelline) gloss to ameliorate the thrust of the prophecies of Merlin.[22] The Guelf thrust of the abbot's *Vita* is countered by (pseudo-)Joachim's *Expositio* (1196?); Dandolo, who clearly believes in the historical reality of Merlin,[23] adds that in 1196 the Emperor Henry VI, was disturbed by his wife's pregnancy, until the abbot Joachim assured him of the child's legitimacy.[24]

This prophecy, composed to assuage the emperor's doubts, still extant as the pseudo-Joachite *Expositio Abbatis Joachimi super Sibillis et Merlino*,[25] a gloss upon the earlier *Dicta Merlini*,[26] or "Sayings of Merlin," included the ambiguous praise of Frederick's miraculous birth.[27] Clearly, by the mid-thirteenth century, Merlin had acquired sufficient authority in Sicily to be chosen as the voice of imperial prophecy, a voice (as the complete title of the *Expositio Abbatis Joachimi super Sibillis et Merlino* implies) nearly as authoritative as that of the ancient Sybil and the contemporary Joachim.

The association of Sybil, Merlin, and the Calabrian abbot seems, at first, quite arbitrary. Salimbene's *Chronicle*, however, records a dialogue between the skeptical Brother Peter and the Joachite Brother Hugh that attests to a widespread belief in the historicity and reliability of all three of these prophets. Accused of relying on the authority of magicians and soothsayers, Hugh presented the claim that "the words of . . . the Sibyl and Merlin and Joachim . . . are not scorned by the Church but received gladly, in so far as they were good, useful, and true words."[28] Taking St. Ambrose's words ("By whomever spoken, truth comes from the Holy Spirit")[29] as his authority, Brother Hugh accepted a fairly eclectic group of prophets and was untroubled by a very modern hesitancy to attribute the same sort of authenticity to the legendary Merlin and the historical Joachim.

While a modern reader might sense an ontological confusion between historical and fictional prophets, a medieval reader would possibly be more likley to feel, as did Brother Hugh, that the proof of prophecy lies in its reliability: the only false prophet is the inaccurate one. The Sybil had a long history of "reliability" and Merlin, although a recent importation into Italy, seems to have met with immediate acceptance. Their association may also reflect Joachim's well-known tripartite schema of world history. In the transition from incarnation to revelation, the ages of the Father, Son, and Holy Ghost seem reassigned to the ages of the prophets. Thus, Sybil and Merlin, voices from the first two eras,[30] are reconciled by Joachim, the master prophet of the third *status*. As the advent of the age of the Holy Ghost is initiated by the appearance of the mendicant orders, Joachim initiates the third age as the ultimate expositor and oracle of the end of time, the *vox clamantis* in Palermo.

Salimbene's advocate of prophecy, Brother Hugh, not only attests to the general truth of Merlin's prophecies concerning Frederick II, but provides a precise analysis of the four termini Merlin had specified in the *Dicta*: (1) Merlin's "In thirty-two years he shall fall" is construed to refer to the Emperor Henry's reign from his coronation to his death, thirty years and eleven days; (2) Merlin's prophecy that Frederick would "live in his prosperity for seventy-two years" was unverifiable, since Frederick was still alive and reigning, but, it was assumed (an assumption soon to be called into question) that Merlin would be shown to be correct; (3) Merlin had prophesied that for "twice fifty he shall be treated gently" which Hugh ingeniously construed to mean fifty plus, rather than fifty times two and argues that this refers to the years of relative peace from the marriage of Henry and Constance to Frederick's eighteenth year as emperor. (The choice of dates is arbitrary, but the interpretation of prophecy often depends on the ingenuity of the exegete more than the accuracy of the seer); (4) Merlin's fourth terminus is that after the eighteenth year of his coronation, "he shall hold the Empire in the face of many enemies." Brother Hugh has no difficulty in showing that Frederick had many enemies after this date, but he focuses on Pope Gregory, who excommunicated the emperor in 1237.[31] Salimbene seems entirely persuaded by these demonstrations of Merlin's accuracy.

While Merlin's *Dicta* are relatively neutral, Pope Gregory was fierce in his excommunication. Encouraged by, and not impossibly responsible for, the rumors that Frederick was accustomed to turn churches into brothels and altars into privies,[32] Gregory spoke of the emperor in terms that echoed the prophecies of Merlin and the Sybil and Joachim's Dragon with Seven Heads.[33]

> Out of the sea[34] . . .comes a beast filled with words of blasphemy, which, formed with the feet of a bear, the mouth of an enraged lion and, in the rest of its body, shaped like a panther, opens its mouth in blasphemy of the Divine Name, nor does it fail to attack with similar shafts the Church and the saints who dwell in heaven.[35]

Compared to the intemperate pope, Salimbene's *Chronicle* is surprisingly tolerant, for although his sympathies tended to be with the Guelfs, he was caught up in the struggle between pope and emperor in more ways than he directly acknowledged.

When after the death of St. Francis, Brother Elias modified the absolute rule of poverty, the "Spirituals" left the order and were officially "suppressed." Joachim of Fiore, whom Salimbene so admired, was adopted as the spiritual father of this splinter group, and Salimbene maintained his affection for both the prophet and his sons. Although—

as the *Expositio* and the chronicles of Salimbene and Dandolo attest—
the Emperor Henry held Joachim in great reverence, neither Salimbene's
veneration for the abbot nor his almost star-struck fascination with the
rich and famous swayed him from his Guelf sympathies. When Brother
Elias was both deposed by the pope and patronized by the excommunicated emperor,[36] Salimbene's sympathies became convictions;
always an enthusiastic Guelf, he developed an unshakable hostility
towards Frederick.

Salimbene's faith in the words of Joachim, Merlin, and the Sybil
was, however, stronger than his partisanship, so he included in his
chronicle, the *Versus Merlini*, the second most widespread Merlin
prophecy in thirteenth-century Italy,[37] and one with a clear imperial bias.
San-Marte[38] and Zumthor[39] agree that the inspiration for this prophecy
is Ghibelline, an argument supported by the verses prophesying the
victory of the empire ("Alamanni imperabit") and the defeat of the
Church ("Ecclesia plorabit"). Much of this prophecy is cryptic, however,
and so uncertain in meaning that Salimbene's English translator leaves
it in the original Latin characterizing it as "a corrupt text of an already
obscure poem."[40]

Obscure as it is, however, the sixty lines of the *Versus Merlini*
introduce the essential features of an Italian Merlin, totally detached
from an English context and reconstituted as the imperial oracle and
the seer of the cities of Italy. Merlin's perceived geographical distance
from Sicily and the court of Frederick II may have given him the
authority of the remote, but his reputation may quite possibly have been
enhanced by the contemporary prestige of his British compatriot,
Frederick's court astrologer, Michael Scot of Balwearie, who, according
to Dante, "veramente / de le magiche frode seppe 'l gioco" (*Inf.* 20.
116–17).[41]

Although the prophecy may be irrecoverably veiled, the primary
intention is clear, and Salimbene fully understood what Merlin meant
to do. The prophecy is placed after the account of the hostilities between
Modena and Parma, hostilities that "took place so that the words of
Merlin, the English magician, might be fulfilled."[42] Incredibly, Salimbene
seems to imply that as the deeds of Christ fulfilled the words of the
Old Testament, so contemporary Italian history is the fulfillment of the
words of Merlin. Clearly, Salimbene was imbued with the methods,
if not the rigor, of Joachim of Fiore, and, like the Master, saw history
as the actualization of a preexistent text. History, therefore, was (and
is) always already written; it is only necessary for time to turn the pages,
so that it may be read. Prophets are those who have been given advance
copies of the text and are able to gloss it before it is given to history's
press for publication.

As history unfolded in Italy, Salimbene found it already written in Merlin's prophetic warnings. The full title of the verses suggests the extent of Merlin's gaze and implies a political vision that extends beyond a limited Ghibelline agenda. In the *Versus Merlini, futura praesagia Lombardiae, Thusciae, Romagnuolae, Marchiae Anconitanae, Apuliae, Marchiae, Franciae, Alamanniae, Provinciae, Hispaniae, per Merlinum recitata*,[43] the prophet surveys the world (at least that portion of it in dispute between pope and emperor), and dissects the consequences of factionalism and tyrannies. Thus, even though Merlin prophesies that "Germany will rule," his Ghibelline prophecy includes moral denunciation and poignant sorrow for divided Italy. If Salimbene the Guelf may not have approved the Ghibelline implications of the prophecy, Salimbene the Franciscan moralist and Italian patriot was inevitably attracted to both Merlin's diagnosis of and concern for the afflicted cities of Italy.[44] The *Versus Merlini* represent the zenith of Merlin's intervention in Italian politics. As incorporated in Salimbene's text, they mark the summit of the imagined alliance of Frederick and Merlin. But the harmony was not destined to last.

The remarkable prophecies that surrounded the emperor's birth were exceeded by those responding to his death. Some, even more credulous than Salimbene, circulated tales of the emperor that repeated the Arthurian themes that had echoed at his birth and were secured by his association with Merlin. Many refused to believe that he had died, and Salimbene records the Sybil's prophecy that "he shall survive. The words will sound among the peoples: 'He lives' and 'He lives not.'"[45] If this mingled uncertainty and expectation recalls the Breton hope, the conclusion of the *Dicta Merlini* ("And in his exit those who cursed him shall be deceived in him"),[46] recalls the wording, if not precisely the spirit, of Geoffrey of Monmouth's account of the passing of Arthur and his *exitus dubius*. Perhaps even more remarkable is the fact that it was rumored that Frederick too slept beneath Mount Etna,[47] where Arthur was reputed to be awaiting his return.[48]

Salimbene's final reference to a Frederician prophecy serves almost as an apology for his earlier credulity. The words of the Sybil, "Vivet, et non vivet," which Brother Hugh had applied to Frederick's father, are now, Salimbene reports, being applied to Frederick by German rumor and an anonymous prophet. The *Dicta Merlini's* proclamation that for "twice fifty he shall be treated gently" was now glossed, not as Brother Hugh's fifty plus two, but as the more grammatically normal, if biologically improbable, fifty times two, an interpretation Salimbene attributes to the Joachites. If then, Frederick was to be treated gently for one hundred years, he could not be dead and the rumors went on to state that he "was still alive in Germany, and that he had a huge German army."[49] But Salimbene's final recorded prophecy as well as this final vision of Frederick as the Last World Emperor comes to an ignominious end. As Salimbene reports, "there was nothing to these rumors"; furthermore, the "prophet" who had circulated them "was an imposter or cheat who pretended such things in order to gain money, and now both he and his followers have been brought to nothing."[50]

Unfortunately for the believers, Merlin had prophesied that "He shall live in his prosperity for seventy-two years"[51] and the uncooperative emperor, frustrating to the end, had chosen to die nearly two decades too soon. Salimbene, persuaded by Hugh's argument that Joachim, Sybil, Merlin, and company were "good, useful, and true," was stumped by Merlin's demonstrable error. Furthermore, like a vatic version of the "domino theory," the collapse of Merlin's authority threatened to challenge the reliability of his companions, Sybil and Joachim. The authority of the biblical prophets may not have been questioned, but the viability of postbiblical prophecy was now seriously to be doubted. Thus, simply by dying too soon, Frederick provoked a skepticism greater than all his assaults on papacy and orthodoxy had been able to achieve.

Salimbene never quite gave up his interest in prophecy and delight in recording it, but after Frederick's untimely death, he was considerably more reluctant to assent to it. He records a time, however, when the prophecies of Merlin reflected both the Ghibelline hopes of a Hohenstaufen messiah and the Guelph fears of a Hohenstaufen Antichrist, a time when both sides had agreed on at least two points— that there was no emperor but Frederick[52] and that Merlin was his prophet.

Contemporaneous with Salimbene's disillusion, the author of *Les Prophecies de Merlin* (c. 1274–79) renewed interest in the British prophet. The peculiar text identifies itself as a translation (into French) of a Latin original undertaken by the otherwise unknown Master Richard of Ireland at the request of Frederick II.[53] Despite this claim of an imperial, Sicilian commission, Lucy Allen Paton has demonstrated a Venetian provenance. A Venetian text masquerading as the product of an Irishman working in Sicily to translate Latin into French for a German emperor may, however, be no less incredible than the prophecies themselves. The elaborate pretense may indicate that the phonier a pseudo-Merlin prophecy the greater the need to demonstrate its authenticity, but the fiction is also testimony to Italy's familiarity with the association of Merlin and Frederick, and to the fascination Frederick still held for Italian readers now nearly a generation after his death.

But, while Frederick in this text becomes a remote, apocalyptic threat, the character of Merlin shifts his factional alliance and becomes unambiguously Guelf.

Fascination with as well as hostility toward the emperor may seem surprising in *Les Prophecies* in view of Venice's determined neutrality in the conflict of pope and emperor, a neutrality based in part on the fact that the republic of Venice "had come to realize that the Empire did not after all constitute a direct threat to her sovereignty,"[54] and a neutrality that was at least a partial cause of the republic's increasing mercantile prosperity. While the author loved his city and its citizens, the *bons mariniers* who are the true heroes of Merlin's prophecies, he detested and feared their powerful neighbor and imperial ally, the notorious Ezzelino da Romano, of whom Salimbene had remarked that even the emperor, although "excessively wicked and perverse. . .was not as cruel as Ezzelino da Romano, who governed for a long time in the Mark of Treviso."[55] In *Les Prophecies*, Ezzelino, the emperor's sometime ally, is the evil ruler who transforms Treviso from the *marche amoureuse* to the *marche doloreuse*. Thus, the author's hostility to the emperor may reflect his own experience of the wars and cruelties in the cities of the Veneto as well as his loyalty to the Church.

While the author's political concerns determine one major theme of *Les Prophecies*, his religious concerns determine his conscientious attempt to demonstrate Merlin's orthodoxy. As a pawn in a demonic plot, happily thwarted, to sire the Antichrist, Merlin's motives and values are never above suspicion. It is, then, to prove his orthodoxy that he willingly shares "insider information," revealing in chapter 84, for example, that ". . .li a[ne]mis d'enfer ne doute riens fors que les vertus de Dieu, la vraie crois, [et] la beneuree Virge Marie, par qui il perdi son esfors et son pooir,"[56] provides an "eye witness" account of the Resurrection and the Harrowing of Hell, and concludes by bestowing the gift of a universal blessing to ward off demonic interventions. "Se il avient aucune tentation a un homme ou a une fame et il facent le signe de la vraie crois desus leur vis, et rementoivent le Pere et le Fil et le Saint Esperit et la beneuree Virge sainte Marie souvent et menu que cele fausse tentacion s'en fuira de sus eus, si que li anemis oubliera ce que li aura commencie."[57]

An intriguing consequence of this practical advice is that Merlin and Christ mutually authorize each other. Merlin's authority is ratified by his devotion to the Sign of the Cross, but at least a part of the efficacy of this Sign seems derived from the authority of Merlin as the bearer of the Sign,[58] a kind of Christian Prometheus stealing a gift from God to share with man.

Merlin finally clears up all doubts of his orthodoxy in Chapter 272, when he acknowledges that his conception was the work of demons,[59] but that Holy Baptism removed him from their power.[60] Having demonstrated Merlin's orthodoxy, the text has established his "divine right" to deliver anti-imperial prophecies. Just as Salimbene's Brother Hugh believed that the truth of a prophecy was adequate evidence of its authority, so *Les Prophecies* establishes Merlin's accuracy by demonstrating his orthodoxy. Since Merlin will move from denouncing the Ghibelline alliance to rebuking the Church and churchmen, he must first establish that he himself is not the Enemy.

His orthodoxy established, Merlin is free to attack the *tireors de cordes* (the "cord pullers," probably cardinals), who are corrupted by their lust and their greed for the *roetes d'argent* ("silver wheels," a new Venetian coinage). Despite the author's affection for Venice and its *bons mariniers*, he had serious doubts about the moral consequences of Venice's increasing material prosperity. Despite the prophetic obfuscations in this somewhat enigmatic text, there is a clear social agenda. The author opposes the good, and generally poor, *bons mariniers* to the seekers after the *roetes d'argent*, the greedy and powerful oppressors of the poor. As a consequence of this greed, both the individual soul and the body politic suffer cruel injury, the soul because it is deprived of consolation and instruction, the body politic, because the *tireors de cordes* deliver "les faus jugemens souvent et menu, non mie selonc reson ne selon[c] justice, mes selons les roetes d'argent."[61]

The *tireors de cordes* and even Ezzelino himself are mere shadows, however, of the overriding threat to the world, the Antichrist that *Les Prophecies* via apocalypse and Joachim figures as the Dragon of Babylon. In a Gospel parody, the Dragon has his dragonnet, who serves simultaneously as his John the Baptist ("preechera la venue dou Dragon [de] Babilloinne")[62] and his perverse Madonna ("sera au nestre de lui, et le fera alaitier et li dourra norrices").[63] The dragonnet prophecies that the Dragon will arrive on the first of March to teach "les choses qui encontre la loy Jhesu Crist doivent estre et il parlera ancontre la virge(s) Marie. . .il aura des lors en avant toute la soutillete des anemis d'enfer dedens le cors. . . .[and, Merlin goes on to warn]. . .estranglera il meismes de ces propres mains .xl. enfans. . .[then, again imitating Christ, he will flee to the]. . .desers de Babilloine avec son mestre, et estudiera illec tant que il ait .xxx. ans accomplis, et des lors en avant vendra a decevoir les gens."[64]

In addition to these echoes of Joachim, the emperor inscribed in *Les Prophecies* echoes the two imperial archetypes that dominate thirteenth-century Italy. Frederick in the authorizing frame of the narrative is the learned patron of the arts, the philosopher-king wisely administering the world from Palermo to Jerusalem, the messiah of the *renovatio mundi* prophesied by Peter of Eboli and others; at the same time within the narrative, he is one of the models for the Dragon of Babylon, the Antichrist that had been defined and condemned by papal propagandists. In a Venice relatively free from his direct intervention and flourishing a generation after his death, the remembered emperor is still a source of fear and hope, a perpetual *stupor mundi*.

At the same time, however, it is clear that *Les Prophecies* marks the decline of Frederick's political influence. He remains a name to conjure with, even though he has long since died, but with his passing, Merlin is no longer useful as the prophet of Italian politics, no longer needed as a Ghibelline partisan. Thus, *Les Prophecies* marks the transformation of the Italian Merlin from a political to a literary figure. Following the lead of the *Versus Merlini, Les Prophecies* removes Merlin from an imperial, Sicilian ambience and relocates him in the north of Italy with a particular interest in the states of the Veneto. As a consequence, the political function of Merlin diminishes from the imperial to the local, as he abandons Palermo for Ferrara, the House of Hohenstaufen for the House of Este. While his patrons are now less likely to be emperors than dukes, he is now the creature of imaginative artists, like the jewels of the Ferrarese court, Boiardo and Ariosto, who, in *Orlando Innamorato* and *Orlando Furioso*, envision a Merlin giving up Ghibelline politics for dynastic fantasies. He may prophesy great things for the House of Este, but *au fond* his role as a politician has been displaced by his role as entertainer.

From this point on, the figure of Merlin may no longer serve a significant role in Italian history, may no longer with Joachim of Fiore be identified as one of the prophets of the Messiah and the Antichrist. Nevertheless, in the works of Boiardo and Ariosto and their literary heirs, he survives the brief millennium he prophesied, and, at last, neither Guelf nor Ghibelline, he joins, like his patrons Arthur and Frederick, the ranks of those of whom the Sybil sounds the rumor, "Vivet et non vivet."

Notes

1. The incident occurred in the Cornish town of Bodmin, according to Hermann of Tournai. The episode is reprinted in E. K. Chambers, *Arthur of Britain* (1927; repr. London, 1966), p. 18 (in translation), and p. 249 (Latin text).

2. P. Zumthor, *Merlin le prophète* (Lausanne, 1943), p. 113.

3. J. S. P. Tatlock, *The Legendary History of Britain: Geoffrey of Monmouth's "Historia Regum Britanniae" and Its Early Vernacular Versions* (Berkeley, 1950), p. 426.

4. Geoffrey of Monmouth, *The History of the Kings of Britain*, trans. L. Thorpe (Harmondsworth, 1966), p. 10.

5. R. W. Hanning, in *The Vision of History in Early Britain: From Gildas to Geoffrey of Monmouth* (New York, 1966), argues that "the ultimate consequence of Arthur's fall is the fall of Britain and the rise of the Saxons. Personal fortune here mirrors and affects national fortune" (p. 140).

6. This is essentially the argument presented in Donald L. Hoffman, "The Third British Emperor," *Arthurian Interpretations* 15 (1984), 1–10.

7. For example, the famous archivolt in Modena, which *may* predate Geoffrey and depicts the rescue of Winlogee from the tower of Mardoc. The date of the archivolt is discussed by M. Stokstad, "Modena Archivolt," in *The Arthurian Encyclopedia*, ed. N. J. Lacy et al. (New York, 1986), pp. 390–91, and by J. Stiennon and R. Lejeune, "La Légende arthurienne dans la sculpture de la cathédrale de Modène," *Cahiers de Civilisation Médiévale* 6 (1963), 281–96. In R. S. Loomis, ed., *Arthurian Literature in the Middle Ages* (Oxford, 1959), plate 2 reproduces a photograph of the archivolt.

There is, in addition, a suggestive reference in 1128 to a defunct Merlino, (*La Storia de Merlino de Paolino Pieri*, ed. I. Sanesi, [Bergamo, 1898], p. xii), but this is more likely to have been a dead "little Merlo" than a namesake of the prophet (demonstrated by Rajna, quoted in *Storia*, ed. Sanesi, p. xii).

8. A. de Stefano, *Federico II e le correnti spirituali del suo tempo* (Parma, 1981), 185.

9. de Stefano, *Federico II*, p. 199.

10. M. Reeves, *The Influence of Prophecy in the Later Middle Ages: A Study in Joachimism* (Oxford, 1969), p. 6.

11. Ibid., p. 7.

12. H. M. Schaller, "Endzeit-Erwartung und Antichrist Vorstellungen in der Politik des 13. Jahrhunderts," in *Stupor Mundi: zur Geschichte Friedrichs II. von Hohenstaufen*, ed. G. G. Wolf (Darmstadt, 1982), p. 426.

13. Godfrey of Viterbo, *Gotifredi Viterbiensis Friderici I. et Heinrici VI*, ed. G. H. Pertz, Scriptores Rerum Germanicarum (Hanover, 1970); E. G. Gardner, *The Arthurian Legend in Italian Literature* (London, 1930), pp. 6–7; L. Meyer, *Les légendes des Matières de Rome, de France et de Bretagne dans le "Pantheon" de Godêfroi de Viterbe* (Paris, 1933), p. 222.

14. E. Kantorowicz, *Frederick the Second: 1194–1250*, trans. E. O. Lorimer (1931; repr. New York, 1957), p. 3.

15. Quoted in T. C. Van Cleve, *The Emperor Frederick II of Hohenstaufen: Immutator Mundi* (Oxford,1972), p. 21.

16. Salimbene de Adam, *Cronica*, ed. F. Bernini, 2 vols. (Bari, 1942), 1:57; *The Chronicle of Salimbene de Adam*, trans. J. L. Baird, G. Baglivi, and J. R. Kane, Medieval & Renaissance Texts & Studies, 40 (Binghamton, 1986), p. 17.

17. The "Sayings of Merlin," or "Dicta Merlini" (also sometimes referred to as the "Verba Merlini") are incorporated in *The Chronicle of Salimbene de Adam*. A somewhat more elegant and annotated translation is provided by B. McGinn, *Visions of the End: Apocalyptic Traditions in the Middle Ages* (New York, 1979), 183–84. A good discussion of the MSS and contexts of this prophecy is found in O. Holder-Egger, "Italienische Prophetien des 13. Jahrhunderts. 1," *Neues Archiv der Gesellschaft für ältere deutsche Geschichtskunde* 15 (1889), 141–78.

18. Van Cleve, *The Emperor Frederick II*, p. 14.

19. Kantorowicz, *Frederick the Second*, p. 5.

20. Salimbene, *Chronicle*, trans. J. L. Baird et al., p. 17.

21. While the *Expositio* may reflect the influence of "Merlin" upon Joachim, a more plausible direction of influence has been seen in a possible Joachite coloring in the Merlin of the (pseudo-)Robert de Boron cycle (Aileen Ann Macdonald, *The Figure of Merlin in Thirteenth-Century French Romance* [Lewiston, N.Y., 1990] pp. 217, 251).

22. The *Vita* edited by H. Grundmann (*Vita b. Joachimi abbatis*, Schriften der Monumenta Germaniae Historica, Band 25, 2. In *Ausgewählte Aufsätze*, Teil 2: *Joachim von Fiore* [Stuttgart, 1977], pp. 342–52) gives an unabashedly Guelf interpretation of the meeting which focuses on the emperor's evils more than on the empress' pregnancy and concludes with the abbot going away muttering, "Quanta mala latent sub cuculla illa" (351).

23. *Andreae Danduli ducis Venetiarum Chronica per extensum descripta, aa. 46–1280 d. C*, ed. E. Pastorello, in L. A. Muratori, ed., *Rerum Italicarum Scriptores: Raccolta degli Storici Italiani dal cinquecento al millecinque cento*, vol. XII, pt. 1 (Bologna, 1938–42). Dandolo dates the conception of Merlin "*a spiritu in specie hominis*" in 443 (p. 57) and his role in the conception of Arthur in 458 (p. 61). As intrigued as the credulous Salimbene by prophetic powers, Dandolo identifies Merlin as he who "*multa oscura revelavit, multaque ventura predixit*" (p. 57) and identifies Arthur's sister, Anna, the mother of Gawain and Morgan, as "*in astronomia peritissimam*" (p. 61).

24. The intriguing account reads as follows: "Henricus imperator, audiens quod coniunx esset gravida, et admirans, cum quinquagesimum transisset annum, consuluit abbatem Ioachim, rogans ut interpretaretur quedam dicta Merlini et Sibile Erictee: quod et fecit, dicens quod Federicus esset filius eius et dicte Constancie, et multa predixit sibi, filio ac sucessoribus suis, et specialiter

quod debebat mori in partibus Melacii, et quando; et sic accidit." (A. Dandolo, *Chronica*, p. 274). ["The emperor Henry, hearing that his wife was pregnant, and being amazed, since she had passed her fiftieth year, consulted the abbot Joachim, asking him to interpret the sayings of Merlin and the Erithrean Sybil: he did that, saying that Frederick was his son by the aforesaid Constance, and predicted many things about him, his son and his successors, and, in particular, that he would die in the region of Melacio, and when; and it happened that way."]

25. The *Expositio* has not yet been either edited or translated, but the introductory letter from Paris, Bibliothèque Nationale, MS. Lat. 3319, has been translated in B. McGinn, *Visions*, p. 184.

26. Edited by Holder-Egger, "Italienische Prophetie," under the title *Verba Merlini*.

27. Salimbene, *Chronicle*, tr. Baird et al., p. 362.

28. Ibid., p. 240.

29. Ibid.

30. While Dandolo gives us a clear 443 date for the birth of Merlin, the date of the Sybil is less clear. It is possible that those creating pseudo-prophecies joined these two as the last of the great pagan and first of the great Christian prophets in their respective homelands.

31. Salimbene, *Chronicle*, tr. Baird et al., p. 235.

32. Van Cleve, *The Emperor Frederick II*, p. 420.

33. M. Reeves and B. Hirsch-Reich, *The "Figurae" of Joachim of Fiore* (Oxford, 1972), pp. 146–51.

34. Is it possible that Godfrey of Viterbo's placing of Arthur's eternal resting place beneath the sea with its implication of an eternal return of the Hohenstaufens may have influenced the pope's choice of a marine origin for the imperial dragon. Imperial dragons also, of course, have an inherent Arthurian resonance; cf. Merlin's first recorded prophecy of the dragons beneath Vortigern's tower and the banner of the Pendragon.

35. Quoted in Van Cleve, *The Emperor Frederick II*, p. 431.

36. J. Moorman, *A History of the Franciscan Order from its Origins to the Year 1517* (Oxford, 1968), p. 101.

37. Zumthor, *Merlin*, p. 97.

38. *Die Sagen von Merlin*, ed. San-Marte, (Halle, 1853), p. 267. The *Versus Merlini*, included in Salimbene's *Chronicle*, have also been edited from all the MSS, by San-Marte, *Die Sagen*, pp. 265–66.

39. Zumthor, *Merlin*, p. 97.

40. Salimbene, *Chronicle*, tr. Baird et al. p. 693.

41. "Who truly knew the game of magic frauds." *Inferno* ed. and trans. C. Singleton (Princeton, 1970) 20:115–117. Michael also figures in Salimbene's chronicle, where his credentials are "proven" in the following story: the emperor asked him the distance from the earth to the heavens, then sent him away for a few months during which the stonemasons lowered the room in which Michael had performed his calculations. On their return, when the emperor repeated his question, Michael Scot was forced to conclude that "either the heavens had risen or the earth had sunk" (Salimbene, *Chronicle*, tr. Baird et al., p. 356).

42. Salimbene, *Chronicle*, tr. Baird et al., p. 547.

43. Ibid., pp. 548–49.

44. While, as is typical of the genre, the *Versus Merlini* are negligible as poetry, their review of the condition of the cities of Italy anticipates the powerful laments for "serva Italia" uttered in Purgatory by Dante's Sordello (6:76–151) and Guido del Duca (14:29–66; 88–126).

45. Salimbene, *Chronicle*, tr. Baird et al., p. 546.

46. Ibid., p. 362.

47. Van Cleve, *The Emperor Frederick II*, pp. 528–29.

48. The legend is first recorded in Italian in the late thriteenth century "Detto del Gatto Lupesco," see *Crestomazia italiana dei primi secoli*, ed. E. Monaci (Città di Castello, 1912), p. 449, and by V. De Bartholomeis, *Rime giullareschi e popolari d'Italia* (Bologna, 1926), p. 24.

49. Salimbene, *Chronicle*, tr. Baird et al., p. 546.

50. Ibid.

51. Ibid., p. 362.

52. Dante may not have entirely accepted either point of view, but he did agree that Frederick was *ultimo imperadore de li Romani* (*Convivio* 135).

53. *Les Prophœcies de Merlin*, ed. L. A. Paton, 2 vols. (New York, 1926–27), 1:57.

54. J. J. Norwich, *A History of Venice* (Harmondsworth, 1983), p. 154.

55. Salimbene, *Chronicle*, tr. Baird et al., p. 597.

56. *Les Prophœcies*, ed. Paton, 1:141. "The enemy of hell fears nothing except the virtue of God, the true cross, and the Blessed Virgin Mary, through whom he lost his influence and power."

57. Ibid. 1:142. "If a man or a woman is faced with any temptation and they make the sign of the true cross, and remember the Father and the Son and the Holy Spirit and the Blessed Virgin Mary right away that false temptation will flee from them, so that the enemy will abandon what he had begun."

58. This syncretism is analogous to the process operating in a far different tradition, the appropriation of the Catholic liturgy in Haitian voodoo rituals. "The famous 'African prayer' (prière Guinin) which opens the most solemn ceremonies, begins with Catholic prayers and interminable invocations of saints: the loa are only summoned afterwards. In giving a Catholic cachet to ceremonies which are not Catholic, voodooists are in no way trying to pull the wool over the eyes of authorities or Church: rather is it that they are in fact convinced of the efficacy of Catholic liturgy and therefore wish their own religion to benefit from it." Alfred Métraux, Voodoo in Haiti, tr. Hugo Charteris (New York, 1972), p. 328. In the same way, the author of Les Prophecies is not dealing in "wool-pulling," but convinced equally of the legitimacy of Merlin and the orthodox Church.

59. This acknowledgment is, of course, also proof that the (pseudo) Robert de Boron's Merlin was by this time known in Italy.

60. Les Prophecies, ed. Paton, 1:307.

61. Ibid., 1:212. "[They deliver] false judgments all the time, not following reason nor justice, but following the wheels of silver."

62. Ibid., 1:62. "Will preach the advent of the Dragon of Babylon."

63. Ibid., 1:62. "Will be born of him and will suckle him and will be a nurse to him."

64. Ibid., 1:62–63. "Things against the law of Jesus Christ will come to be and he will speak against the Virgin Mary. . . he will have from then on all the subtlety of the enemies of hell within his heart and he himself will strangle 40 infants with his own hands, [then, he will flee to the] desert of Babylon with his master, and will study there until he has reached 30 years of age, and then he will come forth to deceive mankind."

A Grave Event:
Henry V, Glastonbury Abbey, and
Joseph of Arimathea's Bones

 — *James P. Carley*

In a series of important articles which grew out of her Ph.D. dissertation Valerie Lagorio traced the development of the Joseph of Arimathea legend in England.[1] She noted how this figure, who had appeared only briefly in the Gospel accounts, became associated with the French Grail legends in the late twelfth and early thirteenth century and how he then was endowed with the attributes normally assigned to founding saints in Pan-Brittonic tradition. Later his name was absorbed into British historical materials and he came to be recognized as the founder of Glastonbury Abbey and evangelizer of Britain who, as such, provided an apostolic claim for the English church. Nor was this association, once established, limited to a local or national level: Joseph's mission to Glastonbury was used for political ends by English delegates at four councils: in 1409 at the Council of Pisa by Robert Hallam, bishop of Salisbury; at Constance in 1417 by Thomas Polton; at Pavia-Siena in 1424 by Richard Fleming, bishop of Lincoln, later archbishop of York; and at Basel in 1434 by Robert Fitzhugh, bishop of London.

In spite of this thorough and politically efficacious anglicization, Joseph's cult does not seem to have been actively fostered at Glastonbury itself; interest in him was sporadic at best. Examining the various accounts of the history of the monastery throughout the later Middle Ages, Lagorio concluded that there were good social, political, and economic reasons for this:

> his slow emergence on the abbey and national scenes can be
> attributed to the absence of any major crisis or period of

rehabilitation at Glastonbury from the mid-thirteenth century until the abbey's dissolution in 1539. . . .With this record of prosperity, Glastonbury had little need to enhance its glory with Arthur's counterpart, Joseph of Arimathea.[2]

It was not until abbacy of Richard Beere (1494–1525) that the Glastonbury community seriously exploited the cult of St. Joseph of Glastonbury; this was a direct result—so Lagorio has suggested—of the crisis arising from the West Country rebellion of 1497.[3]

Given the typical evolution of foundation myths and given Glastonbury's treatment of Arthurian matters as well, one peculiarity stands out in the development of the Joseph legend at Glastonbury. As determinedly as Joseph was proclaimed founding saint, there never appear to have been relics as such. The Glastonbury relic lists, for example, do not mention his name.[4] Melkin's prophecy—presumably put together in the form in which it survives in the fourteenth century—asserted specifically that his tomb had not been found: "Cum reperietur eius sarcophagum integrum illibatum in futuris uidebitur et erit apertum toto orbi terrarum."[5] When William Worcestre visited the monastery in 1480, he copied down a local prayer which makes clear that the situation had not changed in the intervening century:

> Domine Iesu Christe perfeccionem excedens cuiuslibet creature concede nobis famulis tuis ut per opera Sancti Ioseph tibi in et post passionem exhibita possumus in terris ueraciter cognoscere eius natalicia et eius reliquias merito recollendas reperire hic in uita.[6]

The final, and perhaps most conclusive, piece of evidence comes from the Jesuit William Good, who had served as an acolyte at the monastery just before the dissolution:

> Nemo tamen Monachorum unquam sciuit certum locum sepulchri huius Sancti, uel designauit. Reconditum abditissime dixerunt, uel ibi, uel in monte, qui monti acuto uicinus, et cui nomen *Hamden-Hill*: et futurum, ut quando reperietur corpus eius, uniuersus eo mundus confluat prae magnitudine et numero miraculorum quae fient.[7]

The tradition associating Joseph with Montacute continued to circulate well into Reformation times; in his *Description of Somerset* (1633) Thomas Gerard stated that "this place [Montacute] by some latter zealous Recusants hath bin had in greate veneration, for they believe that. . .the body of Joseph of Aremathea. . .was here interred."[8]

The "facts" of the story—that is, that Joseph's relics were never located—seem incontestable, although it is difficult to understand why this is the case. Why would the later medieval community at Glastonbury not undertake some sort of exhumation, the finds of which could be associated with Joseph? Why did Melkin's prophecy put the unearthing of Joseph's grave squarely within an apocalyptic tradition? Surely it would have been more convenient to have physical relics on display to corroborate the so-called ancient writings and to stand as an ecclesiastical parallel to the Arthurian relics.

By the time of John Chinnock's abbacy (1375–1420) the story of Joseph's mission had taken its final localized form as articulated in John's *Cronica*. Soon afterwards, key sections from John and from William of Malmesbury's *De Antiquitate Glastonie Ecclesie* were assembled together in the form of a *Magna Tabula*, which must have been displayed in a prominent location for the edification of visitors.[9] Apart from excerpted historical materials, the *Magna Tabula* contains two small pieces not found elsewhere among Glastonbury documents: one an unpublished list of indulgences and the other a short chapter "De capella sanctorum Michaelis et Ioseph et sanctorum in cimiterio requiescentium."[10] According to this latter text there was an ancient and ruinous chapel in the cemetery, under whose altar numerous relics from the cemetery and elsewhere had been stored. In 1382 Chinnock had it rebuilt and rededicated to the memory of St. Michael and of the saints resting in the cemetery and the chapel, the chief of whom was Joseph of Arimathea. The *Magna Tabula* account, like others already noted, asserts that Joseph's remains had been buried in the cemetery, but also makes clear that his precise burial place remained a mystery. Joseph is simply the chief among the saints whose "reliquias incognitatas" make Glastonbury's cemetery one of the holiest places in the kingdom.

That Chinnock would do something about Joseph seems inevitable, given John of Glastonbury's chronicling activity and given the wider interest which the Glastonbury form of the Joseph story had sparked by the mid-fourteenth century.[11] Lacking evidence concerning locations at which to excavate, his decision to rededicate a decayed chapel full of unidentified bones to the saint seems to have been a brilliant move; it honoured Joseph's relics in the most general sense without any pressure of specificity.

The Joseph story continued to serve Glastonbury well as Chinnock's abbacy progressed. Chinnock, who was president of the English province of Black Monks from 1387 to 1399, used Glastonbury's apostolic link as a means of asserting primacy among English abbots.[12] More importantly, by the beginning of the fifteenth century it became clear that the Glastonbury/Joseph story could be used as part of the English response to recent conciliar developments.[13] The use of the traditional four-nation division—that is, Italia, Germania, Gallia, and Hispania—as a basic organizing structure at the Council of Constance seems originally to have been a ploy to outnumber the Italian partisans of Pope John XXIII.[14] After Sigismund, king of the Romans, allied himself with Henry V, Cardinal Pierre d'Ailly mounted a massive retaliatory campaign against the English, who had already been clamoring for separate status as a fifth *natio*.[15] Thomas Polton, who framed the English response to the French protest presented by Jean Campan on 3 March 1417, dwelt at some length on the antiquity of the faith in England as a grounds for justifying England's right to independent status.[16] His historical arguments were based specifically on Joseph's mission:

> Statim post passionem Christi Joseph ab Arimathia, nobilis decurio, qui Christum de cruce deposuit, cum XII. sociis uineam Domini de mane colendam, Angliam uidelicet ingressus est, et populos ad fidem conuertit. Quibus rex XII. hidas terrae in diocesi Bathoniensi pro uictu assignauit: qui in monasterio Glastoniensi Bathoniensis diocesis, ut scribitur, tumulantur. Super quibus XII. hidis praedictis dictum monasterium antiquitus dotatum dignoscitur. Sed regnum Franciae tempore sancti Dionysii et eius ministerio fidem Christi recepit.[17]

There is nothing unexpected in Polton's account, nothing which does not come directly out of John's history. What is important, however, is the context. John had written for a sympathetic local audience, one which would not have too closely examined either his sources (certain ancient writings and the like) or the precise dovetailing of conflicting stories about Joseph.[18] At Constance, where the debate was acrimonious and the consequences grave, the situation was quite different. Since Polton's general arguments concerning English nationhood did not bear careful scrutiny, especially given the problematic relationship of England with the Celtic realms,[19] Joseph's mission became a crux for the English in the debate—its apostolic aspect carrying great resonance—and a matter whose authority needed to be strongly asserted. In the antagonistic atmosphere of Constance, in other words, unidentifed ancient writings *per se* did not perhaps provide an altogether adequate witness. What was obviously needed, as the case of King Arthur had so neatly demonstrated over two hundred years earlier, was an actual coffin with real bones in it.

Vatican City, Biblioteca Apostolica, MS Reg. lat. 623 is a composite manuscript, made up of at least eight separate parts.[20] What concerns us here is the first booklet consisting of forty-eight folios, written in an *anglicana formata* hand of the early fifteenth century.[21] Folios 1–45r contain a copy of the *Vita B. Thomae* by Bishop John Grandisson of Exeter.[22] This is followed (fols. 45r–47r) by a more or less contemporary copy of a letter written by Abbot Nicholas Frome to Henry V in a similar but not identical hand, after which there are some erased lines. The letter is a response to a request for information made by Henry V to Frome in the late spring or early summer of 1421. Henry, so it appears, had heard that the monks had undertaken an excavation in their ancient cemetery at some point in 1419 and he wished to be apprised of the results. The letter begins with—in fact is dominated by—a long historical preamble, copied verbatim for the most part from materials found in William of Malmesbury's interpolated *De Antiquitate Glastonie Ecclesie* and in John's chronicle. We learn about St. Philip's mission to France, whence he sent Joseph of Arimathea and his companions to England in A.D. 63.[23] Melkin is quoted as an authority on Joseph's death and burial and then segments of the Charter of St. Patrick are used to give a description of the refoundation under St. Phagan and St. Deruvian (the so-called second-century missionaries sent to Britain by Pope Eleutherius), and the reorganization into a communal rule under St. Patrick himself. In this preamble, then, the letter summarizes material which would already be known in a general sense to the king through transcripts of Polton's earlier speech at Constance,[24] if not from Glastonbury documents themselves.[25]

The most important part of the letter concerns the excavation of 1419 which, so the king is informed, took place in the southern part of the cemetery where three coffins were found at a depth of fourteen feet.[26] In two were found the bones of single individuals: the third contained complete relics of twelve corpses. Within the chapel itself there was yet another discovery: the bones of a single individual laid in a beautiful coffin lined with linen cloth. No names are attached to any of the finds, but the description of the coffins must presumably be linked to the earlier part of the text: that is, the reader is required to draw various conclusions based on the resonant juxtaposition of materials. It would seem, then, that the twelve in one coffin are meant to be the original missionaries. But what of the other two coffins? Were these to be understood to contain the remains of St. Phagan and St. Deruvian, about the location of whose relics John had professed himself to be unsure?[27] The description of the burial within the chapel itself seems even more baffling.[28] Whatever else, there are clearly echoes of Melkin's prophecy in this account. According to Melkin, for example, Joseph lies "iuxta meredianum angulum oratorii"; the casket within the chapel was found "sub angulo australi altaris." Melkin's prophecy alludes to the fact that Joseph "iacet in linia bifurcata" which presumably corresponds to the "cista cum panno lineo ad intra circumquaque... adornata." That "clarior noticia de ea [the coffin found in the chapel] haberi poterit in futurum" seems to relate to Melkin's statement (in a section of the prophecy not included in the letter) that "Cum reperietur eius sarcophagum integrum illibatum in futuris uidebitur et erit apertum toto orbi terrarum."

Although precise interpretation of all the details is not possible, it seems clear that the letter was worded in the way it was so that Henry and his advisors would draw the conclusion that Joseph's coffin had been found. Certainly, Polton's speech at Constance had made it expedient for the monks at Glastonbury to find Joseph's burial place and retrieve his relics. Nor is it surprising that Henry V would have wished to know about the results of this excavation—that is, if he had not actually commissioned it. Frome's letter itself, nevertheless, seems at first reading remarkably restrained, if not downright cryptic, in its announcement of the event. The reason for this, I would suggest, is because the letter was meant simply to prepare the way for a major revelation at a later date, on the occasion perhaps of a royal visitation.[29] At this time, the obscure allusions could all be explained and the whole of Melkin's prophecy could take its fulfillment in some suitable— ecclesiastically respectable—form. One can only assume that Henry's death in 1422 put a sudden end to this scheme which, unlike the earlier and parallel Arthurian excavation, was not taken up again.[30]

There is, however, a sequel to the story. In a speech given on 12 February 1424 at Siena, Richard Fleming referred in passing to Joseph of Arimathea's conversion of Britain and his subsequent burial at Glastonbury.[31] On 8 March he expanded on the theme;

Nam statim post passionem Christi Iosep ab Aramatia, nobilis decurio, qui Christum de cruce deposuit, cum XII sociis uineam domini de mane colendam Angliam uidelicet ingressus est et populum ad fidem conuertit, quibus rex XII idas terre in ea, que iam est diocesis Bathenensis, pro uictu assignauit. Ex quibus XII idis magnum illud et famosum Glastoniense monasterium fundatum est, in quo monasterio corpus illius sacrum requiescit et ad convincendas his nouissimis diebus emulorum malicias intra tres annos ultimo iam elapsos sanctum illius corpus quasi integrum in tumulo repertum erat et super illud lamina plumbea et in ea scriptum: Hic requiescit decurio ille Iosep ab Arimatia, qui Christum de cruce deponere meruit et cito post sui fidem et baptisma in Anglia introduxit.[32]

Fleming had obviously heard accounts of the excavation reported in the letter to Henry V. According to his sources, moreover, there had been further developments: in particular, a definite attribution based on a leaden plaque strongly reminiscent of the leaden cross found in Arthur's tomb.[33]

By the time of Basel, however, the English claim had become more modest—mirroring, one can only speculate, the official version now promulgated at Glastonbury itself—and Robert Fitzhugh appealed only to written authority rather than what might now be called archaeological fact.[34] On a more general level, too, there were problems: because of their Continental ambitions the English were unable to find a method of exploiting national (in the modern sense) claims within a conciliar framework.[35] By the time of Basel, moreover, the principle of organization into nations had been rejected and the disputes over Joseph's mission with the Spaniards were—as much else at the council—more or less academic.[36]

Strong incentives removed, the monks themselves had, it appears, retreated to their former position concerning Joseph's burial as articulated by John in his chronicle. Right to the end of the monastery's history the fulfilment of Melkin's prophecy remained something to be safely *in futuris*, something to dream about rather than experience, a local variant on the *rex quondam rexque futurus* theme:

> Igitur qui volet Regis Arturi reditum in Angliam expectare, expectet quoque ut impletum videat quod de Josepho promittit Melkin.[37]

In the edition which follows I have retained the orthography of the manuscript; abbreviations have been silently expanded. In the manuscript itself the large inital capitals in the first and second paragraph have not been filled in, although the appropriate letter has been signalled in each case. Capitalization, punctuation, and paragraph division are editorial and follow standard conventions.

Appendix

Vatican, Biblioteca Apostolica, Reg. lat. 623, fols. 45r–7v

(45r) Abbati Iohanni Chynnock successit dominus Nicholaus Frome, electus in abbatem in crastino Sancti Philiberti, abbatis anno domini millesimo cccc^{mo} xx^{mo} et regis Henrici quinti anno octauo.[38] Cui idem rex tempore ultimo parliamenti sui apud Westmonasterium per seipsum tenti precepit quod informaret eum in scriptis de fodiacione facta in cimiterio monasterii Glastonie tempore absencie sue in Normannia.[39] Quem idem abbas informauit in scriptis in hac forma.

Illustrissime princeps ac metuendissime domine, secundum antiquitates monasterii uestri Glastonie, que primo Ynswytryun et postia uallis Aualonie dicta est, Sanctus Philippus apostolus predicans in Francia misit in Britoniam duodecim ex suis discipulis, quibus et karissimum amicum suum Ioseph ab Armathia prefecit. Qui uenientes in Britanniam / (45v) anno ab incarnacione Domini lxiii, ab assumpcione Beate Marie xv, fidem Cristi fiducialiter predicabant.[40] Rex autem nomine Aruiragus in Britannia ad tunc regnabat, set nolens paternas tradiciones commutare in melius eorum predicacionem renuit. Quia tamen de longe uenerant quandam insulam, ab incolis Inswytryun nuncupatam, ad inhabitandum concessit. Postea alii duo reges, licet pagani, unicuique eorum unam porcionem terre concesserunt.[41] Vnde et duodecim hyde per eos hactenus nuncupantur.[42]

Item, serenissime princeps, anno domini supradicto Ioseph ab Armathia cum predictis discipulis in loco ubi nunc uetusta ecclesia Glastonie cita est capellam cum imagine Sancte Marie erexit muros de uirgis torquatis perficiens. Vnde uirgia ecclesia antiquitus nuncupatur.[43] Habent enim secum omnes ibidem ab antiquo sepulti uirgas in eorum sepulturis, unam scilicet secundum longitudinem corporis, aliam ex transuersa sub pedibus prout liquet clarius intuenti.

Item, excellentissime domine, quoad mortem et sepulturam Sancti Ioseph. Sic antiquitates Glastonie allegant de prophecia Melkany, qui fuit ante Merlinum. Insula Aualonis auida funere paganorum pre ceteris in orbe ad sepulturam eorum omnium sperulis prophecie uaticinantibus decorata et in futurum ornata erit altissimum laudantibus. Abbadare potens in Saphat / (46r) paganorum nobilissimus cum centum quatuor milibus dormicionem ibidem accepit. Inter quos Ioseph de marmore ab Armathia nomine cepit sompnum perpetuum et iacet in linia bifurcata iuxta meredianum angulum oratorii cratibus preparatis super potentem addorandam uirginem supradictis sperulatis locum habitantibus duodecim.[44]

Item, metuendissime domine, de sanctis Pagano et Diruuiano qui baptizarent Lucium regem missi ab Eleutherio Papa et quomodo uenerunt Glastonie. Sanctus Patricius Hibernie apostolus ac primus abbas Glastonie in carta sua ita scribit: "Ego Patricius, humilis seruunculus Dei, anno incarnacionis eiusdem ccccxxv in Hiberniam a sanctissimo Papa Celestino legatus, gracia Dei Hibernicos ad uiam ueritatis conuerti. Et cum eos in fide catholica solidassem, tandem ad Britanniam sum reuersus, ac, ut credo, duce Deo qui uita est et uia, incidi in insulam Inswytryun. In qua inueni sanctum locum ac uetustum a Deo electum et sanctificatum in honorem intemerate uirginis Dei genitricis Marie, ibique quosdam fratres rudimentis catholice fidei imbutos et pie conuersacionis qui successerunt discipulis sanctorum Pagani et Diruuiani, quorum nomina pro uite meritis ueraciter credo scripta in celis. Hii cum essent nobibilibus [sic] orti natalibus, nobilitatem suam fidei operibus ornare cupientes, heremiticam uitam ducere elegerunt. Et quoniam inueni eos humiles / (46v) ac quietos, elegi pocius cum illis 'abiectus esse magis quam in regalibus curiis habitare.'[45] Set et quia omnium nostrum erat 'cor unum et anima una,'[46] eligimus omnes simull habitare, comedere et bibere pariter et in eadem domo dormire. Sicque me[47] licet inuitum sibi pretulerunt. 'Non enim dignus eram soluere corrigias calciamentorum eorum.'[48] Et cum uitam monasticam ita ducerimus [sic] iuxta normulam probabilium patrum, ostenderunt mihi prefati fratres scripta sanctorum Phagani et Deruuiani, in quibus continebatur quod duodecim discipuli sanctorum Philippi et Iacobi ipsam uetustam ecclesiam construxerant in honore prelibate aduocatricis nostre."[49]

Item, illustrissime princeps, quoad exuuias repertas Glastonie sub anno gloriosissimi regiminis et regni uestri septimo. In cimitterio predicte uetuste ecclesie ex parte australi eiusdem tres fuerunt comperte ciste uetuste in terra ad profunditatem uel circiter xiiii pedum.[50] Inter quas cista que iacebat in parte boriali continebat in se ossa mortui et corupti hominis, ossibus secundum ordinem nature debite collocatis. Circa autem ossa capitis fuit in grana herbarum uirencium ac adorancium cum semine eorundem habundanciam.[51] In cista autem que iacebat in medio fuerunt ossa duodecim mortuorum contenta, que fuerunt ita ingeniose et ita subtiliter infra capsulam collocata, quod post extractionem nullus de gremio ibidem sciuit ea iterato in predicta / (47r) capsula collocare. In cista autem tercia, que iacebat ex parte australi, fuerunt ossa unius mortui et corupti in ordine nature iacencia et a medio predicti mortui uersus capud magna habundancia humoris qui sanguis recens inibi presentibus tam per tincturam quam per uisum apparebat; et omnes ciste predicte fuerunt reperte extra predictam capellam. Infra autem capellam sub angulo australi altaris eiusdem fuit alia cista inuenta cum ossibus corupti hominis; que quidem cista cum panno linio ad intra circumquaque fuit pre ceteris excelenticius adornata. Et quia prae omnibus aliis in flauore odoris et in eminencia loci prepollebat in alia magna cista inclusa est, quousque clarior noticia de ea haberi poterit in futurum.

Item, metudendissime domine, Galfridus de gestis Britonum in quarto libro decimo capitulo, ubi loquitur de rege Aruirago, sic ait: "In

tempore uenit Ioseph ab Armathia cum undecim discipulis suis in
insulam Aualonie siue Glastonie." Unde quidam uersificator de illorum
aduentu applaudens ait:

Intrat Aualoniam duodena caterua uirorum.
Flos Armathie Ioseph est primus eorum.
Iosephes ex Ioseph genitus patrem comitatur.
Hiis aliisque decem ius Glastonie propriatur.[52]

Post non multum uero temporis, post informacionem predictam,
rediit dominus / (47v) rex in Franciam et ibi moriebatur penultimo die
mensis Augusti in anno regni sui decimo. Set et ossa eius erant in
Angliam deportata et apud Westmonasterium tumulata.

Translation

Abbot John Chinnock was succeeded by Lord Nicholas Frome, who
was elected as abbot on the day after the Feast of St. Philibert Abbot
in 1420, the eighth year of the reign of King Henry V. At the last time
he held parliament at Westminster the king ordered Abbot Frome to
inform him in writing about the excavation made in the cemetery of
Glastonbury Abbey when he was absent in Normandy. The abbot
informed him in writing as follows.

Most illustrious and dreaded Lord: according to the antiquities of
your monastery of Glastonbury—which was first called Ynyswtryun and
afterwards the Vale of Avalon—the apostle St. Philip, who was preaching
in France, sent twelve of his apostles into Britain, and he appointed
his dearest friend Joseph of Arimathea as leader to them. They came
into Britain in A.D. 63, the fifteenth year after the Assumption of the
Blessed Mary, and courageously began to preach the Christian faith.
A king named Arviragus reigned in Britain at that time, who did not
wish to change the traditions of his forefathers for better ways, and
rejected their preaching. Nevertheless, because they had come from
afar, he gave them as a habitatation an island called by the natives
Inswytryun. Later two other kings, although pagans themselves,
granted to each of them a portion of land. In this way, the Twelve Hides
are named for them up to present times.

Also, most serene Prince, in the aforesaid year Joseph of Arimathea
built with his disciples a chapel containing a statue of St. Mary in the
place where the Old Church of Glastonbury is now situated, making
the walls of twisted wattle. Whence from ancient times it has been called
the wattled church. Indeed, all those buried there from on old have
with them twigs in their tombs, namely one according to the length
of the body, the other in a cross-direction under the feet, just as it is
most clearly apparent to the observer.

Also, most excellent Lord, as for the death and burial of St. Joseph: the *antiquitates* of Glastonbury allege thus concerning the prophecy of Melkin who was before Merlin.[53] The Isle of Avalon, eager for the burial of pagans, at the burial of them all will be decorated beyond others in the world with the soothsaying spheres of prophecy and in the future will be adorned with those who praise the Most High. Abbadare, powerful in Saphat, the most noble of pagans, took his sleep there with 104,000. Among these, Joseph "de marmore,"[54] named from Arimathea, took perpetual sleep and lies in "linea bifurcata"[55] next the southern corner of the oratory with prepared wattle above the powerful and venerable Virgin, the aforesaid twelve sperulated ones inhabiting the place.[56]

Also, most dreaded Lord, concerning St. Phagan and St. Deruvian, who were sent by Pope Eleutherius to baptize King Lucius, and how they came to Glastonbury. St. Patrick, the apostle of Ireland and first abbot of Glastonbury, wrote thus in his Charter: "I Patrick, a humble servant of God, sent by the most holy Pope Celestine to Ireland in A.D. 425, converted the Irish by the grace of God to the way of truth. And when I had made them firm in the Catholic faith, I returned at last to Britain and (as I believe) with God leading me, who is the Life and the Way, I happened upon the island of Inswytrun. There I found a holy and ancient place, chosen and sanctified by God in honor of the undefiled Virgin Mary, the mother of God, and there I encountered some brothers, instructed in the rudiments of the Catholic faith and pious in their lives, who had succeeded the disciples of St. Phagan and St. Deruvian, whose names I truly believe to be written in heaven for the merits of their lives. As they were noble of birth and wished to crown their nobility with works of faith, they decided to lead the eremetic life. Since I found them to be humble and tranquil, I preferred 'to be cast out with them than to live in the courts of kings.' And because we were all of 'one heart and one soul,' we elected to live together, sharing our food and drink and sleeping in the same house. And although I was unwilling, for 'I was not worthy to unloose the latchets of their shoes,' they set me at their head. After we had been leading the monastic life in this way according to the rule of the approved fathers, the aforesaid brothers showed me the writings of St. Phagan and St. Deruvian, which asserted that twelve disciples of St. Philip and St. James had built that old church in honor of our aforesaid advocate the Virgin."

Also, most illustrious prince, concerning the remains discovered at Glastonbury in the seventh year of your most glorious rule and power. In the south side of the cemetery of the Old Church were discovered three ancient coffins in the earth at a depth of about fourteen feet. The coffin which lay in the northern part contained the bones of a decayed and perished man, the bones arranged according to the manner of death. Near the bones of the head there was an abundance in grains of green and sweet-scented herbs with their seeds. In the coffin which lay in the middle there were contained the bones of twelve corpses, which were so ingeniously and so finely arranged within the casket that after their extraction, indeed, nobody there knew how to arrange them again in the aforesaid casket. In the third coffin which lay to the south were the bones of a decayed and perished individual lying in the manner of nature and away from the middle of the aforesaid corpse towards the head a great abundance of fluid, which appeared as fresh blood to those present in that place both by its color and substance. All these coffins were found outside the chapel. Within the chapel, however, under the southern corner of the altar another coffin was found with the bones of a decayed man. This coffin was adorned most excellently beyond the others, with linen cloth inside all over. And because it excelled all the others in delicacy of scent and eminence of place it was enclosed in another large coffin until clearer notice of it will be able to be had in the future.

Also, most feared Prince, in the fourth book, tenth chapter of *De gestis Britonum*—where he speaks about King Arviragus—Geoffrey says thus: "Joseph of Arimathea came at that time into the island of Avalon or Glastonbury with his eleven disciples." Concerning this a certain versifier writes in praise of their coming:

> The twelvefold band of men enters Avalon.
> Joseph, flower of Arimathea, is their chief.
> Josephes, Joseph's son, accompanies his father.
> The right to Glastonbury is held by these and ten others.

Not long after he received the aforesaid information the king returned to France and died there 30 August in the tenth year of his reign. But his bones were carried back into England and buried at Westminster.

Notes

Professor Michael Lapidge first pointed out to me that Vat. Reg. lat. 623 contained a copy of a letter by Nicholas Frome. Dr. Concetta Bianca, Dr. A. I. Doyle, Dr. Robert Dunning, Dr. Lesley Johnson, Professor Philip Rahtz, Professor Felicity Riddy, Professor A. G. Rigg, Dom Aelred Watkin, and Professor Charles Wood have read the typescript of this article and have made many valuable suggestions, for which I thank them.

1. "Pan-Brittonic Hagiography and the Arthurian Grail Cycle," *Traditio* 26 (1970), 29–61; "The Evolving Legend of St Joseph of Glastonbury," *Speculum* 46 (1971), 209–31; "The *Joseph of Arimathie*: English Hagiography in Transition," *Medievalia et Humanistica* 6 (1975), 91–101; "The Glastonbury Legends and the English Arthurian Grail Romances," *Neuphilologische Mitteilungen* 79 (1978), 359–66.

2. Lagorio, "The Evolving Legend of St Joseph," p. 212.

3. Ibid., p. 229.

4. On these lists, both put together in the fourteenth century, see *The Chronicle of Glastonbury Abbey: An Edition, Translation and Study of John of Glastonbury's "Cronica siue Antiquitates Glastoniensis Ecclesie,"* ed. J. P. Carley and trans. D. Townsend (Woodbridge, 1985), p. xlvi.

5. See J. P. Carley, "Melkin the Bard and Esoteric Tradition at Glastonbury Abbey," *The Downside Review* 99 (1981), 1–17, at 3. (For this and succeeding Latin passages—apart from the letter which I have edited and translated—English translations are for the most part readily available. I have not supplied my own translation because what needs to be emphasized are the resonances and echoes which are inevitably lost in translation.) It is worth observing that even in the fourteenth century the monks firmly maintained that there had been a burial at some undisclosed location in the region: see, for example, the verses from a local copy of Petrus Riga's *Aurora* transcribed by John of Glastonbury, which assert categorically that "Ioseph cum fiolis in basilica sepelitur, / A condiscipulis per scripturis bene scitur." (*The Chronicle of Glastonbury Abbey*, ed. Carley, p. 280.)

6. See *William Worcestre, Itineraries,* ed J. H. Harvey (Oxford, 1969), p. 296. In his description of St. Mary's Church Worcestre (*Itineraries*, p. 298) also observed that "Et ex opposito secunde fenestre ex parte meridionali sunt in cimiterio due cruces lapidee concauate vbi ossa Arthuri Regis recondebant vbi in linea bifurcata iacet Iosephus ab Arimathia."

7. Quoted in J. Ussher, *Britannicarum Ecclesiarum Antiquitates* (Dublin, 1639), p. 16. See also J. Armitage Robinson, *Two Glastonbury Legends: King Arthur and St Joseph of Arimathea* (Cambridge, 1926), pp. 46–49, 66–67. On possible reasons why Joseph's burial came to be associated with Hamden Hill or Montacute rather than Glastonbury itself, see J. P. Carley, "The Discovery of the Holy Cross of Waltham at Montacute, the Excavation of Arthur's Grave at Glastonbury Abbey, and Joseph of Arimathea's Burial," *Arthurian Literature* 4 (1985), 64–69.

8. Quoted by A. Watkin, "Last Glimpses of Glastonbury," *The Downside Review* 67 (1949), 76–86, at 84 n. 1. See also Carley, "The Discovery of the Holy Cross of Waltham," p. 68.

9. This manuscript survives as Oxford, Bodleian Library, MS Lat. hist.a.2 and consists of six large sheets fastened on swinging wooden frames. For a description of the contents, see J. A. Bennett, "A Glastonbury Relic," *Proceedings*

of the Somersetshire Archaeological and Natural History Society 34.2 (1888), 117–22; also Robinson, *Two Glastonbury Legends*, pp. 41–42; *The Chronicle of Glastonbury Abbey*, ed. Carley, p. xxii. As Antonia Gransden has pointed out—*Historical Writing in England II* (Ithaca, N.Y., 1982), p. 495—the function of this sort of *tabula* would obviously have been "to increase the church's prestige and perhaps encourage the visitors to give more generously."

10. The text describing the chapel was printed in a somewhat inaccurate version by Bennett, "A Glastonbury Relic," p. 120. My own transcription runs as follows: Scientes igitur sancti patres nostri dignitatem et sanctitatem huius sancti cimiterii quandam capellam in eius medio construxerunt quam in honore Sancti Michaelis et sanctorum inibi requiescentium dedicari fecerunt, sub cuius altare ossa mortuorum ac sanctorum reliquias licet incognitas in magna multitudine cumulauerunt, et missam de cimiterio in ea cotidie celebrari constituerunt. Capella siquidem illa anno domini mccclxxxii° pre uetustate pene consumpta per preceptum domini Iohannis Chinnock abbatis in predictorum sanctorum honore de nouo est reparata, uidelicet in honore Sancti Michaelis animarum principis et in honore sanctorum in predictis cimiterio et capella requiescentium, quorum primus fuit Ioseph ab Arimathia ille nobilis decurio qui et dominum sepeliuit. Ob cuius memoriam predictus abbas fieri fecit in eadem capella tres ymagines, quomodo Ioseph cum adiutorio Sancti Nichodemi dominum de cruce deposuit atque sepeliuit, et secundum illud quod ex tradicione patrum didicimus facta est ymago media secundum longitudinem stature Corporis Christi, Qui det omnibus hic et ubique in Christo quiescentibus et omnibus pro eis orantibus uitam et requiem sempiternam. Amen.

11. Edward III's Arthurian enthusiasm—expressing itself in 1344 in a vow to reestablish the Round Table with 300 knights—may have taken its genesis in his visit to Glastonbury in 1331. In 1345 there was a royal writ issued to John Blome to search for Joseph's body at Glastonbury: "Supplicauit nobis Johannes Blome de London, ut cum sibi (sicut asserit) diuinitus sit injunctum, ut uenerandum corpus decurionis nobilis Josephi ab Arimathia, quod infra septa monasterii Glastoniensis in Christo quiescit humatum, et est ad honorem et multorum aedificationem his temporibus reuelandum, quaerat donec inueniat diligenter. Et quia in quibusdam antiquis scripturis dicitur contineri corpus ejus ibidem fuisse sepultum. Nos si sit ita desiderantes monumentum ejus, et uenerandas ipsius reliquias, qui redemptori nostro morienti tantum exhibebat pietatis et humanitatis obsequium, corpus ejus de cruce deponendo, et illud in monumento suo nouo ponendo, deuotis honoribus praeuenire; et sperantes nobis et toti regno nostro ex reuelatione praedicta gratiam uberiorem prouenire: concessimus et licentiam dedimus (quantum in nobis est) eidem Johanni quod ipse infra praecinctum dicti Monasterii fodere, et illas pretiosas reliquias juxta injunctionem et reuelationem sibi factam quaerere ualeat in locis ubi melius uiderit expedire: dum tamen absque damno dilectorum nobis in Christo, Abbatis et Conuentus dicti Monasterii, et ruina Ecclesiae et domorum suarum ibidem id fieri ualeat; et quod ad id ipsorum Abbatis et Conuentus licentiam habeat et assensum." (Quoted in Ussher, *Britannicarum Ecclesiarum Antiquitates*, pp.

15-16.) The wording suggests that Blome had seen Melkin's prophecy—presumably in a copy of John's *Cronica*—and that the prophecy was the ancient writing to which he was referring and from which he gathered his own inspiration. Around 1350 in his *Historia de mirabilibus gestis Edwardi III* Robert of Avesbury, himself a registrar in the archbishop's court, took up this same theme and traced Arthur's ancestry back to Joseph of Arimathea. His source may also have been John of Glastonbury whose chronicle—as C. T. Wood (in his review of my edition of John of Glastonbury [*Speculum* 62 (1987), 426-30 at 428]) has observed—he would have found instructive: "If Glastonbury wanted to prove its independence of Bath, and this from time immemorial, Joseph as founder was certainly to provide it with unmatchable precedence. Moreover, then to link him genealogically to that king who continued to sleep in front of the abbey's high altar was surely to create a case of such power that, once it reached the archbishop's court, no registrar was apt to forget it." See also Wood, "Fraud and its Consequences: Savaric of Bath and the Reform of Glastonbury," in *The Archaeology and History of Glastonbury Abbey*, ed. L. Abrams and J. P. Carley (Woodbridge, 1991), pp. 273-83, at p. 283.

12. See Lagorio, "The Evolving Legend of St Joseph," p. 220. She took this information, I assume, from Robinson, *Two Glastonbury Legends*, p. 40, whose source I have been unable to trace: no reference to Chinnock's assertion of the Joseph story at a national level appears, for example, in W. A. Pantin's *Documents Illustrating the Activities of the General and Provincial Chapters of the English Black Monks 1214-1540*, 3 vols. (London, 1931-37).

13. On this topic, see J. P. Genet, "English Nationalism: Thomas Polton at the Council of Constance," *Nottingham Medieval Studies* 28 (1984), 60-78. In the context of the Council of Constance, it must be remembered that Henry V's great victory at Agincourt occurred in 1415, and in 1417 he led his second expedition into Normandy, which culminated in the capitulation of Rouen in 1419 and the signing of the Treaty of Troyes.

14. Genet ("English Nationalism," pp. 64-65) observed, however, that the French were never fully supportive of the use of nationes at a conciliar level, fearing that it could lead to further divisions in the church.

15. See C. M. D. Crowder, *Unity, Heresy and Reform, 1378-1460: The Conciliar Response to the Great Schism* (London, 1977), pp. 24-27.

16. Polton held a number of Somerset livings and as early as 1392-93 he had been commissary general of the bishop of Bath and Wells: see A. B. Emden, *A Biographical Register of the University of Oxford to A.D. 1500*, 3 vols. (Oxford, 1957-59), 3:1494-95. He would, therefore, have been in a good position to have first-hand knowledge of the Glastonbury legends as they had crystallized in Chinnock's abbacy. See also Wood, "Fraud and its Consequences," p. 273; Wood suggested that there was a link between Chinnock's headship of the English delegation at Constance and the Joseph story. Joseph's name had already been brought into conciliar discussions by Robert Hallam at the Council of Pisa in 1409—on which see Ussher, *Britannicarum Ecclesiarum Antiquitates*, p. 13—but at that time the matter was less crucial; the stakes were not nearly so high.

17. Quoted in Ussher, *Britannicarum Ecclesiarum Antiquitates*, p. 13. For an English translation of the various documents making up the dispute between the French and English over the nation question, see Crowder, *Unity, Heresy and Reform*, pp. 110–26. Genet, "English Nationalism," pp. 62–63, provides a discussion of manuscripts and early editions of the *Acta Concilii Constanciensis* in which the debate occurs.

18. Although the various inconsistencies were not mentioned by the French delegation at Constance, they were later taken up by the Spanish at the Council of Basel in 1434, where Alonso de Cartagena, dean of Compostella and of Segovia, pointed out, *inter alia*, that according to the Golden Legend Titus did not free Joseph from his imprisonment until A.D. 70, well after his supposed conversion of Britain. On this council, to which Nicholas Frome came as part of the second English delegation, see A. N. E. D. Schofield, "England and the Council of Basel," *Annuarium Historiae Conciliorum* 5 (1973), 1–117.

19. Polton "had to claim the leadership of a *natio generalis* with *natio particularis* material, and he was compelled to hide this inadequacy behind a smoke screen, the identification of *Anglia* with *Britannia*." (Genet, "English Nationalism," p. 75.)

20. For a description see A. Poncelet, *Catalogus Codicum Hagiographicorum Latinorum Bibliothecae Vaticanae* (Brussels, 1910), pp. 391–92. It is one of the manuscripts which belonged to Queen Christina of Sweden: see J. Bignami-Odier, *Les manuscrits de la Reine de Suède au Vatican. Réédition du catalogue de Montfaucon et cotes actuelles*, Studi e testi 238 (Vatican City, 1964), p. 74, no. 1305. I am grateful to Dr. Concetta Bianca for providing me with further details concerning the manuscript as well as a xerox of pertinent sections. Dr. A. I. Doyle confirmed my opinions about the date of the hand. I have not, however, been able to discover the early history of the manuscript or to work out when the English materials joined the other sections.

21. Apart from fols. 57r–6lv (*Passio S. Thomae Martiris* [*Bibliotheca Hagiographica Latina . . . Nouum Supplementum*, ed. H. Fros (Brussels, 1986), no. 8206] written in an English or French hand, s.xii/xiii), and fols. 151–60 (written in an Italian hand dated 1437), the other booklets all appear to be in French hands (s.xiv/xv).

22. *Bibliotheca Hagiographica Latina*, no. 8215b.

23. Lagorio, "The Evolving Legend of St Joseph," pp. 221–23, postulated that the conversion date put forward at Pisa and Constance, although not precisely specified, was understood to be much earlier than A.D. 63 in order to offset the French assertions concerning St. Mary Magdalene, Martha, and Lazarus, and St. Denis in particular. Certainly, Polton maintained that Joseph came to England immediately ("statim") after the Passion.

24. On Henry as orchestrator of the strategies of the English delegates at Constance, see Crowder, *Unity, Heresy and Reform*, p. 26. He also received detailed reports of proceedings.

25. There are only two small details which vary from the standard accounts. First, the letter alludes to the fact that all those buried in the Old Church in ancient times had "uirgas in eorum sepulturis, unam scilicet secundum longitudinem corporis, aliam ex transuersa sub pedibus prout liquet clarius intuenti." Concerning this point it should be observed that a group of eighteen coffins were discovered in 1826 in the Lady Chapel; to the right side of each skeleton was a rod of thorn or hazel, of the same length as the coffin. See R. Willis, *The Architectural History of Glastonbury Abbey* (Cambridge, 1866), pp. 61, 72. Philip Rahtz will discuss this topic in his forthcoming book on Glastonbury Abbey, of which he has been kind enough to show me a preliminary draft. As he has noted: "Such rods or wands have been found in several sites in Britain and Scandinavia with medieval ecclesiastics but their function or symbolism is unknown." In a private communication (24.7.91) he has observed that similar wands discovered in Bordesley Abbey cemetery "are very slender, and might be 'rods of office,' but in Scandinavia they are found in medieval contexts (Lund) in patterns, almost as if they might be runes." Secondly, the last line in this version of Melkin's prophecy gives twelve rather than thirteen "sperulatis habitantibus." This suggests that Frome understood Joseph to be the thirteenth in the group, to be viewed separately from the others. By changing the number, Frome prepared the way for twelve to be found in one coffin and Joseph to occupy an altogether different location. The only complication in this scenario, as Wood has observed, comes in the citation of pseudo-Geoffrey at the end of the letter, where Joseph is quite clearly counted among the twelve. Might Frome simply not have noticed the disparity when he cited these verses? In any case, Polton—like Fleming later at Siena, referred to Joseph "cum XII sociis."

26. According to the account by Giraldus Cambrensis in *De Principis Instructione* (c. 1193) Arthur's tomb was also found at a great depth, at least sixteen feet in the earth. This was to protect it—so Giraldus claimed—from desecration at the hands of the pagan Saxons. In this part of the cemetery, moveover, the level of the ground had been significantly raised during Dunstan's abbacy.

27. See *The Chronicle of Glastonbury Abbey*, ed. Carley, p. 16. In an addendum (fol. 13v) to the unpublished relic list contained in B.L. MS Cotton Titus D. VII there is a reference to another chest containing unidentified relics of various saints: "Memorandum quod cum in ecclesia beate Marie ab antiquis temporibus in quadam cista ueteri fuerint multa ossa sanctorum in tredecim sacellis pre uetustate pene consumptis locata, ad honorem Dei et sanctorum quorum reliquie esse creduntur, eadem ossa eisdem distinctionibus in pannis nouis lineis nouis duplicatis de nouo inclusa fuerunt sexto kalendis Octobris anno domini millesimo ducentesimo quinquagesimo. Incognitum tamen est tamen est [sic] quorum reliquie sint eo quod nulle scripture ibidem reperirentur."

28. At first glance it would seem that the reference is to the Chapel of St. Mary, but it should be remembered that according to the *Magna Tabula* there was also a great collection of ancient bones—including those of Joseph himself—

in the cemetery and under the altar of the refurbished Chapel of St. Michael and St. Joseph. See above, note 10.

29. The model here could well have been the visit made by Edward I in 1278, at which time Arthur was reburied before the High Altar: "Ubi [in sepulcrum incliti regis Arthuri] in duabus cistis ymaginibus et armis ipsorum depictis ossa dicti regis mire grossitudinis et Guennare regine mire pulcritudinis seperatim inuenit. Crastino uero die. . .dominus rex ossa regis et domina regina ossa regine palliis preciosis inuoluta in suis cistis recludentes et suis sigillis signantes preceperunt idem sepulcrum ante maius altare celeriter collocari, retentis tamen exterius capitibus et genis utriusque propter populi deuocionem, apposita interius scriptura huiusmodi." (*The Chronicle of Glastonbury Abbey*, ed. Carley, p. 244.)

30. Wood, "Fraud and its Consequences," p. 282, speculated on reasons for this: "It would appear, though, that this modesty [in not unearthing Joseph's bones and in not claiming possession of the Holy Grail] was not just a product of the normal forger's caution, a fear of claiming things so outrageous that the whole fabricated structure becomes endangered. Rather, given Joseph's role in the crucifixion, and further given the Holy Grail's somewhat heterodox associations, it seems likely that the monks' failures here may well have arisen from religious scruples, from a recognition that there were some frauds that could endanger the faith."

31. See W. Brandmüller, *Das Konzil von Pavia-Siena 1423–1424*, 2 vols. (Münster, 1968–74), 2:293.

32. See ibid., 2:412–13. In several cases I have used variants cited by Brandmüller to give a more accurate reading.

33. In a miscellany compiled by a Glastonbury monk around 1450 there is, moreover, an otherwise unattested verse epitaph to Joseph:

> Hic iacet < excultus > Joseph pater ille sepultus,
> Qui Cristum sciuit ac defunctum sepeliuit;
> Hanc dedit iste domum matri Cristi fabricari,
> Post Eue pomum qua posset homo reparari;
> Pro nobis igitur oret noster pater iste
> Per quem dirigitur tibi laus et honor, pie Criste.

See A. G. Rigg, *A Glastonbury Miscellany of the Fifteenth Century* (Oxford, 1968), p. 117. J. Withrington, "The Arthurian Epitaph in Malory's 'Morte Darthur'," *Arthurian Literature* 7 (1987), 103–44, at 134–36, noted the formal similarities to Arthur's epitaph; he suggested that "it may well be that the Arthurian example served as a model for an epitaph on Joseph of Arimathea, possibly with a view to the future 'recovery' of his body, an event which would enhance the spiritual and political reputation of an ecclesiastical establishment already celebrated as the final resting-place of a hero renowned in chronicle and romance alike."

34. "Certum est in Anglia reperiri libris antiquissimis et archivis, precipue in archivis abbacie notabilis Glasconie diocesis Bathonensis, quod Ioseph ab Arimathia etc." See A. Zellfelder, *England und das Basler Konzil, Mit einem Urkundenanhang* (Berlin, 1913), p. 285.

35. On this topic see Genet, "English Nationalism," pp. 76–77. F. Riddy, "Glastonbury, Joseph of Arimathea and the Grail in John Hardyng's Chronicle," in *The Archaeology and History of Glastonbury Abbey*, ed. Abrams and Carley, pp. 317–31, at 329–30, pointed out that the Joseph story was coming to be used in a somewhat different way in England itself by the mid-fifteenth century: "Hardyng's nationalism is, by comparison [with earlier conciliar forms], secular and chivalric. . . . It looks very much as if Hardyng felt the need to defend the red cross of England against the charge that it had been only recently invented. And so, beyond George, he descries Joseph who validates the antiquity and Englishness of George's red-cross arms." See also L. M. Matheson, "The Arthurian Stories of Lambeth Palace Library MS 84," *Arthurian Literature* 5 (1985), 70–91, at 73–75.

36. See Crowder, *Unity, Heresy and Reform*, pp. 29–30. By this point too (as Crowder observed, p. 35) the conciliar period was more or less over: "Its closing stages, roughly contemporary with the council of Basle, had exhausted interest in their proceedings." Much later, in the seventeenth century, Sir Robert Cotton asserted the precedence of the ambassador of England (in France) over the envoy of Spain based in part on the evidence of Joseph's mission to England. See Kevin Sharpe, *Sir Robert Cotton 1586–1631: History and Politics in Early Modern England* (Oxford, 1979), p. 225.

37. The "sagacious, if ironic comment" of the editors of the *Acta Sanctorum*: quoted by Lagorio, "The Evolving Legend of St Joseph," p. 231.

Notes to Appendix

38. John Chinnock was abbot from 1375–1420, Nicholas Frome from 1420–56: see Ian Keil, "Profiles of Some Abbots of Glastonbury," *The Downside Review* 81 (1963), 355–70, at 356–67. The feast of St. Philibert is August 20.

39. Parliament opened at Westminster on 2 May 1421, in Henry V's presence: see Margaret Wade Labarge, *Henry V: the Cautious Conqueror* (London, 1975), p. 168.

40. *Sanctus. . . predicabant*: Taken from William of Malmesbury's *De Antiquitate*: see *The Early History of Glastonbury: An Edition, Translation and Study of William of Malmesbury's "De Antiquitate Glastonie Ecclesie,"* ed. John Scott (Woodbridge, 1981), p. 44.

41. *Rex. . . concesserunt*: Taken from John of Glastonbury: see *The Chronicle of Glastonbury Abbey*, ed. Carley, p. 50.

42. On the Twelve Hides see *The Chronicle of Glastonbury Abbey*, ed. Carley, p. 274, n. 17, and the references cited therein. See also *The Early History*, ed. Scott, p. 44.

43. *anno. . . nuncupatur*: See *The Early History*, ed. Scott, p. 44.

44. On Melkin's prophecy, see *The Chronicle of Glastonbury Abbey*, ed. Carley p. 54. In other surviving versions of the prophecy there are *tredecim* rather than *duodecim habitantibus*.

45. Ps. 83.11.

46. Act. 4.32.

47. me *superscript*.

48. Mk. 1.7.

49. On St. Patrick's charter see *The Early History of Glastonbury*, ed. Scott, pp. 54–58; *The Chronicle of Glastonbury Abbey*, ed. Carley, pp. 60–64. In John's text an unnecessary *repperi* is inserted after *ibique*, whereas it does not occur either in William or in Frome's letter.

50. I have transcribed $x + 4$ minims as *xiiii* rather than as *xuii*, as this would almost certainly have been the intention by this period. (I owe Dr. Doyle thanks for his judgment on this question.)

51. Presumably an error for *habundancia*.

52. *Galfridus. . . propriatur*: On the presumed Glastonbury copy of Geoffrey containing these interpolated verses to Joseph see *The Chronicle of Glastonbury Abbey*, ed. Carley, p. 50, and cited references.

53. This prophecy, as Robinson long since pointed out, more or less defies translation. For a discussion of the range of possibilities for individual phrases, see Carley, "Melkin the Bard."

54. Robinson, *Two Glastonbury Legends*, p. 61, suggests that the reference is to a marble tomb, but *marmor* could also be translated as "the surface of the sea," or "a lake."

55. For possible meanings of this phrase see Carley, "Melkin the Bard," pp. 8–9. Robert Willis's translation as a linen shirt divided by two flaps (see Robinson, p. 61) seems to relate most directly to the excavation account described in Frome's letter.

56. In an unpublished note, Aelred Watkin suggests that this might contain some sort of reference to a whorl pattern of Celtic crosses in the cemetery. It seems to me that there is an echo in the reference above to the pattern of "uirgas" contained in the ancient burial sites.

The Speaking Knight:
Sir Gawain and Other Animals

 *Felicity Riddy*

Sir Gawain and the Green Knight seems to lie at a cultural crossroads. Intellectual but not bookish, it juggles clerical and courtly values, as many critics have pointed out. My purpose in this essay[1] is to place the poem specifically at the interface between the court and the university, as the product of an aristocratic rhetorical culture that bears the impress of the naturalism bequeathed by thirteenth-century science.[2]

I

Consider the description of the moment at which Gawain cuts off the Green Knight's head. Gripping the Green Knight's huge axe, Gawain raises it and

> Let hit doun lyꜫtly lyꜫt on þe naked,
> Þat þe scharp of þe schalk schyndered þe bones,
> And schrank þurꜫ þe schyire grece, and schade hit in twynne,
> Þat þe bit of þe broun stel bot on þe grounde[3] (ll. 423–26)

Magical the Green Knight may be, but insubstantial he is not: he is compounded, as Gawain is, of bones and flesh. When he returns the blow a year later, the same language is used to create that appalling sense of flesh being sliced by steel:

> Þe scharp schrank to þe flesche þurꜫ þe schyre grece,
> Þat þe schene blod ouer his schulderes schot to þe erþe. (ll. 2313–14)

The person in *Sir Gawain and the Green Knight* is insistently material. Arthur, Gawain, the Green Knight, the lady of the castle and Morgan la Fay are all embodied; they are constituted out of "bones," "blode," "flesch," "grece," "hyde," "felle," "fax," "here."[4] They define themselves, and are defined, as bodies. When Gawain says to his uncle Arthur, "No bounté bot your blod I in my bodé knowe" (l. 357), the language in which he expresses their relationship is literally physical: Arthur's blood courses through his body. The headless Green Knight on his horse is seen as sheer flesh: "He brayed his bulk aboute, / Þat vgly bodi þat bledde" (ll. 440-01), and likewise of Morgan la Fay we are told: "Hir body watz schort and þik / Hir buttokez balȝ and brode" (ll. 966-67). In this material world, honor and shame are not mere abstractions: shame is registered in the face, physically, as a furious blushing. Arthur's humiliation at the Green Knight's mockery of his court is described thus: "Þe blod schot for scham into his schyre face / and lere" (ll. 317-18). Gawain's shame at the end of the poem is similar: "Alle þe blode of his brest blende in his face, /Þat al he schrank for schome þat þe schalk talked" (ll. 2371-2)

Through their physical selves the humans are connected to the palpably and luxuriantly material world of courtly display, to the food, clothing, and armor on which the poet constantly dilates. But their bodies also link them with the natural world which plays so large a part in this poem. In the third fitt Sir Bertilak's animal quarry is created in a language that overlaps with that used for the human body. The deer that Sir Bertilak kills is among "þe grattest of gres" (l. 1326); its flesh, like Sir Bertilak's own and like Gawain's, is "schyree" (l. 1378).[5] It has a "brest" like Bertilak, the lady of the castle and Gawain;[6] like Gawain and Bertilak, it has "schulderes," "hede," and "hals[e]";[7] it shares "thyghes" with Gawain (ll. 579, 1349). The mighty "sides"— flanks—of the deer and the boar (ll. 1356, 1632) connect with the "sides" of the Green Knight and of the lady of the castle (ll. 152, 1830). After the deer has been killed, the huntsmen feed the "felle of þe fayre best" (l. 1359) to the hounds and take the "flesche" (l. 1363) home. This action harks back to Gawain's first sight of the lady the previous evening as "þe fayrest in felle, of flesche and of lyre" (l. 943), linking her with the animal world through that shared vocabulary.

By the fourteenth century a range of scientific discourses—medical, zoological, physical, psychological—connected humans with animals. Aristotle's scientific writings formed the basis of the natural philosophy studied in university arts faculties.[8] Many *quaestiones naturales* survive: these are short problems relating to physical matters which draw on Aristotelian science, on Pliny's *Natural History*, on the encyclopaedic tradition, and on medicine. One early collection of Salernitan "questions," so called because they originated in the medical school at Salerno, were assembled by an English master in an arts faculty around 1200.[9] These questions explore such problems as "Why, when other animals cease to have coitus after conception, do women have intercourse more pleasurably?"; "Why do brute beasts not menstruate?"; "Why is sexual intercourse so pleasurable?"; "Since a woman is humid and cold how does it come about that she is more lustful than a man?"[10] There is an exhilirating curiosity about physical phenomena in all this, as well as a matter-of-fact acceptance of the body's physicality. The "zodiacal man" illustrations to astrological writings, which bring together different but related branches of natural science—astronomy, zoology, and medicine—can be seen as pictorial representations of this attitude to human corporeality. In *Sir Gawain and the Green Knight* the narrative rests on, and never moves very far away from, the view that humans are a species of animal.

One effect, though, of transferring this assumption from academic genres into a romance plot constructed out of a Beheading Game and an Exchange of Winnings is to make the body's materiality vulnerable and poignant, rather than a source of exuberant speculation. *Sir Gawain and the Green Knight* is a poem over which death hangs, not abstracted or generalized, but physical and specific: a prospect of steel slicing through your neck. The killing of the animals in the hunts—disembowelled, skinned, cut up—is a reminder of what it is to be flesh. Gawain adorns his body before leaving Bertilak's castle in the "wlonkest wedes" (l. 2025), including his "cote" (l. 2026) which is "fayre furred withinne wyth fayre pelures" (l. 2029), the skins of other animals. Nevertheless he remains no less flesh—vulnerable to hunger, pain, and cold—than the fox whose "cote" (l. 1921) has been stripped off him at the kill in the third fitt. Gawain's flesh anchors him to time as well as to death; the poem is tied in its opening and closing stanzas into Geoffrey of Monmouth's vision of Arthurian history, so that before and after this story stretches the long flux of the past. And the year's gap between Gawain's giving and receiving the blow, which occurs in other versions of the Beheading Game story, is here elaborated into an account of the mutable seasons which seem to circle but in fact move relentlessly forward, taking Gawain with them towards death:

Þenne al rypez and rotez þat ros vpon fyrst,
And þus ȝirnez þe ȝere in ȝisterdayez mony (ll. 528–29)

The pressure of the body's materiality is felt not only in relation to time and death but also in relation to sex. In the Exchange of

Winnings plot the burden the flesh places on Gawain is no longer that of being cold and lost as he was on the journey from Arthur's court to Bertilak's castle; now the burden is that of being sexual. Gawain is no Galahad, an abstraction untouched by sexual feeling; if he is like any of the knights on the Grail quest it is Perceval, who is plagued by sexual fantasies. That Gawain is sexual is made clear in the way in which he responds to the two women he meets at Bertilak's castle. They are both, as I have already pointed out, represented as bodies: one displaying her "brest and hir bryȝt þrote" (l. 955), while the other has "rugh ronkled chekez" (l. 953), bleared features and those huge buttocks. The narrator's comment that the younger is the "More lykkerwys on to lyk" (l. 968, where "lyk" means "taste") gives us a momentary glimpse of male heterosexual desire, of the directly physical response that Gawain seeks to efface and transcend with his courtesy. Courteous talk provides Gawain with a means of contending with the body's sexuality. It also provides him with a means of defining himself as not merely animal, inescapably animal though he also may be. The poem's position at the interface between the university and the court means that it can explore both the scientific-naturalistic assumption that people are animals, and the aristocratic assumption that some people are more animal than others.

II

Courtly speech, which plays such a striking part in this poem, is used to show how humans can separate themselves from beasts. Gawain is specifically identified as a talker. We see this demonstrated very early in the poem, in the eloquence with which he puts himself forward in Arthur's place in the Beheading Game. That Gawain is a talker is also directly stated early in the second fitt, when Gawain arms himself with the shield and cote-armor that bear his symbol, the pentangle:

> Forþy þe pentangel nwe
> He ber in schelde and cote,
> As tulk of tale most trwe
> And gentylest knyȝt of lote.[11] (ll. 636–39)

Here he is above all a speaking knight; it is his handling of language that makes the pentangle—the endless knot in which the material and the abstract are inextricably enmeshed—particularly his symbol. Not only is Gawain presented as a talker, but a crucial part of the poem's action—the lady's attempt to seduce him—proceeds entirely through conversation. The structure of the third fitt clearly invites the reader to compare the violent physical activity and movement of the hunting scenes with the static and enclosed seduction scenes in which the action proceeds entirely through conversation. The fact that the hunting passages are structurally secondary suggests that, in the contrast between language and action, the balance is weighted in favor of language. The effect is to assert the primary importance of speech as a social activity, and as a means of marking humans off from the beasts with which they otherwise share so much.

Ancient and medieval zoology, for all that it treated humans as a species of animal, knew that speech marked a boundary between them. Pliny, writing about animal and human physiognomy, remarks that "The voice is the source. . . before all things of the power of expressing the thoughts that has made us different from the beasts."[12] This idea, that speech is a defining human activity, is not only a scientific, but a rhetorical commonplace. There is a clear statement of it in the first book of Cicero's *De inventione,* one of the two early works by him which were widely known throughout the medieval period; academic commentaries on the *De inventione* were lectured on in arts faculties in the schools and universities.[13] Cicero describes the origins of the social contract thus:

> For there was a time when men wandered at large in the fields like animals and lived on wild fare. . . . At this juncture a man— great and wise I am sure—became aware of the power latent in man and the wide field offered by his mind for great achievements if one could develop this power and improve it by instruction. Men were scattered in the fields and hidden in sylvan retreats when he assembled and gathered them in accordance with a plan. . . and through reason and eloquence . . . he transformed them from wild savages into a kind and gentle folk. To me, at least, it does not seem possible that a mute and voiceless wisdom could have turned men suddenly from their habits and introduced them to different patterns of life.[14]

Going on to argue the value of rhetoric to the state, he remarks that "Furthermore, I think that man, although lower and weaker than the animals in many respects, excels them most by having the power of speech." Cicero's is of course a self-regarding fantasy of the social contract which gives pride of place in a masculine order to rhetoricians and statesmen like himself. Albert the Great presents a version of the Ciceronian myth in his discussion of the nature of man in book 22 of his *De animalibus:*

Man is the civilized animal *par excellence*, because he communicates with his fellows, he distributes the chores of living according to individual talents, he lives together usually in harmony. . .and in general his life is ordered and perfected by the urbanities of civilized behaviour.[15]

Cicero did not for one moment have in mind an eloquence practised in the bedroom. The shift from public language to private, the contraction of society to two people of good breeding, one male and one female, whose discourse is of love, is the product of medieval aristocratic culture and its own self-regarding fantasies, the influence of which seems to be felt in Albert the Great's talk of the "urbanities of civilized behavior." Nevertheless, aristocratic culture also saw the use of language as a means of separating humans from beasts.

This notion is made explicit in Andreas Capellanus' *De amore*, a twelfth-century text which, like *Sir Gawain and the Green Knight*, mediates clerical and courtly cultures and places speech at a premium.[16] Book I is presented, whether ironically or not, as an art of conversation, in some sense comparable to the new contemporary *artes poetriae*, *artes dictandi*, and *artes praedicandi*. The *De amore* may be only a playful parallel to these academic rhetorical treatises, but nevertheless the form the game takes is one that reveals the value placed on eloquence, not only in the schools but in the courtly milieu as well. At the beginning of the book Andreas suggests that there are three main ways in which love may be acquired: "a handsome appearance, honesty of character, fluent and eloquent speech."[17] Later in the same chapter he goes on to say:

Eloquence of speech frequently impels the hearts of indifferent persons to love. The adorned language of a lover usually unleashes love's darts; it creates a good impression about the speaker's moral worth.[18]

This seems particularly revealing: the ability to talk well is felt in itself to be an index of moral and social refinement. The passage in which Andreas deals with the love of peasants, often quoted, is relevant here:

I briefly append. . .a note about the love of peasants. I maintain that farmers can scarcely ever be found serving in Love's court. They are impelled to acts of love in the natural way like a horse or a mule, just as nature's pressure directs them.[19]

Peasants go to it like animals; men of status talk about love. The ability to defer consummation, to substitute eloquence for intercourse, is what marks men of status off from peasants and beasts. In the discussion between the man and woman of the higher nobility as to whether one should choose the upper half of the beloved's body or the lower, one argument against the lower half rests on the view that in its pleasures "we are in no sense distinguished from the brute animals."[20] All this means that the line which in Cicero separated animals from humans has become in aristocratic culture a class boundary, with those who can speak in a courtly style on one side and those who cannot, whether peasant or animal, on the other. The confrontation in Chrétien de Troyes' *Yvain* between Calogrenant and the giant herdsman, the *vilain* with the elephant's ears, screech-owl's eyes, cat's nose, boar's teeth, and so on, is the classic emblem of this new divide.[21]

The equation between social status and the ability to talk in sexual contexts is true even of women, though the eloquence of the courtly lady has a slightly different function from that of the courtly man. Hers is not an autonomous expression of desire but evidence of her nobility; it means that she is a prize worth pursuing.

> Your kind and gentle reply abundantly reveals your moral worth, for you sought to indulge your nature and to fit your words to your noble birth. Nothing can be more conducive to the praise of a noblewoman than her employment of gentle language when she speaks.[22]

The notion that the way in which the lady talks reveals her *moral* worth as well as her social standing is part of that aristocratic value system which is embedded in a language that equates class with virtue. In the fourteenth century words like "noble," "gentil," "fre," "cortays," all of which are used in *Sir Gawain and the Green Knight*, are class terms.[23] According to the myth of aristocracy, it is the nobleman or noblewoman who is "noble"; the gentleman or gentlewoman who is "gentil"; the frequenter of courts who is "cortays"; the free man or woman who is "fre"; which in *Sir Gawain and the Green Knight* means "noble," "courtly," "good"; the unfree man or woman, the peasant, is a "villein" and therefore villainous, lacking in the moral qualities that are proper to the person of status. When Sir Bertilak welcomes Gawain to his court he is described as "fre of hys speche" (l. 847), that is, he talks courteously, and thus

> wel hym semed, for soþe, as þe segge þu3t,
> To lede a lortschyp in lee of leudez ful gode. (ll. 848–49)[24]

Underlying this are the same assumptions that led Andreas Capellanus to point out that "nothing more clearly contradicts noble birth and noble blood than harsh and discourteous utterance."[25]

III

In a context in which the proper use of language is seen as an aspect of moral as well as of social refinement—because these two things are inseparable—it is possible for the *Gawain*-poet to represent the improper use of language not only as a breach of manners but as a kind of immorality. Gawain's arrival at Bertilak's castle causes a flurry of excitement in the household, in a passage that is often quoted:

> Now schal we semlych se sleȝtez of þewes
> And þe teccheles termes of talkyng noble,
> Wich spede is in speche vnspurd may we lerne,
> Syn we haf fonged þat fyne fader of nurture. (ll. 916–19)

That the "termes of talkyng noble" are described as "teccheles"—spotless—is revealing. It is confirmed by the narrator's observation only a little later, when Gawain and the lady of the castle are seated together at dinner enjoying one another's company and exercising their conversational skills:

> Þurȝ her dere dalyaunce of her derne wordez,
> Wyth clene cortays carp closed fro fylþe. (ll. 1012–13)

Noble, gentle, or "cortays" talk is pure, even though its favorite topic is love. It has an ambiguous relationship to the body, both acknowledging the sexuality which occasions "luf-talkyng," and at the same time seeking to separate itself from sexuality by representing this as "fylþe," as foul and corrupt materiality.[26] In using this word the poet draws briefly on the penitential discourse which he uses so extensively in *Cleanness*; here, though, the function of such discourse is to buttress the aristocratic myth that aristocrats can transcend their animal selves by sheer talk.

The lady of the castle's attack on Gawain is an attack on that myth. In the seduction scenes her moral corruption is disclosed in her corruption of language. This is why the conversation between her and Gawain (which seems at one level to involve nothing more serious than the risk of breaching polite etiquette) at the same time carries a risk of sin: "He cared for his cortaysye, lest craþayn he were,/ And more for his meschef, ȝif he schulde make synne" (ll. 1773–74). Superficially at least, she talks with a courtly adroitness and indirection, but she constantly exploits the opacity of courtly speech for the purposes of sexual innuendo. In other contexts—as, for example, when Criseyde addresses Troilus for the first time at the beginning of book 3 of Chaucer's *Troilus and Criseyde*—courtly speech maintains its purity through its abstractness;[27] its generalized and opaque imprecision provides a means whereby the woman can be created as participating in male erotic fantasies without losing the chastity which in an aristocratic honor system gives her value and thus makes her desirable.

Whereas the language Chaucer gives to Criseyde avoids being specific in an erotically charged situation, in the third fitt of *Sir Gawain and the Green Knight* the lady of the castle is made to narrow down the range of meanings that courtly language can bear so that the specifically sexual and physical nature of her interest in Gawain is unmistakable. The implications of her speech on the first morning are clear: her emphasis on their absolute privacy, his ability to please, and her willingness to be completely amenable show that she has in mind more than just talk, even though her meaning is conveyed without any explicit breach of decorum. Nevertheless, in seizing the sexual initiative and attempting to short-circuit the whole elaborate process of courtly conversation by stopping his mouth with kisses, the lady of the castle is denying Gawain his identity as the speaking knight.

There has been a good deal of debate about how explicit she is when, in the course of her opening gambit, she tells him "ȝe ar welcum to my cors / Yowre awen won to wale" (ll. 1237–38). Norman Davis is surely right to point out that "my cors" is an imitation of a French idiom, the equivalent of a personal pronoun meaning "myself," and that 1237 must mean "I am glad to have you here."[28] Nevertheless, in alluding to herself as "my cors" she reminds the reader and Gawain that she— and he—are bodies; she is implicated in the poem's naturalistic discourse. Her "cors" is the site of all that intrigued scientific curiosity and speculation about the female animal: desiring, menstruating, able to conceive, cold and humid, with genitalia which in the act of sex "open wide and enlarge, though to a lesser degree than the male engorgement," as Albert the Great noted.[29] Gawain has the task of resisting the lure of naturalism. He does it by resolutely ignoring the innuendos her speech contains, by replying as if her language had no sexual meaning, and as if she were not embodied. Not only, though, does Gawain evade the physical implications in what the lady says, but he keeps talking for three days. He has to. If he stopped talking and simply acted he would cross the boundary to where the peasants, the horses, and the mules are. He would no longer be the speaking knight. It is different for Perceval in the French Vulgate *Queste del Saint Graal*. He meets a beautiful, disinherited lady who invites him into a pavilion. Plied with food and wine, he asks her to sleep with him and after some demurral she consents:

"Et je. . .ferai quan que vous plaira. Et sachiez veraiement que
vos ne m'avez mie tant desirree a avoir com je vos desirroie
encor plus. Car vos estes un des chevaliers dou monde a qui
je ai plus baé."[30]

Perceval lies down, naked, beside her but in the nick of time catches
sight of the red cross inlaid on his sword-hilt. He makes the sign of
the cross on his forehead and then the pavilion disappears in a cloud
of smoke and, as the lady takes to a boat, the sea bursts into flames.
A helpful hermit elucidates the meaning of Perceval's experiences to
him; allegorically, the disinherited lady is Lucifer cast out from heaven.
Throughout the *Queste del Saint Graal* hermits and priests allegorize a
text in which the particular and material are only apparently what they
seem; they represent hidden or obscure realities which require to be
interpreted. Events in the story are an aspect of thought, and understanding is the primary object of storytelling. Perceval's struggle is
internal, a matter of the will's assenting to a temptation whose
materiality is only an illusion and which, if resisted, can be made to
disappear.

For Gawain the toils of the body are not so easily escaped. He is,
after all, also an animal. If the lady fails to seduce the speaking knight,
she does succeed in making Gawain take the green girdle that will
protect him from death which, as an animal, he cannot efface or avoid
or talk away. To return to where I began: the girdle holds out to Gawain
the hope that it will stop the axe from slicing through his white flesh,
from cleaving the bones and only coming to rest when it hits the earth
to which all bodies return. When Gawain later realizes what he has
done he sees what connects the Exchange of Winnings with the
Beheading Game: it is the fact of the body. His anger at womankind
is the ancient anger of his sex at its own materiality, for which women
have traditionally borne the blame. The green girdle is for Gawain a
symbol of that materiality, a reminder of "Þe faut and þe fayntyse of
þe flesche crabbed" (l. 2435)—the faultiness and the frailty of that
perverse and untranscendable flesh that makes him one with the deer
and the boar and the fox.

Notes

1. I have given earlier versions of this paper at the 1989 Conference of the
British Branch of the International Arthurian Society in Cambridge, England,
at the University of Liverpool in 1990, and at the Kresge Art Museum, Michigan
State University in 1991. I am grateful to my audiences on all these occasions
for their suggestions for improvement, as well as to James Carley for his tactful

advice. It is with admiration for her exemplary work on Arthurian (and other) literature that I offer this final version to Valerie Lagorio.

2. The poet was possibly a cleric attached to an aristocratic household, since the other poems in the *Gawain* manuscript show a knowledge of the Latin Bible as well as of the noble life. He is almost certain, therefore, to have been an arts graduate or at least attended an arts faculty for a few years even if he did not take a degree. See J. Dunbabin, "Careers and Vocations," in *The History of the University of Oxford, I: The Early Oxford Schools*, ed. J. I. Catto (Oxford, 1984), pp. 565–605.

3. All quotations are from *Sir Gawain and the Green Knight*, ed. J. R. R. Tolkien and E. V. Gordon, rev. N. Davis (Oxford, 1967).

4. See ll. 424 ("bones"); 89, 317, 429, 2314, 2315 ("blod[e]"); 943, 2435 ("flesche"); 425, 2313 ("grece"); 2312 ("hyde"); 943 ("felle"); 181 ("fax"); 183, 190, 436 ("here").

5. Compare ll. 425 and 2313 quoted above.

6. See ll. 143, 955, 1339, 1741, and 2371.

7. For "schulderes," see ll. 156, 1337, 2318; for "hede," see ll. 418, 1353, 2217; for "hals[e]," see ll. 427, 1353, 1639.

8. By the end of the twelfth century many of Aristotle's scientific writings, the *libri naturales*, had been translated into Latin from Arabic and Greek. Aristotle's naturalistic view of human beings and the universe led to the condemnation of the *libri naturales* by the University of Paris in 1210. By 1220 Michael Scot, in Toledo, had translated Aristotle's three major zoological works under the title *De animalibus*, and this text was widely diffused in the schools; William of Moerbeke made another translation from the Greek in 1260. Despite the intermittent hostility of the Paris theologians, Aristotle's scientific works were a major source in the thirteenth century for the zoological writings of Robert Grosseteste, for Robert of Cantimpré's *De natura rerum*, the encyclopaedists Vincent of Beauvais and Bartholomaeus Anglicus, and especially for Albert the Great's *De animalibus*, written between 1258 and 1262, which was the culmination of a life-long curiosity about natural phenomena. For the reception and influence of Aristotle, see B. Dod, "Aristoteles Latinus," in *The Cambridge History of Later Medieval Philosophy*, ed. N. Kretzmann, A. Kenny, and J. Pinborg (Cambridge, 1982), pp. 45–79; C. H. Lohr, "The Medieval Interpretation of Aristotle," in the same volume, pp. 80–98; F. van Steenberghen, *Aristotle in the West: The Origins of Latin Aristotelianism*, trans. L. Johnston (Louvain, 1955) and S. D. Wingate, *The Mediaeval Latin Versions of the Aristotelian Scientific Corpus, with Special Reference to Biological Works* (London, 1931). For Albert the Great, see *Albert the Great, Man and the Beasts: De Animalibus (Books 22–26)*, trans. J. J. Scanlan (Binghamton, N.Y., 1987). For scientific studies at Oxford in the thirteenth and fourteenth centuries see J. A. Weisheipl, "Science in the

Thirteenth Century," in *University of Oxford*, ed. Catto, pp. 435–69; the same author's "Curriculum of the Faculty of Arts at Oxford in the Early Fourteenth Century," *Medieval Studies* 26 (1964), 143–85; and G. Leff, *Paris and Oxford Universities in the Thirteenth and Fourteenth Centuries* (London, 1968), pp. 144–46.

9. See Brian Lawn, *The Salernitan Questions* (Oxford, 1963) and *The Prose Salernitan Questions* (London, 1978). According to Lawn, "more than half of the surviving manuscripts of this early group of questions are of English provenance" (*Salernitan Questions*, p. xi). Lawn also notes the frequent occurrence of Salernitan questions in Quodlibeta of theology faculties in the late thirteenth century, and argues that Quodlibeta, as "a kind of scholastic exercise. . . probably indicated, better than any other, the general intellectual temper of the day, and what questions agitated the minds of those who moved in university circles" (p. 87). I am indebted to my colleague Peter Biller for advice on medieval science in general and Lawn's work in particular.

10. See Lawn, *Prose Salernitan Questions*, pp. 13, 10, 44, and 4. (My translations).

11. According to *MED*, "lote(z)" can mean "manners, demeanour" as well as "speech" (see *MED* lote n. 1 [a] 3 [b]). Nevertheless in all other instances in the poem where "lote" is used in the singular, it clearly means "sound, speech" (see ll. 119, 1623, 1917, 2211) and I assume, with Norman Davis, that this is its meaning at 639.

12. *Pliny: Natural History*, trans A. Rackham, 10 vols. (London and Cambridge, Mass., 1940), III:603 (xi.cii. 271).

13. See James J. Murphy, *Rhetoric in the Middle Ages* (Berkeley, 1974), pp. 106–21, and Mary Dickey, "Som Commentaries on the *De Inventione* and *Ad Herennium* of the Eleventh and Early Twelfth Centuries," *Medieval and Renaissance Studies*, 6 (1968), 1–41. One commentary which is available in a modern edition is Thierry of Chartres, *The Latin Rhetorical Commentaries by Thierry of Chartres*, ed. K. M. Fredborg (Toronto, 1988), pp. 56–215.

14. *Cicero: De inventione, De optime genere oratorum, Topica*, trans. H. M. Hubbell, (London and Cambridge, Mass., 1949), I.ii. 2–3, 5–7.

15. *De animalibus (Books 22–26)*, trans. Scanlan, p. 67.

16. The *De amore* was read in university circles; it has been identified as the work of that name which was condemned, with others, by the bishop of Paris in 1272 on the grounds that Arts students were disputing "manifest and abominable errors. . . conceits and idiotic falsities and propositions" drawn from them. See A. J. Denomy, "The *De Amore* of Andreas Capellanus and the Condemnation of 1277," *Medieval Studies* 8 (1946), 107–49, at 107.

17. *Andreas Capellanus On Love*, ed. and trans. P. G. Walsh (London, 1982), pp. 41–42.

18. *Andreas Capellanus*, trans. Walsh, p. 45.

19. Ibid., p. 223.

20. Ibid., p. 201.

21. Chrétien de Troyes, *Yvain*, ed. T. B. W. Reid (Manchester, 1942), ll. 294–326.

22. *Andreas Capellanus*, trans. Walsh, p. 65.

23. See ll. 623, 917, 1264 ("noble"); ll. 42, 639, 2185 ("gentil"); ll. 803, 1156, 1961 ("fre"); ll. 276, 469, 539, 1511, 1525 ("cortays"). I discuss the class and gender implications of some courtly terms in "Engendering Pity in 'The Franklin's Tale,'" in *The Wife of Bath and All Her Sect*, ed. Ruth Evans and Lesley Johnson (forthcoming).

24. Compare the advice given by the fifteenth-century gentleman Peter Idley to his son, who is also intended to take his place in society at the head of a provincial household: "Of thy tonge be free in gentil speche" (*Peter Idley's Instructions to His Son*, ed. C. D'Evelyn [London, 1935], p. 83). Of Chaucer's Knight we are told that he "Ne nevere yet no vileynye ne sayde / In al his lyf unto no maner wight" (*Canterbury Tales*, General Prologue, 70–71. This and subsequent Chaucer quotations are from *The Riverside Chaucer*, ed. L. D. Benson et al., 3rd ed. [Oxford, 1988]). The Middle English version of *The Book of the Order of Chivalry* says: 'To a knyght apperteyneth to speke nobly and curtoisly. . .Cortosye and Chyualry concorden to gyder / For vylaynous and foule words ben ageynst thordre of chyualrye." (W. Caxton, *The Book of the Order of Chyualry*, ed. A. T. P. Byles, EETS OS 168 [London, 1926], p. 113).

25. *Andreas Capellanus*, trans. Walsh, p. 65.

26. See *MED*, "filth" n. 1 (a) Anything material that is considered foul, unclean, impure or defiling; . . .3 a(b) sexual desire, lust; . . .3b Sinfulness, wickedness, corruption.

27. When Criseyde says "I shal trewely, with al my myght,/Youre bittre tornen al into swetenesse,/If I be she that may yow do gladnesse,/For every wo ye shal recovere a blisse" (III. 178–81), it is impossible to tell exactly what she is promising Troilus. Sexual explicitness is a mark of ill-breeding. At lines 725ff. of the General Prologue to the *Canterbury Tales*, the narrator apologizes to his audience for the improper language that truthful reporting will require him to use. He asks them to "arette it nat my vileynye": don't attribute it to my ill-breeding. He is embarrassed at using "large"—that is, indecent—terms which the well-bred man would normally recast for courtly listeners. For an account of the development in the thirteenth century of a "new gentility," and particularly of polite language in courtly literature, see C. Muscatine, *The Old French Fabliaux* (New Haven and London, 1986), chapter 3.

28. See *Sir Gawain*, rev. Davis, pp. 108–9.

29. See *De animalibus*, trans. Scanlan, 22.i.1 [3], p. 60.

30. *La Queste del Saint Graal*, ed. A. Pauphilet (Paris, 1923), p. 109. "I will...do whatever you desire. And believe me, you have not hungered to possess me one half as much as I have wanted you, for you are one of the knights I was most passionately set on having": trans. P. Matarasso, *The Quest of the Holy Grail* (Harmondsworth, 1969), p. 128. *La Queste del Saint Graal* also lies at the interface between two cultures, monastic and courtly.

Politicizing the Ineffable:
The *Queste del Saint Graal* and Malory's "Tale of the Sankgreal"

 *Martin B. Shichtman*

Ever since Albert Pauphilet acknowledged the influence of Cistercian principles on the *Queste del Saint Graal*, scholarship relating to the text has primarily focused on the nature and conveyance of its religious message.[1] By emphasizing the spirituality of the *Queste*, scholars have, however, overlooked its function as a social and political signifier serving to mediate escalating tensions between the early thirteenth-century Church—and the Cistercian monastic order in particular—and the knightly classes. The *Queste's* discourse of religious certainty positions clerics and knights in a manner allowing for the continued exchange of capital—both symbolic and material—between their two groups. On the other hand, Thomas Malory's fifteenth-century revision of the *Queste*, the "Tale of the Sankgreal," has been generally viewed by scholars as either a failed effort by an unskilled author to reproduce the religiosity of the original or a successful, entirely competent effort to expunge religiosity from the French text in order to promote a vision of terrestrial chivalry.[2] Such scholarly disagreement seems the result of Malory's alterations to the *Queste*, alterations reflecting the uncertainty of the destabilized political situation in England during the fifteenth century. In Malory's "Sankgreal," the assurances offered by the *Queste*—designed to repair fissures between clerical and knightly communities—become subjected to the skepticism and doubt of an age troubled by constant political disruption.

Most studies of the *Queste del Saint Graal* have assumed a philosophical peaceful coexistence between the thirteenth-century

Church and the knightly classes, producing from both groups the expectation of a kind of celestial chivalry.[3] Thus, there has been little discussion as to why the author of the *Queste* would have selected the genre of knightly romance to advance agendas of Cistercian monasticism.[4] Nevertheless, throughout the twelfth and thirteenth centuries, the Church—and its monastic orders—maintained an ambivalent attitude toward knighthood and the affairs of the knightly classes. As Peter Partner notes, "when noblemen of knightly status repented, and in mature years sought the life of the cloister, those within the monastery who had been nourished there from childhood were often reluctant to welcome the recruit. . . .The clergy were absolutely forbidden to shed blood, and to combine the life of an active soldier, killing and plundering like any other soldier, with the life of a monk, was to go against a fundamental principle."[5]

The rise of military orders early in the twelfth century—the Poor Knights of the Temple were given official Church recognition by the Council of Troyes in 1128—seemed an opportunity to celebrate the union of faith and chivalry. But from their beginnings, these orders were, at best, nervously accepted by religious authorities. Even Saint Bernard, an enthusiastic supporter of the military orders, did not hesitate to denounce those whose services he sought. He wrote of knights: "You cover your horses with silks, and I do not know what hanging rags cover your breastplates; you paint your banners, shields and saddles; you decorate your bridles and spurs all over with gold and silver and precious stones, and with such pomp you hasten to death with shameful fury and impudent foolishness. Are these knightly insignia, or are they rather ornaments for women?"[6] In *Sermo exhortatorius ad milites Templi*, he argued for the introduction of military orders primarily as a method of reforming a perverted nobility: "you will find very few men in the vast multitude which throngs to the Holy Land who have not been unbelieving scoundrels, sacrilegious plunderers, homicides, perjurers, adulterers, whose departure from Europe is certainly a double benefit, seeing that people in Europe are glad to see the back of them, and the people to whose assistance they are going in the Holy Land are delighted to see them!"[7] By the latter part of the twelfth century, and well into the thirteenth, the Church faced frequent embarrassment in its association with the military orders. A papal bull was issued during 1160—and, of necessity, reissued in subsequent years— restraining citizens disgusted with the arrogance of the Knights Templar from physically and verbally abusing members of the order. The Third Lateran Council of 1179, led by the criticisms of William of Tyre, attempted to restrict Templar privilege. From 1199 to 1210, Innocent III had to intervene several times in conflicts between Templars and the allied forces of clergy and the citizenry. In 1207, Innocent III publicly criticized the Templars and, in a letter to the Grand Master, demanded restraint in the knights' public dealings. The trials of the Templars, begun in 1307 by Philip IV and concluded in 1312 with Pope Clement V's suppression of the order, were fueled, at least in part, by clerical and popular hostility towards the knights.

On the other hand, the Church—and even the often uncompromising Cistercian order—was willing to engage in commerce with and accept donations from members of the knightly classes. Constance Brittain Bouchard points out that there "were a certain number of men from the very highest nobility, including the duke of Burgundy and even the king, who appeared intermittently in Cistercian charters, and a fairly regular stream of castellans, but the most common were the men referred to as *milites* and their families. . .donors to a Cistercian house were usually not castellans and counts but knights."[8] At the same time the military orders were falling into disrepute, knightly donations to monastic charities were increasing dramatically.

The twelfth and thirteenth centuries saw a monastic revival assisted, in large part, by gifts from knights. Cistercian statutes specified that monasteries be established only on deserted sites—in the wilderness—where members of the order would serve God and support themselves through manual labor.[9] The chronicles of most Cistercian houses testify to adherence with these statutes. But Constance Berman has suggested,

> [p]ersonal names and place names, the existence of churches, the legal terminology describing land units and rights over the land, the existence of political and ecclesiastical taxes, all predicate the existence of lords and peasants in the region for a number of generations before the Cistercians arrived. Thus, in the southern Rouergue where Silvanès was founded, the Cistercians were not primarily engaged in the opening of new lands by clearance and reclamation on what one historian has labeled an "internal frontier.". . .Solitude, if they found it, was the creation of their own efforts to create large, compact, isolated holdings, and if they had no neighbors in the area it was because they had successfully bought out other landholders.[10]

In "Early Cistercian Expansion in Provence: The Abbeys of Aiguebelle, Bonnevaux, Léoncel, and Valcroissant," she further argues that "[t]he pattern which emerges in a study of these four Cistercian houses is in many ways similar to that discovered in earlier research conducted on the Cistercian foundations of the southwestern regions of what is today France. Although there were some potential assarts in the Alps and the possibility of drainage in marshes along the major rivers, most reclamation and resettlement had already taken place by the time the Cistercians arrived in the region."[11] The introduction of Cistercian houses to populated areas, areas of knightly activity, was significant to the support of these houses. As Bouchard demonstrates, "although many knights might have been financially or psychologically ready to make pious gifts for some time, they were prompted to do so only by the actual appearance of Cistercian monks in their immediate neighborhood. Judging from the almost explosive growth of acquisitions in a particular area which might follow the establishment of a grange there, the local knights had. . .a pent-up desire to make such gifts."[12] This pent-up desire to assist in the foundation of monasteries also might well have been, according to Berman, to the advantage of knightly patrons beginning to assume expanded social and political authority:

> Although religious motives for the foundation of these new monastic houses are often cited in the charters, the pious acts of these men also legitimized their expanding power, as well as providing them an outlet for religious aspirations which the older, more aristocratic foundations may well have refused them. It was from this new class of knights, rather than from the older comital families, that most of the order's early recruits for choir monks came; from their tenants, peasants were recruited as lay brothers. Indeed, most Cistercian foundations in southern France were instigated by men of these knightly families, and almost always by laymen rather than clergy.[13]

For the author of the *Queste*, embarrassments provided by the knightly classes and the military orders were apparently offset by the potential of knightly contributions to Cistercian causes. The text serves to demonstrate the methods by which knights, who were generally inclined to sin, could be taught to save themselves.

The *Queste* reflects Cistercian skepticism about the knightly classes as well as the monastic order's struggles to define the parameters of a network with members of these classes. It suggests that if knights would abandon their corrupt ways and allow themselves to be directed by the order's principals, they could begin to participate in the process of salvation. Laurence N. de Looze writes that "the telos of the [Grail] quest is that which terrestrial eyes cannot see, nor human language become: pure signification, immanent and direct, experienced without the intermediary of the signifier;" but he also argues that "[o]nly one knight [Galahad] can look into the Grail, can see Truth revealed."[14] The political thrust of the *Queste* seems to suggest that for *all* knights who follow the precepts of the Cistercian order, who give themselves over to its teachings, the seemingly ambiguous signs of the world—as well as the seemingly ambiguous signs of the transcendental, of the Grail quest—will become stabilized and interpretable. Those rejecting these precepts, rejecting these teachings, risk benightedness both for the present and eternity.

For many readers of the *Queste* Galahad is the perfect knight, a paradigmatic Christ-like figure.[15] But while Galahad is depicted as a marvelous young man of enormous potential, he is never granted absolute omniscience. Like the rest of the knights of the *Queste*, Galahad needs to have signs explained for him. He differs from the other knights only in that he is more educable, more receptive to accepting and understanding the nature of referentiality once it is made clear through religious instruction. Possessing the greatest knightly lineage—he is Lancelot's son—Galahad has also been schooled from early childhood by nuns and clerics. It appears that this schooling, even more than his hereditary gifts, prepares Galahad for the Grail quest. The young knight's willingness to learn, and his humility in taking guidance, is demonstrated vividly in the sequences involving the acquisition of his shield. This shield is guarded by a mysterious knight, dressed entirely in white, who functions both as a chivalric mentor providing arms for Galahad and as a white monk explaining the significance of these arms. Galahad, though he may be "li mieldres chevaliers qui soit ou monde" [the finest knight in Christendom],[16] still must inquire about the nature of the shield he receives. In fact, Galahad initiates conversation with the white knight: "Sire, par cest escu que je port sont maintes aventures merveilleuses avenues en cest pais, si com j'ai oï dire. Si vos voudroie prier par amor et par franchise que vos m'en deissiez la verité et coment et por coi ce est avenu, car je croi bien que vos le sachiez" [Sir, as I have heard it said, many strange adventures have come to pass in these parts by virtue of the shield I bear. I beg you in love and loyalty to disclose to me the meaning of these things and how and why they came about, for I firmly believe you know the truth about it] (*Queste*, pp. 31–32; Matarasso, *Quest*, p. 58). The knight replies: "Certes, sire...je le vos dirai volentiers, car je en sai bien la verité. Or escoutez, s'il vos plaist, Galaad" [You are right Sir...and as I know it I will tell you gladly. So listen Galahad, if it pleases you] (*Queste*, p. 32; Matarasso, *Quest*, p. 58). The knight offers Galahad a long explanation of the history of the shield, a history closely associated with the dissemination of Christianity. The emphasis here is on the fact that meaning—truth— can be disclosed. Signs are shown to be able to carry with them, perfectly, it seems, signification, and apprehension is available to the knight who allows himself to be taught. Tzvetan Todorov addresses the potential of symbolic exchange hinted at in the *Quest*: "The possessors of meaning form a special category among the characters: they are 'sages,' hermits, abbots, and recluses. Just as the knights could not *know*, these latter cannot *act*; none of them participates in a peripety, except in the episodes of interpretation."[17] No sooner does Galahad receive his shield, along with the narrative attesting to its Christian connections, than he becomes involved in ridding a monastery of an evil spirit haunting its cemetery. The mysteries of faith are thus made comprehensible to knights not only for the salvation of their souls but also because they possess social and political currency to repay their instructors.

The *Queste's* portrayal of Perceval deals with the price of salvation for the knight inclined toward sin. Like Galahad, Perceval encounters religious persons who clearly explicate the signs he finds confusing. He, however, initially ignores their teachings. Following a dream in which he imagines a confrontation between himself and two ladies, one riding a lion and the other riding a serpent, Perceval meets an old man dressed in monastic attire—"revestu de sorpeliz et d'aube en semblance de prestre, et en son chief avoit une coronne de blanc samit ausi lee come vos deus doiz" [robed like a priest in surplice and alb and crowned with a band of white silk two fingers deep] (*Queste*, p. 99; Matarasso, *Quest*, p. 119)—who arrives on a ship covered completely in white samite. The old man tells Perceval,

> je i vign por vos veoir et reconforter, et por ce que vos me dioiz vostre estre. Car il n'est riens dont vos soiez a conseillier, se vos la me dites, que je ne vos en conseil si bien come len porroit mielz fere. . . je vos conois mout mielz que vos ne cuidiez. Pieç'a que vos ne feistes chose que je ne sache assez mielz que vos meesmes.
>
> I came thus far to visit and sustain you and to hear from you how you fared. For if you have need of counsel and will confide in me, there is no matter in which I am not supremely fitted to advise you. . . I know you very much better than you think. There is nothing you have done in many a year but I have more inward knowledge of it than yourself. (*Queste*, p. 100; Matarasso, *Quest*, p. 120)

He then proceeds to interpret Perceval's dream and to offer instruction based on the interpretation. But upon meeting a dazzlingly beautiful woman who contradicts the old man, arguing "Ce est uns enchanterres, une mouteploierres de paroles qui fet adés d'une parole cent, et ne dira ja voir qu'il puisse" [He is a sorcerer, a spawner of phrases who makes his words breed a hundredfold and never tells the truth if he can help it] (*Queste*, p. 107; Matarasso, *Quest*, p. 126), Perceval nearly allows his virtue to be compromised. The knight is saved only when he sees a crimson crucifix inlaid on his sword, comes to his senses, crosses himself, and watches the woman, along with her entourage, disappear. Perceval concludes this adventure with an act of self-mutilation; he pierces himself through the left thigh, an act of contrition for transgressions committed—"Biax sire Diex, ce est en amende de ce que je me sui meffet vers vos" [Gracious Lord God, this is to atone for the offense I did Thee] (*Queste*, p. 110; Matarasso, *Quest*, p. 129). As Perceval prays to the Lord for comfort, the old man returns, chastises the knight for his inexperience, his simplicity, explains the events transpired, and provides assurances—"Diex ne l'oublieroit mie, ainz dist qu'il li envoieroit secors prochainement" [God would not forget him but would come to his rescue shortly] (*Queste*, p. 115; Matarasso, *Quest*, p. 133). Perceval's unwillingness to accept the wisdom originally imparted by the old man demands a compensatory personal sacrifice. It is only after compensation is guaranteed that the old man again presents himself, only after compensation is guaranteed that consolation and certainty are offered. Even then, there is a warning: "Car se tu chiez une autre foiz, tu ne troveras pas qui si tost t'en reliet come tu feis ore" [if you fall a second time you will not find any to help you to your feet as promptly as today] (*Queste*, p. 114; Matarasso, *Quest*, p. 133). The social and political implications of the episode are striking. While religious certainty is always available to knights, its value as a purchasable commodity escalates with every indiscretion.

Bors is faced with the problem of negotiating with a false hermit. First, however, he meets a good priest, who warns him away from gluttony, gives him a white frock to wear on his quest, hears his confession—Bors sinned once in the flesh—grants him absolution, imposes suitable penance, performs the holy service, and administers the Eucharist. This good priest establishes a paradigm for clerical/ knightly exchange. In return for Bors' obedience, he guarantees terrestrial and celestial success. As his quest progresses Bors has two dreams. Recognizing he has encountered signs of importance, but unable to determine their significance, he dutifully seeks the explication of a cleric. What Bors finds, however, is a hermit intent on deceiving him. This hermit's inability to produce stable meaning should be immediately apparent to the knight. The hermit takes Bors to a counterfeit "chapel," one lacking the accoutrements which would authorize it as a place of worship, a place where truth resides: "Boorz quiert amont et aval, mes il ne voit ne eve beneoite ne croiz ne nule veraie enseigne de Jhesucrist" [Bors searched high and low but could find no holy water, nor cross, nor veritable symbol of Jesus Christ] (*Queste*, p. 178; Matarasso, *Quest*, p. 191). The dream interpretation supplied by the hermit appears equally suspect in its denigration of chastity. Because Bors has learned the lessons of the good priest, he is not swindled; he does not relinquish capital pursuing pleasures of the flesh. He rejects the advice of the false hermit and instead searches out a genuine monastery, where his dreams are correctly read by an abbot who explains: "se vos fussiez terriens, ja si haute aventure ne vos fust avenue" [if your allegiance had been to the world, so high an adventure would never have been yours] (*Queste*, p. 187; Matarasso, *Quest*, p. 199). The currency of Bors' social and political position as a knight, as well as the currency of his soul, is valued both by authorized and unauthorized advisors, who work in competition with one another. The *Queste* establishes that for the authorized advisor there is never semiotic dissonance; signification is unvarying and absolute. Bors recommends the abbot's insight in an expression of gratitude: "Vos les m'avez si bien devisees que j'en serai meillor toz les jorz de ma vie" [You have explained them so admirably that I shall be a better man for the telling all my days] (*Queste*, p. 187; Matarasso, *Quest*, p. 199).

Lancelot and Gawain, like Galahad, Perceval, and Bors, are offered assistance in the difficult task of deriving meaning from signs. These knights, however, both ultimately reject such assistance and thus cut themselves off from the network within which meaning becomes stabilized. In essence, they insist on problematizing meaning, and this insistence forms the basis of their failures. Although Lancelot attempts, in a number of ways, to enter into negotiations with clerics—often meeting hermits and seeking their advice—he is unwilling to give up his love for Guinevere, a love which, he is told, will deprive him of "la joie des ciex et la compaignie des anges et toutes honors terriannes" [the joys of heaven and the company of angels and every honor that the world can give] (*Queste*, p. 118; Matarasso, *Quest*, p. 136). For Lancelot, the rigidity of the hermits, their uncompromising logocentrism, is unacceptable. Lancelot's discourse is informed by an arbitrary system of signification, a system allowing him to be the best knight in the world while still romantically involved with the wife of his dearest friend, the wife of his king. At the Castle of Corbenic—the residence of the Holy Grail—Lancelot discovers the limits of equivocation. Upon arriving at the castle, Lancelot hears a disembodied voice directing him to enter. His entrance is arrested, however, by his own uncertainty over what he will encounter:

Et quant il est fors issuz, si vient a la porte et troeve les deus lions; si cuide bien qu'il n'en puist partir sans meslee. Lors met la main a l'espee et s'apareille de deffendre. Einsi come Lancelot ot trete l'espee, si resgarde contremont et voit venir une main toute enflammee qui le feri si durement par mi le braz que l'espee li vola de la main.

When he had stepped ashore and walked up to the gate he discovered two lions, and fully expected to have to fight his way out. So he clapped his hand to his sword and prepared to defend himself. No sooner had he drawn his sword than glancing up he saw a flaming hand plunge earthwards, which struck him so hard on the arm that the sword flew out of his grip. (*Queste*, p. 253; Matarasso, *Quest*, p. 269)

The author of the *Queste* leaves no room for Lancelot to misunderstand the signs before him. Disembodied voices and flaming hands from heaven provide direction for the knight. Lessons of hermits are augmented by Divine intervention in orienting Lancelot's efforts at interpretation. It is therefore a demonstration of Lancelot's extraordinary willfulness when he ignores further celestial warnings and attempts to intrude upon the Grail ceremony. For the author of the *Queste*, Lancelot's defiance of the understood contract between clerics and knights, his refusal to submit to monastic principles in exchange for the ability to perceive the significance of signs, must necessarily result in disappointment. Lancelot's encounter with the Grail is undermined by a complete breakdown in his ability to interpret:

Et en ce qu'il vient pres, si sent un souffle de vent ausi chauz, ce li est avis, come s'il fust entremeslez de feu, qui le feri ou vis si durement qu'il li fu bien avis qu'il li eust le viaire ars. Lors n'a pooir d'aler avant, come cil qui est tiex atornez qu'il a perdu le pooir dou cors, et del oïr et del veoir, ne n' a sor lui membre dont il aidier se puisse. Lors sent il plusors mains qui le prennent et l'emportent.

As he drew near he felt a puff of wind which seemed to him shot through with flame, so hot it was, and as it fanned his features with its scorching breath he thought his face was burned. He stood rooted in the ground like a man paralysed, bereft of sight and hearing and powerless in every limb. Then he felt himself seized by many hands and carried away. (*Queste*, p. 256; Matarasso, *Quest*, pp. 262–63)

Robert S. Sturges writes: "Perhaps the most important element of the *Queste* that is not fully interpreted within the text is the Holy Grail itself. The lack of an authoritative reading for the central goal is not due to any lack of meaning for the Grail but to the fact that its meaning is ineffable. That its meaning cannot be expressed is no sign of multiplicity or indeterminacy, either."[18] Galahad, Perceval, and Bors have performed all of the services necessary to understand the nature of signification. Although they cannot communicate their experiences of the Grail, they come away from it filled with insight and appreciation. Lancelot who has judged such payment excessive is reduced to silence after his encounter with the Grail because its meaning(s) is incomprehensible to him.

Of the five major knights in the *Queste del Saint Graal*, Gawain proves to be the worst. Hermits are constantly taking him to task for his flightiness, for his reluctance to commit himself seriously to learning the nature of referentiality. These hermits outline the extent of Gawain's obligation and criticize his irresponsibility:

> Sire, a droit fustes apelez mauvés serjanz et desloiax. Car quant vos fustes mis en l'ordre de chevalerie, len ne vos i mist mie por ce que vos servissiez a nostre criaor et deffendissiez Sainte Eglise et rendissiez a Dieu le tresor que il vos bailla a garder, ce est l'ame de vos. Et por ceste chose vos fist len chevalier, et vos avez mauvesement chevalerie emploiee.

> In justice, Sir, you were called a bad and faithless servant. You were not admitted to the order of chivalry to soldier in the devil's cause thenceforward, but in order to serve our Maker, defend Holy Church and render at last to God that treasure which He entrusted to your safekeeping, namely your soul. To this end you were made a knight, and you, Gawain, have abused your knighthood. (*Queste*, p. 54; Matarasso, *Quest*, p. 79

The hermits suggest that there is a correlation between chivalry and following clerical prescription. But Gawain desires nothing more than the arbitrariness of knightly adventure. He embarks on the Grail quest because he believes that it is simply another opportunity for knight errancy. In condemning Gawain, the *Queste* condemns virtually every knight in Arthur's court, every knight dedicated only to terrestrial chivalry, the one hundred and forty-seven that do not achieve the Grail. It also condemns every knight in thirteenth-century France who refuses to show appropriate respect and support for the Church and its monastic orders.

Whereas the author of the *Queste del Saint Graal* offers knights semiotic security predicated on the philosophies of Cistercian monasticism, Thomas Malory's "Tale of the Sankgreal," reflects the political instability of England during the reigns of Henry VI and Edward IV, arguably the most chaotic period in the nation's history. Whereas the author of the *Queste* offers certainty as a commodity, Malory creates a fictional world in which signs consistently fail to signify. From the opening section of Malory's *Morte Darthur*—in which Igrayne is deceived by Uther appearing in her husband's form—to the concluding section—in which Arthur's and Mordred's troops are confused into battle by an accidentally drawn sword—characters are constantly betrayed by signs they misinterpret. Nowhere is this more true than in Malory's "Sankgreal," where signs become increasingly obscure, interpretation nearly impossible. In the "Sankgreal," Malory indicates that sign systems ultimately break down, prove of no significance. The confidence of Arthur' s knights as they embark on the Grail guest is slowly eroded by semiotic codes which hint at their own accessibility while in fact refusing comprehension.

There has been a tendency—although by no means a universal one—among scholars to romanticize the culture that produced Thomas Malory. Dhira B. Mahoney, for instance, maintains: "That Malory belongs firmly in the fifteenth century has been demonstrated effectively by the criticism of the past two decades. His choice of chivalric subjects was not, as once was thought, an exercise in nostalgia. Arthur B. Ferguson and [Larry] Benson have shown that chivalric ideals were taken extremely seriously in fifteenth-century England, even if they were beginning to have little relationship to the actual facts of political and social life."[19] England's aristocratic classes most likely turned to the chivalric practices of a fictional past to mask the actual facts of political and social life in the fifteenth-century, mask the catastrophic effects of the administration of an insane king—while Henry VI's madness became irrefutably obvious in 1453, the king's mental competence had been questioned from the early 1430s—mask the War of the Roses, mask the corruption that led to popular uprisings, mask humiliations at the hands of the French. England's aristocratic classes most likely turned to the chivalric practices of a fictional past precisely for their nostalgic appeal. Malory seems to recognize the ironies of this nostalgia. For Malory, the Arthurian past provides neither answers nor comfort.

Mary Hynes-Berry argues that "When Malory read the *Queste del Saint Graal* two hundred and fifty years later, he did not understand the full patterns of meaning that controlled [its] intricate network of analogues. He saw the story as a powerful and appealing story. As he put it into English, he emphasized the story element and systematically dispensed with the discursive material. Time and again, he omits explanations by hermits and others—explanations which created the hierarchical patterns of significance for character, event and object analogues."[20] Rather than misunderstanding the "intricate network of analogues" that constituted his source, Malory may well have consciously sought to subvert them, to transform a text whose very structure insists upon the existence of meaning into a story that dwells on meaning's elusiveness. John Plummer seems much closer to appreciating Malory's method in his suggestion that "[h]is compressions of the passages featuring spiritual interpretation of dreams, visions, and historical events are due, I believe, not so much to his impatience with them, and not at all to his mystification by them, as to his inability to feel the confidence of his presumably monastically trained thirteenth-century colleague."[21] Similarly, Felicity Riddy notes that "The haunting possibility of the *Sankgreal*—that the Grail may yield no meaning beyond itself, that at the heart of light there is only silence—lurks beneath the surface of the book's orthodoxies.[22] Malory's reader, like his knights, is forced into the role of chasing after signification, trying to grasp that which is always slipping away. In *The Idea of the Book in the Middle Ages*, Jesse Gellrich writes:

> Certainly many writers before the seventeenth century felt the grounds of signification shifting beneath them: Augustine saw the potential for arbitrary response when he meditated on language as a model for the temporality of the fallen world; Aquinas acknowledged an abiding separation between the transcendent reference of learning and the linguistic *modus quo*. But in both writers a discourse of analysis and reference is forestalled from radical departures because the governing structure within which they worked is never unsettled. In Dante, however, that structure is pointedly questioned as soon as language accepts the factors of its own impossibility, and in Chaucer this situation is before us even more provocatively. A reflection on his work invites a reconsideration of the 'origins' of deconstruction as well as the unavoidable historicism it implies.[23]

For the author of the *Queste*, politics demanded signification be stabilized. For Thomas Malory, political exigencies destroy the possibility of stabilized signification.

Malory's Galahad never needs to interpret; he knows. For Galahad, the puzzling systems of signs which confront questing knights are not a source of difficulty. Filled with messianic certainty, he moves along on his journey rarely stopping to question, never hesitating to draw conclusions. Galahad lives in a world—a world unlike the remainder of Arthur's knights—in which signifier and signified are one and the same, the logocentric world of God's elect. After procuring his shield, Malory's Galahad addresses the white knight with a statement— "Sir. . .by thys shylde bene many mervayles fallen"[24]—rather than an inquiry. The white knight of the *Morte Darthur* responds with no encouraging teacher/student repartee but rather immediately begins the story of the shield's origin. It is apparent that the white knight's discourse is not intended for Galahad at all; Galahad is already aware of his position and his role. Rather, it is meant for Malory's audience, to insure some continuity for the narrative. But continuity is the only comfort that Malory provides. Malory's reader does not share with Galahad a moment of understanding; in fact, the reader can only stand in awe of that which Galahad has already mastered. There is, then, for the reader, a feeling of being left behind, of being somehow inadequate to the monumental task of interpretation. This is a feeling no doubt shared by monks at the monastery where Galahad returns to remove a demon from the graveyard. Unlike Galahad in the *Queste* who asks questions of the monks, soliciting guidance at various times during the exorcism, Malory's character performs the desired task without clerical assistance. Unlike Galahad in the *Queste* who performs this task as a kind of repayment, Malory's character accomplishes it as a gesture of charity. In the "Sankgreal," Galahad is not only, as Stephen Atkinson notes, "remote and inaccessible,"[25] he is unrepresentative, and his actions, blessed though they may be, suggest a deviation from normative behavior.

For Malory's Perceval and Bors, interpretation remains problematic, even as they successfully accomplish portions of their adventures. Although destined to achieve the Holy Grail, these two knights have enormous difficulty sorting out the meanings of the various signs they encounter, sufficient difficulty to indicate to the reader the arbitrariness of signification in the world of Malory's text. Like his counterpart in the *Queste*, Malory's Perceval has his dream of the two ladies explicated by an old man who, dressed in white like a priest, arrives on a ship covered in white samite. This old man, however, offers no explanation of himself; he makes no claim to being supremely suited to advise the knight, no claim to possessing inward knowledge. Thus, when the old man's words are challenged by the dazzlingly beautiful woman, there seems to be far greater authority in her position. Malory's Perceval must select from two seemingly equal and valid readings of the text of his dream; he naturally chooses the second because he finds the reader more to his liking. Upon discovering that he has been deceived, Malory's Perceval, like his French counterpart, mutilates himself. But in the "Sankgreal," the mutilation seems more intended to prevent the selection of future misreadings, intended to save the knight from again being misled by signs. In a speech original to Malory's text, Perceval claims, "Sitthyn my fleyssh woll be my mayster I shall punyssh hit" (*Works*, 2:919). Although Perceval insists in the "Sankgreal" that his gesture is "in recompensacion of that I have myssedone" (*Works*, 2:919), he is offered only disparagement by the old man. There are no words of consolation and certainty, no guarantees that Perceval's sacrifice has been accepted or even acknowledged.

Malory removes from his version of Bors' encounter with the false hermit many of the signs that tip off the *Queste*'s character to the possibility of deception. Thus, Malory's Bors has little information to help him distinguish between a good priest, who assures him of success on the Grail quest, and the bad one who explicates his dreams. Whereas the author of the *Queste* dwells on the suspicious omission of religious objects from the false hermit's place of worship, Malory writes only, "hit there semed an olde, fyeble chapell" (*Works*, 2:963). Whereas the author of the *Queste* infuses the false hermit's discourse with generalizations about the insignificance of virginity, Malory's character poses difficult, specific questions about whether the virginity of a stranger is to be more valued than the life of a beloved relative. Malory's false hermit, because his reading of Bors' dreams and the conclusions he draws from it seem as credible as any of the readings and conclusions reached by genuine religious men, calls into question the very process of interpretation. If false readers of signs cannot be easily differentiated from the true ones, and if signs themselves do not readily yield signification, all certainty has disappeared. The *Queste* demonstrates that, in the competition for knightly capital, authorized advisors are deserving of patronage. Malory demonstrates that it may not even be possible to determine who authorized advisors are.

In the *Queste*, Lancelot intentionally problematizes meaning. In the "Sankgreal," meaning is problematized for him. Malory's Lancelot sees through a glass darkly. His ability to make sense of semiotic systems is obscured as he finds himself confounded by a multitude of possible interpretations. Malory transforms Lancelot into a sympathetic victim who suffers humiliation because he cannot read impossibly complex and confusing signs. In Malory's version of the incident at the Castle of Corbenic, Lancelot hears a voice, sees the lions, draws his sword, and then "So there cam [a dwerf sodenly and smote hym th]e arme so sore [that the suerd felle oute of his hand]" (*Works*, 2:1014). The direct intervention of God in Lancelot's attempts to interpret signs is less obvious in Malory's text than in the *Queste*. There is, therefore, more reason for the knight to maintain a degree of skepticism about the absoluteness of referentiality. By replacing the flaming hand of God with an angry dwarf, Malory allows the reader to appreciate Lancelot's uncertainty about the information available to him. As events unfold, Malory's Lancelot is shown to be in error when he later ignores the voice that warns him away from the Grail chapel, but his skepticism is understandable in the light of his previous adventures, of the variable nature of the signs he has encountered.

Although Malory does little to minimize the extent of Gawain's failure on the Grail quest, he does excise much of the *Queste's* criticisms of the knight. By removing many of the speeches made by hermits castigating Gawain's behavior—including, for instance, the speech referring to the knight as a bad and faithless servant—Malory also absolves this character of some blame.[26] For the author of the *Queste*, Gawain serves as an example of knighthood's unwillingness to recognize appropriately the importance of religion and those who practice it. For Malory, Gawain serves to exemplify the frustration of the great majority who, although they are enthusiastic to discover meaning, find instead ambiguity, confusion, chaos. Malory transforms Gawain, the *Queste's* most miserable failure, into an everyman who ultimately accepts that the fallen, incomprehensible world he lives in will have to suffice.

Accompanying the Cistercian spirituality of the *Queste del Saint Graal* was a political agenda attempting to redefine the sometimes strained relationship between the Church's most demanding monastic order and the members of the knightly classes. In exchange for some of their considerable social and political capital, the *Queste* argued, clerics could offer knights meaning and stability, the truth. Thomas Malory's "The Tale of the Sankgreal," a product of the chaos of fifteenth-century English culture, suggests that meaning and stability may not be accessible at any price, and that the truth is never absolute.

Notes

1. Albert Pauphilet, *Études sur la Queste del Saint Graal Attribuée à Gautier Map* (Paris, 1921); for a discussion on the nature of Christian signification within the text, also see Tzvetan Todorov, *The Poetics of Prose*, trans. Richard Howard (Ithaca, N.Y., 1975); Pauline Matarasso, *The Redemption of Chivalry: A Study of the Queste del Saint Graal* (Geneva, 1979); Emmanuèle Baumgartner, *L'Arbe et le pain: essai sur la Queste del Saint Graal* (Paris, 1981); E. Jane Burns, "Feigned Allegory: Intertextuality in the *Queste del Saint Graal*," *Kentucky Romance Quarterly*

29 (1982), 347–63; E. Jane Burns, *Arthurian Fictions: Rereading the Vulgate Cycle* (Columbus, Ohio, 1985); Laurence N. de Looze, "A Story of Interpretations: *The Queste del Saint Graal* as Metaliterature," *Romanic Review* 76 (1985), 129–47; and Robert S. Sturges, *Medieval Interpretation: Models of Reading in Literary Narrative, 1100–1500* (Carbondale, Ill., 1991).

2. Among Malory's detractors on this matter are Eugène Vinaver, who, in his notes to *The Works of Sir Thomas Malory*, rev. P. J. C. Field, 3rd ed., 3 vols. (Oxford, 1990), 3:1534, calls the "Sankgreal" the author's "least original" tale. Also see Mary Hynes-Berry, "A Tale 'Briefly Drawyne Oute of Freynshe,' " in *Aspects of Malory*, ed. Toshiyuki Takamiya and Derek Brewer (Totowa, N.J., 1981), pp. 93–196; and Terrence McCarthy, "The Sequence of Malory's Tales," in *Aspects of Malory*, pp. 107–24. Scholars who believe that Malory attempted to redefine the relationship between religion and chivalry established in the *Queste* include Larry Benson, *Malory's Morte Darthur* (Cambridge, Mass., 1976); Dhira B. Mahoney, "The Truest and Holiest Tale: Malory's Transformation of *La Queste del Saint Graal*," in *Studies in Malory*, ed. James Spisak (Kalamazoo, Mich., 1985), pp. 109–28; John F. Plummer, "The Quest for Significance in *La Queste del Saint Graal* and Malory's *Tale of the Sankgreal*," in *Continuations: Essays on Medieval French Literature and Language in Honor of John L. Grigsby*, ed. Norris J. Lacy and Gloria Torrini-Roblin (Birmingham, Ala., 1989), pp. 107–19; and, most recently, Christoph Houswitschka, *Politik and Liebe in der Literatur des englischen Spätmittelalters am Beispiel von Thomas Malorys Morte Darthur* (New York, 1991).

3. See, for instance, Fanni Bogdanow, "An Interpretation of the Meaning and Purpose of the Vulgate *Queste del Saint Graal* in the Light of the Mystical Theology of Saint Bernard," in *The Changing Face of Arthurian Romance: Essays on the Arthurian Prose Romances in Memory of Cedric E. Pickford*, ed. Alison Adams, Armel H. Diverres, Karen Stern, and Kenneth Varty (Woodbridge, 1986), pp. 23–46.

4. Sturges addresses this unanimity in *Medieval Interpretation*, p. 70.

5. Peter Partner, *The Murdered Magicians: The Templars and their Myth* (New York, 1982), p. 6.

6. See Malcom Barber, *The Trial of the Templars* (New York, 1978), p. 7.

7. See Partner, *The Murdered Magicians*, p. 7.

8. Constance Brittain Bouchard, *Holy Entrepreneurs: Cistercians, Knights, and Economic Exchange in Twelfth-Century Burgandy* (Ithaca, N.Y., 1991), pp. 165, 169; also see Constance H. Berman, "Fashions in Monastic Patronage: The Popularity of Supporting Cistercian Abbeys for Women in Thirteenth-Century Northern France," *Proceedings of the Annual Meeting of the Western Society for French History* 17 (1990), 36–45.

9. Constance H. Berman, "The Foundation and Early History of the Monastery of Sivanès: The Economic Reality," in *Cistercian Ideals and Reality*, ed. John R. Sommerfeldt (Kalamazoo, Mich., 1978), pp. 280–318, at 293.

10. Berman, "The Foundation and Early History," p. 284.

11. Constance H. Berman, "Early Cistercian Expansion in Provence: The Abbeys of Aiguebelle, Bonnevaux, Léoncal and Valcroissant," in *Heaven on Earth*, ed. E. R. Elder, Studies in Medieval Cistercian History 9 (Kalamazoo, Mich., 1983), pp. 43–54, at 44.

12. Bouchard, *Holy Entrepreneurs*, p. 172.

13. Constance H. Berman, *Medieval Agriculture, the Southern French Countryside, and the Early Cistercians: A Study of Forty-three Monasteries*, (Philadelphia, 1986), p. 35.

14. de Looze, "A Story of Interpretations," p. 135.

15. See, for instance, de Looze, "A Story of Interpretations," p. 135.

16. *La Queste del Saint Graal*, ed. Albert Pauphilet (Paris, 1923), p. 29. The translation of the *Queste* is by P. M. Matarasso, *The Quest of the Holy Grail* (Harmondsworth, 1969), p. 55. Subsequent references will be cited parenthetically in the text of this paper.

17. Todorov, *The Poetics of Prose*, pp. 122–23.

18. Sturges, *Medieval Interpretation*, p. 70.

19. Mahoney, "The Truest and Holiest Tale," p. 119. For a less romantic vision of Malory's fifteenth century, see Felicity Riddy, *Sir Thomas Malory* (New York, 1987), pp. 1–30.

20. Hynes-Berry, "A Tale," p. 95.

21. Plummer, "The Quest for Significance," p. 109. See also Sandra Ness Ihle, *Malory's Grail Quest: Invention and Adaptation in Medieval Prose Romance* (Madison, Wis., 1983).

22. Riddy, *Sir Thomas Malory*, p. 138

23. Jesse M. Gellrich, *The Idea of the Book in the Middle Ages: Language Theory, Mythology, and Fiction* (Ithaca, N.Y., 1985), p. 253.

24. *The Works of Sir Thomas Malory*, ed. Vinaver, 2:879. Subsequent references will be cited parenthetically in the text of this paper.

25. Stephen Atkinson, "Malory's Lancelot and the Quest of the Grail," p. 143.

26. On Malory's reclamation of Gawain, see Martin B. Shichtman, "Malory's Gawain Reconsidered," *Essays in Literature* 11 (1984), 159–76.

"The Prowess of Hands": The Psychology of Alchemy in Malory's "Tale of Sir Gareth"

————————————— *Bonnie Wheeler*

Malory modulates the mood and themes of *Le Morte Darthur* to evoke the high spirit and full vocabulary of traditional "enclosed" romance in the work's third segment, the glittering "Tale of Sir Gareth." Malcontents in Malory's audience whose expectations have been foiled by the dark difficulties of his earlier Arthurian stories are here provided a plenitude of generic fulfillment; "The Tale of Sir Gareth" is the sweet fruit yielded by the twisted vines of his earlier narrative. The lingering aura of meaningfulness achieved by this tale is a function of its situation in the larger work, its relations to romance traditions, and its deployment of provocative symbolism. We emerge from reading the "The Tale of Sir Gareth" with a sense that it is at once absolutely conventional and highly idiosyncratic. It is dense with incident, humorous in dialogue and situation, and rich in decorative effect. Malory's discourse revels in the very literary traditions that it simultaneously reshapes: part of the learned reader's pleasure is sparked by our recognition of Malory's delightful deviousness with romance conventions.

In this essay I propose a new interpretive model for Malory's romance of Sir Gareth, the story of the young, native-born nephew of King Arthur who moves from obscurity to heroic, public maturity. Several structural analyses already detail Malory's conformity to and deviance from romance traditions.[1] Here I am interested in a different context in which to view Malory's discourse, the context of Jungian analysis. In "The Tale of Sir Gareth," I will argue, Malory explores the aesthetic possibilities of the alchemical process to ground his psychology of Sir Gareth's maturing process. For C. G. Jung, the alchemical process both structures and images human change and growth. For Malory, alchemy is undergirding, process, and symbol in the "Tale of Sir Gareth"; the alchemical aesthetic provides structure and contextualizes characters.[2]

This tale provides a powerful scheme of romance-building that is echoed, but not precisely paralleled, in any of Malory's documented sources. The deft decorative quality of the tale is fueled by the tale's extraordinary psychological vision, which finds its theoretical underpinnings in the science of alchemy applied to the hero and his adventures. Alchemy gives us, as well as Malory's contemporary audience, a grid through which the world of "Gareth" can be seen and judged, and through which the psychological processes of becoming-through-*doing* rather than becoming-through-thinking can be understood in terms available to a medieval as well as modern audience. Alchemy gives us, like Jung, access to distinctive theories of personality formation.

Alchemy, or hermetism, was a serious science of the ancient and medieval world. Its primary intention was to take the *prima materia*—the scientist as well as his materials—through a series of operations which would dissolve and reform the material into a nobler and more perfect unity. Only secondarily was alchemy identified with the "puffing art" which the teller debunks in Chaucer's *Canon's Yeoman's Tale*.[3] Alchemy was grounded in the Aristotelian formula which stated that chaotic primary matter found form in the four elements, variously composed. What alchemists added to Aristotle was the notion that blending and reblending these forms, especially through the use of some powerful transmuting agent (usually referred to as the "philosopher's stone") would lead to the noblest of selves as well as the noblest of metals. In the later Middle Ages, alchemy expressed itself increasingly in mystic and allegorical terms, darkly elaborating the process by which metals could be refined through mostly impenetrable allegories of the dissolution and reformation of a mythic Sun King. This process is described in one fashion or another in an enormous range of manuscripts which invariably provide symbolic figurations rather than the more clinically verifiable descriptions preferred by modern science.

These handbooks read like the most arcane mystical tracts; that is no mere accident: the alchemist like the mystic was an adept. Alchemical treatises often contain injunctions against revelations to outsiders similar to that in *The Cloud of Unknowing*, for the elements of the alchemist's craft were privileged and private.[4]

In its consistent emphasis on color, "The Tale of Sir Gareth" suggests that Malory was employing an alchemical scheme. In 1477, the king's alchemist Thomas Norton, whose *Ordinal of Alchemy* survives in thirty-one manuscripts, argued that in alchemy, color is all:

And seth in this arte your chief desyre
Is to have colour which shulde a-bide fire,
ye muste know, bifore ye can that see,
How every colour engendride shalle be.[5]

What does Malory gain by choosing an alchemical scheme to shape the story of Sir Gareth? This is answered quite simply as a visual decoration (alchemy provides a meaningful color sequencing) and most provocatively as a psychological variation (alchemy patterns personality change). Sir Gareth is a knight in the process of becoming, and the analogy of alchemy gives precise rendering, step-by-step, of that process. That much is easily understood. What signals Malory's deeper method is that alchemy presents a progress by analogy through states signalling moments of self-realization. Malory already had created the self-conscious hero in his portrayal of Lancelot. Lancelot and Gareth are distinguished from each other in several ways—as the foreign versus the native knight, as the spiritual versus the worldly knight, and also as the reflectively self-conscious versus the reflexively unself-conscious knight. Instead of overt analysis given by the characters or the narrator, or implicit in the hierarchy of the narrative, Malory chooses to represent changes in his hero through reference to the symbolic scheme of alchemy. Sir Gareth becomes both the subject and object of an alchemical process.

Alchemy charges a perfect dream world with intimations of meaning. Jung found in alchemy a close resemblance to the dream worlds of his patients; it was Jung's own study of alchemy that intensified his understanding and articulation of the theory of archetypes. Further, Jung uncovered in alchemical texts early struggles to describe the workings of the "unconscious." In the alchemical method he identified the transformation process which he called "individuation," wherein the subject achieves at least momentary wholeness through integration of the "conscious" and "unconscious."[6]

In "Gareth," Malory employs the *opus alchymicum* for reasons both thematic and aesthetic. Malory, like Chaucer, was likely to be well acquainted with this *opus*; on the one hand alchemical texts were widely available and easily obtained, and on the other hand, the proliferation of alchemical practitioners suggests that personal exposure to alchemists was not unlikely. The manuscripts, as every commentator irritably notes, annoy with their often incomprehensible intrigue and prolixity, but they are invaluable sources both of secular medieval color symbolism and of a thoroughly articulated secular psychology.[7]

Much of the paraphernalia of alchemy can be pared away in order to concentrate on its central method and symbols as they illuminate "Gareth." Malory is careful throughout the tale to associate Sir Gareth with specific functions and colors which in the end bear the full fruit of alchemical parallels; only by the end can the full scheme be retrospectively analyzed. His overarching scheme, then, is the larger rationale of his narrative habit of retroflective narration which constantly urges the audience to think backwards on the meaning of the hero's previous adventures.

When Gareth first comes to court, he is unformed, unknighted, an inexperienced but noble youth. Like the alchemist's *prima materia*, he is noble in essence but not transmuted by experience. At court he is assigned to the kitchen (a common starting place for romance's hidden heroes) and this place is significant not only in terms of Gareth's unperceived nobility but also in terms of alchemy, for the place where the process takes place is the kitchen, with the ovens which make one stink as the savage Damsel Lyonet accuses Gareth of stinking.[8] Upon leaving the court, Gareth's essential nobility is indicated by his gold armor, just as his lack of transformation is demonstrated by his paucity of weapons until he gains them through successful battle against his oppressor Sir Kay.

An essential elementary step recognized by alchemical treatises is *nigredo*, in which the prime matter is dissolved through a blackening process. Having achieved and then proven his knighthood through battles with foes who at that point in the text are anonymous, Gareth kills his first named knight (named at least by his sobriquet), the Black Knight. Further, Gareth takes upon himself the armor and identity of this Black Knight, thus becoming the *nigredo* of the *opus alchymicum*, the symbolic knight in search of new identity. Once *nigredo* is achieved, alchemical processes can take many forms, but inevitably they move the material through a stage in which the four elements are symbolically subdued and subsumed; it is not surprising, then, that Gareth overcomes, in sequence, the Black, Green, Red, and Blue Knights, who are all brothers. In this context it is important that they are known by color before they are revealed by name.[9] The four elements are frequently envisioned alchemically as four brothers:

Four brothers stand in a long row;
The one to the right carries the weight of earth,
The other that of water; the rest of them
Carry the elements of air and fire.

> If you want all of them to die quickly,
> Only kill one of them, and they will
> Die together, since they are united
> By natural bonds.[10]

Furthermore, alchemy has four regimens, or degrees of heat, each of which is twice as great as the preceding degree. Malory may also have had these in mind by describing the four brothers as progressively stronger and progressively more generous in their gifts to Gareth.

The knight is then ready for a central alchemical test: can the *nigredo* prove equal to—survive—the fire? This process is referred to as *rubedo*, the reddening and heating of the matter. The Red Knight of the Red Lands is doubly significant as Sir Ironside. In general symbolism, iron red is the color of Mars, of violence and martial power. That Malory refers to Gareth as "amated" (1:323) with the Red Knight of the Red Lands suggests a doubling in which Gareth is subduing not only Ironside's violence, but his own. He is being tempered through the fire, and it is crucial that his first act after overcoming this knight is to demonstrate mercy, not vengeance.

The test of Sir Ironside is the seventh test of Gareth's knighthood. Seven is the mystical number in alchemy; Malory makes that numerology significant by reminding us three times that Sir Ironside has the strength of seven men until noon. The *rubedo*, sometimes called the red stone, is often the seventh step of the alchemical process. It is a smoky and rumbling process; Malory tells us at first sight of Ironside's pavilion, that "there was muche smoke and grete noyse" (1:319). Defeating Sir Ironside, Gareth symbolically absorbs his power. He is now prepared to adopt the role of lover.

One conventional symbol with special alchemical significance is the lion, sign not only of power, but in alchemy also an animal transmitting odd overtones of incest. The mythic sun king Sol, who represents the *prima materia* being transformed, is mated with his sister the mythic moon queen, Luna. As Sol is the *spiritus*, so is Luna the *anima*. The mating of this incestuous brother and sister is figured by a double-bodied lion from whose single mouth spew the sulphuric waters of change.[11] The connection of the lion to sexuality and to danger evokes the double she-lions of the "Gareth": Lyonet and Lyones. Gareth for the first time sees Lyones, his immediate passion and eventual bride, at the same moment that he meets the Red Knight of the Red Lands.[12] Change for Gareth is a result of his commitment to his two lion-named ladies: Lyonet propels him out of the kitchen for his first set of adventures, and the love of Lyones provokes the adventures of the second half of the text. Even the lover's sexual misadventure echoes alchemical relations. The act of sex between the allegorical king and queen is described in alchemy as the blood bath of Sol and Luna, an attempt at intercourse that always involves trauma. Just so Gareth's enthusiastic approach to Lyones produces the wounding intervention of Lyonet's magical knight.

In addition to lions, the text produces dwarves. The dwarves particularly associated with the hero in "Gareth" carry not only their traditional romance roles and characteristics but alchemical ones as well, for dwarves are underground gnomes, the metal workers of alchemy.[13] They are peculiarly exempt from ordinary morality; they can, for instance, reveal Gareth's identity when all the ordinary human characters are pledged not to do so. They are figures with what Hanning calls *"engin"*; like magicians, they play by private rules.[14] These tricksters, acting with impunity, are epitomized by the dwarf who dupes our hero into removing the magic ring, thus exposing himself to the court for the first time as "Gareth of Orkeney."

The central and most compelling alchemical symbol in "Gareth" is this magic ring. While such rings are the common property of romancers, the peculiar quality ascribed to Lyones' ring seems unique. It is the ring which transforms the bearer into the Knight of All Colors, a perfect disguise. In alchemy, this is the process called the *cauda pavonis*, the peacock's tail, in which the transmuting agent is *lapis*. A symbol of Christ in the liturgy, the *lapis* is the stone whose prism contains all the hues of the rainbow. In alchemy this is the panchromatic philosopher's stone, whose appearance heralds the moment of transformation. The peacock's tail is often associated with Luna. Not surprisingly, then, with Sol and Luna imaging Gareth and Lyones, the magic ring protects by disguising Gareth in a color prismatic.[15]

Gareth's disguise as the Knight of All Colors excites curiosity but not disapprobation; once more disguise is presented as morally neutral. When Gareth wears the ring in the tournament, he is invincible, unwounded as the lady promises. But the lady only lends her ring. Lyones tells Gareth that she normally wears it since it intensifies her own beauty. Thus we learn that the property of the ring changes with the bearer, illuminating the prime characteristics of each in turn. Lyones' prime characteristic is beauty, while Gareth has two—his prowess at arms and his disguise. The colors into which he changes at the tournament are therefore doubly symbolic, since they represent both the colors of most of the knights he has thus far conquered and subjected and also his capacity for disguise. When, through the dwarf's duping, Gareth takes off the ring near the end of the tournament, his armor turns yellow and his identity is inscribed in gold on his helm.

The achieved process of reformed identity is alchemically marked by the reconciliation of all elements, the transmutation of unrefined gold into refined gold. Gareth, the subject and object of the alchemical process of becoming, has now become fine gold. He has achieved his identity through the test of his actions.

Even the timing has alchemical associations. The tournament is called for Lady's Day, the feast of the Assumption. Malory draws our attention to this date by mentioning it three times in the text. The Assumption is frequently connected with the final process of transmutation in the alchemy of the later Middle Ages. This is natural enough, since Christian alchemists tried to fuse theology and alchemy, and the Assumption represents the highest transformation of ordinary human matter into the heavens' permanence. For Gareth's moment of reformed identity to descend on Assumption Day is therefore particularly adroit.[16]

These multiple points of contact with the *opus alchymicum* serve several purposes for Malory. The overall scheme of alchemy provides a richly decorative romance structure, full of color and vitality. In their specificity the alchemical correspondences give depth to an already jammed narrative, just as their structure gives form to Gareth's world and to his heroic self. Through the use of this progressive symbolism the story takes on the texture of allegory without its explicitness: the dream world has meaning, but that meaning is suggestive rather than exclusive. Most important, the use of the alchemical process allows Malory to present his hero as a knight who can move through a dense environment without any sign from the hero that he is aware of meanings and consequences of that world. Process in the tale is a result of structure as much as characterization.

Following Scudder, critics have tended to read the "Gareth" as a tale in which the hero experiences moral education and moral trans-formation.[17] Malory's precise point throughout "Gareth" seems to me quite the contrary: his hero is elaborating innate (if dormant) virtues rather than developing new ones. It is not Gareth, for example, who learns from the chastity test; it is Lyonet who learns to delay the cure next time. As Scudder says, we find in the tale

> a perfect example of a chivalry neither dragged down by lower traditions nor distraught by inner conflicts. . . [Gareth] charms because his conduct spontaneously illustrates the new code of honor point-by-point, not in copy-book fashion like a set pattern but with the freshness of unconscious living.[18]

It is precisely the "unconscious" of this "living" that alchemical psychology explains. What we find in the tumult of alchemical symbols sprinkled on the tale is a psychology of process and change rendered without regard to *moral* process and change. For a writer whose previous interests have largely been those of ethical process, Malory's change of terms and tone here demonstrates the pluralism of his sense of chivalry as well as the variety of his aesthetic capabilities. His change suggests something else so fundamental that most readers absorb it without notice: unlike Arthur and Lancelot and Tristram, who must (as the adage says) "make their own luck," Gareth is a very lucky knight whose world orchestrates itself to allow his happiness. Some of us have doubtless had the hard fortune of knowing people like him, those who always do the right thing, say the appropriate thing, and get away with all manner of devilment because no one ever brings them to question their own actions.

In his deployment of not only alchemical symbols, but also of the alchemical scheme, Malory anticipated Jung's conclusion that alchemy patterns the unconscious movement of the self. Only in retrospect do the colors, names, dates, and objects of the tale reveal the fullness of this movement. But every reader knows that Gareth has changed, grown, been sharpened and distinguished from his peers; the alchemical process merely serves as a code for Malory's progressive revelations. Gareth offers progressive proof of his virtues throughout the tale, but there are few signs that this character attains deepening awareness or psychological introspection. Gareth's role is to cause such awareness in others, to act as the philosopher's stone, the touchstone, for the court and for society at large. In overcoming the four brother knights of color Gareth does not himself change; the very consistency of his achievement forces his guide, the ill-speaking Lyonet, to change toward him.

The adventures Gareth undertakes after the tournament in which his name is revealed serve other purposes as well. Alchemy is a science of never-ending process. The moment of what Jung calls "total integration" is just that, a moment, so that even after Gareth achieves this integration through the tournament he must continue to demonstrate his values. That these interpolated adventures have thematic purpose is seen next in his identity as an Arthurian knight ridding the land of ills; that they have alchemical significance is suggested not only by the color qualities of the knights he overcomes, but also by his new alchemical role as the touchstone, the refined gold having transforming and curative functions. Thus is the Duke of the Rose "cured" of his "illness," which is excessive and unmotivated loathing of King Arthur and his court.

These episodes also have structural functions. The separation of the tournament from the wedding feast is unexpected in romance;

Gareth leaves both court and lady before he has even claimed Lyones' hand. This is partially explained by Gareth's need to prove himself a useful Arthurian knight; it is also explained by Malory's desire to reinforce the irresolute quality of the tale. Brother turns against brother. This crucial theme is given its most moving expression in the tale's final battle between Gareth and Gawain, and therefore the joy of the wedding feast is not unalloyed.

The function of Gareth as touchstone illuminating court and world transforms the romance from a tale of sheer unconscious, dreamy delight to one of burdened significance, with lightness of tone sustained by Malory's deftness at creating characters with deft tongues. The first example of this wit is perhaps the tale's most important: the nicknaming of Gareth by Sir Kay. The young hero's most unusual physical features are his hands, the "largyste and the fayreste handis that ever man sye" (1:293). Two years later the suitability of his sobriquet—"Beaumains," the fair-handed—is ironically underscored by his mother Morgawse, who points out her son's generosity and strength of hand. We might remember that the alchemical path Gareth followed is called the "handwork" of the scientist and metal, that Gareth's hands embody his grace as well as chivalric accomplishment. It is, inevitably, for his hand that Gareth is given the magic ring; his hands themselves thus acquire magical significance. He is the serious hero of prowess by handiness as Nicholas is the Miller's comic hero of the art of being "hende" in Chaucer.

Certain juxtapositions within the tale and between this tale and Lancelot's are artfully arranged. It is for example notable that Arthur immediately and without question grants Gareth his requests at the beginning of the tale before knowing either who Gareth is or what his requests will be. This is the Arthur of the buried past, found in such stories as the Welsh *Culhwch and Olwen*, whose inclinations of heart toward his own blood are utterly reliable.[19] It is not the Arthur who has learned by dint of difficulty in Malory's earlier tales not to commit himself until he can understand the precise meanings of his commitment. Even Lancelot is more circumspect than Arthur when he later refuses to knight Gareth until Gareth reveals his own name and lineage. The first scene with Arthur is quickly juxtaposed to the next scene with the king, when Lyonet comes to court pleading for a champion. In this instance Arthur laconically refuses to aid the damsel since she refuses to name herself or her sister, although she does name the well-known Red Knight of the Red Lands as her enemy.

The difference between these two episodes involving Arthur is that of felt relation; Malory's highlighting of the issue of blood relation reverberates through the tale and all the rest of his Arthurian history. Gareth quixotically attempts to demonstrate his nobility by separating the nobility of his blood from the nobility of his action. He is compelled by the latter, not the former. The Arthurian world does not, however, tolerate Gareth's naive attempt at social equality, for everyone in his world ruthlessly insists that Gareth's actions of necessity reflect his noble birth; he is not allowed the solipsism of self-creation. Gareth is fused with his family, and only the narrator dares to unglue these relations. The "class solidarity" which Auerbach finds rife in romance is thus reinforced, but to odd effect.[20] The narrator distinguishes between the virtues of Gareth and the vices of Gawain to suggest that noble action may be limited to those of noble blood, but that the reverse equation is not necessarily valid. Gawain's final identification as a murderer demonstrates consanguinity's lack of moral consequence: Lot's children do not share the same nature.

Gareth moves in Malory's most magical world, but not in either his most spiritual or his most courtly ones. Some of these distinctions are clear from the divergent views of love in "The Tale of Sir Lancelot" and in "The Tale of Sir Gareth." Lancelot in his tale is skeptical of love, since he is sure that prowess and passion are opposed values. As he tells the forlorn maiden,

> But for to be a weddyd man, I thynke hit nat, for than I muste couche with hir and leve armys and turnamentis, batellys and adventures. And as for to sey to take my pleasaunce with paramours, that woll I refuse: in prencipall for drede of God, for knyghtes that bene adventures sholde nat be advoutrers nothir lecherous, for than they be nat happy nother fortunate unto the werrys; for other they shall be overcom with a sympler knyght than they be hemself, other ellys they shall sle by unhappe and hir cursednesse bettir men than they be hemself. And so who that usyth paramours shall be unhappy, and all thynge unhappy that is aboute them. (1:270-71)

Lancelot worries about such problems where Gareth simply acts on his inclinations. He wants Lyones; he tries to have her. When prevented, he waits for the wedding. Never is he the ungrudging courtly lover: when Lyones sends him away for a year's testing, Gareth is angry and gives vent to his humiliation.

> "Alas! fayre lady," seyde sir Bewmaynes, "I have nat deserved that ye sholde shew me this straungenesse. And I hadde wente I sholde have had ryght good chere with you, and unto my

power I have deserved thanke. And well I am sure I have
bought your love with parte of the beste bloode within my
body." (1:327)

Though Gareth is here the least conventional of courtly lovers, neither
lady nor narrator call him to task for his rudeness: for none of Malory's
other heroes is such language or attitude permissible.[21] Gareth has
proven more decorous in sexual matters earlier, when he declined Sir
Persaunte's offer of his virgin daughter's bed companionship. There is
slight hesitation and broad humor even there in Gareth's query of the
damsel who came to his bed. "Be ye a pusell or a wyff?" (1:315) he
asks before he decides to send her back to her father, in the display
of courtesy given to Gawain in *Syre Gawene and the Carle of Carelyle*.[22]

Where Lancelot strives for perfection through the Pentecostal Oath
until he plumbs its possibilities, Gareth acts on a simple apprehension
of the Oath which is never cast into question by his adventures. Gareth
never overtly challenges the basic assumptions his society holds about
honor, love, or marriage; it is only by contrast with Lancelot that Gareth's
blithe facility for disregarding the troublesome seems shallow. But if
Gareth does not have Lancelot's complex consciousness, neither does
he share Lancelot's discernible quirks and failures.

Gareth's demonstration of heroism does not diminish Lancelot.
Lancelot's elevation in the Arthurian world was partially achieved at
the expense of Sir Kay, until then a deservedly well-respected knight,
who by the time of this tale has become the lowest of knights. In
"Gareth," a different denigration takes place: here Gareth's eldest
brother Gawain is subject to a complex set of degradations. The strategy
of Gawain's loss of reputation tellingly elucidates the motives and
methods that push "Gareth" beyond the frontier of romance into the
darker paths of tragedy.[23] The final separation of Gawain from his kin
occurs in this tale at a moment of otherwise decorous congruity in which
King Arthur marries all of Gareth's brothers to Lyones' female relatives.
All of Gareth's brothers, that is, except Gawain, who in this tale is
compellingly scorned, though without reason. Most tellingly, in this
moment, he is subjected to the worst of human humiliations—he is in
the end, as in the beginning, ignored.

Although these tensions are felt in "Gareth," the tale finally
reinforces a mood of festivity and play. Malory here achieves what
Henry James in the preface to *The American* calls "experience
liberated, . . . disengaged, disembroiled, disenchanted." In this tale
Malory has presented himself as a revolutionary romancer, a writer who
can summon all the gestures of a genre without committing himself
to its traditional values. Even conventions of love can be reversed

without consequences to the dream quality of the created world. Fantasy fulfillment of almost every sort is given in the tale, measured out in amusing narrative juxtapositions and realistic dialogue.[24]

The romance world of "Gareth" is as infinite as it is unstable; both these qualities are given structure by the tale's analogy to alchemy which always deals with enigmatic emulsions of the unstable and the infinite. The density of incident gives readers the sense of process, progress, and endless interpenetration; readers are seduced into enjoying a world whose values are often antithetical to those of Malory's other Arthurian tales. Disguise, magical paraphernalia, knights with returnable heads—the very motifs of unreliability which the narrative elsewhere rejects as inadequate for serious life and fiction are here incorporated with easy acceptance. All of this serves as groundwork for the next tale, that of Sir Tristram, but it also stands on its own as a catalogue of traditional romance motifs.

This is romance taken beyond the limit of inherited form while employing every technique and motif of that form. Though the characters may not be thoughtful, the writer is cunning. Malory's typical paratactic technique preserves romance as parallel to life, for the act of subordination, of rendering judgments and determining meaning, is largely in the hands of the reader.[25] The game of romance—the young hero winning recognition and the lady—is played out in full measure against the disruptive forces which attain new status in the Arthurian world.

Malory's feat in "The Tale of Sir Gareth" can finally be measured by his tact. The rigor of the alchemical exercise, like the smaller elements of the story, is only available to us in retrospect. But the writer does not use his greater information to condescend to his audience, as Chrétien sometimes seems to do. Malory's mode is always to associate himself with his readers *in the act of reading*. If Gareth pretends to be a Fair Unknown, the writer does not flaunt privileged knowledge of him: to the writer, as to the reader, Gareth is Beaumains until he chooses to unmask himself. And this is true of each character in turn; each is left with disguise preserved until the character chooses to shed it. In this act of respect for his created characters is found respect for his readers. For that tact, readers have always cherished Malory; for that tact we all return to "The Tale of Sir Gareth" to reexperience its multiple charms.

Notes

1. For varying structural models, see Larry D. Benson, *Malory's Morte Darthur* (Cambridge, Mass., 1976); Claude Luttrell, *The Creation of the First Arthurian Romance: A Quest* (London, 1974); Morton Donner, "The Backgrounds

of Malory's Book of Sir Gareth" (Diss. Columbia University, 1956); P. J. C. Field, "The Source of Malory's Tale of Sir Gareth" in *Aspects of Malory*, ed. Toshiyuki Takamiya and Derek Brewer (Woodbridge, Eng., 1981), pp. 57–70; Mark Lambert, *Malory: Style and Vision in Le Morte Darthur* (New Haven, 1975); Vida Scudder, *Le Morte Darthur of Sir Thomas Malory and Its Sources* (New York, 1921); Terence McCarthy, *Reading the Morte Darthur* (Cambridge, 1988). See especially Felicity Riddy, *Sir Thomas Malory* (Leiden, 1987) and *The Works of Sir Thomas Malory*, ed. Eugène Vinaver, rev. P. J. C. Field, 3rd ed. 3 vols., (Oxford, 1990). All quotations from Malory are from this edition and will be cited in the text.

2. I argue in a manuscript in progress that the glitter of the alchemical model intensifies Sir Gareth's value at the very moment that Sir Gawain is displaced as a higher hero. Sir Gareth absorbs the good will Sir Gawain has lost. By the end of the tale, Sir Gawain is defamed, his reputation is tattered. This displacement of Sir Gawain portends the final agonies of the Arthurian court in the midst of its most celebratory moments.

3. The most useful analysis of medieval alchemy, especially in relation to Chaucer, is found in Joseph E. Grennan, "Jargon Transmuted: Alchemy in Chaucer's Canon's Yeoman's Tale" (Diss., Fordham University, 1960). See also Grennan's articles on alchemy and Chaucer, particularly "The Canon's Yeoman and the Cosmic Furnace: Language and Meaning in the *Canon's Yeoman's Tale*," *New Criterion* 4 (1964), 225–40. As Grennan says, "Alchemy, not unlike courtly love, was a literary game as well as a practical pursuit. Not only its grandiose claims, measured by its small achievements, but its high-flown and mystifying language, its stereotyped habits of thought and expression, its conventionalized and practically inflexible rules of procedure—all made it especially vulnerable for ironic exploitation" (p. 229). The use of alchemy as literary game, not always ironically pursued, has largely been closed to general readers because of the arcane quality of alchemical texts.

4. Allen E. Debus, *The Chemical Philosophy: Paracelsian Science and Medicine in The Sixteenth and Seventeenth Centuries* (New York, 1977), p. 14, argues that in the fourteenth and fifteenth centuries, alchemy turned increasingly to allegory and mysticism. In his edition of E. Ashmole's *Theatrum Chemicum Britannicum* (New York, 1967), p. xxii, Debus says that "traditional alchemy with its emphasis on piety, secrecy and allegory reached its apogee in England in the century after the death of Chaucer." The complexity and self-contradictory quality of the alchemical texts is recognized even by their writers; as Thomas Norton says in his *Ordinal of Alchemy* (dated 1477):

> Everyche of them tagthe but oon poynt or tweyne,
> wherby his felows were made certeyne
> How that he was to theyme a brodyre,
> For everyche of them wel undirstonde that odir.
> Alle-so thei wrote not every man to teche,
> But to shew them-silfe bi a secrete speche.
> Truste not therfore to redyng of oon boke,
> But in many auctours werkis ye most loke (ll. 1090–98).

The most useful collections of alchemical texts relevant to Malory's period are: Thomas Norton, *The Ordinal of Alchemy*, ed. John Reidy, EETS, OS 272 (London, 1975); *Theatrum Chemicum Britannicum. Containing severall poeticall pieces of our famous English philosophers, who have written the hermetique mysteries in their own ancient language....*ed. Elias Ashmole (London, 1652), repr. ed. Allen G. Debus, (New York, 1967): *Bibliotheca Chemica Curiosa*, ed. Jeon-Jacques Menget, 2 vols. (Geneva, 1702); *Theatrum chemicum: praecipuos selectorum auctorum tractatus de chemiae et lapidis philosophici antiquitate, veritate...& operationibus, contiens: in gratiam verae chemicae, & medicinae chemicae studiosorum....*, ed. Lazarus Zetzner, 6 vols. (Strausburg, 1659–61); *The Hermetic museum, restored and enlarged: most faithfully instructing all disciples of the sopho-spagyric art how that greatest and truest medicine of the philosopher's stone may be found and held...*, ed. and trans. Arthur E. Waite, 2 vols. (London, 1893). For further bibliography, see Grennan, "Jargon Transmuted"; Eric John Holmyard, *Alchemy* (London, 1957) and the less-reliable Johannes Fabricius, *Alchemy: The Medieval Alchemist and Their Royal Art* (Copenhagen, 1976).

5. Norton, *The Ordinal of Alchemy*, ed. Reidy, ll. 1457–1460.

6. C. G. Jung, *Collected Works*, ed. Herbert Read, Michael Fordham, Gerhard Adler, and William McGuire, 20 vols. (Princeton, 1967–73). See particularly vol. 12, *Psychology and Alchemy*, 2nd ed., trans. R. F. C. Hull (1968); vol. 13, *Alchemical Studies*, trans. R. F. C. Hull (1967); and vol. 14, *Mysterium Coniunctionis: An Inquiry into the Separation and Synthesis of Psychic Opposites in Alchemy*, 2nd ed., trans. R. F. C. Hull (1970).

7. On general color symbolism in the Middle Ages, see particularly Sigmund Skard, "The Use of Color in Literature: A Survey of Research," *Proceedings of the American Philosophical Society* 90 (July 1946), 163–249; Peter Dronke, "Tradition and Innovation in Medieval Western Colour-Imagery," *Eranos Jahrbuch* 41 (1972), 51–107; and Robert J. Blanch, "The Origins and Use of Medieval Color Symbolism," *International Journal of Symbology* 3 (1972), 1–5. The idea of color in the Middle Ages as a substance, rather than a refraction of light, leads to difficulty for interpreters: the meanings of colors hold both a quality and its opposite. For that reason, though the use of color in the "Gareth" is richly suggestive, it is most importantly seen in the context of progression.

8. In *Havelok the Dane*, Havelok, another hidden hero, this one a Fair Unknown, undergoes a similar apprenticeship through social stages from kitchen to kingdom.

9. Alchemy usually moves in stages from black through red and white to gold. Malory subsumes the white stage in his presentation of the Red Knight, Sir Perymones, who, unlike the other brothers who are all surrounded by natural and artificial examples of their own color, is surrounded by white objects. My assumption is that Malory either misunderstood the usual movement through white, or that he was reserving white as a color associated only with the most excellent knights (Lancelot, Galahad) or with spiritual purity.

10. Fabricius, *Alchemy,* p. 24. See also the illustrations in Johann Daniel Mylius, *Philosophia reformata contiens libros biros* (Frankfurt, 1622), trans. Patricia Tahil as *The Alchemical Engravings of Mylius.* . . . , ed. Adam McLean (Edinburgh, 1984).

11. For this image, see Mylius as well as Stanislas Klossowski de Rola, *Alchemy: The Secret Art* (London, 1973), p. 103, n. 2.

12. This is numerologically connected to the frequency with which the lions are mentioned during the *rubedo* process. The tradition of moon- and lion-named ladies is also, of course, part of Malory's romance inheritance; best known to modern audiences is Lunette from Chrétien's *Yvain.* The alchemical model is as relevant to *Yvain* as the "Gareth." For example, in *Yvain,* the merging of Sol and Luna is evoked in the scene in which Gawain and Lunette mate. *Yvain* is full of parallels to "Gareth": a damsel guide who leads the hero to his lady, a magic ring with the power of preserving the bearer's life, tensions among the blood-related Yvain and Gawain, denigration of Gawain and elevation of the young hero Yvain. Professor E. D. Kennedy kindly brought to my attention another alchemical parallel—to Gottfried's *Tristan.* See Gottfried von Strassburg, *Tristan, translated entire for the first time: with the surviving fragments of the Tristran of Thomas, newly translated.* . . . , trans. A. T. Hatto (Baltimore, 1967), pp. 185, 187.

The incest motif is always shrouded in the "Gareth," though it is never far from the reader's mind. Operating in the background of the story is the incest of Arthur and Morgawse and its product, Mordred, whose absence from the tale and from the lists of Gareth's brothers through the tale, is notable.

13. For an interesting discussion of dwarves in the alchemical process, see Mircea Eliade, *The Forge and the Crucible: The Origins and Structures of Alchemy,* trans. Stephen Corrin, 2nd ed. (Chicago, 1978), pp. 102–8.

14. Robert W. Hanning, *The Individual in Twelfth-Century Romance* (New Haven, 1977), pp. 105–38.

15. Fabricius, *Alchemy,* pp. 1–135. The symbolic language of the panchromatic *cauda pavonis* is explicit in the *Cantilena* of George Ripley, trans. in Jung, 14.274ff. Allegories of the peacock's tail as the philosopher's stone permeate the alchemical texts; one example among many is found in *Hermes Bird:*

Ther ys a Stone wych ys called Fagownce,
Od Olde engendered within myne entrayle:
Wych of fyne Golde poyseth a grete unce;
Setryne of Colors like Garnetis of entayle,
Wych makyth men victorius in batalle;
    And who that bereth on hym thys Stone,
    Ys ful assured ageyne his moral Fone.
(*st. 34,* in *Theatrum* ed. Ashmole, p. 220)

16. After his transformation, Gareth has three encounters before his final battle with Gawain. I have not discerned any alchemical significance in the first

adventure, but the killing of the Brown Knight Without Pity parallels the saturnine depression of the alchemist, and the victory over the Duke of the Rose brings in one of alchemy's most central mystical symbols. The rose represents both eternity and the final succumbing of the material to the emotions of the *anima*. The rose is the paramount symbol of alchemy's mystical marriage of elements; Gareth's mastery of its champion is a fitting prelude to his union with Lyones.

17. See Benson, *Malory's Morte Darthur*, pp. 103, 106; Edmund Reiss, *Sir Thomas Malory* (New York, 1966), pp. 105–6; and Susan S. Richardson, "Thematic Unity in Malory's *Morte Darthur*" (Diss. University of Kansas, 1968), p. 75.

18. Scudder, *Le Morte Darthur*, p. 219.

19. In *Culhwch and Olwen*, Arthur is careful before he grants Culhwch's boon the second time to modify his generosity by reserving for himself several private objects, persons and animals.

20. Erich Auerbach, *Mimesis: The Representation of Reality in Western Literature*, trans. Willard R. Trask (Princeton, 1953), p. 121.

21. For analysis of the violations of courtly love norms in the "Gareth," see Charles Moorman, *The Book of Kyng Arthur: The Unity of Malory's Morte Darthur* (Lexington, 1965), pp. 19–21.

22. On the figure of Ironside in that and other romances, see Robert W. Ackerman, "Malory's Ironsyde," *Research Studies* (Washington State University) 32 (1964), 125–34.

23. See Victor Angelescu, "The Relationship of Gareth and Gawain in Malory's *Morte Darthur*," *Notes and Queries* (1961), 8–9, for an argument that Malory's degradation of Gawain is one proof of unity in *Le Morte Darthur*.

24. Benson, *Malory's Morte Darthur*, p. 108, gives an amusing account of this fantasy fulfillment.

25. On the paratactic technique in Malory, see Field, "The Source," especially pp. 31–35, 38–46. Lambert, *Malory* pp. 1–55, follows Field's model in discussing the characteristic effects of parataxis in Malory, while Felicity Riddy historicizes and extends it.

How Many Roads to Camelot?
The Married Knight in Malory's *Morte Darthur*

——————————————————— *Maureen Fries*

In his *Morte Darthur,* Sir Thomas Malory depicts a number of roads which a knight may travel to achieve worship in that complex society which makes up the Round Table. "Worship" is Malory's word for a complicated concept of knightly worth (with a history going back at least as far as the works of Chrétien de Troyes) which involves full personal confidence—a just and justified self-esteem—with societal approval—the earned and continually reinforced esteem of others. The *Morte* depicts three main avenues to such worship. One of these involves kinship with Arthur, a road which brings scant honor in Malory's story. Typical of Arthur's kin is Gawain, knighted early in the book merely because he is Arthur's nephew, whose previous and subsequent career brings him little worship and much shame. "And so anone com in yonge Gawayne and asked the kynge a gyffte.... 'make me knyght that same day that ye shall wedde dame Gwenyver.' 'I woll do hit with a goode wylle,' seyde kynge Arthure, 'and do unto you all the worship that I may, for I muste be reson ye ar my nevew, my sistirs son.' "[1] Far more worship may accrue from a second path, the way of which Lancelot is the prime exemplar; as dramatized in his "Noble Tale," unmarried fidelity to one woman may inspire that courageous combination of mercy and justice which makes Guinevere's lover "moste...honoured of hyghe and lowe": "Wherefore quene Gwenyvere had hym in grete favoure aboven all other knyghtis, and so he loved the quene agayne aboven all other ladyes dayes of his lyff, and for hir he dud many dedys of armys...."[2] But a third possible road to Arthurian glory is the single extended quest which culminates in marriage. It is the treatment of the married knight in the *Morte* that I want to explore in this paper.[3]

The most prominent married knight in Malory is Gareth, whose story is piquantly placed between the tales of Lancelot and Tristram, the two most famous of adulterous warriors.[4] Arriving incognito at his uncle's court (so that he does not depend upon kinship, like his brother Gawain), Gareth spends a year as Kay's kitchen knave. Then, when the damsel Lynet appears to request aid for her sister, Dame Lyonesse, Beaumaynes (as Gareth is called by Kay) asks that he be given her quest and knighted by Lancelot. Continually insulted by Lynet for his kitchen knavery—a scolding obviously intended to provide the traditional impetus to valor— Gareth overcomes more than a dozen strong knights. His justice is tempered, like Lancelot's, with justified mercy, especially in his decision to spare the life of the mighty Red Knight of the Red Lands. Winning in the end not only the approval of Lynet but also the love and the hand of her sister Lyonesse, Gareth, after a final stunning victory at a tournament arranged by the latter, weds his lady amid much pomp and pageantry.[5]

This triumphant conclusion resembles that of the tale of Lancelot, as do many other plot details. Both knights are unproven at the beginning of their quests, and both choose the path of personal merit on their way to Arthurian glory. Gareth's first sight and immediate love for Lyonesse serve, like Lancelot's love for Guinevere, as wellspring for his greatest victories. Like Lancelot, Gareth faces and solves complex dilemmas involving justice and mercy and shows himself especially inclined to pity when a woman is involved. As in the case of Lancelot, Gareth's conquests—ceremoniously praising his prowess—precede his triumphant return to Arthur's court.

Lancelot is himself an important character in Gareth's tale. Within its very first lines he reminds Kay, who has spitefully given the young stranger his mocking nickname, that the newcomer may prove of worship. The senior knight gives his junior gold and clothes during his probationary year, and it is Lancelot Gareth chooses to knight him. During Lyonesse's tournament, Lancelot tells Arthur that, though it lies in his power to put Gareth from his worship, "yet wolde I nat."[6] Finally, Lancelot is several times in the *Morte* described as the knight Gareth loves best.

Even more pronounced is Lancelot's presence in Malory's version of the story of another married knight, La Cote Mal Tayle. In this narrative reconstructed from scattered and interlaced fragments in its French original (the *Tristan en prose*), the scolding damsel and the knight's love object are one rather than the two halves of womanly utility, as guide and as reward, represented by the sisters Lynet and Lyonesse in the "Gareth." La Cote fights against a hundred knights, is taken prisoner, and is delivered from prison by Lancelot (twice). Lancelot marks the progress of La Cote's lady, and thus the knight's own progress, by his successive naming and renaming of her, as first "Maledysaunt" and then "Bien Pensaunt" and finally "Byeaue-Vyvante." In an episode unparalleled in the French source, Lancelot bestows the possessions of the "Castell of Pendragon" upon La Cote. But, when Lancelot also offers the possessions of Sir Plenorys, La Cote refuses (in an echo of Lancelotian nicety) to deprive that knight of his livelihood. So it seems appropriate that Lancelot should promise him a place at the Round Table and that he should wed his lady.[7]

Lancelot also figures in name, if not in deed, in the short and simple annals of Alisaunder le Orphelin, which Malory also reworked from the *Tristan en prose*. Summoned by his cousin Tristram to put himself "in the rule and in the hondis of sir Launcelot,"[8] Alisaunder takes the wrong route, arriving not in London but at the court of King Carados, where he wins a tournament. After several further victories, he acquires the hand and lands of Alys La Beall Pylgryme, by whom he has a son before he is murdered by his uncle, King Mark. In a passage not in the French, Malory's narrator remarks that Alisaunder "had never grace ne fortune to com to kynge Arthurs courte; for and he had com to sir Launcelot, all knyghtes seyde that knew hym that he was one of the strengyste knyghtes that was in kynge Arthurs dayes."[9]

Alisaunder, La Cote, and Gareth's marital successes, turning as they do upon tournament victories, had their analogues in real life, as George Duby has noted: "We should see the tournament...as a kind of exhibition, where eligible bachelors preened themselves under the eyes of the ladies, but especially under the eyes of those who had a woman to bestow."[10] But the presence—and, indeed, prominence—of Lancelot in their stories has no such coefficient, and makes a striking contrast to Malory's insistence upon the lesser heroes' marriages, since Lancelot has previously and specifically rejected marriage for himself: "[B]ut for to be a weddyd man, I thynke hit nat, for than I must couche with hir and leve armys and turnamentis, batellys and adventures."[11] Duby has traced the growth of this concept of the difference between the wedded and unwedded knightly states in the "extremely rich...*History of the Counts of Guines*": "the obligation of the head of the family (*caput generis*) was the careful husbanding of the seed contained in his loins and in those of his legitimate sons."[12] Yet Gareth, perhaps with Lancelot's example in mind, hedges a little in his initial reply to Arthur's seemingly cynical offer to him of Lyonesse "as paramour, other ellys to have hir to his wyff"; once Lyonesse, however, has rather firmly expressed her wish for a legitimate union, he does not hesitate to agree with her.[13] Nor do La Cote or Alisaunder reject the permanent marital couching and family responsibilities Lancelot so persistently refuses. Malory's advocacy of marriage is, moreover, more prominent in the "Gareth," apparently an original tale,[14] than, in the other two, French-derived stories. For instance, the premarital chastity stressed by Lyonet's magical prevention of the consummation of Gareth and Lyonesse's "hoote lustis"[15] matters little in the "Alisaunder," where the hero goes blithely to bed with the damsel of Beale Regard before he meets and marries his Alys.[16]

As has often been noted, English romancers prior to Malory had also strongly supported marriage[17] showing a characteristic, "wariness of if not a distaste for the language and conventions of French courtly love."[18] But Malory presents Gareth's choice of marriage over the more usual Arthurian champion's arrangement in a context which deliberately emphasizes its strangeness for a knight who desires greatness. Arthur, proposing to his nephew that he take Lyonesse "as paramour" before offering the marital alternative, is flanked on one side by his own adulterous (and barren) wife and on the other by Gareth's mother, his own sister and former lover, Morgause. Although the queen and her ladies have still, in Malory, the right to rule in matters of love, neither Guinevere nor Morgause objects to Arthur's immoral proposition.[19] Gareth's publicly made choice of marriage, therefore, suggests not only his own conventional Christian values but the possibility for the return of Arthur's court to moral health—especially since the king, in a seeming endorsement of Gareth's choice (and in a literary echo of the historical role of *caput generis*), promptly weds his other nephews Gaheris and Aggravain to Lyonesse's relatives.[20]

Nor is this Malory's only encomium of marriage. Tristram, who in the French *Tristan en prose* wed Isode of Brittany unhappily, has with her in Malory "suche chere and ryches and all other plesaunce that he had allmoste...forsakyn La Beale Isode."[21] The fatherhood which Malory invents for the Alisaunder he found in his French source suggests a like and mimetic approbation of marital over adulterous values which echoes the historical record. "Quite clearly, the elder (*senior*) made a point of cherishing his lady and of cherishing his children," Duby notes, since the "ethos of...the head of the house" revolved not only around reserving his seed "for the one woman who had been conveyed to his bed in a solemn wedding procession" but also around raising his "eldest son to be a good knight" and providing him with "a good wife."[22] What was true for the Counts of Guines was undoubtedly typical of aristocratic marriage in general.

But in the context of his "hoole" book, Malory is unable to use marriage as a continuing impetus for knightly worship, as, for instance, Chrétien de Troyes had done in such works as the *Erec* and the *Yvain*. Apparently lacking Chrétien's interest in the psychological dilemma of the married knight, he also seems unable to imagine postmarital martial reputations even remotely analogous to Lancelot's for those knights that hero has so prominently aided. Gareth, La Cote, and Alisaunder never even approach the status of a Blioberis or a Lamorak, lesser but mighty warriors significantly involved in extramarital relations similar to Lancelot's. Indeed, in order for Tristram to become—for a time—Lancelot's peer, he must forsake his Breton wife in spite of her "chere and ryches," and resume his adulterous affair with Isode of Cornwall, with its attendant and persistent calls to adventure.

In Malory, wives, as opposed to mistresses, usually neither desire nor condone such adventures, as Gareth's wife shows in her intolerance of the kind of tournament activity by which Tristram triumphs from the beginning, and through which Gareth has just and definitively won her hand. Just after her marriage, "dame Lyonesse desyred of the kynge that none that were wedded sholde juste at that feste."[23] Prudent woman! The "frequent accidents of chivalric sport" had cost the real-life Henry of Bourbourg the loss of three sons out of seven, two killed and one maimed by the loss of an eye (making him "ineligible to assume the honor of his father"), causing that father to hasten a marriage for his youngest son.[24] In his mere handful of further appearances in the *Morte* before his tragic and accidental death at the hands of an unknowing Lancelot, Gareth's only significant role is his aiding of Tristram in his brutal victory over the Round Table party at Lonezep, an action Arthur rightly regards as treasonable.[25] La Cote appears in two or three places besides his own narreme, a figure of little distinction, while Alisaunder, apparently detained by the responsibilities of noble fatherhood as well as marriage, never even arrives at Arthur's court. Nor does marriage bring spiritual distinction: Gareth is mentioned on the Grail quest only to illustrate his brother Gawain's affection for him;[26] and, in the episode of "The Healing of Sir Urry," designed by Malory to demonstrate Lancelot's fullness of grace, the names of Gareth and La Cote serve—among many others—merely to fill out a typical Malorian catalogue (in this case of knights who failed).

That Gareth, at least, might have won a permanent place on the (occasionally shifting) pecking order of the best knights of the world rather than in such a minor catalogue appears from his tale. Sir Persaunt of Inde assures him that, if he matches the Red Knight of the Red Lands, he will become the fourth best knight in the world, succeeding Gawain (who in the Red Knight's ranking is exceeded only by Lancelot, Tristram, and Lamorak). But already, in the tale of "Tristram" which follows his own, Gareth has been displaced by Palomides, while Gawain—in spite of his moral inferiority to his younger brother—remains a contender, and Galahad a later and permanent addition. As Benson notes, "clearly Gareth represents the lowest level [of the High Order of Knighthood]," remaining "a young knight who attains only the first stage of greatness" because he "chooses marriage."[27]

Married knights, deprived of Lancelot's continuing guidance, grow rusty in tournament etiquette, as Gareth proves at Lonezep. Perhaps their haste to rejoin their wives rather than continue on the knightly circuit impedes them, to say nothing of the historically evidenced and previously cited danger to their seed. At the Hallowmass Tournament, "sir Gareth...ded that day grete dedis of armys, for he smote downe and pulled downe thirty knyghtes; but whan he had done that dedis he taryed nat, but so departed, and therefore he loste hys pryse."[28] La Cote and Alisaunder are not even allowed beyond their stories proper such minimal martial mention. The explicit reason advanced for Alisaunder's failure to realize his full potential is his inability to meet and be trained by Lancelot. For all of Malory's choosing marriage as a tidy end to some of his tales, he is unable to reconcile the duties of the *caput generis* with the continuing chivalric glories of his *Morte*: Lancelot and Lancelot's choice of relationship are, and remain, the norm for Arthurian worship.

One may find other indications that Malory was well aware of the gulf in the later Middle Ages between the knightly mystique and the conventionally happy marriage. Edward D. Kennedy, in two studies of Arthur and Guenevere's marriage (a subject which lies outside the present discussion), has commented upon this phenomenon. He notes not only that "Arthur's attitude toward Guenevere changes from the devotion of a loving husband to the indifference of a king whose primary concerns are his realm and the knights of the Round Table,"[29] but also that "the dangers inherent in a uxorious king" as displayed in Edward IV's marriage to Elizabeth Wydeville may have motivated Malory "to omit passages in his sources that show Arthur's love for his queen."[30] Discussing the real-life relationships between marriage and politics in the families of the Nevilles and the Wydevilles in the later fifteenth century, J. R. Lander comments upon the "sordid tangles of matrimonial competition, rivalry for property and influence [which] were the absorbing interest of landed families," emphasizing how, "[i]n the twenty years between 1450 and 1470, the [marital] ambitions of one over-mighty family and of part of another came to dominate national politics."[31]

Similar marriages from political rather than Gareth's amorous motive accrue to Gaheris and Aggravain, his brothers, whose unions with Lyonesse's relatives apparently involve neither love nor choice, but are good financial matches (as would appear from Gareth's wife's wealth and status). Such concerns with matters of money infected all of society from kings down to landed gentry like the Pastons by the end of the Middle Ages. As Frances and Joseph Gies have recently reaffirmed, after the Black Death "[m]arriage remained an economic enterprise, the dowry growing larger and more important than ever. Marriage negotiations among wealthy families of both country and city were deliberate and ceremonious"[32]—as are these of Arthur's nephews. The remarkable record of the Paston letters indicates the importance of (literally) fortunate marriages to heirs or heiresses, and the disasters probably attendant upon the (projected) mesalliance of Anne, younger daughter of John and Margaret Paston, and certainly upon the (actual) union of Margery, their elder daughter, to the Pastons' bailiff, Richard Calle. Even though the bishop decided "in the young couple's favor," and Calle (in a situation we must still find bizarre) retained his post, the family "treated Margery as if she were dead," her mother leaving on her death in 1484 only the same cutoff amount—twenty pounds— to Margery's eldest (and legitimate) child as to her son's illegitimate offspring.[33] A like greed, both for money and for the production of legitimate heirs, infected the kingly class, as Brooke (drawing upon Duby's and his own prior research) has ably documented.[34]

The fifteenth century saw the growth of such mimesis as appears in the marriages of Gareth's brothers throughout all forms of art, and Malory had no reason not to juxtapose it with older romance ideas of chivalry—because, as Benson puts it, fifteenth-century romance was "elevated in style but often mimetically true to the aristocratic life of the time," and although "heightened and idealized," "based firmly enough on reality that the gentlemen for whom Malory wrote could recognize the contours and many of the actual details" of their era.[35] We may recall that it was precisely such gentlemen whose urgent request William Caxton was gratifying when he first decided to render the *Morte Darthur* from manuscript into print.[36] An age which produced the *soi-disant* "bastard feudalism," while honoring love-based marriage in literature, was hardly blind to its difficulties in life, financial and otherwise. Concomitantly, Malory—in this as in so much else a representative man of his time—gives us, in the same manuscript as the "Gareth," some striking examples of wife abuse, of which Sir Pedivere's striking off his wife's head (he suspects her of adultery with her cousin) is perhaps the most memorable example.

In an age as cynical about marriage as is his Arthur in the "Gareth," Malory could therefore hardly have been so sanguine as to consider wedlock a lasting solution to the troubles of the Round Table. Gareth's married love is neither "an index to the noblest elements of the chivalric ideal" nor a really effective "contrast with the adulterous affairs of Lancelot and Tristram," as Wilfred Guerin claims.[37] Adultery, often unexamined, and both simple and incestuous, had been thoroughly ingrained into the Arthurian tradition from at least the time of Geoffrey of Monmouth, and was a continuing concern of both aristocratic and ecclesiastical historical models of marriage.[38] Geoffrey's depiction of the adulterous conception of Arthur by Uther Pendragon and the incestuous union of Mo[r]dred with Guinevere had been succeeded by, among other narremes in the French tradition, the further adulterous/incestuous conception of Mordred by Arthur upon Morgause, and Morgause's later tragic adultery with Lamorak.[39] Adultery was moreover capable of producing both good and bad results, as had been proven through the invention of the love of Lancelot and Guinevere by Chrétien, especially as it was expanded in the French Arthurian Prose *Vulgate* upon which Malory drew for his "hoole boke."

Even more specifically than the *Vulgate*, Malory saw the uses of refined adulterous love as opposed to the uses of knightly marriage— it the former love he praises at the beginning of his "Tale of Sir Launcelot and Queen Guinevere": "But firste reserve the honoure to God, and secundely thy quarell muste com of thy lady. And such love I calle vertuose love."[40] Malory suggests, in the careers of Lancelot, Tristram, Lamorak, and other members of the semi-celibate Arthurian fighting corps, that sexually moderate but unmarried fidelity to one woman, resultant in the discharge of residual passion in almost constant battle, is the surest and most permanent road to Arthurian worship. This affection is not to be confused with ordinary unmarried but promiscuous love, as Malory (unlike his French source, *La mort le roi Artu*) makes clear even when the queen and Lancelot are taken together in her bedroom: "And whether they were abed other at other maner of disportis, me lyste nat thereof make no mencion, for love that tyme was nat as love ys nowadayes."[41] Nor does Lancelot consider the liaison disreputable for most of the *Morte*, as he makes clear in the same speech in which he rejects marriage: "as for to sey to take my pleasaunce with paramours, that woll I refuse: in prencipall for drede of God, for knyghtes that bene adventures sholde nat be advoutrers nothir lecherous, for than they be nat happy nother fortunate unto the werrys."[42] In spite of the claims of proponents of the so-called and recently identified "demise" of even literary courtly love,[43] as a system it served Malory and his knights very well, as long as it maintained the social approval and personal moderation which led to worship. When that failed, the Round Table failed, but that is another story.

From the married knight, with his obligations to maintain his property and beget heirs, in the *Morte* as well as in real fifteenth-century life, the Round Table could expect little support. Even (and perhaps especially) in the Arthurian Prose *Vulgate* which was Malory's chief source, the traditional alternative to the "vertuose love" of a Lancelot was not the wedded man but the celibate Grail knight as he emerged in the thirteenth-century, Cistercian-authored *Queste del Saint Graal*. And even the successes of a Galahad and a Perceval are limited to the Grail quest itself, as Gareth's brilliant successes are limited to his tale.

The very detachability of the "Gareth," Malory's most complete exploration of the relationship between knighthood and marriage, should indicate its limited applicability. Benson has noted its status as the only tale of the eight identified by Eugène Vinaver as comprising the *Morte* which lacks specific links to what precedes and what follows: "one can easily imagine the *Morte Darthur*. . .without, say, the Tale of Gareth."[44] Unlike La Cote and Alisaunder, the other married knights of this study, Gareth is, however, an important character in Malory's work. But his importance stems not from his marriage but from his double role as intimate to Lancelot and brother to Gawain. Abundantly displayed in the "Gareth" and elsewhere, their joint affection for the younger knight is necessary narrative foreshadowing of the tragic sequence in which Lancelot's accidental and unwitting murder of Gareth turns his friend Gawain decisively against him, and thus helps to precipitate the book's disastrous climax. But if, in his whole book, Malory is saying anything about marriage and knighthood in general, and Gareth's marriage in particular, it is that wedlock restrains knightly development, and has kept Gawain's brother in that perpetual state of chivalric juvenescence which makes his unexpected death at the hands of his more accomplished (and deliberately unmarried) friend and mentor, Lancelot, all the more poignant.

Notes

1. *The Works of Sir Thomas Malory*, ed. Eugène Vinaver, rev. P.J.C. Field, 3rd ed., 3 vols. (Oxford, 1990), 1:99, hereafter cited as *Works*.

2. *Works*, 1:287, 253.

3. For a fuller treatment of this subject, see Maureen Fries, "Sir Lancelot and Sir Tristram: Characterization and *Sens* in Malory's *Morte Darthur*" (Diss., SUNY/Buffalo, 1969), Chapter 4, "How Many Roads to Camelot? Of Love and Marriage," pp. 83–106.

4. Both R. M. Lumiansky and his associates, in *Malory's Originality: A Critical Study of Le Morte Darthur* (Baltimore, 1964), *passim*, and (even more) Beverly Kennedy, *Knighthood in the Morte Darthur* (Woodbridge, 1985), also *passim*, maintain that Lancelot's initial relationship with Guinevere is not adulterous—an untenable position, as has recently been well documented by

David R. Miller, "Sir Thomas Malory's *A Noble Tale of Sir Lancelot du Lake* Reconsidered," *Quondam et Futurus: A Journal of Arthurian Interpretations,* 1.1 (1991), 25–43.

5. *Works,* 1:295–363.

6. *Ibid.,* 349.

7. *Ibid.,* 2:459–76.

8. *Ibid.,* 2:638.

9. *Ibid.,* 2:648.

10. George Duby, *Medieval Marriage: Two Models from Twelfth-Century France,* trans. Elborg Foster (Baltimore, 1978), p. 106.

11. *Works,* 1:270.

12. Duby, *Medieval Marriage,* pp. 84 and 96.

13. *Works,* 1:359–60.

14. For a sophisticated discussion of influences on the "Gareth," see Larry D. Benson, *Malory's Morte Darthur* (Cambridge, Mass., 1976), pp. 92–101.

15. *Works,* 1:333.

16. To Alisaunder's credit, however, he does not succumb to Morgan le Fay's intended seduction: "A, Jesu defende me. . . . For I had levir kut away my hangers [testicles] than I wolde do her ony suche pleasure!" *Works,* 2:643.

17. For a very full study of this subject, see Margaret Lanham, "Chastity: A Study of Sexual Morality in the English Medieval Romances" (Diss., Vanderbilt University, 1948).

18. Robert W. Ackerman, " 'The Tale of Gareth' and the Unity of *le Morte Darthur,*" in *Philological Essays: Studies in Old and Middle English Language and Literature in Honor of Herbert Dean Merritt,* ed. James L. Rosier (The Hague, 1970), pp. 196–203, at 202.

19. On the high social tolerance for irregular unions (in spite of their illicit nature often considered valid), see Christopher N. L. Brooke, *The Medieval Idea of Marriage* (Oxford, 1989), especially chapter 3, the section on "Celibacy and Concubinage," pp. 63–77, and chapter 6, "Marriage in Law and Practice," pp. 119–72.

20. *Works,* 1:360–63.

21. *Ibid.,* 1:434.

22. Duby, *Medieval Marriage,* p. 96.

23. *Works*, 1:362.

24. Duby, *Medieval Marriage*, p. 100.

25. For discussion of Tristram's function in the whole *Morte*, see Maureen Fries, "Malory's Tristram as Counter-Hero to the *Morte Darthur*," *Neuphilologische Mitteilungen* 76 (1975), 605–13, and "Indiscreet Objects of Desire: Malory's 'Tristram' and the Necessity of Deceit," in *Studies in Malory*, ed. James W. Spisak (Kalamazoo, 1985), pp. 87–108.

26. *Works*, 2:890.

27. Benson, *Malory's Morte Darthur*, p. 107.

28. *Works*, 2:1088.

29. Edward D. Kennedy, "The Arthur-Guinevere Relationship in Malory's *Morte Darthur*," *Studies in the Literary Imagination* 4, 2 (1971), 29–40, at 29.

30. Edward D. Kennedy, "Malory and the Marriage of Edward IV," *Tennessee Studies in Language and Literature* 12 (1970–71), 155–62, at 157.

31. J. R. Lander, "Marriage and Politics in the Fifteenth Century: The Nevilles and the Wydevilles," *Bulletin of the Institute of Historical Research* 36 (1963), 119–151, at 145. I am indebted to Edward D. Kennedy for this reference. For a fuller consideration of Malory's relation to fifteenth-century chivalric concerns, see Benson, *Malory's Morte Darthur*, ch. 3, "Malory and Chivalry," pp. 137–201.

32. Frances and Joseph Gies, *Marriage and the Family in the Middle Ages* (New York, 1987), pp. 291–92.

33. *The Paston Letters, A.D. 1422–1509*, ed. James Gairdner, 6 vols., (New York, 1965), vol. 5, nos. 843, 842, 884, 713, 721, and vol. 6, no. 978. The affair is conveniently summarized in Gies and Gies, *Marriage and the Family in the Middle Ages*, pp. 265–67. For the successful revolt and marriage to a man she loved in the case of Elizabeth Paston, see the same, pp. 264–65.

34. Brooke, *The Medieval Idea of Marriage*, chapter 6, "Marriage in Law and Practice," pp. 169–172.

35. Benson, *Malory's Morte Darthur*, p. 139.

36. *Works*, 1, "Caxton's Preface," p. 1.

37. Wilfred L. Guerin, " 'The Tale of Gareth': The Chivalric Flowering," in *Malory's Originality*, ed. Lumiansky, pp. 99–117, at 111.

38. The distinction is Duby's, *Medieval Marriage*, chapter 1, "Two Models of Marriage: The Aristocratic and Ecclesiastical," pp. 1–22.

39. For discrepancies between the Mordred incest story and others during the vogue for such narratives in the twelfth and thirteenth centuries, see

Elizabeth Archibald, "Arthur and Mordred: Variations on an Incest Theme," *Arthurian Literature* 8 (1989), 1–27.

40. *Works*, 3:1119.

41. Ibid., 3:1165.

42. Ibid., 1:270–71. For a consideration of the part Lancelot's decline in such virtue plays in the fall of the Round Table, see Maureen Fries, "Tragic Pattern in Malory's *Morte Darthur*: Medieval Narrative as Literary Myth," *ACTA* 5 (1978), 81–99.

43. See, among others, E. T. Donaldson, "The Myth of Courtly Love," in *Speaking of Chaucer* (London, 1970), pp. 154–63; and the essays in *The Meaning of Courtly Love*, ed. F. X. Newman (Albany, 1968).

44. Larry D. Benson, "Le Morte Darthur," in *Critical Approaches to Six Major English Works: Beowulf through Paradise Lost*, ed. R. M. Lumiansky and Herschel Baker (Philadelphia, 1968), pp. 81–131, at 96, 104–105.

PART II
Reinventing The Middle Ages

Spenser for Hire: Arthurian History as Cultural Capital in *The Faerie Queene*

——————————————————— *Laurie A. Finke*

> Mysticism, when transposed from the warm twilight of myth and fiction to the cold searchlight of fact and reason, has usually little left to recommend itself. Its language, unless resounding within its own magic or mystic circle, will often appear poor and even slightly foolish, and its most baffling metaphors and highflown images, when deprived of their iridescent wings, may easily resemble the pathetic and pitiful sight of Baudelaire's Albatross. Political mysticism in particular is exposed to the danger of losing its spell or becoming quite meaningless when taken out of its native surroundings.
>
> *—Ernst Kantorowicz*

Anyone who has tried to teach *The Faerie Queene* to undergraduates must have encountered in students' indifference precisely this sense of deflation Kantorowitz describes in the opening of *The King's Two Bodies*.[1] Removed from its "native surroundings," the poem seems a strange bird indeed. It is not merely the age of Spenser's work that erects such an insurmountable barrier to its enjoyment. After all, we hardly have the same reaction to Shakespeare or Malory, or even to Chaucer, whose writing is two centuries earlier than Spenser's. Rather it is the political mysticism that suffuses *The Faerie Queene* that makes its enjoyment so much an acquired taste. Its combination of allegory, romance, anti-quarianism, religion, and epic appealed to the particular needs and desires of a coterie audience made up of an aging Elizabeth and her courtiers; its purpose was to bear witness to the creation of England as a sovereign nation incorporated in the monarch's body and to

211

participate in forging the "imagined community" that, Benedict Anderson has argued, enabled the development of nationalism.[2] Understood as an act of political patronage and as a species of cultural capital, *The Faerie Queene* emerges clearly only within the network of material, symbolic, and discursive practices that defined social, religious, and political relationships in Elizabeth's court.

This essay examines Spenser's use of Britain's antique past, particularly Arthurian legend and history, to provide a setting for the allegorical romance he dedicated to Elizabeth during the last decade of her life. My purpose is to inquire into the uses of antiquity in the construction of the imagined community of the nation, as well as its function as symbolic capital in the network of patronage relationships through which Elizabeth's ideals of government were translated into specific policies. The fascination the legendary history of Arthur held for the Elizabethans was in direct proportion to the political uses this history could be made to serve. I am particularly interested in exploring the ways in which the history of King Arthur was called upon by Tudor monarchs to legitimate their dynastic ambitions.

Spenser's choice of Prince Arthur as the means through which to "fashion a gentleman or noble person in vertuous and gentle discipline" seems almost inevitable.[3] From the accession of Henry VII, the Tudor monarchs had exploited their links with Britain's Celtic pre-history as a means of bypassing the demands of primogeniture and assuaging doubts about the legitimacy of their claim to the throne. Geoffrey of Monmouth had written that Cadwallader, the last British king, who fled from the Saxons to Brittany was told by an angel's voice that he should not return to Britain "for that God had willed that the Britons should no longer reign in Britain before the time should come whereof Merlin had prophesied unto Arthur."[4] So, when Richard III charged that Henry Tudor was an upstart with "no manner of right, interest, title, or colour" in the throne of England, Henry did not hesitate to send a commission into Wales to produce a genealogy tracing his ancestry through Owen Glendower to King Arthur and finally back to Brutus, the Trojan hero who was the eponymous founder of Britain.[5] This genealogy was supposed to prove Henry Tudor was the monarch prophesied by Merlin who would restore the *British* monarchy. To cement this connection Henry named his first son and presumptive heir Arthur; later he was proclaimed "Arturus secundus."

Elizabeth also found Arthurian history useful. During her reign several genealogies declared her descent from Arthur, Cadwallader, Owen Glendower, and Henry VII, proclaiming her as "the last that remaineth aliue of that lyne."[6] According to Millican, Elizabethan historians used Arthur "in a way that makes the Angevin Anglicization of Arthur of Britain seem pale and sporadic." He describes the Arthurian right of Tudor sovereigns as a "firm historical tradition...sanctioned by Elizabeth herself."[7] However historically suspect this tradition might seem to us, it had the distinct advantage of enabling Elizabeth to forge a myth of legitimacy that linked her family with the founders and true rulers of a Britain conceived of as pristine and originary. It simplified complicated succession arguments by eliminating inconvenient predecessors or claimants. The elaborate symbology of monarchy which Arthurian history fed and which was expressed through elaborate pageants and plays, as well as through poems like *The Faerie Queene*,[8] created a political myth that helped Elizabeth to defuse anxieties about the succession. Arthurian legends provided Elizabeth with a political mystification that appeared to satisfy the demands of patrilineage while redefining those demands through an elaborate historical allegory of the monarch's immortal body.

To be sure, during the last part of the sixteenth century historians also began to question the accuracy of Geoffrey's history of Arthur and of the Trojan myth of origin, but the strength of that critique perhaps gains from hindsight.[9] This skepticism did not immediately sweep away Arthurian history as a vestige of medieval ignorance because Galfridian history still served important political functions, providing the only account of British origins which did not portray the British simply as barbarians colonized first by the Romans, then the Saxons and Normans.[10] Nor did Arthurian legend simply become grist for poems and romances. Geoffrey's account of Arthur circulated among historians, courtiers, politicians, poets, and even commoners side by side with what we might consider more sober history in an uneasy cohabitation well into the next century. For the Renaissance courtier, history, poetry, and government administration were not separate and distinct social practices as they tend to be for us. This is not to suggest that they were thought of as the same thing; rather they circulated freely within the network of interpersonal relations that constituted Elizabeth's court. *The Faerie Queene* cannot simply be "explained" by recourse to its "context," to historical "facts" about coronations, parliaments, antiquarian societies, political intrigues, or religious controversies unproblematically conceived. Rather, the poem emerges out of and circulates within an interactive network of discourses, practices, ideologies, and institutions whose relations to one another are complexly variable, sometimes complementary, and often contradictory. Of particular interest are the relationships between the dominant practices of patronage and the emerging representations of nationalism. Spenser's allegorical view of

Elizabeth as Gloriana and King Arthur as her only potential mate creates in the political sphere what Jean-Joseph Goux calls a "general symbolic equivalent." That is, just as money gives value to commodities in the economic sphere, the monarch in the political sphere stands apart from her subjects in a double relationship of privilege and exclusion, providing "an idealized standard and measure of values."[11] Arthur, while rarely in the forefront of action in the poem and often absent from long stretches of text, provides the universal equivalent that orders and gives value to all the allegorical signifiers in the poem. In *The Faerie Queene*, as at Elizabeth's court, this general symbolic equivalent looked both backward toward medieval political relationships of patronage and forward to a new symbolic economy of the nation.

I

In *The Faerie Queene*, Arthur becomes the model not only of the ideal monarch-in-training but of the ideal patron as well. Spenser writes to Raleigh that "in the person of Prince Arthure I sette forth magnificence in particular, which vertue for that (according to Aristotle and the rest) it is the perfection of all the rest, and conteineth in it them all" (407). For Spenser, Arthur becomes a synecdoche for all princely virtue by reason of his "magnificence" which Aristotle, in the *Nicomachean Ethics*, defines as " 'suitable' expenditure on a grand scale" combined with good taste. Magnificence, for Aristotle, is suited to "persons of high birth and reputation. . .since all these qualities carry greatness and prestige."[12] Princes rule most effectively through expenditure; their willingness to dispense largess freely is the virtue which comprehends all the other princely virtues embodied in the poem—holiness, temperance, chastity, friendship, justice.

The exchange relationships of patronage were the primary means by which those both within and without Elizabeth's government constituted their relationship to it. Indeed, government was in a very real sense the *product* of patronage and could not function without it. Patronage networks predominate when power within a society is to some extent centralized but relatively weak, when the power of the elite to control resources at the periphery is limited by its inability to act autonomously. Nearly everyone in Elizabethan England, whether he was located at the center of power at court or in the periphery, was dependent on a complex network of patron-client relations for advancement, profit, and power.[13] Because patronage relationships are particularistic and diffuse, rather than legal and contractual, and because they define relations between individuals or networks of individuals rather than between organized corporate groups, they characterize a weak sense of national identity.[14] During the Tudor period the discursive and symbolic strategies for representing national sovereignty—as well as the institutional structures for administering it—were beginning to emerge. Elizabeth's powerful personality and political acumen created the illusion of centralization which masked a much deeper structural fragmentation of control. Only through the skillful manipulation of patronage networks could Elizabeth and her ministers govern effectively. Under these circumstances, control of symbolic and discursive representations of the monarch and the state would be crucial.

For this reason, *The Faerie Queene* and the Arthurian mythology it depicts must be understood both as a symbolic representation of the Elizabethan system of patronage and as a species of currency within it. My remarks about patronage in this essay are not limited to literary patronage, which must be seen as part of a much larger institution that controlled the distribution of all sorts of rewards, offices, and honors in exchange for services of all kinds—administrative, financial, military, and cultural. Spenser was not just a poet and antiquarian, he was also a minor government official relegated to the somewhat distant post of secretary to the governor of Ireland and dependent on his patrons for his livelihood.

Seen in this light, Spenser's portrait of Arthur as the ideal patron is a plea for patronage, but it is not directed solely, or even primarily, at Elizabeth. If Arthur's magnificence is a synecdoche for all the chivalrous virtues, then Elizabeth, as the general symbolic equivalent, is the synecdoche that unites all of her courtiers. The poem both represents and appeals to the complex network of patronage relationships that constituted Elizabeth's court, as a glance at the dedications to the 1590 edition of *The Faerie Queene* might suggest. Besides the dedication to Elizabeth, Spenser included seventeen sonnets dedicated to members of Elizabeth's court. The sheer number of the dedications seems excessive; no doubt they suggest that Spenser may have been more than a little anxious about the influence he could command and about his distance from the center of power and patronage. Because the sonnets occupy a space between "literature and the extraliterary realm of court politics," they illustrate how the Elizabethan patronage system operated.[15]

The queen was the source of all patronage, "the most high, mighty, and magnificent empresse." But only a very few courtiers had close access to the queen, so that those more distantly placed—like Spenser—had to rely on the patronage of highly placed clients. The diffusion of patron-client networks was so great under Elizabeth that many courtiers would be at one and the same time both patrons and clients. Carol Stillman has shown that the order of the dedicatory sonnets adheres strictly to the heraldic rules for preference, indicating the rank and dignity of families, offices, and titles. Given the Renaissance obsession with hierarchy and place, these rules of preference and the privileges of rank would be jealously asserted.[16] But rank was not the sole determinant of patronage relationships. For this reason, the sonnet order cannot simply be taken at face value; it must be probed for what it might suggest about the complex patterns of patronage in late sixteenth-century England.

Christopher Hatton and William Cecil, Lord Burghley—the first two dedicatees by virtue of their offices as Lord High Chancellor and Lord High Treasurer—were particularly close to the queen. Burghley exerted powerful control over the dispensing of the queen's patronage throughout her reign, becoming himself a powerful patron, one who might be appealed to even by his peers. One of his clients was another dedicatee, Arthur Lord Grey de Wilton. In 1580 he was appointed lord deputy of Ireland, while Spenser became his secretary.[17] Spenser's patronage, therefore, while it came nominally from the queen, was mediated first by his own relationship with Grey, then by Grey's relationship with Burghley. This distinction among patrons finds its way into the wording of the sonnets. The distance between Spenser and such prominent courtiers as Burghley and Hatton is expressed through the difference between his "ydle rymes" and their impersonal greatness. Burghley becomes the mythical Atlas "on whose mightie shoulders most doth rest/ The burden of this kingdomes gouernement." It is worth noting the repetitive, even formulaic, language that marks both sonnets; the two are virtually indistinguishable in their appeals for protection.[18] The sonnet to Grey however, while preserving the formality and inequality between patron and client, insists on a somewhat more immediate, less impersonal relationship.

> Most Noble Lord the pillor of my life,
>   And Patrone of my Muses pupillage,
>   Through whose large bountie poured on me rife,
>   In the first season of my feeble age,
> I now doe liue, bound yours by vassalage:
>   Sith nothing euer may redeeme, nor reaue
>   Out of your endlesse debt so sure a gage,
>   Vouchsafe in worth this small guift to receaue,
> Which in your noble hands for pledge I leaue,
>   Of all the rest, that I am tyde t'account (412).

In these verses, Spenser indicates that he had already received patronage from Grey; he had been the object of Grey's "large bountie" since "the first season of my feeble age." He feels himself bound to Grey by ties of "vassalage," the clientistic bond par excellence, which binds the vassal to the lord in an immediate and personal way. The rhetorical trick for Spenser in this sonnet is to cast his poem as the compensation for gifts he has received from Grey. The language treads carefully between the language of the gift and that of repayment. He characterizes his poem as a "small guift," but also as a pledge or security (a gage) for debts incurred. The language here illustrates the trickiness of patronage exchanges. Spenser's economic metaphors oscillate between proclaiming the fundamentally economic nature of this transaction and disguising it.

The relationships among Burghley, Grey, and Spenser illustrate just one thread in the complex network of relations the sonnets unfold. Burghley had established relationships with other dedicatees as well. Walsingham began his career at court as Burghley's client.[19] Oxford was Burghley's ward and later married his daughter Anne.[20] Several of the dedicatees shared with Burghley (and Spenser) a Cambridge education, among them Hatton, Essex, and Hunsdon.[21] Yet, despite Burghley's influence, the queen was shrewd enough not to rely solely on one minister. She had other favorites and they too became powerful patrons. Essex and Raleigh are perhaps the most notorious, but we might also include, among the dedicatees, Hatton, Buckhurst, and Oxford. While none achieved Burghley's preeminence, all were the recipients of lavish favors from the queen, enough to make them desirable patrons to less fortunate clients. Raleigh's and Essex's proximity to the queen suggests that, while rank and family ties often determined the shape of patronage networks, they were not definitive. Northumberland, for instance, was Essex's brother-in-law and in the heraldic protocol of the dedications outranks him, but at court Northumberland, the "Wizard earl" with suspected ties to Roman Catholicism, was an outsider.[22] Hunsdon was first cousin to the queen, but remained aloof from court culture.[23] He did not wield anything like the patronage of a favorite like Raleigh, who appears last in the sonnets' order right before the ladies.[24]

A frequent complaint among Elizabeth's courtiers was that she distributed her favors to members of competing court factions.[25] No doubt this dispersal of favor among several contenders, which created factional competition among clients, enabled the queen to maintain power. But it also created competition among patrons because the reputation and success of highly placed clients (themselves powerful patrons) depended on the loyal support that their clients gave in exchange for their patron's favors or protection. Burghley was a formidable rival for all the queen's favorites primarily because of his success in cultivating a clientele. Essex and Raleigh had little love for one another, while the Howards and Dudleys were long-time enemies.[26] Such competition among patrons increased the instability of patronage relationships, which tended already to be flexible and transitory because informal. This instability, however, gave some autonomy and even power to clients. For this reason, an analysis of patronage at Elizabeth's court cannot be limited only to vertical relations of inequality; it must also account for horizontal relationships as well. It may have been Spenser's strategy in dedicating his poem to so many of Elizabeth's courtiers to appeal, through an elaborate fiction of courtesy, simultaneously to the alliances forged by chains of clientage and the competition among patrons to maintain a clientele.

Patron-client relationships involve the exchange of different kinds of resources. Although these resources can be economic, political, or military, they just as often include such intangible resources as power, prestige, influence, or status.[27] This is because to rule effectively in the absence of autonomous structures of power, the elite must convert some of their material wealth into forms of prestige through acts understood as gifts. These "gifts" are converted into labor and services which, in turn, generate more wealth.[28] Because it is almost totally generic (the patron is not even addressed until the couplet), the dedication to Northumberland captures in the abstract the reciprocity required by the exchange of what Pierre Bourdieu has called "symbolic capital."[29]

> The sacred Muses haue made alwaies clame
>   To be the Nourses of nobility,
>   And Registres of euerlasting fame,
>   To all that armes professe and cheualry.
> Then by like right the noble Progeny,
>   Which them succeed in fame and worth, are tyde
>   T'embrace the seruice of sweete Poetry,
>   By whose endeuours they are glorifide,
> And eke from all, of whom it is enuide,
>   To patronize the authour of their praise,
>   Which giues them life, that els would soone haue dide,
>   And crownes their ashes with immortall baies (411).

In this sonnet, what the client/poet offers his patron is "everlasting fame," "worth," and "praise." In exchange, the patron is "tyde" to labor in the "seruice" of "sweete Poetry." The mutual interdependence of patron and client—their reciprocity—is emphasized by the mutual connection of gift and countergift between the first and second quatrain. Curiously, unlike the dedication to his close friend Grey, this dedication does not serve as a reminder of Spenser's dependence upon his patron. Rather he reverses the situation and projects dependency onto his patron. The Muses are the "Nourses of nobility," they create and give life to those who practice "cheualry." The nobility could not exist without poets, that is they could not long continue without the symbolic capital poetry provides. In a culture in which economic activity must be disguised through the exchanges of gifts and represented as voluntary rather than calculating, poetry's metaphoric dimensions—its abilities to transmute, to substitute, to supplement—make it a valuable medium of exchange.

II

In the Northumberland sonnet, Spenser makes the debt incurred for his services as great as it could possibly be: immortal life. His patron's "protection" is simply payment for the poetry "which giues them life, that els would soone haue dide." It is significant that this gift of immortality is the same as that which the Petrarchan poet promises his beloved. During Elizabeth's reign, because she was a female monarch, the elaborate rituals and fictions of courtly love and Petrarchan poetry provided a means by which the economic and political operations of patronage could be disguised as personal and private.[30] Within patronage networks, relationships must be defined within a system of finely articulated and elaborate rituals, codes, and rules, which are usually unspoken or spoken only in elaborately codified languages. Scott describes these elaborate fictions and rituals as the "euphemerization of economic power." Courtly love, as I have argued elsewhere, provided, from the twelfth century on, just such a codified language for "euphemerizing" the economic and political exchanges involved in patronage networks.[31]

Courtly love of the kind usually associated with Arthurian romance works particularly well as a disguise for economic and political relationships in a situation in which traditional gender hierarchies do not coincide with the class hierarchies that control the distribution of power and wealth. Such was the situation during Elizabeth's reign when the traditional subordination of the female to the male was at least superficially contradicted by the accession of a female monarch. Effective rule in this situation required representational strategies that would counter the instability to traditional hierarchies created by Elizabeth's rule.[32]

Courtly love posited an idealized situation in which a male petitioner could prostrate himself before a distant and inaccessible lady. Recasting the all-powerful queen in the role of mistress enables the courtier to recuperate her power by reinscribing it within traditional gender hierarchies. It was a language everyone at court understood to be both erotic and political. The political function of courtly love as a strategy for arbitrating patronage relationships did not preclude the expression of genuine erotic desire; rather the possibility of eroticism gives political power a sexual charge.[33] If the possibility of erotic exchange were not present, however, at least theoretically, the fiction would not work. For twenty years before Spenser wrote *The Faerie Queene*, the conventions of Petrarchan love poetry provided a means by which male courtiers could negotiate their relation of clientage to the queen under the guise of suitors.[34]

The vicissitudes of sexual desire seem an ideal expression for the vicissitudes of life as a client under Elizabeth. The imagery of the lover's suffering described in the allegory of Cupid's masque in the House of Busirane might just as easily describe the futile attempts of most of the 2,500 or so hangers-on at court to secure patronage:

> Emongst them was sterne *Strife*, and *Anger* stout,
> Unquiet *Care*, or fond *Vnthriftihead*,
> Lewd *Losse of Time*, and *Sorrow* seeming dead,
> Inconstant *Chaunge*, and false *Disloyaltie*,
> Consuming *Riotise*, and Guilty *Dread*
> Of heavenly vengeance, faint *Infirmitie*,
> Vile *Povertie*, and lastly *Death* with infamie (3.12.25).

Here Spenser might easily be describing the competition among the many contenders for the patronage the Crown had to dispense, which, while considerable, could not support all those who sought places. The struggle for position was a situation Spenser knew from first-hand experience. For the client unable to secure a place, inconstancy and disloyalty—the petulant behavior of a demanding and cold mistress—might well describe his experience of his queen. Furthermore, while the financial rewards for a successful client could be spectacular—for a Raleigh or an Essex at any rate—the costs of securing patronage could be staggering and might easily bankrupt the unsuccessful. Patronage systems are economies of expenditure and require financial outlays from both patrons and clients in order to secure either material or symbolic capital. Life at court was expensive. Even a peer could overburden himself with the expenditures that accompanied the pursuit of patronage. The "favor" of a royal visit, for instance, was costly. Stone estimates that Burghley spent between £300 and £1000 each time the queen honored him with a visit. £100 was the least one could spend on a present for the queen. Some eager for advancement might spend as much as £1000, as Sir Edward Coke did in 1595 and Sir Thomas Egerton in 1601.[35] It is hardly surprising that such extravagance might end for the unsuccessful in "Vile Povertie" and "Death with infamie."

Book 3 of *The Faerie Queene* stages several scenes of courtly love which depict the extravagant love of a knight for an inaccessible lady or, alternately, the attempts of less desirable ladies (Malecasta, Argante) to secure the services of knights-errant. Without doing violence to Spenser's treatment of love in book 3,[36] we might consider the representations of courtly love as elaborate and complimentary figures for the love of the subject for his monarch and of a client for his patron. Perhaps the most striking of these tableaux is the one depicting the relationship between Belphoebe and Timias, Arthur's squire, after he is wounded by the fosters (3.5). Having cured Timias' sexual wound to his thigh, Belphoebe inflicts another metaphoric wound.

> O foolish Physick, and vnfruitfull paine,
> That heales vp one and makes another wound:
> She his hurt thigh to him recur'd againe,
> But hurt his hart, the which before was sound,
> Through an vnwary dart, which did rebound
> From her faire eyes and gracious countenaunce.
> What bootes it him from death to be vnbound,
> To be captiued in endlesse durance
> Of sorrow and despaire without aleggeaunce? (3.5.42).

The conventional Petrarchan rhetoric in this passage depicts the extravagant suffering of the courtly lover metaphorically figured alternately as an illness, a wound, and a prison. Timias' suffering is increased by his awareness of the gulf that separates Belphoebe's "soveraigne bounty" from his "meane estate" (3.5.44). The language throughout this scene moves between the Petrarchan rhetoric of suffering in love exemplified by stanza 42 and an economic rhetoric of clientage—of *mercede* or reward—as Timias decides the only way out of his dilemma is to die in the "service" of Belphoebe, which he contemplates in a passage almost comical in its overwrought rhetoric.

> Dye rather, dye, and dying do her serue,
> Dying her serue, and liuing her adore;
> Thy life she gaue, thy life she doth deserue:
> Dye rather, dye, then ever from her seruice swerue (3.4.46: 6–9).

While, on the surface, it appears as if the economic metaphors—"meed,"
"service"—define Timias' desire, it is just as plausible to suggest that
love in this passage might serve as a metaphor for an econonic
relationship. Better still, we might speak of a kind of circulation between
discourses of love and those of politics and economics. This reading
is supported by Spenser's remarks to Raleigh in which he states that
in Belphoebe he figures the aspect of Elizabeth as "a most vertuous and
beautifull Lady" (407), a remark which has led many commentators to
identify Timias with Raleigh, one of the queen's most spectacularly
successful clients.[37]

If the portrait of Belphoebe at the center of book 3 offers Elizabeth
an elaborate compliment by figuring the ideal patron as the chaste and
distant beloved of Petrarchan love poetry, book 3 also spawns numerous
deformations of this trope which must be read as criticisms of patronal
excess. The first we encounter is Malecasta in canto 1,

> Whose soueraine beautie hath no liuing pere,
> Thereto so bounteous and so debonaire,
> That neuer any mote with her compaire.
> She hath ordaind this law, which we approue,
> That euery knight, which doth this way repaire,
> In case he have no Ladie, nor no loue,
> Shall doe vnto her seruice neuer to remoue (3.1.26).

Even if the knight does have a lady he serves (like the Redcross knight,
whom we discover being accosted by Malecasta's knights at the
beginning of book 3), he must renounce that love and serve the lady
of the castle unless he can prove by arms that his lady is more beautiful.
Britomart's first adventure is to rescue Holicross from Malecasta's
clutches. Although Malecasta is clearly an antitype of the chaste
Belphoebe, this stanza creates yet another Petrarchan lady who,
superficially at least, differs little from Belphoebe. Her beauty is also
described as "soueraine"; she has no peer and she is "bounteous." The
qualities attributed to Malecasta place less emphasis on her physical
beauty, however, than on her power to command resources and
dispense gifts. Malecasta is a figure for a failed patron; her forceful
acquisition of a clientele clumsily exposes the political and military
machinery the fictions of courtly love were supposed to disguise. Her
knights do not fall in love with her at one glance; rather they must be
coerced into her service. In canto 7, the giantess Argante represents an
even more violent and grotesque double of Belphoebe, who seeks out
"young men, to quench her flaming thrust," to become her "vassall"
in "eternall bondage" (3.7.50).[38]

A more subtle and intricate critique of patronage might be read in the story related by the Squire of Dames who is rescued from Argante by Satyrane in canto 7. Like Timias, the Squire of Dames has fallen in love and he signifies that love using the same vocabulary of service, deserving, and swerving that marked Timias' lament in canto 5.

> That gentle Lady, whom I loue and serue,
> After long suit and weary seruicis,
> Did aske me, how I could her loue deserue,
> And how she might be sure, that I would neuer swerue (3.7.53).

To test him, the lady requires a vow from the Squire of Dames that he will serve other "gentle Dames" and at the end of a year to "bring their names/ And pledges; as the spoiles of my victorious games" (3.7.54). That is, the squire must appear inconstant—by serving other ladies—to prove that he will never "swerve." He is of course wildly successful. At the end of a year he can present to his lady

> Three hundred pledges for my good desartes,
> And thrise three hundred thanks for my good partes (3.7.55).

Still unsatisfied, his lady sends him off on another apparently futile quest. This time he must find an equal number of Dames

> The which, for all the suit I could propound,
> Would me refuse their pledges to afford,
> But did abide for euer chast and sound (3.7.56).

This quest proves more difficult. The squire has been able to find only three: a "Courtisane," who refused him because he could not pay, a nun, and one "Damzell" of "low degree" who is the only woman he can find who "chastity did for it selfe embrace." He despairs of ever matching "the chaste with th'unchaste Ladies train" (3.7.60).

To the modern reader this passage seems to parody the silliness of romance quests and the pointless obedience required by courtly love. Reading this scene within the network of political arrangements I have been exploring, however, reveals the ways in which gender mediates and complicates patronage relationships as well as the ways in which patronage networks construct particular gender roles for social agents. In this case, the demands of those roles are impossibly contradictory. In the first quest, the Squire of Dames must prove his desirability as a lover/client by securing the love of other ladies who will serve as intermediaries between the inaccessible lady and her hopeful client. That is, their sexuality serves as a species of symbolic capital which the squire will accumulate and present as a gift or "pledge" to his lady. But his success cheapens the goods acquired, creating a kind of inflation which renders the symbolic capital worthless. In the second quest he must attempt to revalue what has been devalued by finding patrons who will refuse his service. His very failure to find other "chaste" women gives new value to his lady; her inaccessibility is the mark of her rarity.

This symmetrical pair of quests further exposes the contradictions inherent in the double uses of sexuality as symbolic capital in the Renaissance. The practices of primogeniture that controlled inheritance among the aristocracy demanded strict chastity from women, a chastity that would end in legitimate matrimony with the aim of producing an heir and preserving the lineage.[39] For this reason a woman's chastity constituted an important asset for a family or for a husband. In Elizabeth's case that asset was one that, as an unmarried queen, she perpetually exploited, and her refusal to marry was undoubtedly one of her strategies for extending her rule. If, however, by 1590 the question of the queen's marriage was moot, the practices of masking patronage relations with the fictions of courtly love were still widespread. These practices required sexual display with the promise of erotic fulfillment continually held out, if usually deferred. Women's sexuality, taken out of the circulation of land, goods, and symbolic capital that marked relations at court, represented a threat to the system: the courtesan because she exposes the economic arrangements the fiction of courtly love is supposed to disguise and the nun because her sexuality is not available as symbolic capital. The Squire of Dames' narrative captures these contradictions that complicate the metaphoric transformations of patronage into love.

III

Having placed The Faerie Queene within a system of political relationships at court masked by elaborate fictions of courtesy and love, we might now ask what kind of symbolic capital, besides a flamboyant compliment, Spenser was offering Elizabeth. The simplest answer is that he offers the queen the only marriage she could possibly have accepted, a marriage with Prince Arthur as a synecdoche for Britain's Celtic past. The promised union of Gloriana with Prince Arthur, which is held out by the poem (although never actually fulfilled), weds Britain's history to the promise of its future continuity. Elizabeth was well aware of the liabilities her gender created for her rule. In the early years of her reign, her refusal to marry increased her power because she could exploit the promise of her eligibility without actually surrendering it. This strategy enabled her to hold in tension the contradictions between gender and class hierarchies her reign created. But it also created uncertainty about Elizabeth's successor. At a time when the dynastic continuity of the Tudors was very much in doubt, then, Spenser's poem provides a representational strategy for creating continuity which does not depend on the production of a male heir. Rather, he offers a continuity based on the imagined community of the nation incorporated in the monarch's body.

The nation, Benedict Anderson has argued, is not a self-evident or timeless concept. It has a history and its meanings have changed over time. The nation is an imagined community that had to be invented.[40] It is imagined because even within the smallest nation, its members will never meet—or even hear of—most of its other members. Yet all carry in their minds the image of their community. What distinguishes the nation from other kinds of communities is the *style* in which it is imagined. Under feudalism communal ties were imagined, as I have already suggested, particularistically as networks of kinship and clientage. Even the most hierarchically ordered and exploitative of nations, however, conceives of itself as a "deep, horizontal comradeship"[41] and this emphasis on horizontal rather than vertical relationship, on the sameness of its citizens rather than their differences, is what sets the nation apart from other earlier imagined communities out of which it emerged. The invention of a nation required an array of representations through which the national community can be imagined. In sixteenth-century England, those representations were being forged from the cultural systems that preceded English nationalism—in particular those of religion and dynasticism—and were successfully disseminated through a developing print capitalism which enabled growing numbers of people to relate themselves to others in radically new ways.[42]

This formation of national consciousness is a process which unfolds in stages that might be described by an analogy to the process by which the individual's consciousness is formed. For this reason, the contributions of Lacanian psychoanalysis to our understanding of how subjects are fashioned might illuminate the representational strategies through which the subjects of a nation are fashioned and brought together within an imagined community. It might also clarify Spenser's contributions to this project.[43] Jean-Joseph Goux's work on symbolic economies provides a starting point for this analogy. In *Symbolic*

Economies, Goux attempts to articulate a dynamics of culture that demonstrates the fundamental isomorphisms between the development of a money standard of currency and other forms of centralization dominated by the phallus in the psychoanalytic register, language in the symbolic, and the monarch in the political. He perceives in "the indefinite drift of signs...linking representations...a hierarchy (of values)..., a principle of order and subordination which places the great (manifold and polymorphous) majority of 'signs' (products, actions and gestures, subjects, objects) under the sacred command of a select few among them."[44] Psychoanalysis, for instance, describes a process by which an individual's consciousness is formed by investing a single object—the phallus—with the power to organize and give value to all other objects much as, Goux argues, money is invested with the power to organize and give value to all other commodities. This tendency towards the centralization of value requires the emergence of a "universal symbolic equivalent"—money, the phallus, the monarch. Goux sets out to describe a common process by which "major symbolic elements accede to the hegemony of general equivalents."[45]

Elizabeth's apotheosis into the "Faerie Queene" provides an example of this social dynamic in the register of political representation. In the political realm, the monarch provides a "universal symbolic equivalent" which can mediate the demands of the nation's "subjects."[46] The monarchy was the primary institutional means of representing—of imagining—the English nation. The monarchy—with Arthur and the Faerie Queene as "general equivalent"—becomes a means to allow the "indefinite drift of signs" of Celtic prehistory to be organized and valued as a representation of the nation. The history of that monarchy—particularly its Celtic prehistory—provided the "matter" which would be given representational "form" by the political theory of the king's two bodies.

The Renaissance political theory of the "king's two bodies" provides in the development of national identity the functional equivalent of the mirror stage in the psychoanalytic development of the child. The infant experiences itself as fragmented parts and images with no sense of totality. The achaic *imago* of the fragmented body include representations of castration, mutilation, dismemberment, dislocation, and the bursting open of the body,[47] images, it is worth noting, that appear frequently throughout *The Faerie Queene*. The most elementary structure of the subject, according to Lacan, is "diacritically woven in terms of hetero-geneity."[48] This description of the pre-mirror stage corresponds with Goux's second stage in the dynamic evolution of centralization and the creation of a "universal symbolic equivalent." What he calls the "extended form of value" is dominated by heterogeneity, fragmentation, and conflict in which all values serve as a "mirror" for all other values. No univeral or general equivalent has yet emerged to order the relations among other values. During the mirror stage's drive toward homogeneity and fusion, which occurs around six months, that fragmentation is woven into the image of a whole, coherent, and complete body as the infant perceives in the mirror the unity it cannot comprehend in itself. The fragmentation, however, is never completely resolved into unity. The subject—even as an adult—always registers a discrepancy between a perceived ideal unity which is perfect (the universal equivalent) and its own fragmentation and incoherence.

The theory of the king's two bodies, most succinctly described in the following passage from Plowden's *Reports*, expresses as the *imago* of the nation this disjunction between the perceived perfection of an idealized universal equivalent and the fragmentation and dislocation of the merely human body.

> The King has in him two Bodies, *viz*, a Body natural, and a Body politic. His Body natural (if it be considered in itself) is a Body mortal, subject to all Infirmities that come by Nature or Accident, to the Imbecility of Infancy or old Age, and to the like Defects that happen to the natural Bodies of other People. But his Body politic is a Body that cannot be seen or handled, consisting of Policy and Government, and constituted for the Direction of the People, and the Management of the public weal, and this Body is utterly void of Infancy, and old Age, and other natural Defects and Imbecilities, which the Body natural is subject to, and for this cause, what the king does in his Body politic, cannot be invalidated or frustrated by any Disability in his natural Body.[49]

The king's body politic—the imagined corporate body of the nation— escapes all of the imperfections and shortcomings of a natural body. It is whole, perfect, immortal, static, and unchanging—indeed it is outside of history[50]—providing the temporal continuity that the merely mortal body, immersed in the detritus of history, so plainly lacks. It is not incapacitated by childhood or old age (or by sex in Elizabeth's case) nor can the unity and continuity of the state be disrupted by human mortality. In the pre-national phase as in the pre-mirror stage, political relationships are fragmentary, heterogeneous, and dislocated; stability depends upon networks of patronage and upon the caprices of primogeniture. As with the minor stage, this early stage of development toward national consciousness is accomplished by investing in the monarch an ideal unity which is contradicted by the monarch's and her subjects' experiences of human embodiedness. This perfect body politic provides a means of imagining the nation, supplying a temporal continuity that is belied by the inevitable failures of dynasticism and primogeniture.

Spenser's incorporation of British prehistory into books 2 and 3 of *The Faerie Queene* demonstrates graphically the failures of feudo-dynasticism at the same time it recuperates those failures into its vision of the imagined community of the nation. This is particularly true of book 2's redaction of Galfridian history which Spenser recounts in the *Briton moniments* as "the famous auncestries/ Of my most dreaded Soueraigne" (2.10.1). This nod to the representational strategies of dynasticism and its preoccupation with genealogy is marked from beginning to end by fragmentation, dislocation, and violence. In the words of Harry Berger, it depicts "carnage, anarchy, sedition; murders not only of kings but of fathers, husbands, brothers, children."[51] The individual details—the names, the reigns, the historical "facts"—slip by without coalescing into any obvious pattern. They seem an unrelated, often contradictory, and heterogeneous catalogue of historical events. This effect of interruption and dislocation is only enhanced by the segmentation that marks the Spenserian stanza, an unusual form for chronicle history. The *Briton moniments* reproduces in its narrative the fragmentation and disorder of the Lacanian mirror stage, in Miller's words, the "sunderings of a bodily wholeness."[52] Dynasticism—the unbroken transmission of lineage from father to son—is at best an imperfect means by which to imagine the nation and ensure its unbroken continuity.

If canto 10 presents the "corruption in the soul of a government, . . . the weaknesses of the flesh"[53] that plague the natural body, that failure is recuperated by "mirroring" the mortal bodies of the individual kings of Britain in the perfect temperate body allegorically represented by Alma's house of Temperance, where Arthur discovers his lineage, his history, and his identity. The elaborate geometric and numerical allegory of the human body figured in stanza 22's description of Alma's house emphasizes the unity, harmony, proportion, and symmetry of this perfected body.

> The frame thereof seemd partly circulare,
> And part triangulare, O worke diuine;
> These two the first and last proportions are,
> The one imperfect, mortall, foeminine;
> Th'other immortall, perfect, masculine,

And twixt them both a quadrate was the base
Proportioned equally by seuen and nine;
Nine was the circle set in heauens place,
All which compacted made a goodly diapase (2.9.22).

The body, "imagined" abstractly as the unity of a circle, triangle, and rectangle, of male and female, repeats and completes the harmony—the "goodly diapase"—of the universe, of "heauens place."[54] The allegorical body's perfection contains and neutralizes the fragmentation, disproportion, and violence of the chronicles Arthur discovers within. The perfect temperate body—the body politic—gathers and organizes into a unified vision of the nation and the monarchy the chaotic drifts of history.

Just as the minor stage can never create a perfectly unified subject, however, the constitution of the body politic as a general symbolic equivalent can never banish disorder entirely from the imagined community of the nation. In this vision of the perfected body politic, the natural body lurks as a "dangerous supplement," "extrinsic and subordinate to the body politic, yet essential to its perpetuation."[55] The poem's harmonizing of the "imperfect, mortall foeminine" and the "immortall, perfect masculine" in the allegory of Alma's house is undercut by the chiasmus and the reversal of positive and negative grammatical markers in these two phrases, reminding us that the female constitutes one such "dangerous supplement" because it is "imperfect, mortall." Elizabeth's subjects could never banish entirely their anxieties about their queen's sex or her refusal to produce or name an heir. These anxieties erupted in the periodic rebellions throughout Elizabeth's reign. In *The Faerie Queene*, the logic of supplementarity asserts itself when the allegorical images of incipient nationalism—troped as masculine—give way to the episodic structure of the romance—troped as feminine—in which plots set in motion fail to resolve themselves except as fragments of an endlessly deferred and imaginary wholeness whose image is the union of the Fairy Queen and Arthur of Britain.

Notes

1. Ernst H. Kantorowicz, *The King's Two Bodies: A Study in Mediaeval Political Theology* (Princeton, 1957), p. 3. I thank Martin Shichtman, Robert Markley, and Lindsay Kaplan for their comments on earlier drafts of this essay.

2. Benedict Anderson, *Imagined Communities: Reflections on the Origin and Spread of Nationalism* (London, 1983).

3. "A letter of the Authors expounding his whole intention in the course of this worke: which for that it giueth great light to the Reader, for the better vnderstanding is hereunto annexed," p. 407. All references to *The Faerie Queene* will be from *The Poetical Works of Edmund Spenser*, ed. J. C. Smith and E. de Selincourt (London, 1932). Subsequent references will be cited parenthetically in the text.

4. Geoffrey of Monmouth, *History of the Kings of Britain*, trans. Sebastian Evans (New York, 1958), p. 262.

5. Charles B. Millican, *Spenser and the Table Round: A Study in the Contemporaneous Background for Spenser's Use of the Arthurian Legend* (Cambridge, Mass., 1932) pp. 16, 154; and John J. Parry and Robert A. Caldwell, "Geoffrey of Monmouth," in *Arthurian Literature in the Middle Ages: A Collaborative History*, ed. Roger Sherman Loomis (Oxford, 1959), p. 89.

6. Millican, *Table Round*, p. 38.

7. Ibid., p. 51.

8. For a discussion of the use of Arthurian materials in pageants, spectacles, and plays, see Marie Axton, *The Queen's Two Bodies: Drama and the Elizabethan Succession* (London, 1977).

9. On the historical debates about the veracity of Geoffrey of Monmouth's *Historia* and the matter of Britain see T. D. Kendrick, *British Antiquity* (London, 1950).

10. For an analysis of Arthurian history's function as a *translatio imperii*, see A. Kent Hieatt, "The Passing of Arthur in Malory, Spenser, and Shakespeare," in *The Passing of Arthur: New Essays in Arthurian Tradition*, ed. Christopher Baswell and William Sharpe (New York, 1988), pp. 173–92.

11. Jean-Joseph Goux, *Symbolic Economies: After Marx and Freud*, trans. Jennifer Curtiss Gage (Ithaca, N.Y., 1990), pp. 39–41, 18.

12. Aristotle, *Nicomachean Ethics*, trans. Martin Ostwald (Indianapolis, 1962), pp. 89–91.

13. For analyses of Elizabethan patronage, see Wallace T. MacCaffrey, "Place and Patronage in Elizabethan Politics," in *Elizabethan Government and Society: Essays Presented to Sir John Neale*, ed. S. T. Bindoff, J. Hurtsfield, and C. H. Williams (London, 1961), pp. 95–126; Lawrence Stone, *The Crisis of the Aristocracy: 1558–1641* (Oxford, 1965), pp. 398–504; Leonard Tennenhouse, "Sir Walter Ralegh and the Literature of Clientage," in *Patronage in the Renaissance*, ed. Guy Fitch Lytle and Stephen Orgel (Princeton, 1981), pp. 235–58; and Tennenhouse, *Power on Display: The Politics of Shakespeare's Genres* (London, 1986), pp. 30–36.

14. My discussion of patronage throughout the essay is influenced by the work of social theorists like S. N. Eisenstadt and Luis Roniger, *Patrons, Clients,*

and Friends: Interpersonal Relations and the Structure of Trust in Society* (Cambridge, 1984) and Pierre Bourdieu, *Outline of a Theory of Practice,* trans. Richard Nice (Cambridge, 1977). Eisenstadt and Roniger describe the core characteristics of patron-client relationships which I will be referring to throughout my discussion of patronage; see pp. 48–49.

15. David Lee Miller, *The Poem's Two Bodies: The Poetics of the 1590 Faerie Queene* (Princeton, 1988). p. 50.

16. Carol Stillman, "Politics, Precedence, and the Order of the Dedicatory Sonnets of *The Faerie Queene,*" *Spencer Studies* 5 (1985), 143–48; and, Stone, *Crisis of the Aristocracy,* pp. 21–36.

17. *Dictionary of National Biography,* 8:613. Spenser's choice of heroes enabled him to flatter his friend and patron who was also named Arthur.

18. Miller, *The Poem's Two Bodies,* p. 53.

19. *Dictionary of National Biography,* 20:689–91.

20. Ibid., 20:226.

21. On the importance of Cambridge in supplying Elizabethan government with ministers, see Winthrop S. Hudson, *The Cambridge Connection and the Elizabethan Settlement of 1559* (Durham, N.C., 1980).

22. *Dictionary of National Biography,* 15:856.

23. Ibid., 3:978.

24. In the heraldic protocol the women always follow the men whatever their rank; see Stillman, "The Order of the Dedicatory Sonnets," p. 145.

25. Tennenhouse, *Power on Display,* p. 32.

26. Stone, *The Crisis of the Aristocracy,* p. 399. Robert Dudley, the Earl of Leicester, was one of Spenser's early patrons, but was dead by 1590 so that a dedicatory sonnet in *The Faerie Queene* would have served no purpose. Spenser had, however, dedicated "Virgil's Gnat" to his early patron.

27. Eisenstadt and Roniger, *Patrons, Clients, and Friends,* p. 48.

28. James Scott, *Weapons of the Weak: Everyday Forms of Peasant Resistance,* (New Haven, 1985), p. 307.

29. Bourdieu, *Theory of Practice,* p. 178.

30. See Tennenhouse, "Literature of Clientage" and *Power on Display,* 17–44; and David Starkey, "The Age of the Household: Politics, Society, and the Arts, c. 1350–1550," in *The Later Middle Ages,* ed. Stephen Medcalf (New York, 1981), pp. 252–254.

31. Scott, *Weapons of the Weak*, p. 307 and Laurie Finke, *Feminist Theory, Women's Writing*, (Ithaca, N.Y., 1992), pp. 29-74.

32. Tennenhouse, *Power on Display*, pp. 30-36.

33. See for instance, Stephen Greenblatt's analysis of Sir Thomas Wyatt's love poetry, especially "They flee from me," *Renaissance Self-Fashioning: From More to Shakespeare* (Chicago, 1980), pp. 115-56. Documents cited by both Greenblatt (pp. 161-69) and Tennenhouse (*Power on Display*, pp. 30-36) suggest that the erotic language of courtly love found its way not only into literature, but into personal letters and official communications as well.

34. Louis Adrian Montrose, "Shaping Fantasies: Figurations of Gender and Power in Elizabethan Culture," in *Representing the English Renaissance*, ed. Stephen Greenblatt (Berkeley, 1988) pp. 31-64.

35. Stone, *Crisis of the Aristocracy*, pp. 452-53.

36. Harry Berger Jr., " 'Faerie Queene' Book III: A General Description," *Criticism* 11 (1969), 234-261.

37. James P. Bednarz "Raleigh in Spenser's Historical Allegory," *Spenser Studies* 4 (1983), 49-70.

38. See Judith Anderson, "Arthur, Argante, and the Ideal Vision," in *The Passing of Arthur*, ed. Baswell and Sharpe, pp. 193-205.

39. This is the chastity which is both tested and celebrated in book 3.

40. Anderson, *Imagined Communities*, pp. 15-16.

41. Ibid., p. 16.

42. Ibid., pp. 20-28, 40.

43. Like most allegory, *The Faerie Queene* lends itself rather too well to psychoanalytic readings. Perhaps this has as much to do with Freud's debt to allegorical hermeneutics than to the truth value of psychoanalysis as a philosophical system. At any rate, my argument is indebted to the insightful psychoanalytic readings of *The Faerie Queene* by Miller (*The Poem's Two Bodies*) and Elizabeth J. Bellamy, "Reading Desire Backwards: Belatedness and Spenser's Arthur," *South Atlantic Quarterly* 88 (1989), 789-809.

44. Goux, *Symbolic Economics*, p. 10.

45. Ibid.

46. Ibid., pp. 39-41.

47. Ellie Ragland-Sullivan, *Jacques Lacan and the Philosophy of Psychoanalysis* (Urbana, Ill., 1987), p. 19.

48. Ragland-Sullivan, *Jacques Lacan*, p. 22.

49. Kantorowicz, *King's Two Bodies*, p. 7.

50. Miller, *The Poem's Two Bodies*, p. 202.

51. Harry Berger, *The Allegorical Temper: Vision and Reality in Book II of Spenser's "Faerie Queene"* (New Haven, 1957), p. 90.

52. Miller, *The Poem's Two Bodies*, p. 202.

53. Berger, *The Allegorical Temper*, p. 102.

54. See A. C. Hamilton's gloss of these lines, *The Faerie Queene* (New York, 1977), p. 251.

55. Miller, *The Poem's Two Bodies*, p. 202.

Arthur Before and After the Revolution: The Blome-Stansby Edition of Malory (1634) and *Brittains Glory* (1684)

—————————————————— *David R. Carlson*

At some point during the English revolution, John Milton decided against writing an epic poem on King Arthur. Probably, Milton had good reasons for declining the Arthurian material, although these reasons are no longer clear, and even now there are those who profess to be pleased that he wrote *Paradise Lost* instead of an Arthuriad. In any case, Milton's rejection of the Arthurian material was not perverse or idiosyncratic. Assertions of the perennial popularity of Arthur's story need to be qualified in light of Milton's decision: no major English writer (with due apologies to Sir Richard Blackmore) undertook to write seriously about Arthur between the end of the sixteenth century, with the publication of the final instalments of *The Faerie Queene*, and the invention of Romantic medievalism, towards the end of the eighteenth.[1] This lapse of interest is reflected in the publication history of Malory's *Morte Darthur*. Up to 1634, there had been an edition every generation or so, following the publication of Caxton's *editio princeps* in 1485, with editions by Wynkyn de Worde in 1498 and 1529, William Copland in 1557, and Thomas East in about 1582. After 1634 ensued a gap of nearly two hundred years, closed only by the publication of three editions within a nine-month period in 1816–17.[2] Tastes changed, and what Milton's decision adumbrates—as does the gap generally—is that the Arthurian legend was not endlessly protean or inevitably expedient. The legend had its limitations, and there was this period in English literary history during which it apparently failed to fire the imagination of any significant writer.

In the seventeenth century, during which Milton had to make up his mind, changing political circumstances had consequences for the Arthurian legend. Before the revolution, it was used against the monarchy in the 1634 edition of the *Morte Darthur*; after, in a retelling of the story called *Brittains Glory* printed fifty years later, in 1684, the legend was used to buttress the restored monarchy, but it had to be remade drastically to fit it to this new purpose. These episodes may or may not instantiate Walter Benjamin's pessimistic modernization of the ancient *opima spolia* ("*Even the dead* will not be safe from the enemy if he wins");[3] but at least they instantiate the more basic point that, when the Arthurian legend has been used, it has had to answer to social and political exigencies. These seventeenth-century uses of it provide both positive and negative examples: an instance in which the legend fit the situation at hand, and then one in which the legend could not be made to answer to present conditions except by altering it almost beyond recognition.

The last black-letter edition of the *Morte Darthur*, printed in London in 1634 by William Stansby for Jacob Blome, differed from its Tudor predecessors: it was shorter, fatter, less organized, and less extensively illustrated—it was a more vulgar book. The Tudor editions, beginning with de Worde's, had had as many as twenty-five woodcut illustrations distributed throughout them; the 1634 edition had only a woodcut frontispiece to illustrate it, picturing a round table at which sit several knights, with King Arthur, visible only above waist, apparently standing up through a hole in the middle of the table (fig. 1). The peculiar position that the illustration puts Arthur in is unprecedented in Round Table iconography; its metaphoric intent is clear, however. Arthur's abstract political centrality to the knightly order he founded is rendered in the woodcut by a literal, physical centrality in the table itself. For all the clarity of its symbolic purpose, however, the woodcut makes Arthur's position ridiculous, as Samuel Butler's allusions to it in his post-Restoration satire *Hudibras* (1663) indicate:

> And though Knights Errant, as some think,
> Of old did neither eat nor drink,
> Because when thorough Deserts vast
> And Regions desolate they past,
> Where Belly-timber above ground
> Or under was not to be found,
> Unless they graz'd, there's not one word
> Of their Provision on Record:
> Which made some confidently write,
> They had no stomachs, but to fight,

King *Arthur* and his valiant Knights of the round *Table*.
Sir Triftram. *Sir* Launcelot. *Sir* Galahad. *Sir* Percivall.
Sir Gauwin. *Sir* Ector. *Sir* Bors *Sir* Lionell. *Sir* Griflet.
Sir Gaheris. *Sir* Tor. *Sir* Acolon. *Sir* Ewaine. *Sir* Marhaus.
Sir Pelleas *Sir* Sagris. *Sir* Turquine *Sir* Kay. *Sir* Garerh.

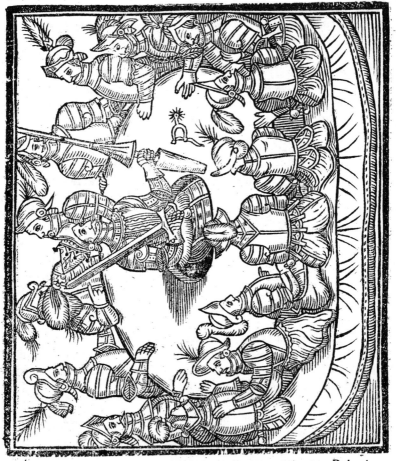

Sir Beaumans. *Sir* Berlunt. *Sir* Palomides. *Sir* Beleobus.
Sir Ballomare. *Sir* Galahalt. *Sir* Lamoracke. *Sir* Fro l.
Sir Superabilis. *Sir* Paginet. *Sir* Belvoure.

Fig. 1. *The Most Ancient and Famous History of the Renowned Prince Arthur King of Britane* (London: Stansby for Blome, 1634 [STC 806]), woodcut frontispiece. By permission of the Folger Shakespeare Library.

'Tis false: For *Arthur* wore in Hall
Round-Table like a Farthingal,
On which, with shirt pull'd out behind,
And eke before, his good Knights din'd.
Though 'twas no Table, some suppose,
But a huge pair of round Trunk-hose;
In which he carry'd as much meat
As he and all his Knights could eat,
When laying by their swords and truncheons,
They took their Breakfasts or their Nuncheons.[4]

As Butler saw, the frontispiece to the 1634 edition of Malory impugns Arthur's authority, his social and political centrality, by implication, by making his central position in the table, as its decorative center-piece, untenable and derisory. The 1634 edition as a whole has this characteristic of its frontispiece. The 1634 Malory refashioned the *Morte Darthur* as an oblique comment on the contemporary political situation—it could hardly have done otherwise, given the conditions under which it was produced—the implication imparted to the book by its particular design being that the position of England's present sovereign was similarly untenable. The 1634 edition was shaped by the volatile, pre-revolutionary political conditions to which it spoke, conditions which had put publishers and printers in a difficult spot, subject to pressure from both sides.

After the Restoration of 1660, Malory's account of Arthur's career did not make its way back into print; evidently, the Arthurian legend in its traditional form was no longer convenient. Its place was supplied by a new version of the story in *Brittains Glory*, and *Brittains Glory* was likewise published with a single woodcut illustration, again showing Arthur and the Round Table (fig. 2). This illustration puts the king back where he belongs. In it, Arthur is restored to the head of his Round Table. Putting him there was no mean feat, in visual terms, given that the table is still recognizably round, strictly headless. Not to mention the illustration's rude foreshortening, it was accomplished in part by means of props: the crown and the ermine mantle. Likewise, making the Arthurian material suitable for the Restoration seems to have been no mean feat. In *Brittains Glory*, it necessitated inventing a new story.

The instability of the Stuart monarchy, culminating in its dispossession twice, had repercussions for those engaged in the business of producing and circulating printed books, for the Stuarts sought to regulate the trade more strictly than their predecessors had. English

Fig. 2. *Brittains Glory* (London: H. B. for J. Wright et al., 1684 [Wing M339]), woodcut frontispiece. By permission of the Master and Fellows, Magdalene College, Cambridge.

authorities had long been concerned about the publication of subversive writings. The history of the relationship between the government and the printing trades in England shows that, by the early sixteenth century, the government recognized the potential power of the press; likewise, the success of the government's early interventions in the book trade signals the conservatism of the early English printers, who had a general interest at least in the preservation of law and order, inasmuch as law and order were good for trade. Their basic conservatism must also have been buttressed by the realization that their commercial survival depended on the good will of the Crown, a point brought home to them from time to time by the breakings-down of presses, nailings-up of shops, and criminal proceedings against members of the trade that did take place.[5]

England's printers had at their disposal means of hurting the authorities, and the authorities knew as much; at the same time, the authorities had at their disposal means of doing physical and commercial damage to the printers; as long as the temptation to one party to injure the other did not become too great, it profited neither to upset the balance; and so the government and the book trade remained on more or less good terms throughout the sixteenth century. Relations between the two parties were codified in the charter incorporating the Company of Stationers in 1557. The incorporation bespeaks the commercial ambitions of the printers, who seem to have been the active party in seeking it, as much as the monarchy's interest in gaining control over the press; for Philip and Mary, acknowledging the spread of "sediciosi et haeretici libri" in England, granted the Company a monopoly over printing in the kingdom, but, at the same time, left policing the terms of the charter up to the Company, acknowledging thereby that the printers themselves had the predominant interest in preserving the arrangement.[6]

The coincidence of self-interest that had insulated the government against seditious and heretical books and the printers against governmental sanctions began to fail in the first decades of the seventeenth century. Dissatisfaction with Stuart governance of the kingdoms increased demand for antigovernment literature: more were willing to speak against the government, and more were willing to hear the government spoken against. Situated as they were between such authors and such audiences, the printers and sellers of books stood to profit by meeting the demand. However, at the same time that such exploitable demand—not to mention genuine commitment to subversion on the part of a few—encouraged the trade to put out "sediciosi et haeretici libri," the government's ability to dispose profitable monopolies and to punish the trade's miscreants encouraged the trade at least to cooperate with the government, if not always to champion its interest. So though there were growing markets for sedition, taking profits from them entailed growing risks.

That the illegitimate trade was flourishing even in spite of the Company's collusion with the Crown is attested by the Stuarts' efforts to impose ever stricter regulations. In September 1623, the king promulgated decrees "for the repressing of sundry intolerable offences. . .occasioned by the disorderly Printing and Selling of Bookes." In them, James forbade anyone to print or import, "or sow, stitch, binde, sell, put [to] sale, or disperse any seditious, schismaticall, or other scandalous Bookes, or Pamphlets whatsoever. . .upon paine of Our indignation and heavy displeasure."[7] In spite of the king's "indignation and heavy displeasure," less than a year later, in August 1624, another even more urgent royal proclamation acknowledged the success that the illicit trade was enjoying: the trade in "Popish," "seditious," and "seditious Puritanicall" books and pamphlets "is growen so common, and practised so licentiously" that the king was compelled to enjoin stricter adherence to the still stricter licencing procedures detailed in the proclamation.[8] Finally, July 1637 saw the promulgation of the most hysterical Stuart decrees on printing, the monarchy's final attempt to control the press. The bill admits that the regulatory efforts of 1623–24 had failed ("divers abuses have sithence arrisen. . .to the disturbance of the peace of the Church and State"), and in a lengthy, obsessively detailed series of articles, it puts forward further remedies. The 1637 decree not only sought to impose royal control over every aspect of the process of printing and distributing books—"no Merchant or other person," it enjoins, for example, "shall presume to open any Dry-fats, Bales, Packs, Maunds, or other Fardals of books" except in the presence of licenced agents of the government or Stationers' Company. It also sought to control even the manufacture of the means of producing printed books: no one was to build a press, and no one was to rent or otherwise allow premises to be used for printing; "no Joyner, or Carpenter, or other person" was to build wooden parts and "no Smith shall forge any Iron-worke for a printing-Presse."[9]

Faced with such obsession, many in the printing trade, particularly the oligarchs of the Stationers' Company, who stood to benefit most, saw fit to link their interests with those of the government; the Stationers' Company did continue to take responsibility for enforcing the regulations promulgated by the government.[10] Nevertheless, the government's iteration and reiteration of its increasingly desperate measures indicate that others in the trade saw fit to link their interests with those opposed to the government; and the government's actions reveal the extent to which its best efforts and the best efforts of the Stationers' Company failed. There remained "a very wide gap between the law and its enforcement."[11]

Jacob Blome and William Stansby, the publisher and printer of the 1634 Malory,[12] were compelled by circumstance to operate in this gap at least in part, and Stansby was repeatedly subject to the law's enforcement, in spite of the fact that neither of them had any apparent abiding commitment one way or the other. Like other printers, they were businessmen. Blome, for example, published both Joseph Henshaw and Thomas Adams, the first a royalist divine who had been chaplain to the duke of Buckingham, George Villiers, until the unpopular royal favorite was assassinated in 1628, and the other probably the greatest of the pre-revolutionary puritan preachers; he published Rachel Speght, a contributor to the feminist response against "Thomas Tel-troth" and his *Arraignment of Women*, but he also published Matthew Griffith's *Bethel: Or, A Forme for Families*, a work as misogynous as the *Arraignment* and which also makes it clear how misogyny served the royalist interest at a time when the radical puritan sects "especially. . .appealed to women, to whom some of them gave equal rights;"[13] and Blome also had dealings with Richard Badger, who, on the eve of the revolution, became printer to Prince Charles and served Archbishop Laud in a similar capacity.[14]

Stansby likewise seems to have worked both sides of the street. On the one hand, he published propagandistic poetry by the royal apologists Richard Niccols and John Stradling; on the other hand, he also took part in the publication of William Perkins, who was "the dominant influence in Puritan thought for the forty years after his death" in 1602,[15] and his role in the publication of Raleigh's *History of the World* led to government seizure of his property.[16] Stansby did business with John Beale, who, during the revolution, in association with Stephen Bulkly, printed fugitively for the crown; but he also harboured the Catholic printer Peter Smith, both before and after Smith's arrest and the destruction of his first press; and Stansby's long-standing association with Nathaniel Butter, the printer of news-sheets, which were almost by definition always subversive in the pre-revolutionary period, led to the nailing up of his shop and the breaking down of his presses in 1622 or 1623 and to action against him by the Stationers' Company again in 1629, in one of the Company's rare prosecutions of evasion of the licencing requirements.[17]

Although neither Blome nor Stansby committed himself to one side or the other in the pre-revolutionary period, their practices, of a sort apparently more common among members of the book trade than commitment, still bespeak conscious evaluation of their political situation. Business conditions—sedition's potential for profit and the risk of commercial ruin that crossing the government entailed—compelled them to be aware of the political import of the work they did. It may be that they regarded the publication of Malory in 1634 as a comparatively safe way to generate profits. Nevertheless, the circumstances in which Blome and Stansby were working made publishing Malory a politically informed affair. Moreover, their contributions to shaping the book implanted a particular political charge in their edition. The 1634 *Morte Darthur* simply reproduces the text bequeathed it by the tradition running back to the Caxton edition of 1485. Aside from the modernization of certain spellings, in other words, no large- or small-scale rewriting of Malory took place at this point.[18] On the other hand, the 1634 edition added a new preface to the book; it restructured the materials; and it dressed the whole in a particular, peculiar material arrangement. These editorial changes altered the meanings that the *Morte Darthur* had for its contemporary audience.

The 1634 Malory is a small, apparently inexpensively produced book that by the characteristics of its design and production signals its address to a broad popular market. Whereas all the antecedent editions had been folios, substantial pieces of property, the objective value of which had been buttressed by illustrations, the 1634 Malory is a short but still not excessively fat quarto, unillustrated except for the frontispiece, of approximately four hundred and seventy unnumbered leaves, printed in single columns of a small, well-used gothic type, with what appears to be cheap ink, on cheap paper; broken characters abound, and in a high proportion of pages in the various copies of the edition that I have been able to examine, print has bled through the paper from one side of the sheets to obscure the text on the other. The book looks more like a piece of anti-establishment, fugitive printing than the opposite, and that all the evidence indicates it to have been a large edition corroborates the implication of the book's design and production: this was a self-consciously popular edition, and was so endowed with the political import that such populism would have had in the early seventeenth century.[19]

The 1634 edition also embodies the first major reorganization of the *Morte Darthur* since the Caxton edition of 1485. The 1634 edition has the same three-tiered hierarchy of parts as the earlier editions—the equivalent of chapters, forming books, forming one "hoole book"—but it distributes its elements differently along these tiers. In the Caxton edition and its sixteenth-century derivatives, five hundred and six chapters make up twenty-one books, averaging twenty-four chapters per book, which in turn make up the single whole book; in the 1634 edition, five hundred and three chapters make up only three parts, of one hundred fifty-three, one hundred seventy-four, and one hundred seventy-six chapters each respectively, which again in turn comprise the whole. The consequent comparative infrequency with which marks of the whole book's hierarchic organization are met in the 1634 edition reduces the importance of the hierarchy; in other words, Caxton's Malory more frequently asserts its hierarchic structure, while reading Malory in the 1634 edition is more like reading a simple sequence of co-equal chapters, all of the same level. In this way too, the 1634 Malory is a less orderly, less disciplined book.

The reorganization was probably dictated by an editorial decision to issue the 1634 edition in three parts. Each of the three comprises a separately designated sequence of signatures, begun anew at the beginning of each part, and each is preceded by a reimpression of the frontispiece and a sequentially numbered title page, facilitating the parts' arrangement for binding—all features that suggest part-issue. Part-issue of books began to be commonly practiced only after the Restoration, in the late 1670s[20] when it served the financial interests of book producers. It enabled them to begin recovering their investment in an edition before publication was complete; and, perhaps more important, part-issue also enhanced sales, persuading consumers to buy large books that they might otherwise resist, by representing such books as a series of small, inexpensive purchases rather than the single large expenditure that they did in fact eventually become. The 1634 Malory represents an early use of this marketing ruse. Like its typography, lack of decoration, quarto format, and other economies of production, the edition's part-issue too bespeaks its makers' intention to reach a comparatively mass readership. Although Blome and Stansby may have been motivated only by the financial advantages to be had by it, part-issue of the book was still a populist gesture, tending to cast a shadow of sedition over the book.

As had not occurred since the Caxton edition, the 1634 Malory contained a preface, an "Advertisement to the Reader, for the better illustration and understanding of this famous Historie," newly written for the edition.[21] Much of this "Advertisement" is a reworking of topics familiar from Caxton's 1485 preface: Arthur's place among the Nine Worthies, his potential value as a source of national pride, and so on; but then in addition, ostensibly "to confute the errours of such as are of an opinion that there was never any such man as King Arthur"— another topic from Caxton—the "Advertisement" retells the early British history, from the cessation of Roman rule to the accession of Arthur's successor. The "Advertisement" makes its early British history speak to contemporary political conditions, obliquely; it fashions a tale out of differences between legitimate and ill-gotten sovereignty, in which usurpation and tyranny, for all the damage they do, are still punished.

The "Advertisement" begins with the cessation of Roman rule over the island, representing it as liberation from a tyrannically imposed servitude: "After this Kingdome had for the space of above foure hundred and eighty yeares, borne the intolerable yoke of the Romane servitude, . . .Vortiger of the Bloud Royall of the Britaine Kings, did (by usurpation and the murther of Constance, the sonne of Constantius) seize upon the crowne." Subsequently, because of his "wicked life and ill gotten Soveraignty, grown odious, and hated by most of his subjects," this usurper Vortigern invited Saxons led by Hengist to come to Britain "to aide and support him"; but the Saxons wanted Britain for themselves, and "Vortigerne the Usurper was deposed, to whom his sonne Vortimer succeeded." Then Vortimer is poisoned by Vortigern's wife Rowan, daughter of the Saxon leader Hengist, "and Vortigerne againe was restored to the Crowne." In the end, Vortigern and Rowan "were burnt in their Castle" and Aurelius Ambrose, legitimate heir "of the race of Constance," which Vortigern had deposed, came to the throne, to be succeeded by "his brother Uter Pendragon," who was in turn succeeded by his son Arthur. Arthur's reign is characterized by great accomplishments at home and abroad; but "whilest he was abroad in these noble and Heroicall Imployments, his Nephew (Mordred) whom hee had put in trust with the Government of his Realme, being puffed up with Ambition, and possessed with Treason, he caused himselfe to be crowned, and usurped the Kingdome." Again, the end of this usurper's "trayterous and rebellious opposition" against legitimate sovereignty is his death, albeit only at a cost: "after two set battailes," Arthur slew Mordred, but only "with the losse of his owne life." Arthur is rewarded, however, for putting down Mordred's usurpation; he is succeeded on the throne by a legitimate heir, "Constantine the fifth, . . . a kinsman to King Arthur."

Vortigern had always been a wicked character for native historians, beginning with the Venerable Bede, the first to name him (*Hist. Ec.* 1.14). More immediate sources for the "Advertisement" exist in the several still influential Elizabethan treatments of the story, including that in John Foxe's *Actes and Monuments*—which represents "wicked Vortigern, who cruelly causing Constans his prince to be murdered, ambitiously invaded the crown," until he was "justly deposed," as an "example to all ages and countries, what it is first to let in foreign nations into their dominion, but especially what it is for princes to join in marriage with infidels," all strictures that might have applied equally against the Stuarts.[22] For the "Advertisement," Vortigern is bad not for having invited the Saxons to Britain; he was already wicked by then: he had had to invite the Saxons to Britain because of his wickedness, expressed most damagingly in his usurpations. Vortigern is bad for the "Advertisement" because of his "ill gotten Soveraignty," since, even though he was of the "Bloud Royall," he had murdered to get to the throne; and in the end, because of it, the morally dissolute king, married to a wicked, foreign-born queen, and in league with foreigners who do not have the nation's best interests at heart—again, all characteristics that might be taken to refer to the first two Stuart kings of England—must be deposed.

Arthur, by contrast, is a legitimate sovereign who comes to the throne by simple inheritance: "Uther Pendragon begat Arthur of the beauteous Igraine (Wife to the duke of Cornwall)." The "Advertisement" downplays the problems about Arthur's conception and the problems caused him later by general ignorance of his problematic parentage (the "Advertisement" states that Arthur had been raised at Uther's court, only "by the helpe" of Merlin); the "Advertisement" restricts Arthur's story to matters of sovereign authority. "Begat" as the legitimate heir to a previous legitimate king, Arthur accedes uncontested to the throne on his father's death, and spends his reign in "noble and Heroicall Imployments," curbing others' "insolent power." Set opposite Arthur is Mordred, Vortigern's latter-day double in a sense, not Arthur's son here, but only his nephew, who, "being puffed up with Ambition, and possessed with Treason," wrongfully "usurped the Kingdome" from its legitimate sovereign, as had Vortigern, and again died because of his wicked usurpation.

In this struggle between legitimate and illegitimate powers that the "Advertisement" effectively took from its circumstance and imposed on the early British history, popular forces have a part to play, in resisting illegitimate sovereigns and putting them down. In the "Advertisement," the agents of political change when wrong is done a legitimate sovereign are named: Vortigern murders Constance; Vortigern's wife Rowan poisons Vortimer; Mordred kills Arthur. In other instances, however, involving illegitimate sovereignty, the agent of change is an impersonal mass of "subjects": "Vortigerne the Usurper was deposed," and his reign was "troublous"; he had "grown odious, and hated by most of his subjects." Here, in the political world called up by the "Advertisement," it falls to hateful subjects to bring down ill-made kings, who forfeit authority by their misdeeds.

That these peculiar emphases imparted to the early British history in the 1634 "Advertisement" were determined by the political conditions under which the edition was prepared is confirmed, albeit indirectly, by *Brittains Glory*, which similarly refashions some of the same materials in light of current circumstance, but with the opposite political import. As the 1634 edition shows, Malory's story of Arthur was susceptible to being presented in a populist editorial context, with an anti-Stuart, if not more generally an antiroyalist coloring. The design, production, and distribution of the 1634 book, and, still more perhaps, the "Advertisement" printed with it, would have encouraged contemporary readers to see the *Morte Darthur* itself and the ancient British history as politically charged, addressing current issues of sovereign legitimacy. From this perspective, the 1634 book appears to use the traditional materials to emphasize what can happen to kings, good ones and bad: sometimes they are overthrown and sometimes killed. It paints a world of usurpation, rebellion, political tension, and struggle. Making an unequivocally pro-royal statement out of these materials—the job *Brittains Glory* attempts in 1684 after the revolution—called for more drastic measures than had been necessary in 1634. The idea seems to have been to use the popularity of Arthur's name and the popular form of the prose pamphlet to broadcast royalist political myths.[23]

In *Brittains Glory*, the story retains a broadly Malorian or at least Galfridian shape, encompassing the whole of Arthur's career, from his conception to his death. The circumstances of his death differ markedly from other versions of the story, but those of his conception retain some familiarity. Here Uther "got" Arthur "on" "Igrayin" by means of the magic of Merlin ("a famous Necromancer of that age"), who had afforded him a single night in the embraces of this wife of another man ("Alfridus Duke of Cornwall"). The difference is that Uther's desire has no immediate or negative political consequences, entailing no strife between him and Igrayin's husband. Alfridus is simply away from home at the time, "in war with the West-Saxons;" when he happens to be killed on this campaign, Uther, "though greatly grieved at the loss of so renowned a subject," was content to marry the widow and legitimate the son (A2r-A2v).[24]

Generally, this is the approach *Brittains Glory* takes: the 1634 Malory emphasises conflicts between legitimate sovereignty and usurpation, and the damages done by wrongfully assumed, misused power; *Brittains Glory* attenuates political conflict within England, when it cannot eliminate it altogether. In the world summoned up by *Brittains Glory*, there is no treacherous adultery, marital infidelity with negative political repercussions: no betrayal of Gorlois by Uther, no betrayal of Lot by Arthur in begetting Mordred, no betrayal of Arthur by Lancelot. *Brittains Glory* has no Lot and no Lancelot, nor figures equivalent to them. Likewise, such openly political opposition to Arthur's rule as arises is external. There is no Mordred; Arthur's opponents are always foreigners. Some resistance to Arthur's accession arises, but only because of his youth; and it is not serious enough to be mentioned more than in passing, for there is no mystery about Arthur's origin and nurture, nor any sword in the stone to justify his accession. Here, he is simply his father's heir: his father having died, "leaving him sole heir of his Dominions," Arthur "thereupon was proclaimed by most of the Nobility, and Crowned King, though some taking advantage of his green years, rebelled, and raised divers Commotions; but he, growing up, and getting the Reins of Government into his hands, did many great Exploits" (A2v).

The bulk of *Brittains Glory* is given over to narration of these "many great Exploits." Broadly, they follow the traditional pattern, but again with differences. Arthur makes his own Round Table, attracting knights to his fealty by offering them continuous entertainment and regular salaries, to be raised later as his "Order" flourishes: Arthur sets the table itself up in his great hall, and

> caused it daily to be furnished with great store of choice provision, for the entertainment of such men of War as would resort thither, and shortly after constituted the Order of the Round Table, allowing a yearly Pension of 100 Mark to such as were truly valiant and would inrole themselves to attend his

service when occasion required, making himself the head or Sovereign of the Order, so that by this means the valiant men of the neighbouring Nations tendered their service to him. (A3v)

The armed might he thus assembles Arthur employs in a series of military campaigns, against Saxon invaders of his own dominions, and then abroad, against the Danish, the Irish, and the French. In *Brittains Glory*, Arthur fights only in just conflicts; never does he turn his forces against his own people, using them instead always either against foreign aggressors, who attack him, or against pirates and terrorists, who vex and victimize his loyal subjects. Arthur is roused to war against the French, for example, when they "(then powerful at Sea) invade[d] our Coast, and with fire and sword spoiled many Sea-Towns, carrying away great booty, as also the people, the men made to row in their Gally, and the women to satiate their prodigious Lust" (B4r). Similarly, the king of the Irish, trying to take advantage of Arthur's absence on a foreign campaign, is routed on Arthur's return and chased from England, "being everywhere assailed by the Country Peasants" along the way (B3v).

The greatest of Arthur's great exploits, however, is his crusade against "infidels" in the holy lands, "to free the Holy City from its pollution" (C1v). He undertakes it at the imprecation of a hermit, who brings him the news that "Turks and Sarazens" are murdering Christians and "polluting the Temple and Holy Sepulchre with their Heathenish Worship," a situation that Arthur calls "intollerable": "Hear you this, my Lords," he asks, "shall we suffer the Enemies of our Lord and Saviour thus to triumph over the professors of his Name?" At the moment, Arthur wanted employment for his military might anyway:

About this time King Arthur finding nothing worthy of his Sword at home, and altogether impatient of ease, studyed how he might imploy it abroad, and whilst he was musing thereon, an Hermit in poor aray came to the Court, and filled it at once with pitty and desire of revenge upon the dismal Relation he made. (C1v)

In the course of his crusade, Arthur first takes Joppa (defeating "a host of 100000 Turks, Jews, and Sarazens") and then Jerusalem, the more difficult but more rewarding job. He defeats a "Turk" champion ("a monstrous Pagan") in a single combat set up to decide the city's fate; but the "Infidels"—"contrary to the promise of their King. . . refusing to stand to what had been sworn"—press the attack. Arthur slaughters them anyway, even as they retreat, and then frees the city, with the result that a great number of miserable men and women were released out of Dungeons, who had for a long time been fed with Bread of Affliction, half-starved, and miserably used by the Infidels, for publikely owning the Name of the Lord, who, not far from thence, purchased them with his precious blood to their unspeakable joy. (C1v–C3r)

While he is abroad on crusade, news reaches him that his ever-perfidious Saxon neighbours "in his absence had cast off their Allegiance, and, being united, invaded his Country, insomuch that his Queen, Son, and those that he had left in charge with the Kingdom, being overthrown in a pitched battel, were fled to the fastnesses of the Snowdown Mountains." Unlike his counterpart in other versions of the story, it costs Arthur nothing to face down this challenge. It entails not even a threat of usurpation (the fidelity of "his Queen, Son, and those that he had left in charge with the Kingdom" being emphasized); and in fact Arthur manages to turn a profit from it. The Saxons simply lay down their arms when news of Arthur's terrible approach reaches them. The whole affair was only a misunderstanding anyway—they thought Arthur had died on Crusade—and they are willing to pay him reparations for his trouble and to secure the future with hostages:

The Kings approache being known to the Saxon Princes (who not long before had news that he was dead in the Holy Land, and thereby were animated to take up Arms) so discouraged them, that withdrawing their Forces, every one retired into his own Province, to study how to appease the victorious Monarch....The King being highly incensed, would at no cheaper a rate pass over their perfideous dealings, than at a personal acknowledgement, and the sum of 2000 Marks each; as also be the better assured of them for the future, that each of them should send his son as an hostage...; and over and above, to make reparation for such damages as could be by any of the Kings Subjects proved to be sustained by their unlawfull Arms. (C3r–C4r)

Hereafter, this Arthur occupies the days remaining to him with good works and pious thoughts. The final chapter heading tells "how King Arthur built many religious Houses, and gave great Cargases to the Poor"; the chapter itself also details "his utmost endeavour to cherish Learning and Arts, to which end at his proper charge he built likewise many Schools and Colledges." He dies peacefully in bed, aged sixty, having reigned forty-nine years (C4r–C4v).

The most striking difference between *Brittains Glory* and other versions lies here, in its treatment of Arthur's death. It makes of Guinevere a Danish king's daughter, chaste but filled with desire for Arthur. She enters into a contract of marital fidelity with her husband, from which neither of them ever strays; and together they produce a male heir. Arthur returns from his successful campaign against the French to find,

> to his unspeakable joy, his fair Queen delivered of a lovely boy, who, by the advice of Merlyn, he named CONSTANTIUS, whose Victories and great Exploits that Prophet fore-told, which, after his fathers death, he succeeding him in his Throne, exactly came to pass. (B4r)

At the boy's birth, Arthur's subjects swear oaths of allegiance to the heir; when Arthur dies, Constantius accedes untroubled to the throne, with a reiteration of his subjects' oaths (C4v).

An untroubled transfer of legitimate sovereignty, from father to son, guaranteed by the oaths of subjects loyal and true: graphically, this final scene reiterates what is important to *Brittains Glory*. There is nothing subtle about it. Its emphasis, throughout, on stable, strong, and glorious monarchy, as well as on happy relations in England between an always sollicitous, always just king and his always dutiful, always deferential subjects, answers back memory of the recent "Revolutions of this Kingdom," mentioned in an epistolary preface.[27]

Brittains Glory remakes the Arthur story thoroughly; and it is clear that the rewriting is again informed by political considerations, even though this 1684 rewriting speaks to a different circumstance from that addressed in the 1634 Blome-Stansby Malory. In 1684, the material was made to mythologize royalist political ideals. The fact that *Brittains Glory* had to change the story so radically tends to confirm that the undoctored Malory that Blome and Stansby published with their "Advertisement" in 1634 was subversive. Because the ancient British history, including Arthur's story, had served to subvert the Stuart monarchy before the revolution, after the revolution it had to be remade. Under another circumstance, those who published *Brittains Glory* might have preferred the expedient of a new edition of Malory or of a less drastic reformulation of the material, one less expensive of imaginative labor than *Brittains Glory* is; but the political situation had so drastically altered by 1684 that a Malory simply edited anew would not have worked, apparently, as if there was something unavoidably inappropriate about the *Morte Darthur*. The 'copyright' on Malory's work was allowed to lapse at this point; when the book began to be published again in 1816–17, nearly two hundred years later, circumstances had again changed.

Notes

1. On Milton and the Arthurian legend, see Nicholas von Maltzahn, *Milton's History of Britain: Republican Historiography in the English Revolution* (Oxford, 1991), esp. pp. 60–72 and 91–117; Von Maltzahn (esp. pp. 95–99) emphasizes early seventeenth-century use of the ancient British history "to express political dissatisfaction with the Stuart kings' conduct and policies." On the other hand, Restoration treatments of the Arthurian materials—Martin Parker's unfinished *Famous History of Arthur King of the Britaines* (1660), the Dryden/Purcell opera *King Arthur* (1691), and Blackmore's poems *Prince Arthur* (1695) and *King Arthur* (1697), as well as the *Brittains Glory* discussed herein—all must deviate significantly from the received tradition to fit the materials to the changed political situation.

2. On the romantic Malorys, see esp. Barry Gaines, "The Editions of Malory in the Early Nineteenth Century," *Papers of the Bibliographical Society of America* 68 (1974), 1–17.

3. Walter Benjamin, "Theses on the Philosophy of History," 6, in *Illuminations*, trans. Harry Zohn (New York, 1969), p. 255.

4. *Hudibras* 1.1.325–44: *Samuel Butler: Hudibras*, ed. John Wilders (Oxford, 1967), p. 11. On the iconography of the frontispiece and Butler's use of it, see my "Arthur's Round Table in *Hudibras*," *Journal of the Warburg and Courtauld Institutes* 49 (1986), 261–64; on the illustrations in the Tudor Malorys, see Muriel Whitaker, "Illustrating Caxton's Malory," in *Studies in Malory*, ed. James W. Spisak (Kalamazoo, 1985), pp. 297–304.

5. On these early relations between England's press and government, see A. W. Pollard, "The Regulation of the Book Trade in the Sixteenth Century," *The Library*, 3rd ser., 7 (1916), 18–43; Graham Pollard, "The Company of Stationers before 1557," *The Library*, 4th ser., 18 (1937), 1–38; Howard W. Winger, "Regulations Relating to the Book Trade in London from 1357 to 1586," *Library Quarterly* 26 (1956), 157–95; and D. M. Loades, "The Press under the Early Tudors: A Study in Censorship and Sedition," *Transactions of the Cambridge Bibliographical Society* 4 (1964), 29–50; and on the introduction of licencing more specifically, see A. W. Pollard, " 'Ad Imprimendum Solum'," *The Library*, 3rd ser., 10 (1919), 57–63.

6. The incorporation charter is edited and translated (from the original Latin) in Edward Arber, *A Transcript of the Registers of the Company of Stationers of London, 1554–1640 A.D.* 5 vols. (London, 1875–94), 1:xxviii–xxxii; on it, see also Graham Pollard, "The Early Constitution of the Stationers' Company," *The Library*, 4th

ser., 18 (1937), 235-60. Emphasis has often been put on the Crown's interest in the incorporation, but Graham Pollard, "The Company of Stationers," esp. p. 35, argues convincingly otherwise; and cf. Loades, "The Press under the Early Tudors," p. 48.

7. W. W. Greg, *A Companion to Arber* (Oxford, 1967), doc. 36, pp. 219-21. Pertinent earlier documents are printed in Arber, *A Transcript*, 2:807-12; and 3:42-49, 699, 679-82; cf. also Greg, *Companion*, nos. 125, 151, 163, 165.

8. Greg, *Companion*, doc. 40.3, p. 228.

9. The document is in Arber, *A Transcript*, 4:529-36.

10. Cf. Blagden, "The Stationers' Company in the Civil War Period," *The Library*, 5th ser., 13 (1958), 7-8: "Officially, the Company was not interested in the calling of the Long Parliament and would have been content with...'The King's Peace;' officially, the Company could only be royalist."

11. Loades, "The Press under the Early Tudors," p. 46.

12. Working arrangements between Blome and Stansby are not altogether clear in the production of the two books that they worked on together, both published during 1634: the Malory (STC 806) and the *Itinerary of Asia and Africa* by Thomas Herbert (STC 13191). It seems most likely, however, that Stansby simply printed the 1634 Malory, while Blome published it, that is, initiated publication of the title, made the editorial decisions embodied in the book itself and described in the prefatory "Advertisement" to it that Blome probably wrote, and took the capital risks for the edition and the responsibility for its distribution. Stansby held exclusive rights to the literary property in the Malory, which he had been assigned nearly ten years previously, in February 1626, by the widow of Thomas Snodham, who had acquired it from the widow of his master Thomas East, Malory's immediately precedent publisher (see Arber, *A Transcript*, 3:413 and 4:152-54). Nevertheless, the title page of the 1634 Malory states that the book was printed by Stansby for Blome. A distinction made in the 1634 Malory's "Advertisement," between editorial decisions left up to "the Compositor and Corrector at the Presse" and decisions taken by the first-person of the unsigned preface, corroborates the likelihood that the edition was effectively Blome's work, simply printed by Stansby for Blome.

13. Christopher Hill, *The Century of Revolution 1603-1714* (Edinburgh, 1961), p. 167. On the controversy raised by the *Arraignment*, see Suzanne Hull, *Chaste, Silent, and Obedient: English Books for Women* (San Marino, Calif., 1982), pp. 111-22. Griffith's book (STC 12368), after corroborating at length its assertion that "wives must be in subjection to their husbands" (pp. 322-34), finally argued that the members of a family so constituted, "as the summe of their dutie,...must feare God and the King, and must not meddle with them that be seditious" (pp. 429-30).

14. For Blome's dealings with Badger, see Arber, *A Transcript*, 4:305 and STC 12368-12370a.

15. J. E. Christopher Hill, "William Perkins and the Poor," in *Puritanism and Revolution* (London, 1958), p. 216; and cf. Louis B. Wright, "William Perkins: Elizabethan Apostle of 'Practical Divinity,'" *Huntington Library Quarterly* 3 (1940), 171–96. In 1622, Stansby printed an edition of Perkins's *A Cloud of Faithful Witnesses* (STC 19679), and he also at one time owned an interest in a "third volume of master Perkins workes," which he sold in 1630 (see Arber, *A Transcript*, 4:238, 431).

16. Arber, *A Transcript*, 5:lxxvii; William A. Jackson, *Records of the Court of the Stationers' Company 1602–1640* (London, 1957), pp. 355–57; and cf. Greg, *Companion*, no. 162.

17. For Stansby's association with Beale, see Arber, *A Transcript*, 4:352; for his association with Smith, see Leona Rostenberg, *The Minority Press and the English Crown: A Study in Repression 1558–1625* (Nieuwkoop, 1971), pp. 98–99; for his association with Butter and its consequences, see Greg, *Companion*, docs. 33.1–4, pp. 209–11, and no. 233 and doc. 52.1, p. 245.

18. The 1634 edition is described in Eugène Vinaver, *Malory*, 2nd ed. (Oxford, 1970), pp. 191–92.

19. On evidence for the size of the edition, see Carlson, "Arthur's Round Table in *Hudibras*," p. 263.

20. The most extensive discussion of English part-issue is that of R. M. Wiles, *Serial Publication in England before 1750* (Cambridge, 1956); in spite of its title, the book does not deal with any instances of part-issue before Samuel Moxon's *Mechanik Exercises*, the first part of which was issued 1 January 1678.

21. The "Advertisement" is here quoted from the 1634 Malory, pt. 1, sigs. [paragraph siglum]3r–[paragraph siglum]4v; it was reprinted in Thomas Wright's edition of Malory, *La Mort d'Arthure*, 3 vols. (London, 1858), 1:i–xxvi.

22. John Foxe, *Actes and Monuments*, ed. George Townsend, 8 vols. (London, 1843), 1:313–14 and 320–23. For other current treatments of the story, see Samuel Schoenbaum, *Middleton's Tragedies* (New York, 1955), pp. 70–74, giving special emphasis to the version in the 1587 *Holinshed's Chronicles*, ed. Henry Ellis, 6 vols. (London, 1807–8), 1:551–67; and Margot Heineman, *Puritanism and Theatre: Thomas Middleton and Opposition Drama under the Early Stuarts* (Cambridge, 1980), pp. 134–50.

23. Choice of this term is intended to evoke Roland Barthes's concept of "myth" (in *Mythologies*, trans. Annette Lavers [New York, 1972], esp. pp. 142–43), as a kind of partisan question-begging, whereby what is in fact a matter for contention is presented as something inevitably and unarguably right. *Brittains Glory* is Wing M339; I quote from the copy in Cambridge, Magdalene College, Pepys Library 1192, the third of four uniform volumes containing what Pepys called "Vulgaria" and "Vulgar ware": popular pamphlet romances, for the most part. *Brittains Glory* (comprising 24 unnumbered pages, collating A–C⁸ 4) is the

eighth of twenty-three items in the volume. For information about the volume and access to it, I am grateful to the staff of the Pepys Library, especially Mrs. E. M. Coleman.

24. This and subsequent parenthetical references following quotations from *Brittains Glory* are to the signatures of the Pepys Library copy.

25. Lancelot's name is in fact mentioned, sig. C2r, but only in a list of Arthur's generals on crusade.

26. The courtship and marriage are narrated at sigs. B3r–B3v.

27. *Brittains Glory*, sig. A1v: "To the reader: Courteous Reader, During the Revolutions of this Kingdom, such have been the Valourous Exploits of the Princes, and other Renowned Warriours, Natives not only in this our Land and neighbouring Countries, but throughout the known World, that all Nations have stood amazed, and trembled at their Prowess. And amongst others, well may the famous ARTHUR that renowned Brittish King take place, though (to lessen the Credit of his great Exploits) some envious Aliens have endeavoured to prove there was never such a man; but since it is evident by Chronologers of the most Antiquity and Integrity, that he was the Son of Uter Pendragon of the Antient Brittish Royal Blood, I shall not use more Arguments to manifest it to the world, but proceed to the Matter of History, as I find it layed down for the Instruction of future Ages."

28. When the block of titles, including the *Morte Darthur*, that East had acquired, and which was subsequently assigned to Snodham and then to Stansby, was sold by Stansby's widow to Bishop in March 1639, the Malory was not among them anymore, as if it had lost all value; the title was not picked up by another publisher. See above, note 12, and Arber, *A Transcript*, 4:458–60.

Reluctant Redactor:
William Dyce Reads the Legend

 *Debra N. Mancoff*

If Tennyson can be characterized as "Arthur's Laureate," then William Dyce must be recognized as the king's court painter.[1] Like Tennyson Dyce recast the legend into a vivid new form, significant to and reflective of the values and needs of his audience. And like that of Tennyson's poetry, the influence of Dyce's paintings endured for over a half century. Taken in tandem, their words and pictures formed a powerful foundation for the Arthurian revival. But unlike Tennyson, Dyce did not turn to the legend on his own volition. The subject was assigned to him in a prestigious commission; his client was the government and his audience the Crown. While Tennyson came to the legend, Dyce was brought to it, and in his cautious approach to the subject and his reluctant embrace of the tradition, his differences from Tennyson are defined.

On 5 September 1848 the Fine Arts Commission (or FAC, the government board, headed by Prince Albert, that oversaw the decoration of the new Palace at Westminster) informed the queen that William Dyce's services were secured to design and execute an ensemble of frescoes, based on the legend of King Arthur, in the Queen's Robing Room, the only chamber in the governmental house reserved for the exclusive use of the monarch. To all parties Dyce seemed the logical choice. He proved his ability in the medium in his first fresco in the new palace; in fact, *The Baptism of Ethelbert* (1846) was so highly regarded by the FAC that other painters were instructed to use Dyce's work as their standard.[2] Dyce was well known and well liked both by the Parliament and the Crown, and had enjoyed governmental appointments and Prince Albert's patronage. In the art world Dyce commanded equal respect. Well travelled and well read, he was known to his contemporaries as a "pre-eminently educated artist"[3] and the foremost practitioner in Britain of the high-minded European tradition of history painting. In the view of the FAC no artist was better qualified to bring the national legend to life on the walls of the monarch's chamber.

In truth, to the modern Arthurian scholar, Dyce lacked what seems to be an essential qualification. Prior to this commission he demonstrated no interest in and no knowledge of the legend. Chosen for his power as a painter, Dyce came to the commission as a new Arthurian reader. From July 1848 to February 1849 Dyce studied the legend, preparing to turn the medieval epic into a modern visual allegory. Dyce's reflections on his texts are recorded in a series of letters written to another painter Charles L. Eastlake, secretary of the FAC.[4] His self-selected course of study, the questions he asked and the answers he found, and, in the end, his revisionist reliance on Malory, reveals the Victorian attitude toward the legend before the appearance of Tennyson's *Idylls of the King*. While the history and result of Dyce's commission have been discussed elsewhere, his process of reading the legend has been neglected.[5] Dyce's inquiry and insights illustrate those of a representative type of Victorian reader at a pivotal point in the legend's emergent popularity. His strategy of definition, justification, selection, and ultimately revision, not only anticipated that of Tennyson, it demonstrates why the *Idylls* were so influential and successful. Dyce raised questions that would be only answered by Tennyson, and his concerns speak for an audience that would be Tennyson's public, revealing not just the desire for revival of the legend, but the desire for its revision.

William Dyce (1806–64) earned his place as the foremost history painter in Victorian Britain through his education and experience, as well as his example.[6] The son of a scientist and lecturer at Marischal College, Dyce seemed destined for learned career. But his interest in painting distracted him from his studies at his father's college, and in 1825 he left his native Aberdeen for London, where he successfully applied to the Royal Academy of Arts as a probationary student. At nineteen Dyce was older than most of his fellow art students, but his education—in the sciences, in classical languages, and in history—distinguished him in a field where university studies were rare.[7]

Dyce did not stay long in London. Within the year he abandoned classes at the Royal Academy to tour Italy. For almost a century travel to the continent, and especially Rome, Venice, and Florence, was regarded as part of an art education and Dyce, with his studious nature, wanted to follow the full curriculum. To the British artist Rome offered a living museum of classical and Renaissance masterworks, a selection unmatched by the limited collections at home. Dyce's first visit was brief, but in 1827 he returned to Italy, and stayed for more than a year. In Rome he studied the antique sculptures in the Vatican collection, the frescoes by Raphael in the Vatican Stanze, and new works by the Nazarenes, a group of expatriate German painters settled in Rome to learn the art of fresco. He also travelled to Venice, Florence, and elsewhere, to see the works of the great painters of the Quattrocento and the Cinquecento, ranging from Masaccio to Raphael. Italian traditions left their powerful mark on Dyce's emerging style, instilling him with a love for the grand grace of the classically proportioned figure, an interest in religious and classical subject matter, and a deep respect for conventions forged more than three centuries earlier.

During the 1830s Dyce drew only modest attention as an artist practicing in the traditional Italianate style. His first wide recognition came not for his painting, but his views on education. In 1836 he was invited to appear before a Select Committee of Parliament to give his opinions on art schools and the state of design training in Great Britain.[8] As a result Dyce was chosen to be the first superintendent of the newly founded Governmental School of Design in 1840. In the next year Dyce appeared before another Select Committee, that which led to the convening of the FAC in 1842. Dyce served as an "expert witness," sharing his knowledge of Continental practice in public art commissions and on the technique of fresco. When, in 1845, he was the first artist to begin work in the new palace, the fresco *The Baptism of Ethelbert* in the Lords Chamber, the selection was probably made more on the basis of his knowledge rather than his practice.[9] It is also significant that to prepare to paint the first Saxon king of Kent to accept the Christian religion, Dyce requested a leave to return to Italy, claiming a need "to go abroad...to see the frescoes of the old Masters."[10]

As a history painter Dyce was bound to certain conventions. Figure type, style, composition, and the mode of communicating the message were all dictated by tradition. The setting of the subject—whether the world of antiquity, the Middle Ages, or modern times—mattered less than the dignity and grandeur conveyed by that subject. History painting gave form to public, not private, ideas. To that end, a standard visual language was employed: classical figures, stable and symmetrical compositions on a large scale, and the reduction of detail (in costume, setting, and individual portrayal) stressing a universal, rather than a specific appearance. To justify the rejection of specificity Sir Joshua Reynolds, first president of the Royal Academy of Arts, argued "a History-painter paints man in general; a Portrait-Painter, a particular

Fig. 1. William Dyce, *The Baptism of Ethelbert* (1846). Fresco. 16′4½″ x 9′4½″. Lords Chamber, Palace at Westminster, London. British Crown Copyright. With Permission of Her Britannic Majesty's Stationery Office.

man and consequently a defective model."[11] The history painter sought the ideal, that which would endure long beyond the actual.

The lexicon for that ideal was based on a canon of masterworks, drawn from the antique world and the Renaissance era. A history painter gave his painting authority and linked it to tradition by quoting a visual precedent from the canon. For example, when Dyce painted *The Baptism of Ethelbert* (fig. 1), he drew on Quattrocento Italy rather than Saxon England for his prototype. His visual source was Masaccio's *Baptism of the Neophytes* (1425) in the Brancacci Chapel at Santa Maria del Carmine in Florence, a stop on his tour of 1845. Although the subject and the sentiment of Dyce's *Baptism* are thoroughly national, the form and composition is essentially *Italiante*. The figures have an illusionistic weight and a proportional power that obeys a classical rather than a medieval aesthetic and the balanced composition and the triumphal arch gracing the background echoes a Renaissance setting. Neither Dyce nor the FAC saw an anachronism in this translation of a national medieval subject into an Italianate classical image. Through the conventions of history painting the subject, celebrating the venerable alliance of Christianity and the monarchy, transcended its chronological origins and was transformed into a message for all times.

Dyce's allegiance to the conventions of history colored his view of the Arthurian legend. As the first British artist since the medieval era to undertake a large-scale Arthurian program, he lacked a prototype for his visual precedent. Antiquities of medieval origin had archaeological interest, but did not comply with the conventional aesthetic, and academic rule warned against choosing the specific over the universal. Manuscripts were conceived on a totally different scale, and to the mind of the history painter a book did not encompass the depth and scope of a wall. Dyce knew that the German Nazarenes, particularly Pieter Cornelius and Julius Schnorr von Carolsfeld, painted their national legends in fresco by veneering the medieval subject over classical form and composition.[12] His *Baptism of Ethelbert* marked a similar amalgam of form and subject. The absence of a visual prototype proved no barrier to Dyce, but he needed the means to transform the sprawling Arthurian narrative into a cogent and universalized discourse on the dignity of humanity. To achieve his end Dyce became an Arhturian redactor, reducing the legend to a new Victorian order.

In the 1840s an Arthurian reader could choose from a wide range of sources. Since the previous century the legend had been recovered and reconstructed from literary fragments, old texts, and translations. Available texts were diverse and reflected the evolution of the revival in literature. The literary anthology, such as Thomas Percy's *Reliques of Ancient English Poetry* (1765) or George Ellis's *Specimens of Early English Romances* (1805), offered examples of medieval ballads and romance (in drastically edited or summarized form) with commentary on source, style, and meaning. Historical studies, such as Sharon Turner's *History of the Anglo-Saxons* (1807), Edward Davies' *The Mythology and Rites of the British Druids* (1809), and Algernon Herbert's *Britannia After the Romans* (1836–41) sought to reconstruct Arthur's world and inquired into his historicity. A vital development was seen in the sphere of literary analysis, ranging from the pioneering studies of Thomas Warton's *Observations on the Faerie Queene of Spenser* (1762) and Richard Hurd's *Letters on Chivalry and Romance* (1762) through John Dunlop's *History of Fiction* (1816). Extending this line of critical inquiry were the essays written as prefaces for the publication of "recovered" texts, seen in Sir Walter Scott's "Introduction" to *Sir Tristrem* (1804) and Sir Frederic Madden's essay for *Syr Gawayne; A Collection of Ancient Romance Poems* (1839).

To the scholarly community of the early nineteenth century one text was essential to Arthurian recovery: Sir Thomas Malory's *Le Morte Darthur*. Out of print since 1634, copies of Malory's text were rare.[13] In describing it as a book "in the hands of most antiquaries and collectors," in 1804, Walter Scott marked both its appeal and its limited audience.[14] Plans were announced for the republication of Malory's text. Between 1807 and 1817, both Scott and Robert Southey picked up and abandoned several projects, but by the end of this process, three new editions of *Le Morte Darthur* were in print: *The History of the Renowned Prince Arthur, King of Britain* (Walker and Edwards: 1816), *La Mort d'Arthur* (R. Wilks: 1816), and *The Byrth, Lyf, and Actes of King Arthur* (Longman, Hurst, Rees, Orme, and Brown: 1817). Of the three, the Longman's edition emerged as authoritative. Edited by poet laureate Robert Southey, it was a handsome quarto production (the others were small—pocket sized—with minute print on cheap paper) based on the 1485 Caxton *Le Morte Darthur*.[15] Artists found little practical application for Malory's text, no matter the edition, and in the first half of the century, Arthurian subjects in art were drawn from Spenser's *The Faerie Queene* rather than Malory's *Le Morte Darthur*.

The richness and diversity of Arthurian legend in the early Victorian era drew an ever widening audience. But this diversity engendered confusion. If the legend was to function as a national story and the character of Arthur to serve as a national hero, a singular vision needed to be forged. It was Tennyson's vision that dispelled the confusion. Serving as the primary Victorian "revitalizer" of the legend Tennyson's mode of interpretation went beyond a simple act of recovery. He gave his generation their own legend, "infusing it with contemporary standards of conduct" and "using it as a vehicle to debate Victorian concerns."[16] Rebecca Cochran differentiates between the role of the "revitalizer," whose defining bond is with the audience, as opposed to an "innovator," whose defining bond is with the revived text.[17] Tennyson stood in as the reader of the legend for his Victorian public, and functioned as their intervening author, providing a lens through which a unified version of the legend could finally be read.

This bond is best illustrated in "The Epic." Tennyson wrote, "The Epic" to frame the publication of "Morte d'Arthur" in the collection *Poems* (1842). Working as a prologue, the first part of "The Epic" challenges the act of revival, demanding "Why take the style of those heroic times?/ For nature brings not back the mastodon,/Nor we those times; and why should any man/Remodel models?" (ll. 35–39).[18] The response to the challenge is a recitation of the poem "Morte d'Arthur," which, when heard, inspires the narrator of "The Epic" to dream of Arthur's return.

> There came a bark that blowing forward, bore
> King Arthur, like a modern gentleman
> Of stateliest port; and all the people cried,
> "Arthur is come again; he cannot die."
> Then those that stood upon the hills behind
> Repeated—"Come again, and thrice as fair";
> And, further inland, voices echoes—"Come
> With all good things, and war will be no more." (ll. 344–51)[19]

"The Epic" cast a matrix for the modern Arthur, but Tennyson's presentation encompassed more than bringing the king out of Avalon. Linda K. Hughes asserts that Tennyson used "The Epic" to guarantee a favorable reception for his present and projected Arthurian work, that with it he "primed" his audience for accepting him as the new Arthurian interpreter as well as accepting his Arthurian poetry.[20] The frame of "The Epic" justified Tennyson's endeavor and declared the scope of his intentions. As the "revitalizer" of the legend, Tennyson set the legend in motion again, inverting Arthur's last journey so that he could "come again." To this end Tennyson redefined the legend's central figure, but at the same time he offered his readers a model of response, in the cheering crowds eager and able to recognize and reverence the king.

Given Tennyson's newly established hegemony over the revival of the legend in the 1840's, it might be speculated that Dyce followed his lead. But no documentary evidence links Dyce to Tennyson. The poet's name is not mentioned in Dyce's letters or in James Stirling Dyce's memoir of his father's life. Dyce never drew on Tennyson's poetry for painting subjects and Tennyson's name as an Arthurian interpreter is not recorded in the records of the FAC. Yet it is hard to believe that a well read and educated man like Dyce remained unaware of Tennyson's work, especially given Tennyson's status as Arthurian revitalizer and Dyce's commission as Arthurian painter. While it is clear from Dyce's subjects and writings that he was not a devoted reader of modern literature, such an explanation is insufficient. It is more likely that Dyce's adherence to the conventions of history painting influenced his selection of sources, leading to him to works deemed authentic and enduring by viture of their venerability rather than new works, despite their popularity. For his own preparation Dyce, for the most part, rejected literature for historical studies of pre- and post-Roman Britain culture and mythology. For the Arthurian narrative he chose a single source, Malory's *Le Morte Darthur*.

It is hard to judge the extent of Dyce's familiarity with Malory's text before the Robing Room Commission. His early work reveals no interest in or knowledge of the legend. In fact, unlike most of the other artists employed at the Palace at Westminster, Dyce rarely turned to medieval literature or history to inform his painting. The few subjects in his oeuvre that mark the exception depend on other interests and extenuating circumstances. For example, *Paolo and Francesca* (1837; National Gallery of Scotland, Edinburgh) was more likely inspired by his respect for Italian tradition than his interest in Dante as a medieval poet, while his Lords Chamber fresco *The Baptism of Ethelbert* (1846) was painted on commission, with the subject chosen by the FAC.

However, the origin of the Robing Room iconography has been traced to Dyce, suggesting that he knew Malory's text well enough in 1848 to have opinions about its potential for artists. According to his son, the painter regarded the text as a national saga and stated to his patron Prince Albert "that the stories of King Arthur, and in particular Sir Thomas Malory's 'Morte d'Arthur,' would supply to English Painters subjects of legendary history. . . for their great interest, their antiquity, and national chivalrous character."[21] Within a week's time, Albert—president of the FAC—took the idea to the Commissioners. They ultimately agreed that Dyce should carry out his idea in the Robing Room.

The speed with which Dyce produced a set of reflections on the Arthurian legend for the FAC stands as evidence of prior preparation for the project. Less than two weeks' time separates the FAC's announcement of the Robing Room program (9 July 1848) and Dyce's first letter detailing his plans. In six pages he raises the most important considerations for his commission: those of source and interpretation. His letter is a position statement. Malory's book is his first concern: he gives it canonical status, declaring *Le Morte Darthur* "of course must be my text Book." After a brief narrative summary of the last section of the book, which he says contains "all that is striking or original in [Arthur's] history," he offers two modes of interpretation: a "historically consecutive" approach, attempting to illustrate the narrative, or the allegorical approach, using the legend as the source for the personification of "certain moral qualities." Dyce makes no secret of his preference, noting that the historical view is of interest only to the "Antiquary," but the allegorical is "favored by hints scattered here and there throughout the work" and "belongs to all time."[22]

Definition, recognition, and response were also of primary importance to Dyce. Like Tennyson, Dyce felt it necessary to identify Arthur before he could revive him. This is evident in his first letter of 20 July, when he probes the issue of Arthur's historicity. For his research Dyce turned to two popular historical texts, Algernon Herbert's *Britannia After the Romans; Being an Attempt to Illustrate the Religious and Political Revolutions of that Province in the Fifth and Succeeding Centuries* (1836) and Edward Davies' *The Mythology and the Rites of the British Druids* (1809). Dyce's thoughts—and reservations—about Arthur's place in history typify those of his era.

Dyce began his search for the "real" Arthur, hoping not to find him. Writing "at one time I had some hopes that the researches of those who conceived that Arthur was not a real, but a mystical personage might be turned to account in determining, the general plan of the series of pictures:—but in this expectation I was disappointed," Dyce reflects both his concerns as a history painter and as a practical-minded Victorian.[23] Using a mythical Arthur in his ensemble of pictures, Dyce the painter would be released from historical setting and archaeological accuracy. He could place Arthur and his circle in the timeless realm of the distant past, and the heroes he created could speak with the force of powerful form and grand gesture, like the classical figures of antiquity or the Renaissance. In seeking the tangible dimensions of Arthur's past, Dyce the Victorian combined an insatiable curiosity about bizarre religious and social practices with a predisposition toward disdain and reprehension.

Despite his claim of disappointment, Dyce's sources did not let him down. Evidence for Arthur's historicity was slight *and* disturbing. Dyce identified Arthur as a symbol of suspect beliefs. From Herbert he took the term "Arthurism," "a perversion of Christianity," while from Davies he learned of "Arkite" mythology, designating Arthur "a representative of the Deified Patriarch Noah and his wife Qwenever (sic) the ark." Arthur as Pagan—or even worse, as heretic—would hardly suit the demands of his royal patrons, so Dyce developed a stance, in accord with Davies and Herbert, that there were two Arthurs: one of history and the other of chivalric legend. Discovery of the pagan image of Arthur also stregthened his argument for choosing an allegorical approach to painting, over that of explicit narrative, for fear of "embodying some politics—some religious creed in extinct species of Paganism, about which we know very litte."[24]

The subject of the Grail quest posed similar problems. Although in his letter of 20 July Dyce saw in it the force of "a religious allegory," "a sort of 'Pilgrims Progress' of the middle ages,"[25] his research taught him otherwise. Herbert called the Quest part of a literature that was "tedious and odious," "a blasphemous imposture," part of an attempt "to pass off the mysteries of Bardism for direct inspirations of the Holy Ghost."[26] Little wonder Dyce changed his mind!

The shift of stance is evident in his letter of 23 November (58), when he declares his intention to illustrate the virtue of piety with a scene from the Grail quest. He calls the subject corrupt, "little else than a tolerably intelligible religious allegory, strongly tinctured with the monastic ideas of the 13th. century, and seemingly, to some extent, intended to throw discredit on Chivalric greatness."[27] But to ignore it would eliminate the section of the legend Herbert called "the most ancient of the Arthurian Romances," tracing it back to eighth-century origins, in Bardic, Welsh, and ultimately Breton versions.[28]

The age and authenticity attributed to the Grail quest convinced Dyce that he was "right in giving so great prominence to the subject of the St. Greal" (sic), but also led him to formulate a scheme that kept "out of sight the particular adventures of the St. Greal, which regarded either as Arthurism myths or as Christian allegories, appeared to me to involve matters of religious and antiquarian controversy, which had better be avoided."[29] His solution—the design *Piety: The Knights of the Round Table Departing on the Quest for the Holy Grail* (1849; fig. 2)— updates the subject through elimination and suppression of the suspect elements. For a source, Dyce turned to *Le Morte Darthur*, book 13, chapter 7, when Arthur and the whole court gather as the knights commence their journey. Nothing indicates the object of their quest. There is no vision of the Grail, no Grail Maiden, no angels or heavenly beings to inspire and guide their travels. Priests are present, but relegated to a minor position, half hidden behind Arthur as he laments "Ye have set me in great sorrow, for I have doubt that my true fellowship shall never

Fig. 2. William Dyce, *Piety: The Knights of the Round Table Departing on the Quest for the Holy Grail* (1849). Watercolor. 9⅛" x 17⅜". National Gallery of Scotland.

meet again."[30] In *Piety* Dyce envisioned the Quest as a Protestant endeavor, free from ancient heresy or any endorsement of Catholicism.

A decade later Tennyson struggled with the same issues. Immediately after the 1859 publication of the first four *Idylls*, the poet was urged to continue his Arthuriad by returning to the knight he made popular in 1842. *Blackwoods Magazine* urged him to write more about Galahad, that "noble type of true Christian chivalry—of that work of heaven on earth which only pure hearts can love, only clean hands can do!"[31] His friends concurred, but when the duke of Argyll decreed "the 'Grail' ought to be written forthwith," Tennyson responded "I doubt whether such a subject could be handled in these days, without incurring a charge of irreverence. It would be too much like playing with sacred things. The old writers *believed* in the Sangreal"[32] (original emphasis). Another decade elapsed before the publication of "The Holy Grail" (1869). Drawn out of the poet's belief that "[t]he natural, if people cared, could always be made to account for the supernatural," Tennyson's account the Grail quest rejects the impulse behind its ancient source.[33] As David Staines observes, "unable to accept the Grail as a symbol of divine grace, Tennyson accepted the plot of the quest as the basis for a study of human responses to the spiritual world."[34] Dyce had already come to a similar resolution. In *Religion: The Vision of Sir Galahad and His Company* (1851; fig. 3), Christ appears to the Grail knight and his companions flanked by the historical Gospel writers, illustrating a practical means to come to an understanding of Christian mysteries.

Fig. 3. William Dyce, *Religion: The Vision of Sir Galahad and His Company* (1851). Fresco. 11'2½" x 14'6". Queen's Robing Room, Palace at Westminster, London. British Crown Copyright. With Permission of Her Britannic Majesty's Stationery Office.

Religion also demonstrates Dyce's adherence to the conventions of history painting. The figures are tall, solid, and heroically proportioned, classical bodies in medieval raiment. The composition is like a shallow stage on which the subject is portrayed through simple, eloquent gesture. The structural axes of the pictorial design (the triangle uniting Christ at the apex with Galahad and his companions at the base; the X uniting the authors of the Gospel with the seekers of the Grail) demonstrate the most common types used during the Renaissance. More than any other element, Dyce's use of an authoritative quotation links his work with high art tradition. The unification of a spiritual realm with a terrestrial setting recalls the disposition of figures and space in Raphael's *Disputa* (1509) in the Stanza della Segnatura in the Vatican. In his visual choices Dyce asserted the legend's universality through the conventions of his art (form, composition, and reference). Depicting what Reynolds called the "general" rather than the "particular," Dyce transformed a subject he feared to be "little else than a tolerably intelligible religious allegory" into an icon for all times.[35]

Dyce's commitment to Malory's text as his singular source never wavered. *Le Morte Darthur* combined national significance with a high-minded message, but at the same time portrayed the human experience with sympathy and drama. Dyce called it, "a vivid and intelligible picture of human life, with its greatness, its crimes, and its misery."[36] But Malory's tale also contained much that offended his moral sensibilities and despite his high praise, he found Malory's narrative difficult to adapt, for it turned on "incidents which, if they are not undesirable for representation under any circumstance, are at least scarcely appropriate in (the Queen's) apartment."[37] To use Malory as his source, Dyce felt compelled to edit the legend, expelling all that would be offensive to his patrons, purging Malory's world of its "crimes" and "misery," while preserving its "greatness."

That Dyce found the morality of Malory's narrative suspect is evident in the terse and dismissive tone used in the summary of events he provided for the Commissioners in the first letter on 20 July.[38] This passage also indicates the direction of the editorial changes he wished to make.

> On the discovery of Gwenevir's infidelity her Paramour Launcelot is obliged to fly and Gwenevir is condemned to death. Thereupon Launcelot summoning his companions, returns, rescues the Queen and carries her off. On his way to his Castle of Togense Garde, he is met by the Abbot of Glastonbury, who persuades him to restore her to Arthur. This Launcelot does, and after obtaining the pardon of the Queen, condemns himself to banishment from England. On his departure Sir Gauvain, Sir Gaheris, Sir Mordred (nephews of Arthur) and other Knights who were jealous of Launcelot's fame and greatness, are offended that Arthur had allowed him to escape so easily; they induce the King to make war on Launcelot. Arthur accordingly sets sail for France with his Knights and soldiers leaving Mordred (with whom no doubt, the scheme of pursuing Launcelot originated) viceroy during his absence. No sooner has Arthur left England than Mordred seizes the Crown and proclaims himself King.—Whereupon Arthur, returns, and a battle is fought in which Mordred is slain and Arthur is mortally wounded and disappears.
>
> Gwenever whose crime has caused all Arthur's misfortunes and death, is stung by remorse, and dies penitent in a Nunnery at Arnesbury;—before her death having converted Launcelot who had returned to England in search of her.[39]

As Dyce tells it, *Le Morte Darthur* is less a saga of "Chivalric greatness" than a catalogue of adultery, abduction, jealously, weak leadership, trickery, murder, and false Catholic redemption. His omissions (and substitutions) are revealing: Mordred is Arthur's nephew, not his son by incest; Guenevere does not refuse Launcelot in the end, she converts him; Launcelot does not grieve after Arthur's death, but simply searches for Guenevere; there is no messianic promise of Arthur's return, he just disappears. Certainly, Dyce loaded his account as part of his strategy to argue for allegorical representation; he prefaced the summary with the statement "If the historical plan be adopted the following is an outline of the story I should have to deal with."[40] But his inclusions and omissions serve to show the difficulties inherent in an ethical Victorian reading of Malory's narrative. Even at the most preliminary stage Dyce felt compelled to censor, censure, and revise.

Dyce builds his alternative reading—indicative of what he calls "moral signification"—on high art convention. In proposing to "consider the Companions of the Round table as personficiations of certain moral qualities and select for representation such adventures of Arthur and his Knights as best exemplified the courage magnanimity, courtesy temperance fidelity, devoutness and other qualities, which make up the ancient idea of Chivalric greatness," he relied on a traditional visual code of meaning. Since classical times, specific figures signified specific abstract concepts: Athena as wisdom; Hercules as strength; Apollo as inspiration. While Arthurian characters—and their attributes—were less known than their classical counterparts, narrative reference to Malory's *Le Morte Darthur*, as well as to canonical works of art, allowed Dyce to create a new abstract signification.

Dyce's linkage of Arthurian heroes with specific attributes became an editorial act, reforming their vices through omission while celebrating their virtues through illustration. Lancelot's adultery, for example, was absolved by his "Generosity" in *King Arthur Unhorsed, Spared by Sir Launcelot* (1852; fig. 4), while Tristram's struggle over duty and desire disappeared in view of his "Courtesy," seen in *Sir Tristram Harping to La Beale Isoud* (1852). While Galahad, as seen above, could personify "religion" without any change, and Arthur represented "Hospitality," for Gawain, Dyce chose an incident where the rash knight was chastised for acting without thinking and tried by a court of Guenevere and her women.[41] This simple form of allegory allowed Dyce to revise the narrative and give it the moral signification appropriate to his time and expected in the commission, and at the same time, to support his and his audience's notion of "an ancient idea of Chivalric greatness."

It is ultimately in the figure of Arthur that Dyce perceived this notion of "greatness," but in his portrayal of the king the differences

Fig. 4. William Dyce, *Generosity: King Arthur Unhorsed Spared by Sir Launcelot* (1852). Fresco. 11′2½″ x 5′10″. Queen's Robing Room, Palace at Westminster, London. British Crown Copyright. With Permission of Her Britannic Majesty's Stationery Office.

between what Dyce could do and what Tennyson would do are evident.[42] Including the rejected watercolor *Piety* with the five completed frescoes, Dyce painted Arthur three times: in *Piety* bidding a sorrowful farewell to his knights, in *Hospitality: The Admission of Sir Tristram to the Fellowship of the Round Table*, raising a sword in a gesture that welcomed the Cornish knight and promised his investiture, and in *Generosity: King Arthur Unhorsed Spared By Sir Launcelot* (fig. 4) as a fallen warrior on the brink of defeat. These three images offer a thin character protrait. In the first two Arthur stands in for a location, bidding welcome and farewell to those who come and go. His gestures indicate simple responses, sorrow at the departure, joy at the arrival. These are emotions, not virtues, and they teach little about either Arthur or the noble human spirit.

In *Generosity* Arthur sprawls on ground at the base of the composition. Here he embodies not an emotion, but a virtue: dignity even in defeat. With hauberk shattered and surcoat torn, Arthur's massive chest is exposed, declaring his vulnerability, but at the same time affirming his potent masculine force in a time-honored artistic sign, the mature male nude. His proportions and position are made eloquent thorugh Dyce's system of referents. The grand scale of Arthur's physique recalls the Hellenistic fragment *Belvedere Torso*, and his posture, in the opposition of the collapsing torso with the upward thrust of the supporting arm, echoes the *Dying Gaul*, a figure from the commemorative altar of Attalos at Pergamon. Both works had been part of the Vatican collection since the 1500s and both were regarded as standard examples in the classical canon. Dyce knew them and consciously used them to amplify his portrayal of Arthur as an exemplary tragic hero for all times, no different than Promteheus, Phocion, Laocoön, or Philoctetes. This grand and moral Arthur would be humanized by Tennyson. The same Arthur who represented the highest in man, "who submitted to death to elevate humanity" would also forgive his friends and "the spouse who had brought him great pain."[43] While Dyce's art demanded that every gesture, every facet of character be grand and timeless, Tennyson's allowed greater nuance. Hughes has observed that in the *Idylls* Tennyson "took a grand form of the past...and domesticated it," stressing the individuality rather than the universality, of life's experience, depicting a cast of legendary characters "more human and accessible, less grand and remote," who "could be imitated by ordinary urban citizens of the mid-nineteenth century."[44] In this Tennyson met the history painter's main objective—to inspire the viewer to higher action by example—but Tennyson did so by speaking his audience's language. Dyce, on the other hand, sought to teach his spectators a language through the legend, and in this limited the scope of his intelligibility.

When Dyce read the legend, he did so as a history painter. Bound both by the conventions of his art and the terms of his commission, he imposed on the legend an external moral standard and united the acts of reading and revising into one. But the result cannot be dismissed as just an expurgated version of the Arthurian legend, free from moral transgressions, religious or spiritual challenges, and ungentlemanly conduct, for the process by which Dyce achieved his revision offers insight to expectations about the legend held by the Victorian public. Active in promoting the legend as a catalogue of "Chivalric greatness," as seen in the acts of Arthur and his companions, Dyce also represents why his contemporaries looked to the legend. But Dyce's mode of representation looked back, not forward. Analogous to Tennyson's "The Epic" rather than the *Idylls*, Dyce's interpretation was an act of justification and recognition. True revival, infusing the legend with contemporary standards, rather than just bringing it into conformance with acknowledged conventions, would be Tennyson's work, answering Dyce's search for "a vivid and intelligible picture of human life, with its greatness, its crimes, and its misery."[45]

Notes

1. The reference to Tennyson is borrowed from J. Phillip Eggers's study *King Arthur's Laureate: A Study of Tennyson's "Idylls of the King"* (New York, 1971).

2. Upon completion of the fresco the FAC declared that "Mr. Dyce's fresco is to be referred in a great degree to the style and design and colouring which he has adopted. . .we deem it important, without wishing to impose undue restrictions on the invention or taste of the other artists. . .(that they make their works) agree sufficiently with. . .the specimen already executed." *Sixth Report*, 4 August 1846, pp. 7–8.

3. Francis T. Palgrave, *Essays on Art* (New York, 1967), p. 142.

4. These letters are transcribed in vol. 3, ch. 27 of the unpublished typescript by the artist's son James Stirling Dyce, "Life, Correspondence, and Writings of William Dyce, R.A. 1806–1864, Painter, Musician, and Scholar, by His Son," 4 vols., in the collection of the City Art Gallery of Aberdeen, Department of Manuscripts. Those written by Dyce are numbered 49–53; 58. The responses are not numbered, but interspersed according to date. None are paginated. The unorthodox spellings, punctuation, and emphases are in the typescript and can be attributed either to the painter or the typist.

5. For an art historical analysis of these works, see Debra N. Mancoff, "An Ancient Idea of Chivalric Greatness: The Arthurian Revival and Victorian History Painting," in *The Arthurian Tradition: Essays in Convergence*, ed. Mary Flowers Breswell and John Bugge (Tuscoloosa and London, 1988), pp. 127–43, and *The Arthurian Revival in Victorian Art* (New York 1990), pp. 101–35.

6. The use of the term "history painter" refers to the traditional ranking of subjects formulated by André Félibien des Avaux in his *Entretiens sur les vies et sur les ouvrages des plus excellens peintres anciens et modernes* (1666-68), a treatise written as a handbook for training young painters at the Academie Royale. This hierarchy, placing history at the top and descending through portraits, genre, landscape, animals, and still life, was adopted by academies throughout Europe. To be a history painter was to embrace the highest art tradition. *Histoire*, depicting the noble capacity of human action, at first encompassed subjects based from the Bible or classical mythology or history, but in the late eighteenth and early nineteenth centuries, sources came to include, and even emphasize national epics. History as a subject is not to be confused with historical. For a discussion of the origins of this tradition and its place in British art, see Mancoff, *The Arthurian Revival*, pp. 79-86.

7. For a full discussion of Dyce's youth and training see, "The Early Years 1806-1832" in Marcia Pointon, *William Dyce, 1806-1864: A Critical Biography* (Oxford, 1979), pp. 3-24.

8. In 1836 Dyce was appointed Master at the Trustees' Academy in Edinburgh. With fellow Master Charles Heath Wilson he authored a report on the possible reorganization of the Academy, including a section on design education. This report brought Dyce to the attention of the Select Committee of Parliament and was published as *Letter to Lord Meadowbank and the Committee of the Honourable Board of Trustees for the Encouragement of Arts and Manufactures* (Edinburgh, 1837). See Pointon, *William Dyce*, pp. 41–42. For the actions of the select committee, see Mancoff, *The Arthurian Revival*, p. 286.

9. Dyce was also one of the few artists experienced in the technique of fresco in Britain in the 1840s. This interest likely emerged during his second Italian trip, perhaps through contact with the Nazarenes, who revived practice in the medium. At the time of the FAC's deliberations Dyce was working on a fresco at Lambeth Palace (*The Consecration of Archbishop Parker*, now destroyed), and it was for that work that he was called in as an expert witness on the medium.

10. Dyce to D. L. Eastlake, 8 July 1845, in J. S. Dyce "Life, Correspondence," 3:49.

11. "Fourth Discourse," 10 December 1771, in *Discourses on Art*, ed. Robert W. Wark (New Haven, 1981), p. 70.

12. For the work of Cornelius and Schnorr von Carolsfeld, see Keith Andrews, *The Nazarenes: A Brotherhood of German Painters in Rome* (Oxford, 1964).

13. For a full account of publications of *Le Morte Darthur*, see Barry Gaines, "The Editions of Malory in the Early Nineteenth Century," in *Papers of the Bibliographical Society of America* 68 (1974), 1–17. See also Carlson's essay in this volume.

14. As quoted in James Douglas Merriman, *The Flower of Kings: A Study of the Arthurian Legend in England Between 1485 and 1835* (Lawrence, Kan., 1973), p. 81.

15. Both the Walker and Edwards editions and the Wilks edition were based on the 1634 Stansby text, which Merriman describes as corrupt (*The Flower of Kings*, p. 129). Error and careless printing further contributed to departures from Malory's original works and the Wilks edition was expurgated in regard to protecting a readership of "youth" and the "Fair sex" by editor Joseph Haslewood. Merriman, *The Flower of Kings*, pp. 129–30. For an overview of activity in Arthurian writing after the republication of Malory, see ibid., 137–77 and Eggers, *King Arthur's Laureate*, pp. 218–25.

16. Rebecca Cochran, "William Morris: Arthurian Innovator," in *The Arthurian Revival: Essays on Form, Tradition and Transformation*, ed. Debra N. Mancoff (London and New York, 1992), pp. 75–96, at 79–80.

17. Rebecca Cochran observes: "Writers who attempt to revive or revitalize the Arthurian legend reinvent it by infusing it with contemporary values, concerns, and standards of conduct. Thus revitalizers function as mediators between the older material and a new readership. Innovators might be considered revisionists rather than inventors. As more active interpreters, what is of primary interest is the relationship between their sources and the new texts they produce." "Who's Arthur? Whose Arthur?" presented at the 27th International Congress of Medieval Studies, May 1992, Western Michigan State University, Kalamazoo, Michigan, in the session "The Arthurian Revival: Tradition and Invention."

18. Alfred Tennyson, "The Epic," in *The Poetical Works of Tennyson*, ed. G. Robert Stange, Cambridge Edition (Boston, 1974), pp. 63–64.

19. Alfred Tennyson, "The Epic," p. 68.

20. Linda K. Hughes, "Tennyson's Urban Arthurians: Victorian Audiences and the 'City Built to Music,' " in *King Arthur Through the Ages*, ed. Valerie M. Lagorio and Mildred Leake Day, 2 vols. (London and New York, 1990), 2:39–61, at 42.

21. As quoted in J. S .Dyce, "Life, Correspondence," 3:992.

22. Dyce to C. L. Eastlake, 20 July 1848, in J. S. Dyce, "Life, Correspondence," 3:49.

23. Ibid.

24. Ibid. Dyce asserts Davies' opinion the Arthur of the romances and the real Arthur were not the same, "but that the Romanists confounded them." Herbert, he notes, "does not admit the existence of the Arthur history" but does allow he might have been "the object of the bards" for a "new species of Druidism," founded "on the ruins of Christianity when the Romans left Britain."

25. Ibid.

26. Algernon Herbert, *Britannia After the Romans; Being an Attempt to Illustrate the Religious and Political Revolutions of that Province in the Fifth and Succeeding Centuries* (London, 1836), p. vi.

27. Dyce to C. L. Eastlake, 23 November 1848, in J. S. Dyce, "Life, Correspondence," 3:58.

28. Ibid.

29. Ibid.

30. Dyce to J. T. Coleridge, 17 April 1849, in J. S. Dyce, "Life, Correspondence," 3:np. While Dyce paraphrased (and truncated) the passage in his letter to Coleridge, he preferred to read Malory in Southey's authoritative edition. On 19 February 1849 (3:53) he identifies his source as "Southey's reprint of Caxton's edition," a copy of which he sends to Eastlake "with the places marked."

31. *Blackwoods Magazine* 86 (November 1859), 610.

32. As quoted in Hallam Tennyson, *Alfred Lord Tennyson: A Memoir by His Son*, 2 vols. (New York, 1897), 1:456–57.

33. Ibid., 2:63.

34. David Staines, *Tennyson's Camelot: The ''Idylls of the King'' and Its Medieval Sources* (Waterloo, Ontario, 1982), p. 78.

35. Dyce to C. L. Eastlake, 28 November 1848, in J. S. Dyce, "Life, Correspondence," 3:58.

36. Dyce to C. L. Eastlake, 20 July 1848, in J. S. Dyce, "Life, Correspondence," 3:49.

37. Dyce to C. L. Eastlake, 15 August 1848, in J. S. Dyce, "Life, Correspondence," 3:51.

38. Dyce to C. L. Eastlake, 20 July 1848, in J. S. Dyce, "Life, Correspondence," 3:49.

39. Ibid.

40. Ibid.

41. Sir Thomas Malory, *The Byrth, Lyf, and Actes of King Arthur: of His Noble Knyghtes of the Rounde Table*, ed. Robert Southey, 2 vols. (London, 1817), 1:79–80.

42. Dyce hoped to portray Arthur as "the Head of all Chivalry" in a modern adaptation of the Nine Worthies, but the FAC rejected this proposal.

43. Hughes, "Tennyson's Urban Arthurians," p. 49.

44. Ibid., pp. 42–44.

45. Dyce to C. L. Eastlake, 20 July 1848, in J. S. Dyce, "Life, Correspondence," 3:49.

The Snake in the Woodpile: Tennyson's Vivien as Victorian Prostitute

 *Rebecca Umland*

It is curious that the harshest critics and the most ardent admirers of Tennyson's *Idylls of the King* agree on one point: that the poet infused the Arthurian legend with Victorian standards of conduct and explored issues of concern to his audience. Published serially between 1859 and 1885, the poems earned the immediate approbation of most Victorian readers because of Tennyson's revitalizing efforts. As Linda K. Hughes argues in her discussion of the Victorian reception of the work, the success of the *Idylls* can be attributed to Tennyson's ability to discern and meet the expectations of his audience.[1] Typical reactions to the first four idylls support Hughes' claim. A notice published in the October 1859 issue of *Bentley's Quarterly Review* serves as an example: "He will bring his subject to *us*, not require us to go back through all the ages to a world of legend."[2] The contemporary quality of these poems did not escape the criticism of one of the work's most outspoken detractors, A. C. Swinburne, who condemned it on just such grounds when he referred to it as the "'Morte d'Albert,'" suggesting that the depiction of Arthur was a thinly disguised portrait of the prince consort.[3]

Modern critics agree that the *Idylls* embody not medieval but rather Victorian values, at least those of a middle-class, conservative readership that placed a high premium on stability and maintaining the *status quo* in the domestic and public realms. Clyde de L. Ryals, for instance, labels the work a modern philosophical poem,[4] and David Staines attributes its success to Tennyson's growing independence from his medieval sources.[5] Alice Chandler argues that the work does not conform to what she identifies as the "medieval ideal" that prevails in some nineteenth-century literature because Tennyson simply uses the Arthurian legend as a vehicle to express Victorian issues and values.[6] What these assertions emphasize is that the *Idylls*, by virtue of their lengthy serial publication and in their complexity, may serve as a register of Victorian social, moral, and political concerns.

Major themes that reflect the values of Tennyson's readers include the views on religious faith, the ideal political leader, and the exploration of sexual mores, particularly on the part of Tennyson's Arthurian female figures. In addition, Tennyson purges the Grail material of Malory's medieval Catholicism in order to cater to a largely middle-class, Protestant audience. He also emphasizes the subjective nature of religious conviction in an effort to answer the growing skepticism of his age.[7] Throughout the *Idylls*, the poet explores the qualities that comprise the ideal political ruler, presented in the figure of Arthur. He stresses the Carlylean principles of the divinely inspired, visionary, strong leader who ought to be recognized and obeyed by his subordinates.[8] This concern reflects the Victorian compulsion for order and inspired leadership. Finally, a pervasive issue is that of the degree to which the domestic realm, with women as its moral guardians, either preserves or destroys the moral and sociopolitical fabric of society.

Related to this issue, and encoded in the text by the use of euphemistic language and by a setting in the remote past, is the exploration of various modes of sexual conduct by the female characters in the *Idylls*. Tennyson thus raises a very topical question regarding proper sexual behavior for women and the moral and social implications of sexual license. In doing so, however, he was scarcely alone. As Michel Foucault has argued, the Victorians hardly "repressed" discussions of sexuality, but rather transformed sex into "discourse" in order to regulate and control it as one might manage the parameters of a debate.[9] Following Foucault, Jeffrey Weeks points out that the Victorian era has been branded as repressed, puritanical, and—because of its consumption of pornography—hypocritical, "[y]et simultaneously and apparently paradoxically it was during the nineteenth century that the debate about sexuality exploded. Far from the age experiencing a regime of silence and total suppression, sexuality became a major issue in Victorian social and political practice."[10] Week's assertion is corroborated by the vast attention the Victorians paid to sexual issues, especially to the problems of prostitution and venereal disease in parliamentary debates, medical journals, and newspapers. Given this preoccupation, it is not surprising that Tennyson should have contributed to this discourse, examining and reflecting middle-class attitudes towards sexuality.

One of Tennyson's major departures from his primary source, Malory, is his depiction of Arthur as the "blameless king" whose ideals are undermined almost exclusively by the adultery of Lancelot and Guinevere. Tennyson purges the legend of any unsavory elements relating to Arthur's character: he removes the illegitimacy of his conception and birth, and erases the king's incestuous liaison with Morgause. Arthur's other minor sexual infractions that are recounted in Malory also vanish: as the king reminds Guinevere, "I was ever virgin save for thee.[11]

Tennyson's harsh condemnation of the adultery between Lancelot and the queen has long been acknowledged as a reflection of Victorian middle-class values, with their concern for domestic stability. Weeks attributes this obsession with the woman's role as preserver of morality to the reorganization and increased significance of the family structure, in part due to new marriage laws (especially after 1836) which were more binding and thus resulted in longer marriages (24–25). Later, the revised divorce laws of 1857, which made it easier for *women* to obtain a dissolution of marriage, were widely perceived as a threat to the social structure. As presiders over hearth and home, women who violated their duties or disrupted the domestic order by sexual indulgence were perceived as the worst possible threat to society. Martha Vicinus observes: "The woman who broke the family circle, be she prostitute, adulterer or divorcee, threatened society's very fabric. The most unforgivable sin. . .was the married woman who committed adultery."[12] Given this attitude, it is no accident that Arthur likens Guinevere to an insidious disease that infects and destroys his kingdom.

In addition to the adultery theme, however, is the sexual incontinence which finds expression in the seduction of Merlin. If the sin between Lancelot and Guinevere is responsible for the irrational suspicion Geraint harbors against his saintly spouse, Enid, and for the madness of Balin and of Pelleas, Vivien's effort to empower herself by using her sexual wiles against Merlin also poses a threat to Arthur's order, in that this seduction suggests the social and moral chaos that can ensue from the deviation of a standard of conduct that binds a culture together. The code which Arthur expects his knights to obey includes a chaste, married life.[13] Because Merlin succumbs to Vivien's charm, he becomes incapacitated and is unable to assist Arthur in his efforts to reform his kingdom, another dictate included in the king's creed. An examination of Vivien's character as it is presented in "Merlin and Vivien," of her role in the *Idylls* as a whole, of Tennyson's careful planning of her entrance into the larger scheme of the work, and of Victorian reactions to her, suggests the implications of her behavior as they can be applied to *the* social problem with which the Victorians were confronted.

Vivien's rebellion against Arthur, her antagonism towards his principles, and her use of her sexuality to achieve personal gain, have prompted readers to view her as a prototype of the archetypal temptresses—Lilith, Eve, and Delilah—or even as a modernized version of Milton's Satan or Keats' Lamia.[14] The poem offers support for these assertions, to be sure. Merlin, regretting that he had ever mentioned the existence of a potent charm to the inquisitive and persistent Vivien, laments: "Too much I trusted when I told you that, / And stirr'd this vice in you which ruin'd man / Thro' woman the first hour" ("Merlin and Vivien," ll. 359–61). In addition, snake and serpent imagery abound in this poem, as a few examples will show. Vivien, having followed the brooding Merlin into the forest of Broceliande, begins her seduction of the mage by situating herself in his lap:

> And lissome Vivien, holding by his heel,
> Writhed toward him, slided up his knee and sat,
> Behind his ankle twined her hollow feet
> Together, curved an arm about his neck,
> Clung like a snake ("Merlin and Vivien," ll. 236–40)

After Vivien has spewed forth her venomous slander against various members of Camelot she is transformed, in Merlin's eyes, from a beautiful and agile snake to a repulsive viper, and her base accusations (several of which are actually true), prompt an angry response from him: "And hearing 'harlot' mutter'd twice or thrice, / [She] Leapt from her session on his lap, and stood / Stiff as a viper frozen; loathsome sight" ("Merlin and Vivien," ll. 841–43).

Finally, Vivien's resemblance to biblical temptresses is underscored by her successful seduction of Merlin, despite his recognition of her baseness. Tennyson's use of a lexicon of sexual euphemisms does not prevent this scene from being understood:

> and in the change of glare and gloom
> Her eyes and neck glittering went and came;
> Till now the storm, its burst of passion spent,
> Moaning and calling out of other lands,
> Had left the ravaged woodland yet once more
> To peace; and what should not have been had been,
> For Merlin, overtalk'd and overworn,
> Had yielded, told her all the charm, and slept.
> ("Merlin and Vivien," ll. 957–64)

This highly-suggestive language, which includes the metaphors of "yielding" and "spending" reveals prevailing Victorian views of sexual intercourse as an illicit activity that saps a man's physical and mental strength, thus diminishing his ability to function in his higher daily enterprises. (The tropes of forest and storm function as a means to clarify the "exchange" that occurs in this scene.) As Steven Marcus notes, the most common Victorian metaphor for orgasm was, not coincidentally, an economic one—that of "spending."[15] The "exchange" between Merlin and Vivien consists of him "yielding" the potent charm in "return" for her sexual favors. Put in another way, Merlin's charm holds a high "market value" which Vivien "purchases" as a "profit" to herself. The analogy to prostitution can hardly be denied.

The poem acquires a special significance when it is read as Tennyson's discursive commentary on the contemporary problem of prostitution—its related causes and its potential effects on Victorian society. That this issue might have been very much on Tennyson's mind when he composed the poem is suggested by the pervasiveness of the problem and the attention it was attracting in the public arena. For instance, Weeks observes: "From the 1850s sexuality, particularly in the wide area of venereal disease and prostitution...enters the heart of Parliamentary debates.[16] E. M. Sigsworth and T. J. Wyke cite data about the scope of this social aberration. Police statistics from 1857 list 8,600 prostitutes in London, a staggering figure. But Sigsworth and Wyke contend that even this number must have been very conservative: "These, however, relate only to prostitutes known to the police and, as Memynge commented of the 1857 Metropolitan figure, 'this is far from being even an approximate return of the loose women.... It scarcely does more than record the circulating harlotry of the Haymarket and Regent Street.' "[17] Finally, the highly controversial Contagious Diseases Acts, which debated whether prostitutes should be required to carry certificates of proof that they were free of disease, raged throughout the second half of the nineteenth century. Considering this sociohistorical context and Tennyson's presentation of Vivien's character, it is possible to view her idyll as Tennyson's acknowledgment of the problem.

Tennyson's first installment of Arthurian idylls, published in 1859, focused on four major female figures: Enid, Elaine, Vivien, and Guinevere, indicating that from its inception, Tennyson intended *Idylls of the King* to explore the role of women in maintaining or undermining the social order. Tennyson clearly recognized that his readership, a large component of which was female, was interested in domestic issues, and the inclusion of poems devoted to the virtues and vices of his female characters was surely calculated to appeal to his audience. But even before 1859, Tennyson had planned to print the "Enid" and "Vivien" poems (the latter was originally titled "Nimüe") as a pair that would reveal the extremes of moral behavior. As Robert Martin recounts in his biography of Tennyson, the poet had printed privately six copies of "Enid and Nimüe: The True and the False," but he withdrew them, as the following excerpt from a letter reveals:

> a blustering mouth...a man, a friend it was said, to whom I read or showed the Nimüe...appears to have gone brawling about town, saying that such a poem would corrupt the young, that no ladies could buy it or read it,...I should indeed have thought that the truth & purity of the wife in the first poem might well have served as antidote to the untruth of the woman in the second.[18]

Always sensitive to criticism, Tennyson withheld this publication and instead issued the four idylls in order to suggest the range of behavior he intended to present in the completed *Idylls*.[19] What is more significant here, however, is that the anonymous friend so readily recognized Vivien as a despicable woman, one unfit for a female readership. That Tennyson published the Vivien idyll two years later shows that, while he does not deny that the protagonist *is* such a dubious character, he fails to agree that the subject is too offensive for his readers. Perhaps he believed that his use of euphemistic language, along with the employment of an antiquated setting for the poem, rendered it acceptable for his audience.

Another of Tennyson's acquaintances, the Reverend B. Jowett, extended praise for the Vivien idyll, but his response underscores the fact that she was readily recognized as a harlot: "Of the other poems I admire 'Vivien' the most (the naughty one), which seems to me a work of wonderful power and skill. It is most elegant and fanciful. I am not surprised at your Delilah reducing the wise man, she is quite equal to it."[20] The fact that Jowett relished the poem because, in part, he acknowledges it as "the naughty one" stands as testimony to the ease with which Vivien's true role was recognized; it also serves as yet another example of the split between Victorian public values and their private pursuit of erotic pleasures.

Jowett's positive reaction, however, was scarcely typical. While this first installment of idylls was generally received with enthusiasm,[21] "Vivien" did offend some critics, precisely because of its "vulgarity." In his study of the *Idylls*, J. Phillip Eggers remarks that "even those who thought highly of the idyll tended to find Vivien deplorable" and he then cites a *Blackwood's* review which he claims "in a bizarre note of Victorian self-consciousness" viewed the poem as "one more sign of the corruption it saw everywhere."[22]

It is the condemnation of a more astute critic that points to the clear recognition that Vivien serves as a prototype of a Victorian prostitute. In his essay, "Under the Microscope," Swinburne takes to task Tennyson's modernization of the Arthurian story and identifies within this context Vivien's character. "She is such a sordid creature as plucks men passing by the sleeve." He continues to berate the poem for its "loathsome dialogue in which Merlin and Vivien discuss the nightly transgression against chastity, within doors and without, of the various knights of Arthur's court," and then descries the poem for "describing the erotic fluctuations and vacillations of a dotard under the moral and physical manipulation of a prostitute." Finally, Vivien is "unspeakably repulsive and unfit for artistic treatment."[23] Granted, Swinburne's venom in this essay is partly due to the fact that he is defending his own poetry against charges of immorality (an attack launched largely by Robert Buchanan's invective against the Pre-Raphaelites), but his perception of Vivien as a harlot is corroborated by the other responses discussed earlier.

That Tennyson himself understood Vivien to be a depiction of such a woman is further witnessed by the fact that, according to the *Concordance* to his poetical and dramatic works, the word "harlot" and its variations (e.g., "harlot-like," "harlot-bride," "harlotry") appears only thirteen times.[24] Eight of these thirteen instances occur in the *Idylls*; four of the eight are employed in "Merlin and Vivien" (ll. 821, 831, 843, 972). It is likewise important that the other four uses of the word occur in those idylls that also present sexually licentious women: in "Pelleas and Ettarre" which portrays Ettarre's casual sex with Gawain (ll. 466, 470), and in "The Last Tournament" which features the adulterous Isolt of Ireland (ll. 81, 428).

Hallam Tennyson remarked, "My father created the character of Vivien with much care—as the evil genius of the Round Table—who in her lustfulness of the flesh could not believe in anything either good or great.[25] Tennyson composed "Vivien" in 1856 but, as mentioned previously, he did not publish the poem until 1859. Still unsatisfied with this version of her character and her role in the *Idylls*, the poet added substantial portions to the "Merlin and Vivien" idyll before its inclusion in the completed work (1886). In order to emphasize her role in the larger scheme of *Idylls of the King*, he decided to introduce her character at the conclusion of the poem that precedes "Merlin and Vivien" in the finished collection ("Balin and Balan"). In 1873, Tennyson added to the poem lines 188–194 (a narrative passage that connects Merlin's moral weakness with his melancholy, itself a result of his prescience of the downfall of Arthur's order). More significant, however, is the poet's inclusion of lines 6–146 (added in 1875), a passage which recounts Vivien's unhappy advent into this world and her unfortunate tutelage under the evil King Mark. Vivien recalls the events of her life as she exchanges words with Mark, offering her own assessment of these events at the same time:

> As Love, if Love be perfect, casts out fear,
> So Hate, if Hate be perfect, casts our fear.
> My father died in battle against the King,
> My mother on his corpse in open field;
> She bore me there, for born from death was I
> Among the dead and sown upon the wind—
> And then on thee! and shown the truth betimes,
> That old true filth, and bottom of the well,
> Where truth is hidden. Gracious lessons thine
> And maxims of the mud! "This Arthur pure!"
> . . . .
> To me this narrow grizzled fork of thine
> Is cleaner-fashion'd—Well, I loved thee first;
> That warps the wit. (ll. 40–49, 59–61)

This passage offers a motivation for Vivien's animosity towards Arthur and, in its psychological explanation of her character, adds some small touch of sympathy to this depiction of her. But it is precisely this personal history that adheres closely to the paradigm of the prostitute outlined in the 14 November 1857 issue of the main Victorian medical journal, *Lancet*, cited by Sigsworth and Wyke: "In London there are now hundreds of such women in every phase of degradation, whose history is comprised of these words: seduction—desertion—prostitution."[26] Evidently this was the best the Victorians could do by way of a sociological theory to explain this prevailing problem.

During her discourse with Mark in the passage above, Vivien recounts how her father, a rebellious king who opposed Arthur, was slain in battle against him. After this, Vivien's mother gave birth to her and died. Thus, although her parents had enjoyed a high social rank, the fact that her father was a renegade and that she was orphaned in infancy, renders Vivien a member of a disenfranchised social group and makes her as vulnerable to evil influences as Rossetti's Jenny or Hardy's Tess. And, indeed, her "adoption" by Mark proves that, once abandoned by her parents, Vivien was seduced—physically, as lines 45–46 and 60–61 indicate—but also morally, as she was indoctrinated into Mark's philosophy of envy and spite, which results in her equation of Filth with Truth. "Gracious lessons thine / And maxims of the mud! (ll. 47–48) shows the degree to which Vivien has been sullied by her contact with Mark, the character who *truly* stands in opposition to Arthur and his dictates. In fact, the cowardly and dishonorable acts committed in the *Idylls* become known as "Mark's way"; he is also labeled the "lustful king," as he serves as the antithesis to Arthur, the "blameless king."

Vivien's life does conform to the paradigm of prostitution outlined in the *Lancet* article. Her life began as an orphaned infant. She was seduced by Mark and at last became a prostitute of his will when, angry and vengeful because Arthur had scorned his effort to become a member of the Round Table, he sends Vivien to Camelot to accomplish his revenge for him. At the opening of the "Merlin and Vivien" idyll, Mark addresses his pupil before sending her to Arthur's court: "Here are snakes within the grass; / And you methinks, O Vivien, save ye fear / That monkish manhood, and the mask of pure / Worn by his court, can stir them till they sting" (ll. 33–36). Furthermore, the means by which Vivien attempts to undermine Camelot include flattery (of Guinevere, Arthur, and Merlin), the spreading of insidious rumors about the sexual impurity of the king's *entourage* and, appropriately, seduction, first directed at Arthur (without success) but finally at Merlin. Vivien has, indeed, become a prostitute for Mark, ostensibly motivated by her desire for personal fame, which she believes will gain her the social acceptance which many disenfranchised members of a culture seek. That she at last shares Mark's spite and subversiveness also complies with the psychological proclivities of a scorned and rejected fringe element in a rigid society which demands conformity.

What, then, does Tennyson's portrait of Vivien reflect about the moral fabric of Victorian society? To what degree does the "fallen woman" in various guises—be she adulterer or prostitute—pose a threat to her culture? Certainly, Camelot is toppled by the sexual license of its members, and the blame is particularly directed at the women who deviate from the standard (a)sexual norm. But here a distinction should be made, I would argue, between Vivien's *actual* contribution to the demise of Arthur's order and the *potential* threat she poses. For it is finally the adulterous Guinevere, and not Vivien, who is *most* culpable for the moral corruption of the realm.

In the poem, "Guinevere," Arthur berates his queen for her adultery and holds her directly responsible (albeit, unfairly so, to many twentieth-century readers, though probably not to most of his Victorian contemporaries) for the ruination of his order. In fact, he goes so far as to compare her with a (venereal?) disease that infects the court. The adultress, he asserts, is "like a *new disease*, unknown to men, / Creeps no *precaution* used, among the *crowd*, / Makes wicked lightnings of her eyes, and saps / The fealty of our friends, and stirs the pulse / With devil's leaps, and *poisons* half the young" (ll. 515–19, emphasis mine). Guinevere has enjoyed all the advantages of a privileged birth and an exalted position in life, but she has betrayed both her public duty of assisting Arthur in his creation of a moral atmosphere that would encourage the propogation of his ideals, and her private vows to the husband who deserves her love and fidelity. Arthur laments to his queen: "For thou hast spoilt the purpose of my life" (l. 450), and places the blame on Guinevere: "Then came thy shameful sin with Lancelot; / Then came the sin of Tristram and Isolt; / Then others, following these my mightiest knights, / And drawing foul ensample from fair names, / Sinn'd also, till the loathsome opposite / Of all my heart had destined did obtain / And all thro' thee!" (ll. 484–490). Thus, according to the moral vision presented by Tennyson in the *Idylls*, Guinevere's behavior results in even more serious consequences than Vivien's seduction of Merlin.

For what, finally, is the result of Merlin's entrapment? Here, as in Malory's work, it would appear that the actual effects of his absence are scarcely felt. If one reads the poem allegorically, as some readers have been inclined to do, it may be argued that Merlin's fate represents the overpowering of the intellect by the flesh, but Tennyson himself cautioned against reading the *Idylls* in order to discern a strict, tightly structured allegory.[27] Practically speaking, while this seduction may hold potentially serious consequences, these are not realized in the larger scheme of the *Idylls*. As the concluding line of "Merlin and Vivien" suggests, the mage is just one more "fool" who should have known better than to succumb to flattery and seduction. It is Arthur, and no other, who serves as the ideal Victorian man, who remains uncorrupted by the immorality around him.

"Merlin and Vivien" may well reflect the shameful problem of prostitution, just as "Guinevere" reveals the ultimate danger of the adulterous wife. In the *Idylls*, we see that Tennyson has accepted the prevailing cultural view of women as potential threats to society. As a prostitute, Vivien is capable of corrupting the culture of which she is a marginal part. A conservative poet, Tennyson reflected and espoused the middle-class views of his audience but, finally, despite his portrayal of this social aberration, he does not absolve Vivien or challenge the accepted views of his readers. Nor does the poet excuse any of the women (e.g., Guinevere, Isolt of Ireland) who, despite extenuating circumstances, violate the rigid social and sexual mores of Tennyson's Victorian/Arthurian world. In his insistence upon maintaining and even reinforcing the view that women must be held accountable, at last, for the socioeconomic cohesion of society, Tennyson contributed to the continuance and proliferation of attitudes that culminated in what Bram Dijkstra identifies as "a veritable iconography of misogyny" in pictorial art at the end of the nineteenth century. Though Dijkstra's study focuses on the visual arts, he also claims "that the images of the painters also echoed in the words of the writers working during this period.[28] Therefore, if Tennyson incurred some resistence from his inclusion of a prostitute in his *Idylls*, his presentation of Vivien does no more than reflect an odious type and a proper Victorian response to it.

That Tennyson was able to employ the Arthurian legend as a vehicle to present difficult, if pervasive, issues stands as testimony to one of strengths of the *Matter of Britain*—its flexibility. For even if one concludes that *Idylls of the King* is flawed as an Arthurian work, it would be more difficult to dismiss it as anything short of one of the most lucrative and significant registers of Victorian thought, a reflection of its age that affords it an importance which rivals Tennyson's other *magnum opus*— *In Memoriam*—dedicated to the other Arthur in his life.

Notes

1. Linda K. Hughes, "Tennyson's Urban Arthurians: Victorian Audiences and the 'City Built to Music'," in *King Arthur Through the Ages*, ed. Valerie M. Lagorio and Mildred Leake Day, 2 vols. (New York, 1990), 2:39–61, at 44.

2. Ibid.

3. Algernon Charles Swinburne, "Under the Microscope," repr. in *Swinburne Replies*, ed. Clyde Kenneth Hyder (Syracuse, 1966), p. 56.

4. Clyde de L. Ryals, *From the Great Deep: Essays on 'Idylls of the King'* (Athens, 1967), pp. vii–viii. Most recent critics concur that the poem is essentially modern. See also, for instance, John Rosenberg's study, *Fall of Camelot: A Study of Tennyson's Idylls of the King"* (Cambridge, 1973).

5. David Staines, *Tennyson's Camelot: The 'Idylls of the King' and Its Medieval Sources* (Waterloo, Ontario 1982). Staines specifically notes that "*Vivien* is almost completely original, being only loosely related to a small incident recorded by Malory. . .though the finished idyll receives a different emphasis and tone with the introduction of Guinevere's adultery" (p. 40). Two essential points are made

here: that Tennyson's expanded depiction of the beguiling of Merlin is unprecedented in the poet's sources, and that it is Guinevere's adultery, in the final version of the *Idylls*, that is the most devastating to Arthur's realm.

6. Alice Chandler, *A Dream of Order: The Medieval Ideal in Nineteenth-Century English Literature* (Lincoln, 1970), p. 232.

7. Tennyson was extremely reluctant to compose an idyll on the subject of the Grail. Hallam Tennyson quotes his father: "I doubt whether a subject as the San Graal could be handled in these days without incurring a charge of irreverence." See *Alfred Lord Tennyson: A Memoir by His Son*, 2 vols. (New York, 1897) 2:126. In addition, each of Tennyson's characters who sees the Grail sees it differently and always alone, suggesting the subjective nature of religious experience, and the poet's desire to satisfy skeptics. Again, Hallam Tennyson quotes the poet: "There is no single fact or incident in the 'Idylls,' however seemingly mystical, which cannot be explained as without any mystery whatever" (*A Memoir*, 2:127).

8. Tennyson is especially indebted to chapter 8 of Carlyle's *On Heroes, Hero-Worship and the Heroic in History*, titled "The Hero as King."

9. Michel Foucault, *The History of Sexuality, vol. 1: An Introduction*, trans. Robert Hurley (New York, 1978).

10. Jeffrey Weeks, *Sex, Politics and Society: The Regulation of Sexuality Since 1800* (London, 1981), p. 19.

11. Alfred Tennyson, *The Poetical Works of Tennyson*, ed. G. Robert Stange (Boston, 1974). "Guinevere" l. 554. Subsequent references to Tennyson's work will be taken from this edition and cited by line number in brackets after the quotation.

12. *Suffer and Be Still: Women in the Victorian Age* ed. Martha Vicinus (Bloomington, 1972), p. xiv.

13. Arthur recites his creed in full in "Guinevere," ll. 464–80.

14. This connection is posited primarily because of 9. l.91 of *Paradise Lost*, in which Milton describes Satan as a "wily snake." Vivien may also be compared, of course, with Keats' Lamia, but the transformation of her, in Merlin's view, suggests that Tennyson created a more puritanical version of Keats' serpent. The assumption that Vivien is modelled on the biblical temptresses is nearly universal, but for a summary of this view, and a provocative questioning of it, see William W. Bonney's "Torpor and Tropology in Tennyson's 'Merlin and Vivien,'" *Victorian Poetry* 23 (1985), 351–67.

15. Steven Marcus, *The Other Victorians: A Study of Sexuality and Pornography in Mid-Nineteenth Century England* (Bloomington, 1964). Marcus quotes one of the most outspoken Victorian authorities on sexuality, Dr. William Acton. In

286   REBECCA UMLAND

his opening chapter, Marcus summarizes Acton's views, which suggest strongly
that overindulgence in sex created severe physical and mental disorders, the
most common of which Acton referred to as "spermatorrhea," the result of too
much "spending." Among the symptoms are exhaustion and mental fatigue—
such as that which afflicts Merlin after his seduction by Vivien. Before Marcus'
study, Peter T. Cominos had also made use of Acton's writings, connecting
prevailing socioeconomic theories with Victorian sexual mores. See "Late
Victorian Sexual Respectability and the Social System," *International Review of
Social History* 8 (1963), 18–48, 216–250. Cominos argues that with the publication
of the first four *Idylls* in 1859, Tennyson "was said to have won the governing
classes" (p. 43). Although Marcus considers Acton's views to be representative,
this has been challenged by more recent studies: see especially, Peter Gay's
The Bourgeois Experience: Victorian to Freud, vol. 1: *Education of the Senses* (New
York, 1984); M. Jeanne Peterson, "Dr. Acton's Enemy: Medicine, Sex, and Society
in Victorian England," *Victorian Studies* 29 (1986) 569–90; and Carol Zisowitz
Stearns and Peter N. Stearns, "Victorian Sexuality: Can Historians Do It Better?"
Journal of Social History 18 (1985), 625–34. Finally, for an excellent overview of
the debate regarding Victorian sexuality, see John Maynard, *Charlotte Bronte and
Sexuality* (Cambridge, 1984), especially chapter 1, "Coming of Age in the
Nineteenth Century," and its accompanying notes.

16. Weeks, *Sex, Politics and Society*, p. 20.

17. E. M. Sigsworth and T. J. Wyke, "A Study of Victorian Prostitution and
Venereal Disease," in *Suffer and Be Still*, ed. Vicinus, p. 79.

18. Tennyson's letter to the duchess of Argyll, which Martin dates in late
May of 1857. See Robert Bernard Martin, *Tennyson: The Unquiet Heart* (Oxford,
1980), p. 422.

19. This contrast of characters also suggests that early on the poet intended
to create a hierarchy of women in the work. The major female figures, I believe,
are ranked in descending order as follows: Enid, Lynette, Elaine, Ettarre, Isolt,
and Vivien. Guinevere's character is thrown into relief by this hierarchy, though
she does not fit it: she is capable of the best and worst behavior.

20. Quoted in Tennyson, *A Memoir*, 1:449.

21. For good summaries of the Victorian reception of the work, see J. Phillip
Eggers, *King Arthur's Laureate* (New York, 1971), pp. 53–104 and Hughes,
"Tennyson's Urban Arthurians." Also see Hughes' article, " 'All That Makes a
Man': Tennyson's 'Idylls of the King' as a Primer for Modern Gentlemen,"
Arthurian Interpretations 1 (1986), 54–63.

22. Eggers, *King Arthur's Laureate*, p. 83.

23. Swinburne, "Under the Microscope," pp. 59–60.

24. Arthur E. Baker, *A Concordance to the Poetical and Dramatic Works of Alfred
Lord Tennyson*, repr. (New York, 1967), p. 302.

25. Alfred Tennyson *Idylls of the King*. Annotated by Alfred Tennyson. ed. Hallam Tennyson (London, 1908), p. 478.

26. Sigsworth and Wyke, "A Study," p. 84.

27. In *A Memoir*, Hallam Tennyson quotes his father: "They [the reviewers] have taken my hobby, and ridden it too hard, and have explained some things too allegorically, although there is an allegorical or perhaps rather a parabolic drift in the poem. . . . I hate to be tied down to say, '*This* means *that*,' because the thought within the image is much more than any one interpretation" (2: 126–27).

28. Bram Dijkstra, *Idols of Perversity: Fantasies of Feminine Evil in Fin-de-Siecle Culture*, (New York, 1986) p. viii. This is one of the most thorough and insightful studies of Victorian attitudes towards women, the reasons for them, and their implications in late nineteenth and early twentieth-century art and thought that I have seen. In his "Preface," for instance, Dijkstra even asserts tht "the intellectual assumptions which underlay the turn of the century's cultural war on woman also permitted the implementation of the genocidal race theories of Nazi Germany," p. (vii). Dijkstra's claim that there is a symbiotic exchange between painters and poets is in accord with Debra N. Mancoff's premise that William Dyce, the Victorian painter, followed Tennyson's strategies in popularizing Arthurian subjects. See *The Arthurian Revival in Victorian Art* (New York, 1990), p. xx.

Feminism, Homosexuality, and Homophobia in *The Mists of Avalon*

James Noble

In a recent article on the feminism of *The Mists of Avalon*,[1] Karin Fuog credits Marion Zimmer Bradley with having successfully challenged some of the cultural stereotypes and assumptions about women that have come to be associated with the Arthurian legend during the course of its long, patriarchal history.[2] Worthy of particular commendation, Fuog argues, is Bradley's success in demythologizing the mystique of female sexuality by rendering its mysteries intelligible and by representing sexuality as a potential source of personal power and pride for women.[3]

As many readers familiar with the legend have been startled to discover, however, Bradley's treatment of the issue of sexual identity transcends gender so as to include a representation of Lancelot as latent homosexual. The concept of a gay Lancelot (Lancelet) is as daring as it is rich in potential, given that homosexuality is a form of sexual expression as alien and incomprehensible to patriarchy as female sexuality and as subject to cultural myths, stereotypes, and misapprehensions that have long needed to be explored and/or exploded. If such were Bradley's intentions in transforming the legendary lover of Gwenhwyfar into a closet homosexual, however, her efforts fall disappointingly short of the mark: indeed, in the final analysis, Bradley's representation of Lancelot's situation would seem to be a clear-cut case of patriarchal homophobia posing as sympathetic liberalism.[4]

On the surface of things, Bradley's characterization of Lancelot challenges the archetypal cultural image of the homosexual as a lisping, limp-wristed, effeminate male whose interests and ideologies set him apart from the stereotypical heterosexual male. Bradley sees to it, in fact, that Lancelot's sexual orientation is no more readily apparent to the reader when s/he first meets him than it is to any of the characters Lancelot encounters in the novel itself. When Lancelot first enters the narrative, Morgaine is immediately struck by the fact that "she had never seen so masculine a creature before" (147). Indeed, he seems to be all "man" in the sense in which that term is so often and so unfortunately employed: not surprisingly perhaps, given that he is said to be a fearsome warrior, Lancelot refuses Viviane's invitation to stay in Avalon for seven years on the grounds that he would rather be "where the real struggles of life are taking place" (146), which is to say, in Britain fighting the Saxons. Furthermore, he seems to be a radically independent figure who insists upon following his own course, whether or not that course is one that even so influential a figure as the Lady of the Lake would have him pursue. He has lived, he announces chauvinistically, "in a world where men do not wait for a woman's bidding to go and come" (146), and he is determined to remain a member of such a society. Surprisingly, moreover, in light of what is later to be disclosed about his sexual identity, Lancelot demonstrates what appears to be a "normal" heterosexual impulse when we first meet him; indeed, Bradley makes quite a lot of the fact that Lancelot finds himself physically attracted to Morgaine during their afternoon spent together in the shadow of the Ring Stones and of his disappointment that Morgaine should be pledged to the Goddess and therefore incapable of entering into sexual relations with him (153–56).

Before Morgaine is afforded a second opportunity to engage in the kind of intimacy with Lancelot that had been denied to them on Avalon, Lancelot has met Gwenhwyfar. Although she is but a child at the time of their first meeting, Morgaine notes that Lancelot looks upon Gwenhwyfar as he had only a short time earlier looked upon her, "with love, desire, almost worship" (158). She notes a similar response on Lancelot's part to the adult Gwenhwyfar when he delivers her to Arthur as his future High Queen: "Lancelot looked at her as if she were the statue of the Virgin on the altar at church" (272). This reverential response to women surfaces again when Lancelot tells Morgaine during their final intimate encounter that he cannot engage in intercourse with her, as she wants him to do, because to relate to her in that fashion would be to risk causing her "hurt or dishonor" (324). Most telling of all, however, is Gwenhwyfar's disclosure towards the end of the novel to the effect that her relations with Lancelot over the years have seldom involved intercourse:

> It was not his body she desired. Morgause. . .would never have believed how little difference *that* had made to either of them.

> Seldom, indeed, had he ever taken her in that way which was sin and dishonor—only in those first years, when they had had Arthur's acquiesence, to try and see if Gwenhwyfar could bear a son to the kingdom. There had been other ways to find pleasure, which she somehow felt less of a sin, less violation of Arthur's marriage rights in her body (854).

"The other ways" in question here, which Lancelot practises with Morgaine on the only occasion in which they actually engage in sexual relations, strike Morgaine as unnatural in that

> it seemed to him that this was the way it should be. . . as if nothing mattered but their bodies, that there was no greater joining with all of life. To the priestess, reared in Avalon and attuned to the greater tides of life and eternity, this careful, sensuous, deliberate lovemaking seemed almost blasphemy, a refusal to give themselves up to the will of the Goddess (324–25).

Morgaine's reflections on this occasion would seem designed to echo an earlier observation about Lancelot to the effect that he is a man who "has denied the touch of the Goddess in himself" (147). Since Bradley makes it quite evident in his initial conversation with Viviane in the novel that Lancelot's problems with the Goddess stem from the nature of his childhood relations with his mother, who, from his perspective, had always been "a stern Goddess" to him when what he had wanted was "a loving mother" (144), one wonders if Bradley is not suggesting that Lancelot's inability to engage in anything but "careful, sensuous, deliberate lovemaking" with women and to treat them with a reverence that denies them (or at least Morgaine) the opportunity to find fulfillment in their sexual relations with him is not somehow related to the problematic nature of his relations with his mother.

As close as she comes, however, to giving voice to the Freudian and decidedly homophobic notion that the homosexual's "problem" with women originates in an emasculating childhood experience with his mother, Bradley chooses to have Lancelot simply confess to Morgaine that his sexual orientation has always been homosexual, even though he tried for a long time to deny the fact by flinging himself into sexual experiments with any woman who would have him (481). As he goes on to explain, however, these experiments have seldom been very satisfying for him—nor, I think we can presume, based on Morgaine's experience, for the women in question—given that "there were few women who could rouse me even a little." That is, Lancelot continues, "till I saw—her. . . .With her, I know myself all man" (481).

The her is Gwenhwyfar, of course, although by the time we hear this statement from Lancelot's mouth, Bradley has seen to it that we know enough not to dissociate Lancelot's feelings for Gwenhwyfar from his feelings for Arthur. As he admits to Morgaine, Lancelot finds fulfillment in his relations with Gwenhwyfar and a sense that he is, to use his own words, "all man" when he is with her only because of the nature of his initial sexual encounter with her, which, in Bradley's version of the legend, had also been a sexual encounter with Arthur:

> "But you do not know all," he whispered. "As we lay together— never, never had anything so—so—." He swallowed and fumbled to put into words what Morgaine could not bear to hear. "I—I touched Arthur—I touched him. I love her, oh, God I love her, mistake me not, but had she not been Arthur's wife, had it not been for—I doubt even *she*—" He choked and could not finish his sentence (482).

No less telling than this passage in terms of what it reveals about his feelings for Arthur is Lancelot's admission to Morgaine that he is powerless to do anything to alter the situation which his relationship with Gwenhwyfar poses for all concerned: "I should take Gwenhwyfar and be gone from here, before it becomes a scandal to all the courts of the world, that I love the wife of my king, and yet. . .yet it is Arthur I cannot leave. . .I know not but what I love her only because I can come close, thus, to *him*" (482). Although the news of his Beltane *ménage à trois* with Arthur and Gwenhwyfar comes as a tremendous shock to her, Morgaine has known for some time before she hears the admission from his own lips that Lancelot's love for Gwenhwyfar is somehow related to his feelings for Arthur. The realization had first come to her (and the reader) on Arthur's wedding day when she had found herself reflecting with respect to Lancelot's wedding gift to Arthur: "How he loves Arthur; this is why he is so tormented. It is not that he desires Gwenhwyfar that tortures him; it is that he loves Arthur no less" (295).

Although Bradley continues to deal with the issue throughout the remainder of the novel, the episode in which Lancelot discloses his sexual orientation to Morgaine and actually gives voice to his feelings for Arthur constitutes a critical stage in Bradley's attempt to demythologize Lancelot's sexuality. For what he declares to be the first time in his life, Lancelot gives verbal expression to a reality about himself that he has long suppressed and attempted to negate by entering into sexual relations with women. Morgaine's response to Lancelot's confession is to shrink back from its implications in horror: "Morgaine put out her hand to stop him. There were things she could not bear to know" (482). Ironically, given what she seems to be attempting to accomplish in her characterization of Lancelot, Bradley's response to Lancelot's self-disclosure is not very different from Morgaine's, for, like Morgaine, Bradley chooses to do nothing with the declaration Lancelot makes about his situation or to see in it any possibilities for resolution or self-realization.

By way of contrast, female characters in the novel who experience similar moments of self-awareness with respect to their sexuality are inevitably empowered by the experience. As Fuog has suggested, Nimue does not achieve self-actualization until she has come face to face with her identity as a sexual being: "Instead of the traditional feelings of 'lost' virginity or submissive giving, Nimue's feeling after making love with Kevin is one of overwhelming triumph. Woman has not lost in the sexual encounter, but rather gained power and knowledge, both deemed dangerous for her to possess under a patriarchal system."[5] Similarly, Igraine is empowered by the experience of taking on a personal sexual identity for the first time in her life when she decides to act upon her feelings for Uther: "She felt no fear now, and no shame; what had been with Gorlois duty and acceptance had become delight almost unendurable, as if she had been reunited with some hidden part of her own body and soul" (105). Furthermore, Morgaine is not only "healed" (417) by voluntarily engaging in sexual relations with Kevin, but also regenerated when she later gives expression to a long-suppressed sexual identity by entering into a relationship with Accolon: "Or is it only that when he touches me, speaks to me, I feel myself woman and alive again after all this time when I have felt myself old, barren, half dead in this marriage to a dead man and a dead life?" (587).

Bradley sees to it, however, that Lancelot is afforded no such opportunity to experience the vitality and power, the self-affirmation and sense of self worth that she identifies in her treatment of her female characters as the inevitable consequence of having come fully to grips with their sexuality. Given that she has Lancelot emerge, however fleetingly and haltingly, from the proverbial closet in the encounter with Morgaine now under discussion, Bradley might well have seen fit to carry through to its logical conclusion her attempt to demythologize his sexuality by having Lancelot act upon the impulse to which he gives expression in this episode; in the remaining half of the novel, she might easily have had him enter into an empowering sexual relationship with another man—if not with Arthur, the object of his affections, then with Gareth, who worships Lancelot, or with any of the other knights in Arthur's court who can express nothing but admiration for Lancelot.

Instead, however, in two significant departures from the traditional storyline of the legend, Bradley chooses to make Lancelot suffer even more than his confession to Morgaine suggests that he has already suffered as a consequence of his sexual otherness. In the first instance, Bradley deprives Lancelot of Arthur's friendship, not surprisingly perhaps, by making sexuality the knife which severs the cord that has long bound Lancelot and Arthur together. In one of her petulant rages, Gwenhwyfar accuses Arthur of having invited Lancelot into their bed on that memorable Beltane eve not in the hopes that Lancelot's presence there might give her pleasure and make her pregnant, but because Arthur has always been sexually attracted to Lancelot:

> "Can you swear that when you brought him to our bed...I saw it then, you touched him with more love than ever you have given the woman my father forced on you—when you led me into this sin, can you swear it was not your own sin, and all your fine talk no more than a cover for that very sin that brought down fire from Heaven on the city of Sodom?" (547)

Although Arthur's initial response to Gwenhywfar's charge is utter incredulity (He stared at her, still deathly white. "You are certainly mad, my lady"), when Gwenhwyfar repeats the accusation for a second time Arthur explodes with a violence that is uncharacteristic of him: "Say that again...and wife or no, love or no, I will kill you, my Gwenhwyfar!" (547). Just what Bradley intends the reader to make of Arthur's response to Gwenhwyfar's accusation is hard to say: on the one hand, it is so uncharacteristically vehement it would almost seem to be a case of Arthur's "protest[ing] too much" against the charge that Gwenhwyfar has levelled against him; on the other hand, it is a reaction so altogether typical of patriarchy's response to the threat of being branded a homosexual that Bradley probably intended it to constitute no more than a firm declaration of Arthur's heterosexuality and of the fact that, although his interaction with Lancelot during the Beltane lovefest may have afforded him a homoerotic experience, it was not a form of contact Arthur had ever expected to have with Lancelot or that he had engineered for the purposes of indulging in a sexual liaison with him.

Whatever this episode may tell us about the nature of Arthur's sexuality, it is an event which radically alters the nature of Lancelot's relations with Arthur from this point forward in Bradley's narrative. When Lancelot returns to court for the first time after the episode between Gwenhwyfar and Arthur, what Gwenhwyfar is later to describe as "the old closeness" (841) between the two men has disappeared: Bradley tells us that Lancelot "raised his eyes to Arthur, and for a moment, Gwenhwyfar thought Arthur would embrace him; but then Arthur drew back and let his hand drop. Lancelot gazed at him, startled..." (563).

Lancelot has good reason to be startled by Arthur's response, for Lancelot has always been careful not to say or do anything to make Arthur think that Lancelot's feelings for him are anything other than feelings of close friendship and comraderie. Indeed, that which torments Lancelot as much as anything else in the novel is the knowledge that he cannot tell Arthur how he feels about him. When Morgaine suggests that surely Lancelot ought to be discussing the matter of his sexuality with another man, rather than with her, Lancelot replies:

> "No man, I think, has ever felt such—God knows I hear enough of what men desire, they talk of nothing else, and now and then some man reveals something strange he may desire, but never, never, nothing so strange and evil as this! I am *damned*....This is my punishment for desiring the wife of my king, that I should be held in this terrible bondage—even Arthur if he knew, would hate and despise me. He knows I love Gwenhwyfar, but this not even he could forgive, and Gwenhwyfar—who knows if she, even she, would not hate and despise me." (483)

Faced with the options with which Bradley affords him, Lancelot has no alternative but to suffer his "terrible bondage" in silence. Not content to leave him suffering in silence, however, Bradley improvises on the traditional storyline of the Arthurian legend yet once more by forcing Lancelot into an unhappy marriage. For reasons that are obvious to the reader but to no one in the novel except Lancelot and Morgaine, Lancelot agrees to marry Elaine out of a sense of honor to her and duty to her father but, as Bradley takes some pains to tell us, at a cost to himself that is tremendous. At his wedding he is said by Morgaine to look "wretched, thin, and pallid with despair" (543), and, when asked sometime later if he is happy in his marriage, Lancelot replies sardonically: "Happy? What man alive is happy? I do as best I can" (563). Nor, as Elaine eventually reveals, does Lancelot spend any more time with her after they are married than is necessary: "I had more time to speak with Lancelot before Pentecost than in all the years of our marriage. This is the first time in all these years that I have had more than a week of his company!" (628).

Lancelot's fate, given the circumstances which prevail as a consequence of his strained relations with Arthur and of his marriage to Elaine, is to live the exilic life of the Anglo-Saxon Wanderer he sings about during a visit to Arthur's court some years after his marriage and immediately preceding the Grail guest:

> What sorrow is like to the sorrow of one who is alone?
>
> For what is the fair meadow of my home to me
> When I cannot see the face of my king
> And the weight on my arm is but a band of gold
> When the heart is empty of the weight of love.
> And so I shall go roaming
>
> With none to bear me company
> But the memory of those I loved
> And the songs I sang out of a full heart
> And the cuckoo's cry in memory (687–88).

Although Arthur embraces Lancelot at the conclusion of his song, telling him "But you are again with your king and your friend, Galahad" (688), the reconciliation is short-lived, since Lancelot almost immediatly departs with the other knights in search of the Grail, removing himself from Arthur once again. The madness Lancelot experiences during his Grail quest is further testimony to the sense of disorientation which has been his life experience, for, as he tells Morgaine upon his return to Camelot, "I think it was not the first time—there were times, during those years with Elaine, that I hardly knew what I did" (806).

Whereas Bradley would seem to want her readers to believe towards the end of the novel that Lancelot's experience of the Grail ultimately brings him the peace he has always longed for but never been able to achieve because of his sexual orientation, one must recognize that, in deciding to enter the priesthood, Lancelot is once again denying his sexuality; in fact, he is attempting to negate it altogether at this stage by surrounding himself with a company of men who, by virtue of their monastic vows, have likewise declared their intention to be asexual. But such is the fate, Bradley leaves us to infer, of those cursed, like Lancelot, with a sexual orientation that denies them a place within the mainstream of patriarchy.

For all her efforts to demythologize Lancelot's sexual otherness, Bradley has done little in *The Mists of Avalon* to challenge existing cultural stereotypes and assumptions about homosexuality. Whereas she can perhaps be credited with having addressed mimetically in her characterization of Lancelot the popular misconception that ruggedly handsome men engaged in the pursuit of "manly" professions who are capable of engaging in sexual relations with women and of fathering children cannot possibly be homosexual, Bradley's attempt to demythologize the phenomenon of homosexuality amounts, in the final analysis, to little more than tokenism. Indeed, in a very real sense, her treatment of Lancelot is more homophobic than it is anything else, given that Bradley takes such pains to emphasize the extent to which Lancelot is disempowered by his sexual orientation and given that she repeatedly invents opportunities to accentuate the suffering that accompanies this disempowerment. The practice is one that bears thinking about, since Bradley might just as easily have exercised such options as she exercises in the case of Nimue, Igraine, Morgaine, and Morgause to create situations that would have permitted Lancelot not only to come to terms with his sexuality, but also to claim it as a source of personal power and pride. In short, if Bradley's treatment of Lancelot does not suggest, at least by implication, that he *deserves* to suffer as he does because of his sexual orientation, it is a treatment which ultimately acquiesces to a value system one might have expected to see challenged in a much more radical fashion in a contemporary treatment of the Arthurian legend which specifically addresses itself to the plight of the homosexual living within the confines and social constructs of a patriarchal order.[6]

Notes

1. Marion Zimmer Bradley, *The Mists of Avalon* (New York, 1982). All textual references to the novel in this paper will appear in parentheses in the text of the essay.

2. Karin E. C. Fuog, "Imprisoned in the Phallic Oak: Marion Zimmer Bradley and Merlin's Seductress," *Quondam et Futurus: A Journal of Arthurian Interpretations* 1 (1991), 73–88.

3. Fuog, "Imprisoned," p. 81.

4. A recent example of the traditional patriarchal response to homosexuality is to be found in Oliver Stone's film *JFK*, where the conspirators are depicted as a group of tawdry gay Louisianans with John Birch leanings: see Michael H. Hodges, "In Hollywood, Does Homosexuality Equal Villainy?," *The Detroit News*, 15 January 1992, pp. E1 and E4.

5. Fuog, "Imprisoned," p. 80.

6. I am obliged to my colleague, Dr. Robert Moore, for reading an early draft of this essay and offering a number of helpful suggestions.

Camelot 3000
and the Future of Arthur

 *Charles T. Wood*

In 1989, when Valerie Lagorio sought to explore what she called "Camelot, U.S.A.," she emphasized not just the timelessness of Arthurian myth, but also what she stressed was "its essential apocalyptic thrust."[1] And her evidence, extensive, ranged from Norris Lacy's *Arthurian Encyclopedia* to Michael Jackson's possibly more apocalyptic Victory Tour. Included among her popular treasures was DC Comics' *Camelot 3000*, a twelve-issue maxi-series which first appeared in 1982–85 and which Warner Books subsequently reissued as a single-volume paperback in 1988. Although its title page insisted that its story would be "continuing legends chronicled by Sir Thomas Malory,"[2] Lagorio was surely right in terming the results "a far remove" from more traditional adaptations, "with Morgan Le Fay a fitting amalgam of Sheena the queen of the jungle, and the Dragon Lady, and visual sound effects of 'zap, kaboom, pow' reverberating throughout Camelot."[3] Since—GASP!—that's not the half of it, the present article seeks to honor Professor Lagorio by devoting more space to *Camelot 3000* than was available in her 1989 overview.

Because comic books are usually cooperative ventures, it is often difficult to establish their authorship. In the present instance, the front cover of the Warner Books reissue carried the information "Mike W. Barr & Brian Bolland, *Camelot 3000*," thereby implying that these two are its authors, an impression which is strengthened on its last page, where they are termed "Creators." Yet the title page credits no less than six people: Mike W. Barr and Brian Bolland as "writer/co-creators/artists"; Bruce D. Patterson and Terry Austin as "embellishers";

John Constanza as "letterer"; and Tatjana Wood as "colorist." Nevertheless, the introductions to both versions make it clear that Barr comes closest to being the "true" author, and his own account, from 1982, demonstrates the extent to which his own experiences, his own culture, have helped to alter the text he inherited from Malory:

> Mike W. Barr (who is writing this page, whether he refers to himself in the third person or not)...went to college after graduating from high school. In this he is not alone,...[but] Mike *stayed* there a bit longer than most....Why Mike stayed so long...is not germane to this page, save that a conflict in a far-off kingdom known as VietNam had a lot to do with it. Anyway, in his never-ending search for electives to fill his schedule, Mike, one day in early 1975, stumbled across a course called *Seminar: Arthurian Literature.* Thinking that this sounded like a pleasant way to while away a few hours—and having always nurtured a fondness for the stories of King Arthur and Company anyway—he took the course, and found himself reading...*Le Morte D'Arthur* by Sir Thomas Malory....Those of you who have read *LMDA* or seen either...*Camelot* or...*Excalibur* are aware that *LMDA* concerns itself with the "definitive" telling of King Arthur and His Knights of the Table Round.
>
> Mike knew this too, after reading it, and thought that *LMDA*, with its heroic, yet bittersweet tone, its magnificently agonized characters, and its overall tone of high adventure, was some of the best fun he'd had since discovering comics....[H]e began trying to find a new way to tell the Arthurian Legend....
>
> [M]any talented and capable folks have already adapted *LMDA* in one way or another, from such far-ranging works as *The Once and Future King,* by T. H. White, to Hal Foster's *Prince Valiant,* subtitled *In the Days of King Arthur....*[T]he glitch was in how...to be *original* in the telling. And for a time, that seemed insurmountable, until...Mike was reading the end of *LMDA,* including the part about King Arthur not having died at Glastonbury Tor, but rather sleeping, recovering from his wounds, and waiting for the time of England's greatest need.
>
> "Of course," shouted Mike, as a kind of epiphany (look it up) broke over him. His jaw dropped with the simplicity of it. He would do a *sequel!*[4]

This testimony suggests that *Camelot 3000* had a surprisingly complex background. In a sense, only chance and Vietnam brought Barr to Sally Slocum's seminar at the University of Akron,[5] but at the same time he also admits to a preexisting fondness for "King Arthur and Company." Although he is not entirely precise about the sources of this affection, they appear to have included T. H. White, Lerner and Loewe, and Hal Foster. Strikingly, however, none before Malory seems ever to have introduced him to the sleeping Arthur. As he reports on the nature of his knowledge in the introduction to the later Warner Books edition:

> Since my writing of the comic book series known as *Camelot 3000*, I have come to be regarded as something of an expert on the Arthurian mythos. . . . For better or worse (probably worse, regarding my standing amongst the academics), I must confess this is not true. My knowledge. . .comes entirely from one course. . .and. . .more sources than can readily be documented, many of which have been lost to time. Rather than looking upon this as a flaw, I chose to regard it as the continuation of a great tradition. After all, the legends of King Arthur did not spring from one carefully-organized and uniformly-coordinated source. Over the centuries, chroniclers added to and subtracted from the mythos as they chose. . . .Therefore, in the writing of *Camelot 3000*, I took from the legends precisely what I could use. . .and ignored or ruthlessly discarded that which I could not. My understanding of the Arthurian mythos, then, is that of a perhaps more-than-usually-well-informed layman, but no more.[6]

What come through clearly, too, are Barr's assumptions about his intended audience. It was to be sufficiently well educated to appreciate the humor of his pseudo-*New Yorker* style, and it was to be flattered by his straightforward use of unusual terms ("mythos") and British forms ("amongst"). At the same time, though, he seems to have known that, while readers might accept it, he was pushing things when he used a word like "epiphany," and his professed worries about the attitude of "the academics," not to mention his casual approach to the Slocum seminar, demonstrate that he expected his audience to include more than a few rednecks and/or perpetual sophomores.

Given *Camelot 3000's* presumptively limited circulation in academic circles, a brief sketch of Barr's creation is needed if we are fully to appreciate the ways in which he has altered this inherited text. In the year 3000 Earth is devastatingly invaded by aliens from an unknown tenth planet ruled by Morgan Le Fay. But a youthful Tom Prentice manages to escape from London and make it to Somerset, where he seeks refuge in the tunnels of the Glastonbury Historical Dig. Pursued

The Awakening Arthur Surprises Tom Prentice at the Glastonbury Historical Dig

Excalibur Returns at the Salisbury Down Nuclear Plant

by aliens, he there stumbles on a sarcophagus out of which Arthur emerges. When Britain's king wonders how long he's been asleep and explains who he is, Tom replies: "Listen, mister, whoever you are, we've gotta get out of here—Fast!"[7]

After dispatching the aliens, they hasten to Stonehenge, where Arthur rouses Merlin. All three then proceed to the Salisbury Down nuclear plant where the Lady of the Lake rises from the cooling tank, bearing Excalibur. Before Arthur can take it, however, both lady and sword disappear, with the latter soon reemerging as the sword in the stone in the middle of the United Nations General Assembly. After Arthur draws it, Merlin uses reincarnation to bring back Guinevere and six members of the Round Table: Lancelot, Kay, Percival, Galahad, Gawain, and Tristan.

Just as Arthur soon remarries Guinevere, so too does the love triangle with Lancelot resurface, albeit with a few new complications. Jordan Matthew, the UN Security Director, turns out to be Modred, and this time he enters into a conspiracy with Morgan and the world's four most powerful leaders to destroy the new Camelot. When Tom Prentice is afflicted with radiation sickness in the ensuing battles, Arthur makes him a knight of the Round Table and orders a quest for the Holy Grail to cure him. Percival finds it, of course; Tom is cured; but Modred manages subsequently to steal the Grail, taking it to the tenth planet. A rescue by rocket is soon organized, and Arthur, after killing Modred, finds the ultimate way to rid the universe of Morgan Le Fay as well. When she promises revenge, he stands over a stone with sword upraised, saying: "In years agone, I did take Excalibur from a stone." Then, as he brings it crashing down, he exclaims: "And now I shall return it!"[8] The result resembles matter meeting anti-matter since, as the thermonuclear mushroom cloud rises, everything is destroyed, including Arthur.

By now, Kay, Percival, and Galahad have also departed this life, but back on Earth peace is celebrated and things return to normal. Gawain rejoins his pre-reincarnation family; Tristan gets together with Isolde; and Tom begins the daunting task of rebuilding London. As for Lancelot and Guinevere, when she discovers she is pregnant, she can only comment: "Lance, I hope it's *his*," to which, after agonized hesitation, he responds: "So do I."[9] Even the tenth planet is not forgotten, for out of its rubble emerges a reptilian creature which stumbles forward to wrap its octopus-like arm around the sword it proceeds to pull from a stone. The creature raises it on high as the text on the final page reads: "And the road goes ever on."[10]

Although this tale is not exactly Malory's Matter of Britain, it seems just as clear that this sequel depends on modifications of, and elaborations on, his text, one now well over five hundred years old. Moreover, the changes involved are not simple ones. Rather, they reflect the work's pop-culture context and intended market even more than they display Barr and Bolland's uniquely creative vision. Indeed, because they do, we should at least briefly explore the role of DC Comics as publisher of the whole enterprise.

Barr's first comments demonstrate that from the beginning he was aiming at a reasonably sophisticated audience, and DC Comics did everything possible to support that intention. Thus the original version (like the book that followed) was printed on special heavy-stock paper that permitted a sharpness of detail and vivid colors impossible to reproduce on the kind of low-quality newsprint normally used. More tellingly, each issue was sold only at specialty shops, and insofar as that decision placed *Camelot 3000* outside the jurisdiction of the Comics Code Authority, the industry's self-censorship body, Barr and Bolland had the freedom needed to take "an honest look at adult themes— including, but not limited to, sex."[11]

The intended adult tone, a high one at that, becomes apparent with the opening words of the first issue, for they read: " 'This is the way the world ends,' wrote the poet T. S. Eliot, 'not with a bang, but a *whimper.*' The citizens of London, England in the year 3000 would have certainly preferred the whimper to the *bang.*"[12] Still, sophisticated as this use of Eliot may be, the need to identify him as a poet—or London as a city in England—suggests that Barr and DC Comics were not about to overestimate the cultural literacy of their market. Indeed, presumed audience outlook appears to have shaped some of the ways in which Malory has been updated.

Most noticeable, perhaps, is the transformation experienced by the six knights who abandon their modern identities to take on those of the Arthurian past. Since, in present terminology, their prototypes were a bunch of dead white males, a few changes must have seemed in order. Thus, even though Lancelot inhabits the body of Jules Futrelle,[13] a French industrialist and the world's richest man, Sir Kay runs a seedy Chicago hash house and is in hock to the mob; Galahad is a Japanese samurai; and Gawain is a South African black from Johannesburg, presumably the descendant of Zulu warriors. Percival, however, is purely a product of science fiction (the genre, incidentally, to which Warner Books assigns *Camelot 3000*), for he is a so-called "neo-man," a monstrous form of being that the UN creates out of political prisoners in Australia and then employs in its defense forces. Last, though surely not least in this rainbow coalition, Tristan turns out to be Amber March, a prospective Canadian bride who discovers her true identity only at

Guinevere and Lancelot Renew Their Love to the Distress of Arthur

the altar. One senses immediately, therefore, that this sex change is likely to cause plot complications when Isolde appears, not the least of which will be the new dimensions that this mythic couple will now give their forbidden love.

Be that as it may, these transformations would appear to have significant implications. That is, politicians in the 1980s may have railed against what they claimed were the disastrous consequences of all equal-opportunity programs, and electoral results may have seemed to confirm that judgment, but if Barr and Bolland's relentless insistence on the diversity of their Round Table proved no barrier to sales, one can only conclude that pop culture was not inhospitable to their implicit efforts to create new career opportunities for minorities and women.

Here, as it happens, since the original *Camelot 3000* had a letters section, this conclusion can be at least partially corroborated by reader-response theory. Since these letters are absolutely silent on the subject, they suggest that no one found anything amiss with the racial backgrounds of Gawain and Galahad.[14] On Tristan's gender, however, there was frequent comment, but to understand it fully one must first grasp how Barr chose to present his/her "plight." For his Tristan, it must be emphasized, is a person torn.

That reality emerges soon after Tristan's appearance when s/he protests to a dangerously smitten Tom: "I'm *not* a woman! I'm a *man*! I just have the *body* of a woman!"[15] In fact, later on s/he comes close to betraying the Round Table when Morgan promises: "I'll correct the mistake Nature made in your reincarnation. My magicks will make you a man again!. . . A *man*! I know how your present form tortures you."[16]

Nowhere does this torture take more acute form than when Isolde reappears in the form of Claire Locklyn, Jordan Matthew's secretary. Given Locklyn's harlequin glasses and Apache-style punk hairdo, Tristan refuses to accept her true identity, but after Isolde has embraced and passionately kissed her startled lover, s/he can only shout: "*NO*! I *want* to—and I *hate* myself for it! Was I so *evil* in my first life? What did I do to deserve *this*?"[17] The realities of a lesbian relationship then continue to horrify him/her until the final pages where, in a bedroom filled with roses, both women find it possible to make joyous and ecstatic love.

On the other hand, Tristan also constantly insists that s/he is still a knight. For example, when Arthur is directing his first attack against the aliens, he orders: "Gawain and Percival, repel the ground assault," but with thoughtless chauvinism he quickly adds: "You, too, Tristan! But be careful!" In response, Tristan can only grumble through clenched teeth: "He thinks I'll be no good in battle! He'll learn!"[18] As, indeed, he does, especially after he orders Tristan to vamp and distract one of the men guarding the rocket they need for their flight to the tenth planet. S/he reluctantly attempts it, but when the guard gets suspicious, suddenly s/he knees him brutally and follows up with a vicious double-fisted uppercut that lays him flat as s/he taunts: "You'd let yourself be beaten by a *woman*?" Then, as s/he daintily reties the bow at the back of her neck, s/he adds: "You don't *deserve* to be a man!"[19]

Reader response to the new Tristan proved both lively and supportive. Only one unreconstructed male wrote off the whole situation, explaining that "if I were reincarnated into a body like that, I don't think I would have any problem getting used to it."[20] Women chimed in with supportive comments ranging from: "The difficulties of Tristan's misplaced reincarnation. . .are delightful,"[21] to a somewhat foggy, yet notably positive:

> I think your Tristan dilemma is infinitely intriguing! His/Her's is truly one of human bondage, that of having the waking consciousness of a man while contained in a woman's body. The emotional range of this character is always amazing to witness, never knowing how Tristan will react to any given situation. This is the focal point of the series for me.[22]

Strikingly, correspondents showed no distaste for the lesbian possibilities that began to surface with Isolde's reappearance. On the contrary, most displayed a tolerant, often thoughtful understanding. As Mike Sopp, a frequent contributor, put it:

> If somebody had told me *Camelot 3000* #7 would show two women kissing passionately,. . .I probably would have muttered, "Oh well, DC is no better than the other ones. Cheap thrills hiding under the word adult."
>
> I would have been wrong. (You don't know how proud I am to say that.)
>
> I'm not a prude. I realize that sexual intercourse between two people not necessarily one man and one woman. . .is commonplace today. Since comic books are designed to reflect humanity it is only natural, and right, that they include these subjects.[23]

Women proved equally accepting. As one from France pointed out, she saw nothing to be gained in endless bickering about Tristan's femininity since "not all women wear lipstick and silk nightgowns, nor are all who wear lipstick and silk nightgowns women."[24] In fact, the only display of female disapproval came not in comments about Tristan's gender identification or sexual orientation, but, rather, in a concern over the negative implications of Tom Prentice's infatuation with this knight who had once been a Canadian bride:

> In answer to my letter in *C-3000* #9 in which I said I found Tom's crush on Amber/Tristan "unconvincing," you said that one couldn't "blame Tom for being distracted by the physical evidence." This is, however, *exactly* what I am blaming him for.

Granted, Tom is but a young man. Granted, Tristan is more than striking to look at. Granted, you do call it a "crush." I would still like to think that by the 30th century even young men in crushes will give more weight to personality and character than to the "physical evidence."[25]

As such comments suggest, a good part of *Camelot 3000's* success appears to have resulted from its capacity to be seen simultaneously as pure science-fiction fantasy and also as a vehicle through which contemporary concerns could be explored at a dispassionate distance. Still, not all correspondents fully grasped the simultaneity involved:

You know, it's occurred to me that perhaps King Arthur awoke from his long sleep *too far ahead* in the future! Sure, there are problems in the year 3000, perhaps more immediately pressing than those that face us today. . . . But the problems we *do* face— inflation, unemployment, the possibility of nuclear holocaust, and a deep and basic distrust of our elected officials in all branches of government—are not being adequately dealt with by any of our current leaders. Boy, we could use a man like Arthur today!. . . I guess it's just wishful thinking.[26]

Whatever the writer's doubts here, the fact is that *Camelot 3000* does cover most of his concerns, and a good many more as well. For example, if the leaders of the world's four leading powers conspire with the UN's Jordan Matthew/Modred to overthrow Arthur, Brian Bolland's artwork underscores the extent to which contemporary parallels were meant to be seen. President Marks of the United States may wear a wig and an Uncle Sam suit, but his Stetson, six-guns, and cowboy manners lodge his ancestry firmly in LBJ. The Soviet Union's Premier Syerov bears a striking resemblance to Leonid Brezhnev; Africa's Supreme Rakma to Idi Amin; and China's Chairperson Feng to Jiang Qing, Mao Zedong's widow. Surely this gang of four was not created by accident.

Even more strikingly, perhaps, the whole story takes place within the context of movie versions of World War II—seen here not just as "the good war," but more particularly as that time when the actions and ideals of "little people" really made a difference. As early as the first page Tom stands in the bombed-out ruins of London, lamenting: "Lord, what I wouldn't give to be out of here and on the way to France to join the Resistance!"[27] Luckily, though, he then manages to commandeer a spacecar and flees with his parents on the motorway. Just as they near the exit for Glastonbury Tor, Tom's father cries out: "*Careful,* Tom! I don't want to die at the hands of the aliens *or* in an accident!"—to which Tom responds with a geographic confusion worthy

The New Round Table
Rear: Percival and Kay; front, left to right, Tristan, Lancelot, Tom Prentice, Galahad, Gawain, and Arthur.

of Chrétien de Troyes: "Don't worry, Dad. We'll make the Channel by morning."[28]

Although Tom's reawakening of Arthur means that his life in the Maquis is not to be, the echoes of "the good war" continue, most notably when Lancelot tells Guinevere that, despite their love, she must marry Arthur. When she hesitates, he points out: "Arthur needs you. You are part of what makes him king, and he must have your strength." If the allusion to Humphrey Bogart's Rick in *Casablanca* is evident already, it becomes overpowering when she responds: "But what about *us*?" With shoulders slouched and hands in pockets Lancelot walks slowly away as he nobly responds: "We have our memories."[29] As far as one knows, those memories don't include Paris, but it must have been a city much on the minds of Barr and Bolland as they sought to convey something of the Arthurian ideal while at the same time preparing fans of pop culture so that they would more fully grasp the tragedy inherent in the subsequent renewal of Gwen and Lance's illicit love.

Nevertheless, if cinematic versions of World War II provide context for the good guys in *Camelot 3000*, the baddies owe much of their villainy to much more immediate memories of Vietnam. Thus, while Modred is evil from the very beginning, the extent of that evil is brought home only when he orders the death of Arthur and his followers with a chilling: "Terminate them, with *extreme prejudice*."[30] These words, so reminiscent of CIA directives against the Viet Cong, owe their resonance to sources other than movies.

Beyond Vietnam, however, the range of ills stressed seems accurately to reflect the resentful judgments of "little people" on political conduct today. When a woman outside the UN complains: "And all they do is *talk*! Why don't they *do* something?" a noxious TV reporter cuts in with: "And in a dramatic surge of unity, the General Assembly has voted 912 to 0 to bitterly *censure* the invading aliens!"[31] When UN guards call for reinforcements, what come are

> Neo-men! Criminals, dissidents, and undesirables, genetically changed to loyal, virtually brainless servants of the powers-that-be! Hated by the citizenry. . ., the neo-men are the perfect enforcement tool of an administration that likes things nice and quiet. Of course, trivialities like initiative and value judgments are sacrificed for such mindless allegiance, but isn't that a small price to pay?[32]

This frustration and distrust form one of the major themes in *Camelot 3000*. Abstractly, the discontent is with modernity itself and with a world grown too complex and that has substituted anonymous hordes of bureaucrats for heroes. More specific targets include: politicians and government in general; the United Nations in particular; the intrusive stupidities of the media; and especially the frequently perverse consequences of science and technology, not the least of which are the neo-men just cited.

Essential to this vision is that "apocalyptic thrust" that Professor Lagorio finds so characteristic of all Arthurian literature. When Arthur marvels at the wonders of modern science, Gawain tells him: "Not all the products of technology are benevolent, sire, as World War III, late in the 23rd century proved. Billions upon billions were slain."[33] Even more striking in its hostility to science is Morgan Le Fay's explanation to Modred of how she took over Chiron, the tenth planet. Before her arrival its aliens had been benignly peaceful, but, as she says: "I took the liberty of discharging their natural bent toward magic and turning it toward science, they would learn the rules of logic and the mind while the path of sorcery on this world would be trod by my feet alone."[34] A bit unfocused though this statement may be, its message about science is crystal clear.

Given these themes, it seems hardly surprising that little people in the year 3000 should have welcomed Arthur with as much enthusiasm as did the pop culture of the 1980s. For example, when he first appears at the United Nations, after a TV reporter exclaims: "It. . .it's *incredible*, folks! Do you *see* it?" an unidentified narrative voice takes over with:

> And all over the world they do. All over the world, in people who have too long been denied a *dream* in this over-populated, much-beleaguered globe, something stirs in them now, as if daring them to *hope*, something in their subconscious, something only half-learned, and long *forgotten*. But as they *see*. . ., they *remember*.[35]

Barr's Arthur is, after all, a man who knows how to cut through the crap, and he usually does so in ways that speak directly to the frustrations cited above. After the knights of the Round Table have seized the rocket needed for the trip to Chiron, Galahad may cry in despair that its power cells need recharging, but Arthur, rejecting science, quickly solves the problem by thrusting his sword into them as he says: "I will show you that Excalibur's might is not confined to *destruction!*"[36] Then off they go to the apocalyptic Final Battle, though in this version there *is* a happy ending. Arthur survives, albeit as a mutant, while the greatest tragic lovers in medieval literature—Lancelot and Guinevere, Tristan and Isolde—find lasting peace in each other's arms. Understandably, perhaps, the world of DC Comics demands a certain amount of textual alteration when confronted by the apocalyptic thrust of tragedy.

In conclusion, Barr and Bolland have unquestionably revisioned Arthur as *the* hero of all time, a man much more excitingly active than was his prototype in most medieval versions of the story. More disturbingly, *Camelot 3000* so stresses the need for Arthur's leadership that, given the cultural context of the twentieth century, one begins to fear that his creators may have unconsciously been seeking the return of authoritarianism at best, fascism at worst. For in this version the actions of Britain's most famous king seem nowhere to depend on the will of the people, the role of which is limited only to cheering and/or grateful adulation. Still, that muted note finds no echo in the comments of *Camelot 3000*'s readers. Just as Barr and Bolland's fans betray few signs of racism, sexism, or homophobia, so, too, do they appear to love pretty much the same person who has always been there. *Camelot 3000* becomes bastardized Malory at its worst when it depicts Arthur wielding Excalibur like Wonder Woman's bracelets to ward off bullets and death rays, and yet viewers of such scenes appear to have responded to them with a not-inaccurate grasp of their hero's once-and-future appeal. As Stephen Scott Beau Smith expressed the point in a letter from rural West Virginia:

> I think I have figured out the "charm" that seems to make King Arthur such an interesting character. He seems to be the smartest and yet at the same time the dumbest man in the book. What I mean by that is I have never seen a person more bred for leadership than Arthur, yet when it comes to a decision of the common nature, he is a total loss. I like the guy, he's got class![37]

It would appear, then, that Arthur has the staying power to survive even the indignities visited upon him by popular culture. Unacquainted with the original "legends chronicled by Sir Thomas Malory" though Mr. Smith may be, he remains held in thrall by the story of a mythic figure who combines the idealistic statecraft of the public king with the blind human frailties of the private man. Doubtless Professor Lagorio could phrase Smith's sentiments with greater elegance, at least when not distracted by her ukulele, but one suspects that even she would find it hard to put them better.

Notes

1. V. M. Lagorio, "King Arthur and Camelot, U.S.A. in the Twentieth Century," *Medievalism in American Culture*, ed. B. Rosenthal and P. E. Szarmach (Binghamton, N.Y., 1989), pp. 151–69, at 151–52.

2. I am grateful to DC Comics Inc. for permission to quote and use artwork from Mike W. Barr (author) and Brian Bolland (artist), *Camelot 3000* throughout this article. Since this is my first quote, I should mention that publishing texts from comic books presents almost as many editorial challenges as do medieval

manuscripts. When *Camelot 3000* appeared (though less so now), lettering was invariably in block capitals; boldface was frequently used for emphasis and other emotive purposes; and final sentence punctuation, when not question marks or exclamation points, usually consisted of double dashes or three periods (not ellipses) that heightened continuity from one speaker's balloon to the next. Indeed, the very placement of these balloons on the page and the distribution of text between and among them are forms of punctuation. In what follows, I have used only normal capitalization and eliminated or italicized much of the boldface. Usually I have also substituted normal punctuation at the end of sentences. I hope, nonetheless, that some of the original flavor comes through. To that end I have retained the work's usages on names (e.g., "Isolde") and have not attempted to correct occasional lapses in spelling and grammar.

3. Lagorio, "Camelot, U.S.A.," p. 159.

4. M. W. Barr and B. Bolland, *Camelot 3000* (DC Comics version), 1.26. Since all citations will now be to this work, I should explain how I have distinguished, where necessary, between the original and book versions. The Warner book has no overall pagination, but since it repeats that of each original issue, I have cited only issue numbers (the same as chapter ones in the books) followed by the page reference. Thus "3.15" means issue or chapter 3, page 15. Material that appears only in one version is identified as to source through the use of either "DC Comics" or "Warner Books" followed by the place where the material cited may be found. Lastly, in comic book publishing "Creator" is in fact a technical term that identifies the person or persons most responsible for the original concept. A creator continues to receive credit for a strip even after he or she has stopped scripting or drawing it. I am indebted to Ian M. Spackman for this and other technical information about the publication of comics.

5. DC Comics, 1.27.

6. Warner Books, iv.

7. 1.9. Tom's character, like Michael Jackson's on his Victory Tour, is partially based on Luke Skywalker's in *Star Wars,* but he is more rooted in Tom of Warwick from Lerner and Loewe's *Camelot.*

8. 12.20.

9. 12.29–30.

10. 12.32.

11. According to Don and Maggie Thompson, co-editors of *Comic Buyers' Guide*: see Warner Books, ii.

12. 1.2. Starting with a quotation, frequently from "the Bard of Avon," is a frequent practice in adult comic books.

13. DC Comics, 6, appendix, explains that "Jules" was "Mike's tribute to the great French detective Jules Maigret," while "Futrelle came from the name of detective author Jacques Futrelle."

14. Note, though, that one complaint about Galahad does appear in DC Comics, 8, appendix. As a Japanese, he was presumably not a Christian and, further, he was just about to commit hara-kiri when reincarnation intervened. Patricia Fogelman therefore protested that he was wrong both in background and intended deed for "the Perfect Christian Knight," and she also felt he enjoyed killing too much, not a good trait for a saint. All in all, then, these seem religious objections from an Arthurian purist, not racial slurs.

15. 6.24.

16. 6.2.

17. From Barr's decision to use the form "Isolde" one infers that he expected his audience to be more familiar with Wagner than Malory. In fact, some readers complained, preferring "Iseult" or "Yseult."

18. 4.15.

19. 10.9. Visual details such as Tristan's bow demonstrate the extent to which Brian Bolland is as fully the "Creator" of *Camelot 3000* as is Mike Barr. Again and again he adds dimensions impossible to convey in text alone.

20. DC Comics, 11, appendix.

21. DC Comics, 8, appendix.

22. DC Comics, 8, appendix.

23. DC Comics, 10, appendix.

24. DC Comics, 11, appendix.

25. DC Comics, 11, appendix.

26. DC Comics, 7, appendix.

27. 1.1–2.

28. 1.2.

29. 6.8.

30. 10.7.

31. 1.24–25.

32. 2.4.

33. 11.5.

34. 5.12.

35. 2.2–3. The King and Kennedy echoes here need no comment.

36. 10.12.

37. DC Comics, 8, appendix.

INDEX